Letters on Familiar Matters

Aldo S. Bernardo is Distinguished Service Professor in the Department of Romance Languages and Literature at the State University of New York at Binghamton. He is the translator of Rerum familiarium libri I–VIII *(1975), also available from The Johns Hopkins University Press. The third book in the series,* Letters on Familiar Matters: Rerum familiarium libri XVII–XXIV, *is forthcoming.*

Francesco Petrarca

Letters on Familiar Matters

Rerum familiarium libri IX–XVI

TRANSLATED BY ALDO S. BERNARDO

THE JOHNS HOPKINS UNIVERSITY PRESS, 1982

BALTIMORE AND LONDON

This book has been brought to publication
with the generous assistance of the State
University of New York.

Library of Congress Cataloging in Publication Data

Petrarca, Francesco, 1304–1374.
    Rerum familiarium libri.

    Vol. 2– has title: Letters on familiar matters.
    Vol. 2– published by Johns Hopkins University Press.
    Bibliography: v. 1, p. 437–439.
    Contents: v. [1] I-VIII—v. [2] IX-XVI
    1. Petrarca, Francesco, 1304–1374—Correspondence.
2. Authors, Italian—To 1500—Correspondence.
I. Title. II. Title: Letters on familiar matters.
PQ4496.E29E23 1975   851'.1   75–2418
ISBN 0–87395–295–2 (v. 1)   AACR2
ISBN 0–8018–2750–7 (Johns Hopkins: v. 2)

To Reta

Contents

Book XI

Book XII

Preface

Book IX of the present volume was translated by Eleanor Sypher, whom I had invited to collaborate in the project because of her work as a classicist. Circumstances made the collaboration unfeasible, and so I proceeded alone. Book IX has since undergone considerable revision, and it is only right that I assume full responsibility for its inevitable defects, given the nature and difficulty of Petrarch's Latin.

The same criteria were applied in the preparation of this volume as were used in the first. The Latin text is that of the definitive edition by V. Rossi and U. Bosco. The paragraphing is once again in the actual paragraphing of that edition (not the numbered paragraphs given in the margins). Despite its awkwardness in English, such paragraphing still allows ready reference to the Latin text without extending the length of the volume.

As with the first volume, annotations, aside from brief identification of correspondents not indicated in the first volume, were not included, in order to minimize costs. A fourth volume containing such annotations is a possibility. Meanwhile, the reader is once again referred to the definitive edition for identifications of textual citations, to the detailed notes appended by Ugo Dotti to his Italian translation of the first eleven books, to the rich, if somewhat outdated, notes of the nineteenth-century Fracassetti translation, or to those appended to the selections contained in the Ricciardi edition.[1]

In arriving at the present translation I found it useful to check difficult passages against the Italian translations of Fracassetti, Dotti, and Bianchi, and the English translations of Wilkins and Bishop.[2] I also made limited use of the C. Day Lewis translation for a number of citations from the *Aeneid*, as well as the translation of H. T. Riley for a few passages from the *Pharsalia*.

While idiomatic expression was a basic concern in my renditions, it was sacrificed to the principle of faithfulness to the Latin text whenever such expression seemed to interfere with Petrarch's desired meaning. I also found it expeditious and useful to make extensive use of the computer-assisted technique I developed for this series as described in the first volume. The system accelerates the translation process to a surprising degree. Were it not for a series of personal misfortunes during the six years since the appearance of volume 1, the present volume would have been ready at least three years ago. I hope to have volume 3 ready well within the next three years, at which time I propose to turn to the translation of the *Seniles*, whose first three books are already completed.

As was the case in the first volume, all names appear as they are in the Latin text. Thus Virgil, Ovid, Horace, Juvenal, Terence, and Seneca appear respectively as Maro, Naso, Flaccus, the Satirist, the Comic, and the Tragedian; while names with diphthongs retain the medieval form, viz., Lelius, Sceva, etc., except for a few commonly used names such as Caesar, Aeneas, etc. The same general principle applies to Petrarch's spelling of Roman names ending in *ci* for which he prefers *ti*, viz., Fabritius, Martia, etc. As for the names appearing in the salutations, I generally observed the following criteria: names referring to persons of special renown have been anglicized (Charles IV, Clement VI, etc.), those of foreign correspondents are given in the language of their country (Philippe de Vitry, Jan ze Středa, etc.), names of Italians retain their Italian form. The forms agree with Wilkins's list of addressees.[3]

I find it impossible to acknowledge fully the debt of gratitude I owe to my wife, Reta, for the present work. Were it not for her persistent encouragement and the long hours so selflessly spent with me in proofreading, revising, improving and preparing the typescript, the present volume would never have appeared. I am also grateful to The Johns Hopkins University Press for daring to accept a series that most presses would hesitate to consider in these days of astronomical printing costs, as well as to Charles S. Singleton for his timely assistance.

Notes

1. *Le Familiari*, vols. 1–3 ed. V. Rossi, and vol. 4 ed. Rossi and U. Bosco (Florence: Sansoni, 1933–42); *Le Familiari*, trans. U. Dotti, 2 vols. (Urbino: Argalia, 1974); *Lettere di Francesco Petrarca*, trans. G. Fracassetti, 5 vols. (Florence: LeMonnier, 1863–66).

2. Francesco Petrarca, *Opere*, trans. Enrico Bianchi (Florence: Sansone, 1975); Ernest H. Wilkins, *Petrarch at Vaucluse* (Chicago: University of Chicago Press, 1958); *Letters from Petrarch*, trans. Morris Bishop (Bloomington: Indiana University Press, 1966).

3. Ernest H. Wilkins, *Petrarch's Correspondence*, Medioevo e Umanesimo, No. 3 (Padua: Antenore, 1960), pp. 12–14.

Introduction

The 104 letters contained in Books IX–XVI of Petrarch's *Familiares* were written between the late 1340s (the earliest being 1348) and the early 1350s (the latest being 1354). The longest books are XI and XII, with seventeen letters apiece. The shortest is Book X, with six letters. The eight books fall within the period that E. H. Wilkins designates as Period III in Petrarch's life, defined as "Residence alternately in Italy and Provence" extending from 1341 to 1353 and covering three periods of residence in Parma and three in Vaucluse. The actual span of time starts in Wilkins's Period IIIE and reaches what he designates as Period IVA, during which time Petrarch visited the following places for a variety of reasons: Parma, Verona, Valserena, Padua, Treviso, Venice, Carpi, Lake Garda, Mantua, Luzzara, Rome, Florence, Bolsena, Viterbo, Arezzo, Vicenza, Lonigo, Ferrara, Piacenza, Mont Genèvre, Avignon, Vaucluse, Montrieux, Aix, St-Maximin, and Milan.[1] It is also in these books that we find the beginnings of Petrarch's correspondence with two men who were to be his closest friends in later life, Giovanni Boccaccio and Francesco Nelli. The correspondence with Boccaccio focuses on his attempt to have the government of Florence restore Petrarch's patrimony and to invite him to return to his native city. The thirteen letters to Nelli (Francesco of the Church of the Holy Apostles) deal with a variety of subjects.

Books IX and X contain the intrusion of letters from other periods, thereby continuing the trend begun in Book V, which practically disregarded all chronology. Most striking in this regard are letters IX, 15–16, which were not written until Petrarch had left Vaucluse never to return, and had settled in Milan in 1354. From XI, 10 to XVI, 10, however, the collection is arranged, according to Wilkins, "with a remarkable degree of chronological precision."[2] Of the sixty-nine letters forming this particular group, fifty-one are dated either from Vaucluse or Avignon, while the remainder indicate no place of writing. These mark the longest uninterrupted series of letters written by Petrarch from any one place.

As shown in the first volume of this series, Petrarch had entertained the possibility of forming a collection of his own correspondence ever since his discovery of three of Cicero's letter collections in 1345. Inasmuch as he viewed such a project as an artistic undertaking rather than as a mere recopying of his letters in chronological order, it was not until five years later that he was ready to begin serious work on the project. On January 13 of that year he wrote in Padua a long letter to his friend "Socrates," dedicating the collection (still in embryo form) to him and describing some of the principles and procedures used in initiating the collection. In Wilkins's words, "He thought of the collection not as a series of documents but as a work of art in itself, every element of which was to be made as perfect as he could make it: this idea governed his decisions as to inclusion, revision, and arrangement, and all other relevant decisions."[3] In point of fact, among the very first letters to be included as part of the collection were letters invented between 1350 and 1351 to provide the collection with the impression of a distinct chronology starting in his youthful years.[4] It was indeed his letters to Charles IV (X, 1 and XII, 1) and to his brother (X, 3–5, written several months earlier) that prompted Petrarch to extend his collection from ten to twelve books, a number deriving from what Billanovich calls "the sacred models of the *Aeneid* and the *Thebaid*." The concept of a collection divided into twenty-four books came to Petrarch only in 1359 when his greater knowledge of Homer caused him to view the Homeric model of twenty-four books as the ideal length.[5]

In his last study on Petrarch's humanism (before his untimely death in 1979), Guido Martellotti repeats the assertion, generally accepted by scholars, that the years between 1342 and 1350 were decisive in the intellectual and spiritual development of Petrarch.[6] There was his coronation in Rome in 1341, which had bestowed upon him an international renown surpassing even what he had hoped to achieve symbolically by means of the coronation.[7] Then there were the religious vows taken by his brother, Gherardo, in 1342, the same year as the initial composition of the *Secretum*. It was also during this same period that he seriously began to consider the possibility of a return to Italy, especially following the loss of so many friends, presumably including Laura, in the plague of 1348. Finally, there were the interesting encounters with Boccaccio and other Florentine admirers before and after his journey to Rome in 1350 as well as the touching gesture by the Florentines, orchestrated by Boccaccio and others, restoring Petrarch's patrimony and offering him a professorial chair at the Studio.[8] How deeply this must have affected Petrarch may be seen in the date appended to his formal response (*Fam.* XI, 5)—April 6, the mysterious date that haunted his life.

While most scholars agree that Petrarch's essential conflict during this period consisted primarily of those elements described in the *Secretum*, others have felt that, since that work concludes without a resolution, the conflict went far beyond the contents of his self-confession.[9] For Martellotti the *Secretum* represented Petrarch's first serious but unsuccessful attempt to reconcile classical and Christian cultures, but in that very attempt may be seen his gradual evolution away from an exclusive admiration for the Romans toward an eventual acceptance of other voices.[10] In many ways, the heart of the problem was Petrarch's unrealistic desire to see the rebirth of Rome and of all she stood for, especially following the year of the Jubilee in 1350, when his visit to Rome made such a deep and lasting impression on him.[11]

The matter reached a climax with an event that Martellotti describes as having most profound repercussions in Petrarch's life and in his political orientation: the attempt of Cola di Rienzo in 1347 to reestablish Rome as a Republic. Even in one of his last works, the *Invectiva contra eum qui maledixit Italie*, Petrarch recalls the moment when the entire world, and particularly the likes of his "barbarian" opponent, held its breath wondering whether Cola would really revive the ancient queen of the world. "If at one time this revival had been unheard of," he exclaims, "it recently appeared possible when a single man of most humble origin, with scarcely any financial means, and—as events proved—possessing greater courage than constancy, dared to support the republic on his weak shoulders and to assume the protection of the tottering empire."[12] So great was Petrarch's enthusiasm in 1347 that he actually took leave of his friends in Avignon and left France intending to join Cola's movement. Vibrations of his admiration for Cola may still be felt in the relatively late XIII, 10, written some five years after Cola's attempt.

While the failure of Cola's coup proved a deep blow, it caused Petrarch to realize that he no longer had to remain a "prisoner" of the Curia in Avignon. There followed what Martellotti calls "the period of lively polemics in defense of his own reputation as man and scholar, while his voice becomes more authoritative in the field of studies and also in that of politics as a result of his at times truly important diplomatic missions willingly assigned him by his new patrons."[13] The contents of his letters during this period consequently become increasingly political, and though they often reflect some patron's interest, they all appear inspired by the deeply felt ideal of a homeland that can still peacefully return to the lost path of its ancient grandeur.

In short, during the period covered by these eight books of the *Familiares* we observe Petrarch not only deciding to start a collection of his letters as a genre, in imitation of Cicero, but undergoing a series of personal experiences and making a number of irrevocable decisions that were to have a profound effect on his life. Among the most significant of these was his decision to transfer from the Guelf atmosphere of Avignon to the Ghibelline environment of Milan and other Italian states. The period preceding the final move was filled with all kinds of inner conflicts that were recorded in practically everything he wrote at this time, and that dramatically reflected his profound humanity and his stature as humanist and citizen of the world. It is at this moment that he develops what Martellotti calls his sense of mission as a man of letters who draws strength and authority from his studies to dispense to the powerful men of action of his day warnings and advice, praise and condemnation, and to serve as an interpreter of ancient wisdom among the moderns.[14]

The three most frequent themes appearing in Books IX–XVI are (1) an almost biblical longing for deliverance from the Babylon that is Avignon, (2) a need for repose and tranquillity, and (3) a burning desire to return to Italy, especially to Rome. Other recurring subjects include the spiritual blessings enjoyed by his brother; the endless attraction of Vaucluse; a deep concern for the welfare of his few remaining intimate friends, with the concomitant desire to spend his last years as near to them as possible; a series of strong appeals to the highest civic and ecclesiastical authorities to intervene in behalf of such causes as the unification of Italy, Rome, or the Kingdom of Sicily; the defense of a helpless religious order; the sharing of benefices with friends; the education of his illegitimate son; the defense of letters and poetry against the uninitiated; the establishment of peace between states and even between men of renown; and several disquisitions on such philosophical issues as the meaning of life, the effects of time and death on earthly ambitions, the essence of true friendship, and the value of travel as a means of personal growth.

There is little doubt that the clearest image of Petrarch that emerges from these books is that of the man of letters dispensing his wisdom and knowledge. Aside from the scholar skilled at citing exempla and quotations from ancient and ecclesiastical writers, these books reflect a Petrarch remarkably well informed about current events in nearly every country or state. This can best be seen in XV, 7 where with expert strokes of the pen he depicts for Stefano Colonna the political situation in at least twenty areas of France and Italy in addition to Britain, Germany, the Balearics, Sardinia, Corsica, Sicily, Spain, Rhodes, Crete, Greece, Cyprus, Armenia, Jerusalem, with passing reference to Asia and Africa. Adding to these credentials Petrarch's self-awareness of his role and function as the Sage of his day, as expressed in XIII, 7, it is no wonder that he feels qualified to advise the high and mighty as well as the lowly on all kinds of subjects besides political and social ones.

Among the more interesting examples of personal advice given by Petrarch in these books are the following: the dangers of lust and adultery (IX, 4); the distinction between religious and secular poetry (X, 4); the best training and education for a young prince (XII, 2); the best education for a young man (XIII, 2–3); how a person whose faith is wavering may avoid intellectual pitfalls (XVI, 4); how to control the drive for success and advancement at the highest social and political levels (XI, 14–15; XIII, 4; XIV, 1; XVI, 1).

There are also letters containing fascinating insights into Petrarch's personal attitudes and values. In speaking of his disgust with papal Avignon, he exclaims in XII, 11, "whoever has once experienced disgust for this accursed city will find nowhere in the entire world a disagreeable place, unless perhaps the Babylonian poison has permeated to his very marrow through long habit. . . ." What makes this statement particularly interesting is that in IX, 6 he had already confessed that the poison had indeed affected him. Then there are the descriptions of his preferred life-style as practiced in his beloved retreat at Vaucluse (XI, 12; XII, 8; XIII, 8; XV, 8). There is even confirmation of the seemingly unimportant but actually significant bit of information that his intimate friends called him Silvanus (X, 4). A reader cannot help marvel at his modern sense of the nature of poetry as revealed in XII, 5: "I consider it a great accomplishment to express great concepts with words, and to reveal with artistically combined words the beauty hidden in the mind." Dog lovers will find the description of a dog's behavior at its master's departure a veritable gem (XIII, 11). Of considerable interest is the reference to the unusual honor being bestowed upon him by the Neapolitan government, which was constructing in the vicinity of Vesuvius "a new Parnassus bearing my name" (XII, 15). Petrarch's strong sense of fleeting time and approaching death is expressed in a particularly forceful manner in XV, 11 when he asks, "Do you realize the value of a single day for the soul of a dying person?" Similarly his concept of virtue receives its clearest definition in XI, 3 in which he expresses his preference for the definition of the Stoics who had defined it as "feeling rightly about God and acting rightly among men." The last letter of this group, XVI, 14, provides support for this definition with its unequivocal assertion that a good life is far more important than a good literary style.

Petrarch's apparent restlessness, uncertainty, wavering, sense of isolation, imprisonment, and persecution, continuous appeals for assistance in selecting a final resting place for himself and his books, and intense desire for both tranquillity and glory as reflected in Books IX–XVI reveal the extent to which he was indeed a victim of the intense conflict so beautifully defined in his famous outcry: "et veggio 'l meglio, et al peggior m'appiglio" (And I see the best and to the worst I cling). (*Canzoniere*, CCLXIV, 136.)

Notes

1. Ernest H. Wilkins, "Peregrinus ubique," in *The Making of the "Canzoniere" and Other Petrarchan Studies* (Rome: Storia e Letteratura, 1951), pp. 1–8; also in the same volume, "A Chronological Conspectus of Certain Writings of Petrarch," pp. 347–59; and "The Chronology of the *Familiares* and the *Seniles*," pp. 368–78.

2. Wilkins, "The Chronology," p. 374.

3. Ernest H. Wilkins, *Life of Petrarch* (Chicago: University of Chicago Press, 1961), pp. 87–88.

4. Giuseppe Billanovich, *Petrarca letterato*, I: *Lo scrittoio del Petrarca* (Rome: Storia e Letteratura, 1947), p. 48.

5. Ibid., pp. 5, 20, 23. The first chapter (pp. 3–55) gives a fascinating account of how Petrarch formed the collection.

6. "L'Umanesimo del Petrarca," *Il Veltro* 1–2 (1980): 80.

7. Wilkins, "The Coronation of Petrarch," in *The Making of the "Canzoniere,"* pp. 9–69.

8. Billanovich, pp. 94–99.

9. Francesco Rico, *Vida u obra de Petrarca* (Chapel Hill: University of North Carolina Press, 1974), pp. 517–35. For Rico's view of the period under discussion, see p. 484; and for his dating of the *Secretum* between 1347 and 1352, p. 471. See also Aldo S. Bernardo, *Petrarch, Laura and the "Triumphs"* (Albany: SUNY Press, 1974), pp. 77–81.

10. Martellotti, "L'Umanesimo," p. 77.

11. Marguerite Waller, *Petrarch's Poetics and Literary Theory* (Amherst: University of Massachusetts Press, 1980), pp. 4–5 and passim for a contemporary analysis of Petrarch's attitude toward Rome.

12. Francesco Petrarca, *Prose*, ed. G. Martellotti, P. G. Ricci, E. Carrara, and E. Bianchi (Milan and Naples: Ricciardi, 1955), p. 777.

13. Martellotti, "L'Umanesimo," p. 81.

14. Ibid., p. 82.

Letters on Familiar Matters

Fam. IX, 1.

To Manfredo Pio, Lord of Carpi, * cured of a serious illness, an appeal.*

At the moment I am suffering the frequent insults and assaults of fortune and the no less frequent ones of winged fame. With poisoned arrows the one batters my spirit, the other strikes my ears, and both at the same time beat and threaten me in turn. Once they mingled joy with sorrow, sweetness with bitterness; now, alas, all things are sad and bitter. Fortune, ignorant of sweetness, pierces my soul with its harsh stings; fame, ignorant of pleasure, speaks only of grief to me. We know for certain that the only shield against fortune is virtue, which I often realize how much I lack as a result of deadly wounds. Yet with what weapons can I elude fame since I have no wings? It is a winged monster. I chose as my remedy never to inquire about anything or anyone, but that too was useless; for although I had bridled my tongue, I had not blocked my ears. And so without my asking I heard much I preferred not to hear—the diseases, funerals and serious misfortunes of my friends; the mere recollection of such matters is a punishment. Nonetheless, that distressing bearer of news was for once kinder to me by bringing me word of your recovery before that of your illness. I learned that you had risen before knowing that you had fallen. Thus, happy about the present, unconcerned about the past—for there can be no dread or anxiety over the past—yet astounded, as the person who unknowingly avoided a steep precipice, I am dumbstruck and trembling with delight at the thought of the crisis I escaped. Thanks be to Him who allowed your health to be tested, yet not destroyed, so as not to burden us with grief! By thus increasing our joy since the danger was past, He made us subsequently ever more eager for you and you dearer to us. If possible, I would like to exchange for a time my Muses for a knowledge of herbs so that I might provide you in your present condition with a health restorative. The famous physician being sent to you will accomplish, God willing, what I would like to do; I myself shall follow as soon as possible since you consider this too a likely remedy. In the meantime, I have decided to insert in this letter a unique cure I find popular with doctors—if you accept it in good faith, do not expect

*Manfredo Pio, one of the many contemporary rulers with whom Petrarch was intimate, was a member of the Pio family of Carpi. In 1329 he was made Lord of Carpi and Modena by Ludwig the Bavarian. In 1336 he abdicated his rule over Modena but retained that of Carpi.

sounder advice from any Hippocrates! It is composed more or less of these ingredients. First of all, you must willingly entrust yourself and your concerns to divine judgment, raising your spirit to heaven and casting your anchor of hope in Him; by Him alone can you be granted, not only salvation, but your present condition. And you must not despair that He who showed such concern for you from the beginning will take wonderful care of you in your last days. Secondly, you must realize that it behooves a courageous man, accustomed to battling with fortune, to despise illness and death and all mortal things, lifting himself above human misfortunes on the wings of his spirit, which often appears healthy even in a sick and afflicted body. In the midst of biting pains and even at the point of death, it has given clear evidence that happiness is possible even in circumstances said to be wretched, and that true spiritual virtue is unshaken by bodily distress. Finally you must remember that mental disposition usually has an influence on the body, whether it is ill or healthy. There are some men who shorten their life span by secretly consuming their own hearts—no greater madness can be imagined—while others prolong their flowering years in noble joy, delaying death and old age, which they will bravely bear when they reach their end according to the law of nature. I wish you would adopt their ways. Lay aside useless grief, drive away empty cares, scatter the soul's destructive clouds and, in short, rid yourself of whatever upsets you or disturbs your serenity, repeating to each man in the midst of the storms of this life and in this exile of ours the famous Virgilian line: "Hold on, and find salvation in the hope of better things." Farewell, enjoy good health and remember me.

30 July.

Fam. IX, 2.

To his Socrates,* a remembrance of friends past and present.

May I address you for once with my groans suppressed and my sighs at rest, with unbroken voice and dry eyes; hear me as if I were a man escaped from shipwreck and weary of complaints and sitting on the shore, still dejected but now drying his tears and examining the small remains of a large fortune. I am not speaking of those most pleasant and glorious riches of friendships that only recently I seemed to possess in such abundance as to appear richer even than the very kings and lords of the earth, and that I suddenly lost. Since whoever mourns his diminished pleasures is insufferable, I proceed to the subject of the essential comforts of life which seemed mine but were not. My mother had borne my two brothers, friendship had supplied others; death indeed carried off the first of my natural brothers as an infant, now the Carthusian abbey has taken the second as a grown man. Actually it has returned my Gherardo, taken not from me but from the world, to God; he is in fact no less dear to you than his only brother, and no less loved by you than by me. As for the others, I shall not mention those two who have caused my recent tears—one lies dead in the Apennines and the other wanders aimlessly; just as the death of the first is certain, so the life of the second is uncertain. I shall also not mention four others: Tommaso, of course, and Barbato, and Lelius, and my Guido. Of these, Sicilian Messina had given me the first, Abruzzan Sulmona the second, Rome the third, the Genoese shore the fourth; but death snatched the first from me at a tender age, the tenacious bond of marriage the second, affairs of state the third, politics and a desire for gain the fourth. Two others besides these had come my way, Francesco and Giovanni, both second to none in talent or in honorable friendships, both my fellow countrymen, both perfect equals of the most refined men in their learning and in their elegant manners. The country that gave them to me snatched them away; for they are so attached to their native land and taken by its sweetness that, although I have numerous and great pledges of their love, there is absolutely no hope of enjoying their company outside their city walls. Therefore, since our talk is about well-matched friends, whose companionship is simpler and more enjoyable than others, you can see that, unless I am mistaken, the entire matter finally is reduced to you alone. But you, my Socrates, you alone the Ausonian soil did not give me—a

*See I, 1.

fact posterity might wonder at—as it did the others, but instead Nunia of Campinia, barren of Ceres, Bacchus, and Minerva yet fruitful in men. Nor should the ignorant reader perhaps think I said Campania; I mean Campinia, of lower Germany as people now say, really the farthest region of Belgian Gaul which lies between the left bank of the Rhine, Holland, and Brabantia. A poor country, it prided itself on rich talent, and in it nature seemed to follow its own law of creating great souls from any mud and under any heaven. Thus, this country bore for me such an illustrious man, and brought him to light at the very time I was being born far away in another part of the globe. Though your origin was foreign, the gentleness of your spirit, your extensive sociability and especially your love for me has made you in large measure Italian. It is wonderful that a great kinship of minds and union of wills may exist among those born so far apart, as is now proven by the testimony of twenty years. Your name was given you because of the dignity and cheerfulness of your character; although the art of music in which you excel suggested the name of Aristoxenus, the judgment of friends prevailed that you be called our Socrates. It has been pleasant to have recalled this—not for you but for myself and for others. Now by putting the Alps between us, spiteful fate tries to separate you from me, you who have been almost the only consolation and solace of my troubled life. If fate succeeds, I am alone. Do not let this happen, I beg you by all the saints, and I implore you to use all the sharpness of your mind to prevent it. We are really separated by too great a distance of place and time, thereby losing the one choice fruit of good fortune and the one remedy for adversity—living together. I have often said and written much about this to our Olimpius, but fearing that it was in vain, I also wrote and said as much to you as well. Since I trust that what I said has been fixed in your memory, I shall now simply refresh and stimulate it with a few words. Therefore I urge you whom I used to consult together with others now to take counsel with yourself alone—you are the defender and prosecutor, the judge and juryman of the sentence to which I gladly submit. You know that I have two residences in Italy; if neither pleases you, then you decide where we shall be more comfortable provided feeling not interfere with good judgment. I am never so entrenched that I could not be moved by a faithful friend's pleasant nudge. For this reason, unless I am mistaken, you must weigh the matter quite carefully. See if there is any way to reunite scattered friends; if there be none, I pray that meanwhile you free yourself and me from this chore and permit me

to do what no star can prevent, to see you in your letters; for you see me so often in mine that by now I would be a bore for you if it were not for your love.
Farewell.

12 March, from Verona.

Fam. IX, 3.

To his friends, that it is often more troublesome to spend one's old age where one's youth was spent.

The relics of my old misdeeds harass me. I wish to declare my respectability but am unable to do so; I enjoy no trust in the present, laboring as I do under my reputation in times past. A persistent lady friend besieges my threshold, and the more she is driven away, the more she returns and hides in ambush throughout the night. You can swear you wish to live a chaste life; she will believe that you prefer another and that, as someone who does not know celibacy, you would as soon do without life as without the company of a woman. My former friends group around my popular doorway, calling out to me, interrupting me, and excitedly announcing a holiday and a party with well-born ladies. At first they are astonished, marveling at your reply that you do not care for such things; next they mock you and drag you by force where you would prefer not to go. They resemble those incapable of imagining in their contemporaries changed feelings and approaching old age—to which they pay no heed in themselves since their minds are still juvenile. Bailiffs and administrators of my domestic affairs advise that, on the one hand, I must guard against future losses and, on the other, that I must repair past ones. When I cite that saying of Anaxagoras, "I would not be safe unless such things were destroyed," they consider me either a hypocrite or a madman. Fatherly friends worry about my settling down and point out thousands of ways to get ahead and to make money, saying that one must make good use of time and actively take advantage of fortune. When I swear that I am satisfied with my possessions, some scorn me as a silly and worthless man; others believe that I am hiding a scheme behind a facade in order not to share any profits with anyone who may learn about them. Why should I dwell upon major annoyances when the mere presence of minor ones troubles me? Thus far I am incapable of persuading my tailor or cobbler that I wish a garment or a shoe larger than usual; they think I am speaking from false modesty and, though they promise much, they follow not my request but their own opinion. Thus am I, as an old man, hard pressed by the evils of my youth. When I ponder what might be a possible remedy, only one road to safety lies open— I must escape to some place on earth where the fact that I have a sane mind would not be incredible, where I could at last be what I am, and not always forced to be what I once was. Often a change of position has relieved the weary and a change of air the sickly; grafted trees become domesticated and transplanted vegetables regain strength. As far as I am concerned, my friends, that is now my plan. For, although against the opinion of many, I feel that often old age is spent more peacefully elsewhere than where one's youth was spent.

Avignon, 25 September.

Fam. IX, 4.

To a friend, a warning against dangerous loves.

Fear and grief now call forth my words; I could have perhaps endured one without the other in silence. Indeed I know, I know what seems so enchanting to you and to those dedicated to this way of life, and forces you to abandon the level road for steep places, blinded by false knowledge and victims of habit. Anything easily obtained repels you, difficult things delight you all the more if they seem nearly impossible to obtain; you scorn what is accessible, you seek what is hidden. Wherever a jealous husband or an anxious mother and a worried father are known to keep close watch, wherever feminine purity is fortified by an impassable hedge, the thought of storming such a stronghold with gifts and flattery or leaping inside it by some new trick must be numbered among the sweetest of all the well-known pranks of youth. For some hunters it is customary not to touch a sleeping deer or a hare lying in the briars; the chase of game excites the interest of the pursuers. Thus your love, as Horace elegantly put it, "disregards what stands before it and pursues what flees." You desert your wives, you seek those of others; meanwhile your wives have their own suitors, sleek and alert. Thus you might everywhere see fulfilled that prophecy of Jeremiah, "They have become as horses and stallions in heat; each man neighed after his neighbor's wife." And yours are truly neighings and bestiality, unchecked and unbridled lust; the prophet very aptly described the behavior of our youth, to which another says in vain, "Be not as the horse and the mule which have no understanding." I shall add this one thing, though with bitter distaste, that sometimes equine lust has shown more restraint and, if I may say so, more sense of modesty than human lust. If we read of many who were intimate with their sisters and who penetrated a second time the wombs of their unfortunate mothers, such recollection is unpleasant. Notorious among these is the crime of Semiramis who, it is believed, was killed by her son in a chaste rage when she tried at an advanced age to make love to him. Recently there was someone—I know not whether to call him a man—known to me by face and name, who must be protected from all notoriety. When he attempted to defile his married daughter who was by that time a mother, he bit and clawed her almost to death because she had repulsed his foul and ungodly urge. On the other hand, one can read in very famous writers about a stallion which through the herdman's cunning had its eyes blindfolded and was forced to mate with its mother. When the blinders were finally removed, and the stallion recognized its mother, it instantly turned away as though from a crime, and hurled itself to the ground injuring itself so badly that, as it were, it gave up the spirit. In Varro's *De re rustica*, we see another horse deceived by a similar trick, taking revenge, not upon itself but against the very one who had deceived it. When the blindfold was removed, he immediately attacked him and bit him to death, as Varro says. How much more worthily these deeds might have been said of men, and those related previously be said of beasts! So the point of the subject is that no animal is nobler than man as long as the latter remembers he is a man; when he forgets that, nothing is more vile and more base, nothing worse than the man driven by his natural impulses and uncontrolled by the restraints of reason.

But let us pass over these painful stories; let my discussion return to the vauntings and pursuits of young men. I mean adultery, which is concealed under the veil of love; it hides under a pretty name a shameful crime which, not only in our era abounding in evils of every description but in the many centuries before us, was so common that someone not inappropriately wrote, "This is something that can be neither permitted nor prohibited." Long ago Annaeus Seneca said with regard to the distinctive features of his own epoch, "If no mistress has made a man distinguished and if he does not give a ring to another man's wife, the matrons call him a vulgar person of foul desire and a lover of maidservants." This bane which started at that time now is so commonplace that a young man whose adulterous liaison has not succeeded, however rich and handsome and well born he may be, is considered wretched by his friends, as if he were abandoned and driven away not by modesty but by contempt, and as though the beloved's chastity were a reproach to the lover. This is the source of that ardor of young men and that shameless anxiety as if it were a contest not for carnal passion but for honor. This is the source of the hardships, the sighs, the very bitter rejections; and yet, conquest is often still more bitter. For even as the affair proceeds with Venus smiling and Cupid propitious, what is the heat of jealousy, what are the stings of suspicions, and what that restlessness of spirit day by day and hour by hour, and what the very quick alternation between war and peace in the kingdom of love? Even were such things, through force of bad habit, to be counted among the delights of the nobility, what are those punishments they are so unable to avoid, deriving either from public justice or from the personal rage of husbands? For how many indeed was that desired night unexpectedly their last? How often have we heard or seen—alas too often—that wantonness and those sweet embraces end in painful wounds? If I want to offer examples of this, I need not canvas histories so much as alleys and households. I am saddened by one of these which is so recent and so notorious that, were ancient or modern examples lacking, the terrible fate of this illustrious man ought to frighten all those following in his footsteps. Because of the outcome, I mourn the wretched and unworthy fate of a man who had loved us; I mourn the unjust stain on his military career and the irreparable damage to his friends, but above all his indelible and everlasting disgrace. While otherwise prudent, he submitted not only eagerly and passionately, which is common to all lovers, but quite blindly and insanely to a woman's wiles. What makes me indignant is that it was all for a woman whose favor was not reserved for him alone but shared with many. His was not a new love, but an old one, and if he had had any sense he would have felt that excess had made it a bore. The unlucky man, shiftier than the wind and not even mindful that the wind does not usually enter a place whence it cannot issue, thrust himself into such narrow straits that there was no means of defense or avenue of escape, nor even an opportunity for a seemly death. And so, not only helpless but naked, he was the noble victim of an angry wife, and a great shame and grief for us all. I long for him whom we have lost, and I regret the foresight he lacked in destroying himself. What the Roman people once mourned in Claudius Marcellus, I think must be mourned in this man—not death which is common to all, not swords which many have often survived with great honor, but such folly at an age which ought to have gone beyond youth's impetuosity and beyond youth itself that had long passed. I know not which infernal Alecto with her murky torches kindled his heart, now so cold, nor which dreadful Tartareans buzzing around his eyes with screeching wings robbed him of the vision of approaching death. This tragedy is truly the sort one can weep over, but not change. Laying aside my grief without remedy, I turn to you to speak briefly of my apprehension for you in the hope of finding a remedy.

Indeed to discuss love at length with you would be empty ostentation, you whom experience and skill have made the Ovid or Catullus, the Propertius or Tibullus of our era. Now is the time to mention to you something about which these or others have spoken, especially Horace in his well-known satire on the necessity of fleeing the love of married women for young men. This would be enough to induce nausea in a full stomach. I shall include one example about which you may not have yet read, so that you might understand this most ancient passion which mortal madness daily revives. In the *Cis-tellaria*, Plautus has two ordinary women conversing, one ignorant and inexperienced in love, the other very learned. The first one asks,

> *Please tell me, is the beginning of love bitter?*

The other woman replies:

> *By Castor, love is most fertile in honey and gall;*
> *It gives a sweet taste and heaps up bitterness to satiety.*

But someone might perhaps say that this could be attributed to her sex, which is not up to struggling with the passions of the spirit. Hear then what the stronger sex says a little later:

> *I believe that love was first invented among men as a torture.*
> *I make this conjecture from my own experience, so that*
>   *I need not look farther,*
> *I exceed and surpass all men in my mental torment.*
> *I am hurled, crucified, driven*
> *. . . and turned upside down*
> *On the wheel of love, I am wretchedly weakened,*
> *I am tolerated, dismissed, distracted, destroyed,*
> *So that I am not in my right mind.*
> *Wherever I am, there I am not; wherever I am not, there is my*
>   *heart. . . .*
> *In this way love deludes the weary in spirit,*
> *It banishes, drives, grasps, ravages, restrains,*
> *It throws away, it gives abundantly: what it gives,*
>   *it does not give; it deludes:*
> *Whatever it once urged, it opposes,*
> *Whatever it advised against, that it offers.*

Thus he spoke. What then? Do these seem to you the words of a calm mind? Believe me, whoever speaks like that is in a bad way. But someone might say the poet invented it. Who denies it? Yet the law of poetry allows nothing to be created unless it agrees with nature, and therefore I believe speaking from experience that nothing more natural could be created, nothing truer could be said. And so, to be truthful, since I deeply fear the hooks baited for your throat and the sirens' songs sweet to your ears and the fetters entangling your feet, I ask and implore you for your own salvation that you take counsel with yourself, and be properly warned by this example of perfidy which has added to my distress. From this tragedy, draw at least some good because, just as no case could have been more painful, none could have been more distinguished. When your neighbor's house is in flames, delay not in throwing water on your own. Fire is fast-spreading, creeping easily when winds blow strongly. This is obviously happening to you now. Enough of these things at which my pen recoils although I have much more to say about them face to face. I shall close with a quotation from another comedy by Plautus:

> *No one prohibits anyone from using a public road,*
> *Provided you make no inroads through a fenced-in estate;*

and whatever follows at that point concerning this opinion. Do you wish the source? The name of the comedy is the *Gurgulio*. In short, I recommend something for you of which I seem to have persuaded myself. Whatever warm cinder from the old flame of my heart had survived, reflection has smothered, time has soothed, death has recently destroyed. Know that I have sounded the retreat from whatever pertains to this battle of human life. For now, I am not about to write you anything more. You know who and where I am, you understand against what I warn you, you see what I fear for you. Farewell; be alert and be on your guard.

Fam. IX, 5.

To Ugolino, Bishop of Parma,* a self-defense against the slander directed against him, on the nature of harmful acts, and against suspicion.

Although grief is often terse, sometimes too it is mute when the anguish of a sad and sluggish mind has blocked the voice's passageway with a heavy bolt. When this obstacle of frozen sorrow is dissolved, however, in the warmth of a wounded spirit, words find the way and often grief becomes quite eloquent. I am an example of either sort of behavior. I was long silent because of my excessive grief; now, as you see, I am relieving my sad and heavy heart with lengthy discourse. I have spent nearly my entire life trying not to harm anyone or to be suspicious of anyone, even if I could not be useful to many as I would have wanted most of all. How can I therefore patiently dissimulate that you, dear father, certainly did not conceive on your own this superficial suspicion of me, utterly undeserved? Nature lavished a gentle spirit and an honest disposition upon you, but you are inspired by the hissings of certain serpents and covered by the incurable poison of certain vipers unless you reject it. It is my intention to discuss justice with you; indeed it is still the month of December, a time in antiquity when even the slaves bought with money were given the freedom to say anything they wished against their masters. If what you read pleases you, you will consider this letter, bare of ornament and any smear of verbal rouge, the pledge and security of my affection; it comes from a part of my mind which is clear and clean, yet to tell the truth not at all calm but deeply disturbed by the many whirlwinds of detractors. Otherwise let my grief and the occasion cause you to forgive me. So as not to detain you longer, tell me the origin of such a rumor about me. Why did I deserve this from you, my dear father: that where there was no trace of deceit, tracks of suspicion became visible? What did I ever do? What did you see in me that offended your eyes? What did you hear from me too harsh for your respect or too bland for my conscience? What did you ever hear from my lips, I ask, that was suspect? For I doubt not that day after day you have heard many and

---

*Ugolino dei Rossi, whose family were lords of Parma until 1335, was made Bishop of Parma in 1323. Petrarch was first canon and then archdeacon of the cathedral of Parma, and therefore under the Bishop, but had supported the new lords of Parma (Alberto and Mastino della Scala).

diverse things about me from the mouths of those constantly barking at you from all sides, murmuring innumerable lies and flattery in your ears. If you still have your good sense, if it has not vanished in the unwholesome breezes of flatterers, you ought to weigh my deeds against their words. If no harshness of deed or word is obvious on my part, if no cloud on my brow indicates a troubled spirit, why such delight in imagining the opposite of what you see? You take me for an enemy when I wish to be your friend, and would be, if one-sided love could make a friendship. A malicious interpreter sees everything in a bad light. Why do you, such a distinguished, wise, and venerable man, trust another rather than yourself with regard to me? I beg you, close your ears to insinuations and ask your heart in silence about my conduct. It will deny I am your enemy and will confess I am your friend, declaring as your true enemies those who have on their lips hidden poison and bile, well mixed with honey, so that they might secretly stain a magnanimous spirit and tarnish a bright fame with infamous verbal venom, not without a loss of friendships which is among the greatest noble spirits can experience. But I can have no business with those whose thoughts, deeds, and words I equally despise. With you, dear father, as I said, with you lies my suit, and certainly with an unprejudiced judge however much I myself am suspect. You alone I appoint as defendant, witness, and judge. Even with me as the defendant, you remain both witness and judge; in this way the case will be tried for each side and the judge will remain unchanged. And so that I might expedite the trial from this point, I really hold nothing against you except the crime of suspicion with which you offend my innocence. Against me you have many, and perhaps serious, charges if you believe your attendants, but absolutely nothing, I think, if you follow your judgment. Therefore, if you acquit me, I have what I sought; but if your verdict condemns me, I appeal to your conscience: that will certainly acquit me.

I am accused of having come to the Roman Curia with the intention of harming you, and of remaining here with the same purpose in mind, so as to secretly slander you; all this will come to light in good time, as they say. Astonishing impudence! Novel crime foreign to my nature! Ever-blind envy! Absurd fabrication, abhorrent to all my principles! Since as a boy in law school—today those studies no longer interest me—I learned that the first inquiry in a trial must concern the defendant, as if this were the basis for the verdict itself, I suppose that it would be worthwhile investigating with you, dear father, who I am, not really all of me but only that part bearing the brunt of the attack: that is to say, to what extent I am accustomed to do harm, and am desirous of doing it. Here is my question: since from my early youth I suffered many harsh and undeserved offenses—and the way they were carried out increases the injustice—at the hands of those from whom I neither deserved nor feared any such thing, to whom did I ever return evil for evil, against whom did I invent falsehoods, for whom did I set traps, whose inheritance or person did I ever seek through violent means? No matter how carefully an investigator inquires, I think he will find nothing I can be accused of, aside from some simple complaints even a sheep or a dove would not find offensive. I have often desisted, and even when I could speak freely I have quietly restrained my grief, often to the point of cowardice. Except for a few letters in which I answer the insults of my critics, without naming them so as not to bite permanently into their reputations, there is no other instance where I, in avenging my grief and hurts, seem forgetful of humane conduct or of dignity. Thanks be to Him who gave me such confidence in the sincerity of my own conscience that I can furnish without further hesitation evidence of my innocence, not only with winged words but with written permanent ones which may perhaps fall into my enemies' hands. I am aware that if those who constantly torment me with patent lies found any small pretext, even a single word, to catch me in error, they would eagerly grasp it with both hands. Let them do so and with my consent if I ever took a harsher vengeance for the many wrongs inflicted upon me by my rivals during my life (though I often could have) than did the dying Africanus for the wrongs done to his country. I certainly have tried not to depend on anything desired by the multitude because I had learned from the Satirist that revenge befits a petty and weak, mean and womanly mind. If my resentment at an offense ever penetrated rather deeply, I consoled myself with the divine promise, "Vengeance is mine, I shall exact my due." I thought it vain for man to attempt what the heavenly Avenger had promised to do Himself. And so, am I now to be considered as gentle to my enemies as I am dangerous to my friends, a lamb among wolves and a wolf among lambs? What indeed did escape from work and the city, eagerness for solitude and leisure, love of peace and tranquillity profit me, if at this moment I must be classed a master criminal? Alas, how intensely I am experiencing what I had heard from many learned men—that the art of living is the most difficult of all! It is, by heaven, and nothing is truer! What do we mortals ever accomplish as we wish? Our inclinations are deceived by the proximity of their opposites; labor often results in loss, and rarely do the promise and the result correspond. See what I have received when I ought to have won a reputation for integrity: the suspicion of exercising new machinations and malicious cunning against the very finest men. Perhaps—as has often reached my ears by chance when I was in the company of great men, great by fortune but not by talent—perhaps, I say, by this time I appear to many as a necromancer and magician. I no doubt appear so because I am frequently alone and because, as those experts say and I do not deny, I read the works of Virgil, an opinion which elicits in me bile mixed with laughter. I have indeed read them. There is the reason for mistrust; there is the reason for the bad reputation of studies! Now I am less surprised at the accusation of magician hurled at Apuleius of Madaura, which he refuted in his very elegant book. I have no need for such an elaborate defense; I am not yet dragged to trial but slandered in dark corners by hushed whispers. And you think it is light sport that the skiff of my reputation is dashed again and again on these rocks of ignorance? Exercise your talent, pass sleepless nights, write something which might soon fall into unfriendly hands, only to earn the name of magician if you say anything at all which the ignorant do not understand. Although this is rather amusing, I would prefer to be called a magician than a speaker and doer of evil; and if we lay aside these things, a transgression of the will is more serious to the spirit than a transgression of the intellect, and a greater disgrace to my customs than to my studies. Without my knowing it, I have borne both of these. I say this, in case it is possible to be dishonored by the dishonorable. Is it not then enough to cite none other than the brief and bristly poem which Persius begins with the exclamation, "O human anxieties, O how great the vanity in things!"? Truly there is nothing solid, nothing certain since I quite inadvertently fell into the very pit I had always so carefully avoided, and no effort was of any avail in evading the fangs of my snarling critic. For I did escape, I was silent, I lay hidden; but envy sniffed out my tracks and even broke into these secret and silent retreats to attack me.

Enough about the person on trial; let us proceed to the accusation. Since nothing explicit is presented against me, as I hear tell, the case is argued on the basis of suspicions, and in a manner they call conjectural. I believe that, first, there must be some inquiry into what may be driving me to harm you; but if it is established that there is nothing, let it be resolved that I neither did any harm, nor wished to harm, nor had cause for wishing to do so. Unless I am mistaken, all things men do to harm one another proceed either from preconceived hatred or sudden wrath, or from envy or hope or fear. Aside from these, I know not what a cause for doing harm could be except perhaps a kind of bloodthirsty, inhuman ferocity and a most wretched passion for committing crime; but it is offensive to suspect this in a man of sound mind. If you agree, let us touch briefly on the first five causes. I wonder, dear father, whence and from what roots came my hatred of you. What have you done to deserve my hatred? Indeed, long before I was given the highest position after yours in your church—I who perhaps deserved the last—you not only committed no offense, mother of hatred, against me but always held me in great esteem, often preferring me over many who were more powerful and of higher station. It is ridiculous, therefore, to offer this as a reason for my hatred of you, but I know of no other. What indeed is the point in speaking about anger, since we have been discussing hatred, the more concealed evil? Could fewer meetings and, after long intervals, ever pleasant and peaceful associations have left any room for wrath? What shall I say about envy except that I have never envied any man, something I can say most confidently and truthfully? I wish I were as free of the charge of disparager as I am of the charge of envy. But if this is true of my more fiery years when innumerable reasons for rivalry emerge, what do you think of my behavior now when, after mastering the strong gusts of juvenile passions, I am so nearly safe in port, as the comic poet says? I repeat once more, and I call on God and my conscience as witnesses that I am not deceiving myself: I envy no one, being more content with my own lot than that of everyone I know. I fear that envy is my enemy rather than my friend; that is, I am more envied than envious. Moreover, not only do I not envy you, dear father, but I even have a filial compassion for you, to speak frankly, and for all who are likewise burdened by the cares of pastoral office. But I feel this somewhat more intensely for you since you must bear, in addition to the regular ecclesiastical burdens, those of your fellow citizens as well as the civil discords with which your city teems, a common scourge of those who rule in their own city. It remains now to comment upon hope and fear. In the first place, I have nothing to gain from your downfall. Please believe what I say; it never occurred nor ever will occur to me to exchange my tranquillity for your preoccupations, my peace for your labors, my poverty for your riches. Nor should you think that I envy your good fortune, for there is no man in your situation whose position I would like to have, and which I would not obstinately refuse were it offered me. If I lie to you, let me be struck down by a thunderbolt! Perhaps someone else might be surprised; you doubtless are not, since you know well the hardness of the seat on which you sit. Nor would I say this so decisively, had I not known intimately the supreme head of the Roman See and these resplendent cardinals and prelates of other cities, an intimacy which does not allow me to be mistaken in my estimation of their imaginary happiness. I shall add a saying of Pope Adrian, since everyone is familiar with the words of the emperor who, according to Valerius Maximus, "upon meditating at length on the crown given to him and holding it for a long time before he placed it on his head, said, 'O famous but unlucky crown! If anyone really knew your hidden danger, he would not pick you up even from the ground.'" But less familiar is the saying of Pope Adrian IV that I read in some philosophical anecdotes. He used to say, "No man is more unhappy than the Roman pontiff, nothing is more wretched than his condition, and were nothing else to harm him, it is fated that he die very quickly by toil alone." For in that chair, he would declare, he had encountered so much unhappiness as pope that, in comparison to his present condition, all preceding affliction seemed pure pleasure and a life of happiness. He repeatedly said that the see of the Roman pontiff is thorny; his cape bristles everywhere with very sharp stings and is so heavy that it chafes, presses, and weakens his powerful shoulders; the crown and gold embroidery seem quite bright because they are on fire; he often added that from the time he had risen step by step from cloistered priest through all the offices to the highest one, the pontificate, he enjoyed none of the happiness and calm of his former life. He used to say, "On His anvil and with His hammer the Lord has broadened me, but now if it is His will, let Him give support with His hand to the weight He has imposed upon my infirmity because it is unbearable to me." I have given this in context in nearly the same words as were written down by the person who heard them spoken. What shall I say except that Adrian was a most harsh and severe judge of his own position but a worthy one who, when he put down his heavy burden, was quickly carried to the eternal See? But, to return to you, allow me to boast. If I envied you your office, I would not know what I could do with it now, but often through these years past I could have risen to a station not only equal to yours but richer. I not only always scorned such an ascent, but I abhorred it; and I preferred lowly freedom to distinguished servitude, something I was never ashamed to admit. Perhaps I might have remained silent about this matter except that someone still lives who believed me worthy of that position and who dispassionately begged me not to consider myself unworthy, a man unaccustomed to begging but to being begged humbly and suppliantly even by kings themselves. If I am lying, he can testify to it. What shall I say about fear since all my hopes depend on you? It is typical of the ingrate to fear someone whom you know from experience is kind, as long as you are not aware of any reason for there being a change of heart. I love and revere you and, if you wish it so, I have respect, but not fear, for you except insofar as love does not exist without fear. And certainly I have always believed that you preferred to be loved than feared. It is a principle of mine to fear no man greatly unless I decide to love him. Therefore, may you read this, dear father, with the realization that I would not write this to you or to the Roman pope or to anyone at all unless I had read what I write in the depths of my heart.

I may be said to have forgotten one thing by those men who, as Julius Caesar writes in a letter, "were always deadly enemies of yours and of mine and in their craftiness cause," not, as he wrote, "the republic to reach this state," but rather our intimacy and friendship. For they maintain that in the Curia I once opposed you when you were having a serious quarrel, an inevitable evil among neighbors, with the Correggi. Nor were they lying in this one instance. But I call your memory to bear witness, since you were present throughout. Did I then let slip from my mouth anything too stinging or irreverent? If it ever did, I confess—and this may be viewed as greatness of soul or rashness—that I was much more apt to slander you to your face than behind your back. I defended a just cause, unless love deceives me; but if it were unjust—every lover is blind—I did not perceive the injustice. I certainly defended the cause of a family very kind and dear to me, at whose invitation and under whose auspices I first came to those places. Because of their love, as you see, I made a foreign country my own—if there is any country that a man may call his own—I made it second to none between the Alps and the Apennines and it, I believe, considered my loyalty second to none. I think no one will argue with me about this, especially you whom a trusting friendship delights above all else. See what an opinion I have of your character: I think that you esteem me more as your adversary, but loyal to those to whom I ought to be, than as one devoted to you and disloyal to them. Moreover, I defended that cause not as an advocate but as a friend, and I did so not with shrewdness or insults or any sarcasm or attacks against your reputation, but with a simple and unassuming statement of facts. The result was that, a rarity in lawsuits, no opportunity for new suspicions about you was offered either to the Supreme Pontiff or to the College of Cardinals before whom the suit was argued. My defense was against you, but you were present and unknown to me in that tempest. Although you were a bishop, you had not yet become my bishop. Later indeed, having refused more important offers often gratuitously granted me by heavenly largesse, I chose to become your archdeacon. Unless I am mistaken, you even have this one sound proof of my sympathetic attitude toward you: for with what madness would I, who bristle at the very name of lawsuit, have willingly chosen a never-ending suit and a powerful opponent? If I believed you to be my enemy, I would never have preferred above all others this place where I was a recent arrival, and you were the most established and most powerful citizen with the exception of the pope. But I would certainly have believed that you were my enemy if I knew that I was your enemy; for it is stupid to expect good will from the man you hate. I came to you and to your church with the intention of being at peace, not of quarreling and competing; your character was pleasant, your civility delightful, but I wish it had always had worthy advisers. Nothing about you was displeasing or is displeasing to me except perhaps excessive credulity and levity of mind. If that is a fault, it is not in the least a serious one unless aggravated by rash advice. For if it obeys wise counselors, it is often beneficial and never immoderate. I came then not unaware, but certain, of your kindness and hopeful about your wisdom; nor did I come as to an angry enemy but as to a gracious father whom I used to think so valued virtue that I was esteemed, indeed most esteemed, for having loyally defended the cause of so many distinguished friends, even though against you. Nor did my hope prove false; I found a father, I cherished and shall continue to cherish a father to the end unless forbidden to do so. Such being the case, please lay aside your anger; I ask you not to suspect that I am now planning what I never before had in mind, or that, having been a most faithful defender of friends when I was as yet unknown to you, I could now with total disregard of my character be your most deceitful accuser just when I have become known and dear to you, am held in the greatest esteem, and have become your eye, as they say. It is the duty of a healthy eye not to court danger for the head, but rather to be farsighted, showing what must be avoided and where to be cautious; nor does a healthy head hate its eye, but instead protects it more than the other parts of the body with particular and affectionate care.

It remains for me to answer the slander of those who, without having any proof, and to avoid boredom, even find fault with the time I spend in the Curia, as though it was for your harm and destruction. Rather it was to serve you, given the opportunity, if you wished to make use of my services. For I hear that there are some men close to you—O people vigilant about others' concerns but careless of their own!—who pose questions and answer one another concerning my affairs, as if their eyes could read into my heart. The questioning goes as follows: "Why is the archdeacon absent so long? What is he doing in the Curia?" The reply is: "No doubt he is plotting something evil against the Bishop." If this discussion were about a poet, I could now make use of poetic entreaties; but I am addressing a bishop and must speak more conservatively. And so, against their tongues with which they artfully plot, against their vain hearts, against their throats which open like sepulchres, against their mouths in which there is no truth because they are full of abuse, bitterness, and falsehood, hiding trouble and pain under the tongue, shall I find any remedy except that of the Psalmist who cried out in his tribulations to the Lord: "O Lord, deliver my soul from lying lips, and from the treacherous tongue"? Those other words of the Psalmist also return each day to my lips, always with a new impact, and often cause me to raise supplicant hands to heaven: "Redeem me from the calumny of men, that I may keep your precepts." I shall repeat these and similar words, even while seeming to be silent; nor shall I cease praying until either wickedness, falling back into man's heart, closes his mouth, or the mouths of those who speak falsely are closed by some divine judgment. Up to this point, I have been more violent against them than I wished and perhaps than I ought to be, but the indignity of the matter forced me to it. Yet hereafter, because I see that my business is with those who carry their feelings on their lips, I shall keep mine in my ears, sometimes even on my tongue; and I shall strike back with equal force at those who provoke me for no reason, since a lie is all the more powerful the more fragile and obtuse it is, while the truth is very sharp and cutting. I shall find consolation in thinking that this would never have happened to me if I did not appear more than I am to those bleary and crooked eyes, or certainly more than they want me to be. The worst lot is the one envy does not touch. They say that when Plato was envied by his contemporaries he asked Socrates how he might be safe from envy. Socrates answered, "Live as Thersites," a truly elegant reply by that happy and learned man to his student's question. But in truth, it is much better to imitate Achilles' virtue and be envied than Thersites' sloth and not be envied. Whoever decides to live his life free from envy must forego the pursuit of virtue; I believe this to be the only way. But while fleeing envy on that path, he necessarily falls into contempt. The life of man generally requires him to labor under both evils. To put an end to this discourse which is more necessary than pleasant, I laugh at their question, I detest their answer; and not unjustly, for their question is stupid and their answer poisonous. Yet I accept your question if perchance you ask it, and I reply with my usual candor. "What are you doing in the Curia?" I am languishing, tortured, tormented, offended and—no loss is more serious than this, though none more common—I am wasting time, with which I had decided to be very thrifty. But I consider it important not to overlook the wishes and prayers of friends. Finally, if you should ask what I do, I would not so easily be able to say what I do as what I do not do. Certainly I am hurting no one but myself; I intend to harm no one, and not only not to harm you but to be of assistance to you if I can. Thus your error is to suspect my good will, your cruelty is to hate me. I really do not fear your hatred, provided suspicion vanish. By all the saints in heaven, I beg you, keep it distant from you as an unfortunate and noxious burden. If you have the time, study examples from the ancients, and you will see the many and great afflictions that arise from suspicion; I have not the time for them now. Yet how quickly my memory, unaided by books, serves me so that our discussion need not be completely without illustrations! Hippolytus, a truly chaste young man suspected of incest because of the false accusation of his stepmother, was killed by his unfortunate father. Procris, a most devoted wife, died because of her unknowing husband's fiery jealousy over empty suspicions. To recount more recent and verifiable examples, newly freed citizens drove into exile Tarquinius Collatinus, a most patriotic citizen and an illustrious defender of liberty, because of a capricious suspicion concerning a name. Because of a slight suspicion, too, Hannibal slew his loyal helmsman; a famous Sicilian mountain named after the buried helmsman bears witness to the crime. Demetrius, son of King Philip of Macedonia, beloved even by his enemies because of his noble character, was ordered killed by his credulous father, who was won over by the insinuations of his other son. Time would fail me should I continue with ancient exempla. Even our era has produced contemporary examples that demonstrate how dangerous suspicion always is to friendships. If possible then, please include me among your friends, something I used to take for granted. Should you be hesitant about my loyalty, do as you will. Should you judge me unworthy, cut me off politely; do not drive me from among your friends into the ranks of your enemies, for my flight will surely mean damage not to my reputation, which is slight, but to yours, which is truly great. You will indeed be accused of pride if you make an enemy of one who wishes to be your friend.

28 December, on the Day of the Innocents.

Fam. IX, 6.

To Luca, clergyman of Piacenza.*

Your letters are always agreeable to me, particularly when they arrive as though from heaven bringing comfort to one living in hell. I am held here, I confess, by the hooks of my sins, nor can any stratagem free me. This is scarcely surprising, although unfortunate to someone aware of the nooses of the Curia. But as I am more unhappy here, so am I more gravely indignant and despondent that treachery holds such sway that it dares, and can, persuade any sane person that not only am I prolonging my stay of my own accord but, being infected with the poison of the Curia, am abusing another's reputation; and that what I never considered doing in my leisure and in tranquil times, which often spawn wicked desires, I have begun to do now, having suddenly changed my ways and interests, in this flurry of activities that scarcely gives me time to breathe. For I hear from many sources that our revered father and bishop feels about me otherwise than I deserve and than I wish. For this, I blame not him, but my misfortune and others' wickedness. Since I often pass the day in intimate conversation with you, you can attest before the others what my opinion has always been of his mind and character, provided he would return to himself and his true nature once he is rid of flatterers (that bane shared by popes and princes alike). I therefore have given you this very important task, which I hope you will loyally fulfill. Present to him this lengthy letter which I have written under the influence of anger and grief. If it will find in him that disposition of mind befitting his nobility, his position, and his age, it will eradicate his unfounded suspicion and make certain it never grows again. I beg you, speak to him in person. Farewell.

*Don Luca, whose surname is unknown, was rector of San Stefano in Parma. Petrarch became friends with him during his first stay in Parma in 1341. Later, in 1352, Petrarch transferred a canonry in Modena to him.

Fam. IX, 7.

To the same correspondent, * *concerning suspicion.*

Here is a story I learned from you some time ago. Fire, wind, water, and suspicion were journeying together. When they had reached a crossroads and each wished to take its own path, they said, "Look, we are going separate ways, but let us decide upon a signal so that we might meet again." Then fire said, "Wherever smoke appears, look for me there." But wind replied, "Wherever you see foliage and stalks moving, there I am." And water remarked, "Wherever you catch sight of a rush, I am not far distant." To them suspicion observed, "As for me, I am the easiest to find. You are in constant motion, I am not moved; if I go somewhere once, I stay there." You understand me, my friend; I am throwing your fable back to you after these many years. If the last part were true without exception, I would have poured forth many words in vain. Therefore I wish you to exercise your wits in this matter. We shall see what he will respond to my letter. A tongue or pen, however, will not disclose everything; for a person's face and forehead, posture, complexion, tone, foot, hand, eyes, and eyebrows say much, but nothing to the person who is absent. Since you are there, take care not to prove me wrong. Certainly I seem to have done my duty; suspicion is poison to friendship, and I am trying to eradicate it completely with a measure of truth. Whether he keeps his ear open or closed will be his affair. But consider this one task your responsibility, that you investigate vigorously to which side he will turn and inform me of his plan. Basically, I do not care much what men think or say about me, provided I am not pricked by pangs of conscience. As long as I am at peace with my conscience, I shall not fear external wars. Through the letter I have begun to straighten his slanted opinion. I shall persist if he relents, but I shall cease if he remains obdurate; for he will be obdurate in vain. No one is easily forced to have trust, and often suspicion increases by finding excuses. Farewell.

13 January, from Avignon.

---

*See preceding letter.

Fam. IX, 8.

To Giovanni da Bunio, attorney, * *a friendly letter.*

From our youth to the present time, fortune has begrudged me your face. You were nonetheless always present in my thoughts and—to use the words of our once common studies—I had private rights to you, something which neither distance of place nor passage of time was able to take away from me, nor will death, I believe. I address you then with that youthful intimacy of ours and, with my former privilege restored, as they say, I pick up my pen once again. For we have not communicated for twenty years or more, as you know, which is a period sufficiently long for silence, not to say for a lifetime. I will have to place the blame on me or you or someone else, or else on fortune which has long forced us on paths so athwart and opposed that neither saw, let alone obtained, traces of the other. Now your best wishes for my present state are extended in a brotherly spirit, as you do with everything else. But, my friend, my state, if it is spoken of as a state, is nothing but a tumbledown ruin; and this is the just lot and unavoidable necessity which is no greater for me than for all who are born. Horace has said, "One day is hastened along by the next," and we are dragged along by the course of time without being aware of it. Certainly if there be any good reason for which my friends' congratulations are owed me, I would not doubt that you would sincerely rejoice for me. But how much ought I in turn to congratulate you! In very few words you have described yourself as truly happy, certainly healthy, cheerful and poor, yet rich in spirit. For however much even the rich spirit be praised—whence that poetic saying equating the riches of kings to the riches of the spirit—the living truth nevertheless asserts, "Blessed are the poor in spirit." What more can be said? You are happy and well, if you have turned your mind to this. Farewell.

17 June, from Parma.

*Giovanni da Bunio was a friend from Petrarch's law school years in Bologna. Little or nothing is known about him except what is contained in this letter.

Fam. IX, 9.

To his Socrates, * *that everything must be shared with a friend,
especially friendship.*

I am not a friend unless I share with you my most precious possessions; nothing is more precious than a friend; therefore I am not a
friend unless I share a friend. This is an old saying: "Everything is
held in common among friends." But of how little worth are those
things of seemingly great value which the multitude admires—gold,
silver, necklaces, rings, bracelets, embossed signets, Corinthian vases,
glittering jewels, perfectly rounded pearls, snowy marble, carved
ivory, paintings, lifelike statues, the gleaming purple, and other
things of that nature which are the earth's dregs and dirt or the pride
of sooty artisans! A friend is a particular good, unique and inestimable, which winds may not blow away, nor frosts wither, nor
storms crush; but, as with pure gold, it is refined in the flames of
persecution and hardship. This is a good which does not delight
superficially as so many do, but penetrates the spirit itself with its
sweetness, somehow becoming part of us. Understanding this, Horace called Virgil half of his own soul; and in Lucan that devoted general did not blush at calling his beloved wife the best part of himself,
although perhaps he used words more tender than befits such a man.
I turn again to the friend. If in forming true friendship simultaneous
willing and unwilling is required, who will deny that two persons become one with as much harmony of wills as may scarcely be found
in one and the same mind? A rare occurrence, I do not deny, but this
is so not only in this case, but in nearly everything under the sun for
which abundance and scarcity affect their value. And so, as there is
almost nothing rarer, so there is nothing dearer than true friendship,
which as a gift of heaven becomes the one anchor of a stormy life,
the one respite from toil that can make happiness sweeter and sadness more bearable. In short, a friend is another self, the support of
our condition, the light of our soul, guide of our mind, torch of our
studies, pacifier of all dissensions, partner in our troubles and tasks,
companion in our travels, and a consolation to our households, present not only at home but also in the country and in war, on land
and on sea, an enduring and immortal solace not only during one's
lifetime but also beyond the grave. Indeed, whoever dies leaving
friends behind seems to live especially after he has died. Since this is
so, however great a friend's generosity and kindness, if he clings too

*See I, 1.

tenaciously to this rare boon, if he is similar to that man who either through his fault or, as Juvenal says, "through the fault of his people never shares a friend and keeps him only for himself," he does not deserve the full glory of friendship. Now in pondering upon this, I have decided to share with you, my dearest brother, someone whom his own excellence, and not my merit, made my friend. To describe him to you in a few words, he is Pierre by name, Auvergnat by country, a monk by religion, an abbot by position, black in his habit, white in spirit, quick of wit, sweet of speech, knowledgeable in learning, prudent in judgment, affable at table, young in age, old in seriousness, venerable for honesty. Approach him, I beg you, using this guide whom I sent to you especially for this reason. He will instantly recognize my Socrates about whom I have often spoken; you will rejoice to have found a man such as we have long sought in vain. You will thank me who made you the partner in such an event, although I clearly see how imprudent I am being, uniting two such men whose association and shared admiration of each other's excellence might perhaps diminish their opinion of me. But as long as your love, whose increase I hope for, does not diminish, let your opinion be as it will. Of such magnitude is my faith in you. Farewell.

Mantua, 28 June.

Fam. IX, 10.

To his Lelius,* in praise of a friend.

Dearest Lelius, if you knew when and where I write this, the very circumstances of time and place would excuse my pen and put a spur to you who are always ready and willing to satisfy my desires. It is a stormy night, and I am at Luzzara where I arrived yesterday evening at sunset after setting out from Mantua. It is summertime and Cancer is preparing to send his quiver-bearing friend to Leo; nonetheless you will be surprised to hear that with the south wind blowing daily and the Alpine snows dissolving, this town in the vicinity of the temporarily swollen Po was almost inaccessible to us. Everything was covered with mud, and even dangerous were the paths to the fountains from which we could scarcely restrain our horses. Here indeed I have been received much more agreeably than I thought possible. A messenger of the lords of Mantua, whose grandeur often overcomes even nature itself, had been waiting for me. A sumptuous dinner was laid out: imported wine, exotic dishes, courteous hosts, pleasant faces—in short, everything elegant except the place, where the summer foretells what it may be like in winter. Now in fact it is the home of flies and mosquitoes, whose buzzing advised a hasty departure from the feast. An army of frogs came to attack; you could see them coming from their hiding places into the midst of the banquet and jumping about in the dining room. I escaped to bed having feasted not only on conversation, as Apuleius once did at Milo's in Ipata, but on the tastiest delicacies. And although a very short night urged me to sleep, nevertheless my love for this man made me force my heavy eyes and tired fingers to write you this letter. For he is very dear to me, as you know, and as your admirer he is eager to meet you. He believes, however, that to be worthy of your good graces, he must depend on the aid of my friendship. Because he places hope in you and needs your assistance, dear Lelius, do please let him know what he desires to know, find what he hopes, receive what he seeks, enjoy what he needs. And so, farewell, and remember me.

Luzzara, 28 June, at midnight.

*See III, 19.

Fam. IX, 11.

To Niccolò da Lucca,* that virtue and the reputation of virtue are the best promoters of friendship.

This admirer of yours and of all good men, the promoter and careful propagator of noble friendships, with great enthusiam urged me to write you. Because I refused for some time, uncertain of where to begin or with what words to address a man known to me through reputation alone, he finally prevailed upon me to take up my pen and write you whatever occurred to me. When he saw I had done this, he went away happy and gratified in his desire. As I was considering how to weave artfully from nothing a friendly letter, wondering what we had in common, needing a reason and a subject to write on, the first thing to come to mind was that well-known and excellent maxim of Cicero's, "Nothing is more lovable than virtue, nothing more alluring," and then that its power is such that we often love those whom we have never seen. From that point all wonder and hesitation immediately vanished, and a field broad and favorable for writing appeared: more widely known than your face is your virtue. I see it, and you through it, with clearer eyes; through its merit you are known by me and dear to me. If we cannot love unless we see something with mortal eyes, the first and most important step in loving is lost; no man will love God or himself, for no man ever saw God, his own spirit, or his own face. There is no question that the difference lies in this: just as we love ourselves, whom we have not seen, as a natural act, so we love others for their virtue and fame, the companion and messenger of virtue. It was virtue that compelled Masinissa, most renowned of kings, forgetful of his country and his duties in which the human mind finds particular delight, to request a meeting with Scipio Africanus. The general's inspiring presence caused him to pass over from the Carthaginian to the Roman side. It was the same virtue of Africanus who was present at the trial—a marvel indeed resulting from disparity of minds and customs—that dismissed a suit with a most honorific verdict, since he was indeed a friend not of himself but of virtue, admiring it even in an enemy. And it was the same virtue that dignified the banquet in which Africanus participated, to the glorious admiration of a foreign king and a harsh enemy. Finally it was the same virtue that dignified

---

*Niccolò da Lucca (Niccolosio Bartolomei) was a successful merchant and politician in Lucca and Venice. His humanistic education and interests led him to enjoy contacts with many men of letters, including Petrarch.

Africanus's exile by rendering a band of cutthroats suppliant and prostrate. In short, virtue engendered in the hearts of men the opinion that Scipio was of divine origin, giving rise not only to sincere praise but to legends about him. This is what gives fame to truly deserving men while they are alive on earth, what raises the dead to heaven calling forth from their graves those who will be victorious in eternity. I am relating matters that are more credible. How great and lively is the interest, how intense usually the partisanship, between those who read and those who hear the tales of heroes! Because we so love and praise, not the person we saw, but the person we believed in through fame, we seem to have seen the hero a thousand times. That writer was not ignorant who said: "When wars shall be read of, [these deeds] will excite both hopes and fears, and wishes destined to be of no avail: and all, moved, shall read of your fate as though approaching and not concluded, and still, great Pompey, shall wish you success." This is a great thing; what follows is even greater, since fame as mediatrix makes us accept not only those whom we have never seen or those whom we could not see, but also those whom we rightfully hate. What I say succinctly must be more extensively developed. Fame herself, transforming hatred into love, has subdued strong and highly fortified cities; fame often put an end to serious wars, achieving a victory unattainable by arms yet very pleasing even to the vanquished. It opened the iron gates of the Falisci to Camillus; it bound in friendship, as much as is possible among enemies, King Pyrrhus and the Roman generals, brave Curius and unbending Fabritius; it unexpectedly dissuaded Porsenna, that arrogant ruler of Etruria, from his relentless siege; it prostrated at the feet of Julius Caesar the chieftains of Gaul, who perhaps could have still ventured something dangerous; it directed Pompey the Great to Posidonius's house and Alexander of Macedon to Diogenes' tub; it assigned a most glorious surname with the consent of all mankind to the Emperor Titus, and restored the empire taken from Germanicus to his son although he was unworthy. It once subjected the people of the Orient and many men to the will of a single widow; within our own time it caused Saladin, king of Egypt, not only to be benevolent but munificent toward some of our own people. And to cull some examples from Jewish history, because of fame that great admirer of Solomon came to Jerusalem from a distance to see what she had only heard; and the ambassadors of Maccabeus crossed the seas to make friends with the Romans. Here I am being as apprehensive now about my ending as I was anxious about my beginning! I feared the lack of subject matter, but now I fear that it is excessive and plan to cut it short; so many examples come to my mind from everywhere, from all lands and all ages. In conclusion, why is it so surprising if your virtue, proved by the loyalty of many, but especially by the loyalty of our common friend, leads me captivated by sweetness into friendship with you, especially when we consider that nothing we admired in those men just mentioned stands in the way: neither age, nor nationality, nor war, nor a great difference in fortune or dissimilarity of interests. It was pleasing to my spirit to converse with you in this letter, and it will be still more pleasant to speak with you face to face, if chance should bring us together. But now I am being drawn once again to my usual tasks. And so, farewell, and remember me.

Fam. IX, 12.

To an unknown correspondent, on the great variety of customs and opinions.

I ought to marvel that love so deceives you with regard to me, except that it has often deceived the most learned men, conquered the strongest and subdued the most exalted. You forced me to write to a stranger and it turned out well; I seem to have acquired a good and lasting friend with a brief letter. Since success spawns confidence, as happens in almost all matters, you now urge me to write to another, a great man as you say, whom I still have not seen or spoken to or met, as though certain that he will have the same opinion of me as you. You do not consider that he might have a different opinion either through greater understanding or lesser love. And so you drag my reputation, which I maintain in some fashion among those who respect my good name, against its will to the tribunal of an impartial judge. Your reason for so doing—my having recently written to that other person at your insistence—is invalidated by his nationality alone, even were we to admit that all other circumstances that might be dissimilar were similar. The person to whom I wrote was Italian, the one to whom you ask me to write is Dalmatian, accustomed to a different environment and style. We share the same sea, but not the same shore, spirit, and character, in short not the same way of living and speaking. As the lofty Alps separate us from the French and Germans, and the stormy Tyrrhenian from the Africans, so the Adriatic, which Horace, who lived near it, rightly called restless, divides us from the Dalmatians and Pannonians. You see with your own eyes the great diversity, and even had I some modest reasons for writing to the first, I really have none for writing to the other. From time to time, I am in the habit of writing to my known and intimate friends; more often, of replying to them, not so much from a desire for praise as in the hope for some indulgence and for the far from small pleasure of conversing. I am not in the habit of inflicting these bare and unadorned letters of mine on strangers, particularly on such men as you describe. Spare then, my friend, spare my reputation, I beg you; for among those who cherish it, I know you do not hold last place. In loving me too much, you are forcing it forward, thrusting it into danger. If it pleases you to be mistaken about me, do not seek a partner; if nothing interests you without an ally, be content with old ones if there are any. Seek not new ones and, happy in your mistake as someone said, lead not others into error, especially those who cannot be compelled, who take greater pleasure in solid truth than in flattering misconception. Furthermore, do not allow your delight to perish because of excessive curiosity, since by some accident you may arrive where you do not wish to be, where, in short, the ignorance of your friend, whom your love smears with pleasing cosmetics and covers in charming dress, will be exposed by a stricter judge, and where at the same time the veil under which I hide from your eyes and the error in which you delight will be removed. Consequently, what you willingly believe about me, believe freely, believe peacefully, and do not summon at whim someone who may clothe you with new opinions after stripping you of your old customary ones. He may transport you as if you were a foreigner, even though an experienced settler, from your lands to his, which may be more tranquil but not as congenial to your spirit. It is not proper for good taste to seek what may be distasteful. Farewell.

Fam. IX, 13.

To Philippe de Vitry, musician, * *rebuking the ineptness of those persons so restricted to one corner of the world as to consider even a glorious absence undesirable.*

My friendly words will strike friendly ears as true rather than flattering, as sincere rather than elegant. Great is the frankness of friendship, great its security. Whoever loves much fears nothing; or rather great love fears and notices everything, especially what it suspects might offend the loved one. Indeed Seneca observed about his own friend that "I do not love him, lest I offend him." Nothing less do I wish than to offend you. But never let it be said that you may be offended by the truth, you who have always been a very dedicated and eager seeker of the truth. I hope you will rather take delight in it, and with the strength of your virtue find a remedy for the frailty of your mind, so that, as a great philosopher of our age who rejects the prejudices of the raving multitude, you may at length speak not only as a man but as a true philosopher. What, I ask, remains to man that might be called not eternal, but lasting, when old age penetrates even the mind? With reason and with experience as my teacher, with even a famous historian as witness, I have learned that "all that is born dies, all that grows ages." But I considered the human spirit exempt from the inevitable fate of mortal things, as something not earthly but celestial and as something formed of eternal substance that rises on high by its own strength and by the wings of its own nature, so to speak, and despises death, which creeps and rages along the ground. What I had read in the poet about some ancient peoples in Italy whose "sluggish old age does not weaken their strength of mind" I once applied more extensively to the entire human race. You compel me to doubt this opinion. For you seem, O distinguished sir—I shall state clearly what I mean—you seem to me, I say, to have aged not so much in body as in mind. But if this could happen to you amidst such wealth of learning and virtues, what are we to think will happen to those naked and defenseless ones with no consolation in their virtue and no assistance from letters, suited to nothing other than increasing the numbers of the multitude, born only to eat food,

---

*Philippe de Vitry (1291–1361) was a chaplain of John XXII and of the Cardinal of Boulogne, and eventually Bishop of Meaux (1351) and secretary to Charles IV. He was a man of learning and poetic ability, a composer of religious songs, and translator of Ovid's *Metamorphoses*. In Petrarch's fourth eclogue he is "Gallus."

as Horace so aptly said? You will not deny that the mind can also die if it can grow old, since without doubt old age is the last part of life and a descent, as it were, to death. Once we concede this, you see what follows: both the sweetness of life as a whole and the hope of immortality are snatched away. It was this hope alone that kept me from grieving at being a man, subject on the one hand to temporal death and on the other to a more noble destiny, and, as faith teaches us as well as nature, destined ultimately to live with both the eternal and blessed life. I am well aware that you are wondering where my words are leading with such long digressions. If I really know you and your mind, you already understand what I am saying, or am about to say, since by this time your conscience is taunting you.

As you know, the famous clergyman Gui, bishop of Porto, apostolic legate to the Holy See, is here. Already I can picture your expression; a modest blush is spreading over your face. You did not realize that I would examine your letter, which is in his possession. Had you suspected this, you would never have spoken so weakly, so humbly and, forgive my strong words, so effeminately, if not out of respect for me, at least out of respect for the Muses who are my guests. If these do not now arm themselves with their verses, the reason is not patience but rather lack of time. I ask you, what do you say to this? Examine the meaning of your words with me; I am dealing with you, as they say, with evidence in hand. You make accusations against this common lord of ours; you sting and you blame, you deplore with an excessively intolerable irresolution, not his absence but—as you call it—his exile, and you disgrace with an unfortunate word his truly sacred pilgrimage, which could not be more glorious. Surely this is that old age which I lament in you, my friend. You would never have spoken that way when I first knew you. Your extraordinary passion and ardor for examining secrets and mysteries, in which you seemed second to none, has cooled. Is there, then, no middle path between restless curiosity and extreme sluggishness? Once India used to appear not too distant to you. At one time with eager mind, you used to take measure of Thoprobanes and whatever unknown places exist in the Eastern Ocean. At other times, you used to sigh for Ultima Thule hidden on unknown shores, after the Orkneys, Ireland, and whatever lands the Mediterranean washes lost their appeal for you because of their very proximity. Why, indeed, is it surprising if the earth seemed too small for the mind of a very learned man who turns with indefatigable eagerness toward that celestial pole continually rotating above us guided by an icy rudder, or toward that other pole which—if the Antipodes exist—men clearly behold in the southern region, or finally toward the oblique path of the sun and toward the fixed and wandering stars? Is there anything that passage of time does not destroy? To be in Italy may seem to you a wretched exile, whereas to be far from it might more likely resemble an exile but for the fact that any soil is a strong man's fatherland. With your permission, I would like to suggest that the Parisian Petit-Pont and its arch, not quite in the shape of a tortoise shell, is too appealing to you; the murmur of the Seine flowing under it delights your hearing too much; finally the dust of France lies too heavily on your shoes. In my opinion, you seem to have forgotten that man who, when asked where he was from, answered that he was a citizen of the world. You are so thoroughly French that you call leaving France for any reason whatsoever an exile. I do not deny that the appeal of our native land is implanted in us, and I do know that illustrious men were by no means destitute of this feeling. I read in Livy, the historian, that Camillus, restorer of Rome and of the empire, equal to any of the most powerful leaders, was silent in his Ardean exile, confessing that he was tormented by the memory of, and by the desire for, his native land; I read in the poetry of Virgil that Diomedes attributed to the gods' envy the fact that he would not again see his Calydon; I read that Ovid deplored his absence from his native land, not in a few words but in a complete volume; and I read that Cicero endured his exile with so little manliness that the eloquence of Cicero seemed to lack Ciceronian talent. Besides all this, I know that characteristic of irresolute and weak souls, when honorable reasons are lacking, is an inability to break their fetters and rise above them, or to subordinate the pleasures of the eyes to virtue, which is pleasure of the mind. There are a great number of foreign and Roman generals and philosophers who spent their lives in constant travels to increase either their military or intellectual reputation; but because I recall more willingly what is closer to my profession, I shall mention some of the philosophers. When Plato left Athens—where, if it is proper to say so, he was worshiped as a terrestrial god—he first went to Egypt, then to Italy. How great a hardship for a man accustomed to a sedentary life! But through all the difficulties of his journey, he used his desire for learning as a vehicle. Then there is the famous trip of Democritus, and the more famous one of Pythagoras, who never returned home once he had left, being more inflamed with the love of truth than of country; accordingly he traveled throughout Egypt, as Cicero narrates, visited the Persian magi, traversed countless foreign lands on foot, and crossed many seas. If you wish to know the ultimate destination of his travels, it was Italy herself where he lived the last twenty years of his life in the very place where you lament a single year's stay by our friend as a tearful exile and truly wasted time. Rouse yourself, rouse yourself, I beg you, awaken your sleeping mind and lift your fallen spirit! You will see the extent to which you are victimized by a cloud of vulgar opinions, when you say those things which I wish I had not read. His is not an exile, as you think, but an honorable sojourn, praiseworthy and dignified, an occasion for everlasting fame with minimal effort. At present, it is difficult to persuade you of this since you think nothing splendid or agreeable, as I see it, except Paris and those few clods of your small field to which you have devoted your mind. But when you become once again your old self and, with the multitude excluded, begin to judge for yourself and have confidence in yourself, I shall renew my confidence in you. Give me back my old companion and the old Philippe. By my being silent, truth will do the pleading. Now this quarrel of mine is not with you but with another Philippe, your enemy. Therefore, be forgiving if you perhaps read something said more freely than the contemporary custom for flattery allows. As Brutus says in a letter to Cicero: "To speak eloquently is indeed beneficial to those who know not what is or is not to be feared."

Let us return to your exiled friend, about whom you are so disturbed and anxious. I wish you could see him, more magnificent than usual, advancing with head held high through Italian cities. I wish you could see the concourse of people and rulers attending him with honor; I wish you could hear the joyful voices of those who everywhere applaud and support him. You would be ashamed of your cowardly words, and would not call him an exile, but more accurately the author of peace and tranquillity and the savior of the state. Since the causes of war between the kingdoms of Hungary and Sicily gushed from deep wells of hatred, dragging a large portion of Europe into danger, and since deadly insurrections had to be suppressed by timely assistance in order to be quelled, no one else could be found for so important a task. If you consider this judgment of the pope, this opinion of the College of Cardinals, this public hope and this joy to be wretched and painful for him, I know not what you would call happy and fortunate. But I beg you, tell me in the name of reason, which ought to control your feelings, what leisure can you compare to this task, what pleasures to these causes, what repose to these labors? Let the epicurean multitude proclaim what it will; I prefer such a noble mission to all delights and pleasures which sleep or food, ambition or passion might offer. For all virtue, all glory, all noble delights are difficult to attain; by descending, a person arrives at obscene pleasures, by ascending, at honorable ones. Therefore, do not deplore the truly enviable fortune of this man; instead, consider yourself an exile and lament it, since you have so distanced yourself from the contemplation of his glory. Even now I might mourn and pity in equal measure your misfortune and your exile, were it not that in pitying him you silently judged your own situation to be happy. On the other hand, I fear to pity one who is happy lest this be useless compassion, unless perhaps it is in fact the greatest mercy to have compassion on someone who is falsely joyful. What is more, if you have become sedentary before your time, nonetheless be just and allow this man, whom I know for certain you love with your entire mind, to have preferred to an inert immobility this magnificent journey. He is at the prime of life, possessing a strong body, a famous lineage, a lofty talent, and a burning desire for knowledge. Driven by these goads, he left the Seine and the Rhone, and even visited unknown regions. Daring to spurn his teacher, his playmate and his nurse, he attempted manly pursuits, following the distinguished, although difficult, path of unbending virtue.

Lest you think that only philosophers undertook such journeys and that, therefore, this man born of royal blood must be distinguished from their humble condition, I shall cite examples which are even more illustrious. Scipio was twenty-four when his courage belied his age and he set out for Spain against four strong Carthaginian armies and against an equal number of outstanding commanders. After his return laden with countless victories and happy in the praises he had earned, he could have been content to remain at home as a famous private citizen. But since Hannibal was thundering through Italy, he preferred to cross over into Africa against the will of the Senate—which might amaze you—and against the judgment of Fabius Maximus, both tremendous obstacles. As victor in the midst of extremely difficult circumstances, he followed his own calling to greater glory in order to return with security rather than riches for his country, and with a surname for himself; for he went as Cornelius and returned as Africanus. Hannibal himself, whose journey was troublesome and almost fatal for us, left home as a boy in his eagerness to acquire fame and to extend his empire, and returned an old man. What of Alexander of Macedonia, who never did return home? What of Pompey the Great, whose travels throughout his entire life left scarcely a corner of the world unexplored? What of Julius Caesar and his ten-year journey through Gaul, Germany, and Britain? You know from histories, as your ancestors knew from their defeats, how glorious it was for him, how frightful for you. It is well known that his next march lasting four years, briefer in time but greater in importance and extensiveness, led him to the height of power in the midst of innumerable worldwide upheavals, so that even after the fall of the empire its name still lives on. Neoptolemus went to Troy, scorning the entreaties and tears of his grandfather. Had he obeyed them, his father and his country would have remained unavenged. Ulysses too went to Troy, and even further, crossing lands and seas; nor did he stop before he had founded a city bearing his name on a most distant western shore. At home he had an aged father, a young son, a youthful wife beset by suitors, while he fought with Circe's poisonous cups, the sirens' songs, the violent Cyclops, sea monsters, and tempests. This man, famous for his wanderings, put aside his affections, neglected his throne, and scorned his responsibilities. Rather than grow old at home, he preferred to age between Scylla and Charybdis, among the black whirlpools of Avernus, and in the midst of such difficult circumstances and locations as to weary even the reader's mind. He did all this for no other reason than to return one day to his country more learned in his old age. And truly, if experience makes men learned, if it is the mother of the arts, what skill or what praiseworthy achievement might a person expect who remained the perpetual keeper of his paternal home? It is proper for the good peasant to remain in his own country, to understand the quality of his land, the behavior of his cattle, the quality of his waters and his trees, the success of his crops, the advantages of the seasons, the changes in the weather, and finally his rakes, hoes, and ploughs. But it is characteristic of a noble spirit that aspires to lofty goals to have seen many lands and the customs of many men, and to have assimilated them. What you have read in Apuleius is very true: "Not unjustly did the divine father of ancient Greek poetry, wishing to present a man of utmost wisdom, sing that the greatest virtues were achieved by the person who had witnessed the downfall of many cities and known many peoples." In imitation of this, you know the many cities and shores to which our poet led his Aeneas.

You who are now the sole French poet, have pity on this Ulysses or Aeneas of yours, who has been a testing ground for your talent and material for your pen, because he has seen something other than Paris. You do not realize what a pleasing spectacle it was, and will be, for him to see with his own eyes what he imagined in his mind. We know what the Emperor Hadrian used to do. Those places that through reading or reputation he considered famous, he quite eagerly wished to see personally; nor did the weight of empire hinder him from doing so. As Cicero says in the *Tusculans*, "If those men who have seen the mouth of the Pontus and the narrows through which passed that ship named 'Argo, because in it sailed the glorious Argives seeking the golden fleece of a ram,' or if those who saw the ocean's mouth 'where the greedy water divides Europe and Libya' think they have accomplished something," what must our bishop think who has seen the Italian Alps, once shattered by Phoenician fire and vinegar? With unimpeded vision, he took measure of the broad, smiling fields of Cisalpine Gaul and of Milan, a city illustrious and flourishing and founded by your ancestors, as writings through many centuries prove; he took measure of Brescia and Verona and in their midst Lake Garda—the former being extraordinary creations of men, the latter of nature. From there he went on to Padua, founded by the Trojan Antenor. He next visited that wonderful, beautiful, and greatest city of all on the Venetian shores, then little Treviso girded by rivers and pleasant with summer delights, which he chose as his residence, not so much for his own convenience as to provide for the comfort and needs of foreign visitors. Next he went beyond Aquileia to quell northern insurrections; crossing the Noric Alps he traveled far and wide throughout Germany and reached the Danube, once the boundary of the empire, equal to the Nile, proud with its thousand springs and seething with dreadful whirlpools. Having recently returned amidst great praise, he has this very day transferred the body of St. Anthony the Minor amid the devotion of an immense throng; that was the sole reason for his somewhat protracted sojourn in Padua. Tomorrow he will resume his journey so that, just as he saw the roaring of the Adriatic, he will witness the Tyrrhenian tempests. First he will cross the Po, king of rivers—unless he views the Seine as such; he will then proceed to Ravenna, said to be the most ancient of cities, then to Rimini and Perugia, a most powerful city; and passing through others on the way he will finally arrive at the capital and mistress of the world, Rome. Whoever has not seen it admires others thoughtlessly. If the good fortune of the Romans at times rendered the appearance of the city more splendid, the year of the Jubilee will render it more sacred than ever before. Even though you call him an exile, he appears to me a most fortunate traveler. He will cross the thresholds of the apostolic churches and he will tread upon ground dark with the holy blood of martyrs; or he will view a likeness of the Lord's face preserved on a woman's veil or depicted on the walls of the mother of churches; he will gaze at the spot where Christ appeared to the fugitive Peter and see on the hard stone his footsteps which all nations will worship eternally; he will enter the Holy of Holies, a shrine filled with heavenly grace; he will admire the Vatican and the cave of Calixtus built from saints' bones; he will look at the Savior's cradle and a relic of His circumcision, and a wonderfully shining vessel of the Virgin's milk; he will see Agnes's ring and meditate upon the miracle of conquered lust; he will contemplate the maimed head of the Baptist, Lawrence's grill, and Stephen's remains, which were brought from elsewhere so that both of them might rest peacefully in a single tomb; he will behold where Peter was crucified, where from Paul's spilt blood sprang forth fountains of pure water, where a stream of olive oil emptied into the Tiber when the Lord was born, where the foundations of a magnificent church were laid on the traces of a summer snowfall, where mighty temples collapsed at the Virgin Birth, where Simon in a fall from heaven disgraced the innocent rock; and he will be shown Silvester's hiding place and the site of Constantine's vision as well as the divinely prescribed cure for his incurable malady, and countless other things. A part of these I once included in two lengthy letters to a friend, and later rendered in verse.

If ever his mind descends to the earthly from the heavenly, he will notice the palaces, although in ruins, of Roman leaders and emperors, the palaces of the Scipios, Caesars, Fabii, and the remains of others which have no limit or number; he will marvel at the Seven Hills, enclosed by a single wall and once the ruler of all the earth, the mountains and the seas, and the broad highways once too narrow for lines of prisoners; he will see the triumphal arches laden with plunder from subjugated kings and people; he will climb the Capitoline, head and citadel of all lands, where once existed a shrine to Jove; now it is Ara Coeli where, as they say, the Christ child appeared to Caesar Augustus. Indeed this is what he will see; but you, every time you contemplate the fields of St-Germain and the hill of Ste-Geneviève, will think you have seen all that the sun shines upon from its rising to its setting, happy in your illusion, if indeed there can be any happiness in error. Upon his departure from Rome—to tell you all—he intends to visit the Etruscan cities—Viterbo, which lies in a green valley surrounded by icy and tepid springs; Orvieto, remarkable because of its recent monument and located on the summit of a wide, steep plateau; Siena too, emulous of Rome because of its nursing she-wolf and seven hills, whose beauty exceeds that of any city built on high (nor in my judgment does the charm of any French city rival hers); nearby Florence, the work of Roman generals, about which I shall say nothing for now so that love of country will not make you mistrustful of me, or me of you. From there, after crossing the Apennines once again, he intends to return here, passing through learned Bologna in order to convene a solemn council of the prelates in his legation; and so he will at last arrive in Milan and bearing left will cross the Apennines for the third time to see Genoa, truly deserving a visit, for no city is more fearless, and could today more rightfully be called a city of kings, if civil harmony existed there; then around the Gulf of Liguria, sunnier than all others, through forests of cedar and palm, over the fragrant and resounding shore he will reach the borders of Italy in order to return to France. These are not signs of a hurried mind affected by boredom. You can see how he is traveling in a circuitous manner, how delight at his arrival is obvious in many places, how his noble mind is refreshed by the sight of a variety of things. Thus, your exiled friend has reason for great joy in having seen many great and memorable things, in having everywhere exalted his illustrious name with his presence, something which usually diminishes fame. In this too Italy has cause for rejoicing since in the midst of the clouds of our age she has been calmed by him as though by a lucky star. This land which, from the beginning of history, as you yourself well know, was always praised above other lands according to the testimony of every author, has now found in our day a great supporter where it was not expecting one. Believe me, upon his return you will marvel at his discussions of Italian affairs. For this reason if you long impatiently for such a father, if you lament your loneliness and the rust growing on your mind because of excessive neglect, I can forgive human weakness. If because of him, however, you envy us, or because of us you envy him, then indeed you deserve to be gnawed by a satirist's tooth, since another's joy torments you. Accordingly, whatever is, is short-lived. Next summer will bring you victory, restoring to you the one it will take away from us. Nonetheless no amount of time will eradicate his image from our hearts. And consider how much more happily and more worldly he will be upon his return, how much more eminent not only to others but even to himself, since he will have seen so much with his own eyes and will have seasoned French urbanity with Italian dignity! Ashamed of your childish complaints, you will turn that elegant eloquence of yours into applause. There was no excuse for them except that they were written in the vernacular, showing that you followed not your own judgment but that of the rabble whose opinion was always blind and base.

Farewell, enjoy good health, and remember me. The physician Marco, compatriot of Virgil, sends greetings.

Padua, 15 February.

Fam. IX, 14.

To Luca da Piacenza, clergyman, in praise of love*
for the solitary life.

I feel your anguish as much in your words as in your silence. This I know: many are persecuting you on account of me; but why me? I confess I do not know, unless perhaps they are offended by my name which, although unimportant and obscure, may nonetheless appear to them greater and more famous than blind envy can bear. I no longer marvel at it; as the great seas surge with perpetual waves, so do names which are great or seem to be great. Let us yield to these tempests not from fear but from disdain which, when it grows to excess, creates nausea. We shall go and take refuge, but not ingloriously; for our names, unless I am mistaken, will be heard tormenting the envious everywhere more distinctly from the hiding places than from the cities. Have no doubt, God will conceal us in a safe port and will protect us from the slander of men so that we might keep His commandments. I have directed all my attention to this, I work for it day and night; God will not deny a devout prayer. Indeed I might accomplish the entire matter more easily if you would give your approval, which seems in the offing. Know that I am convinced, my friend, that you are a good man, otherwise I would not have embraced your friendship. If I had unknowingly stumbled upon it by chance, I either would have renouned it as our ancestors did or gently severed it following the advice of Cato; I would not have broken it off rudely. With this understood, I am in accord with whatever you do or say. But remember that never did you say anything so pleasing to me with such effectiveness and, insofar as I could understand, with all the power and strength of your mind, as your recent words urging me and you to pursue solitude. My friend, you speak well, wisely, truly, seriously, soundly; for I know, speaking specifically about us rather than generally, that only with difficulty can we live well and die well without solitude; and that we must now turn our thoughts to death no less than to life, and to the destination no less than to the journey. Nature, our guide, made us solitary; why do we refuse her and follow indirect paths? May hope of a longer life not deceive us, nor that saying of David's which has by now deluded countless people; it assigns seventy years to one's life and even eighty years to men of strength. I do not oppose this; all sayings of the prophet are true, but the majority of mankind does not reach fifty. How many thousands of occu-

*See IX, 6.

pations, what an array of undertakings that prophetic authority interrupted! What David set as the outside limit we have interpreted as the mean, and what he promised to the few and the strong we promise to all! Let vain hopes cease, let no one deceive us, in fact let us not deceive ourselves; may that saying of Cicero's not apply to us: "Everyone covets the good fortune of Metellus." God can indeed give us extraordinary and magnificent gifts, but we must nevertheless aspire to simple things out of moderation and mankind's common lot. But even if life were very long, you can easily judge how far we are from its end if you look back and begin measuring the future by considering the past. As for your request for the *De vita solitaria* as a substantial aid to your purpose, there was no need even to mention it. Whatever has emerged from this talent of mine is at your disposal and ready for you, although it has not yet been made public. The same holds for the works of the ancients, which I possess in great numbers. Therefore, since I presently lack the time to say anything more concerning this, keep firmly in mind that my friendship for you has increased wonderfully because you have written so effectively on solitude. Now for my sake you must persist in your convictions with perseverance and with courage. Farewell.

Fam. IX, 15.

To Guglielmo da Verona, orator,* in gratitude.

I am grateful to you, O illustrious sir, for being so indulgent with me; for I much prefer assistance in my studies than in my pleasures, although studies do have their own honest and honorable pleasures, which in my opinion are better known to you than to any man. I greatly need that book for my series on illustrious men to which I have devoted my modest abilities. Therefore hurry, I beg you; you know the preciousness of time for those who weigh their hours and minutes. I send you too my special gratitude for reminding me about such an important responsibility. I tried to do as you advised, and I would have done so even on my own. In fact I had already begun to do so, but you know my slowness and contempt for such things. Just as I hope to die a death which is not total, so in all my activities does almost everything that happens on earth seem to be a silly fable and an utterly empty dream. I thus needed an incentive, which, knowing my ways, you provided through your friendship, and drove me despite my hesitation to do a good turn. How effective it will be, the outcome itself will show. If we can have any confidence in intuition, your honest advice will not have to be without result. Farewell.

*Guglielmo da Pastrengo (Guglielmo da Verona) was born in 1290 and died in 1362. A notary and judge, he was also among the first humanists and a devotee of the ancients. He was one of the first to write a universal encyclopedia (*De origini-bus rerum*) of authors from every age, nation and persuasion. Petrarch addressed six metrical letters to him.

Fam. IX, 16.

To the same correspondent, * *on false hope.*

Our plan has failed; hope, the daily plague of mortals, has deluded us. Nothing is more false, and yet nothing enjoys greater credibility. Are you surprised? You certainly should not be. I speak of something that is well known and common. But if you were to ask the cause for this evil, it is human greed, the companion of hope, which orders us to believe everything because it covets everything. And so, hope was false, greed credulous, and we were deceived. You did what you could, but the rashness, injustice, and cruelty of others have overcome that prudence, loyalty, and piety of yours with which you honored me according to our native custom: an array of three enemies, a well-known battle, an unworthy victory! But let us retreat lest we aggravate the injustice through our impatience. Nothing remains to be said except what a certain wise man supposedly said: when human assistance fails we must seek divine assistance. Farewell, and remember me.

*See preceding letter.

Fam. X, 1.

To Charles IV, Emperor of the Romans,* an appeal to cross into Italy.

The present letter, O most glorious Caesar, shudders at the precipice confronting it, conscious as it is of its author, whence it came, and whither it may be going. Is it any wonder that, born in the shadows, it is shaken by the splendor of your most illustrious name? But since love expels all fear, it will see the light, if for no other reason, as the bearer of my affection. I beg you to read it, O glory of our age; read it and do not fear from me the flatteries, public bane of kings, which I understand are hateful to you. Prepare your ears instead for laments, for you will hear a querulous discourse, not a flattering one. Why have you become unmindful of us, and, if I may say so, of yourself? Where has your concern for Italy gone? We truly hoped that you, like a messenger from heaven, would be a resolute defender of our freedom. You flee instead; when there is need for action, you waste time in tedious deliberations. See, O Caesar, the confidence with which I, an insignificant and unknown man, deal with you. I beg you not to become enraged at the liberty I am taking, but rather to rejoice over your character and your ways, which give me such confidence. Why, then, to continue where I left off, do you spend so much time in deliberations as if certain of the future? You do not know how little time is needed for the greatest events to evolve; what has developed over many centuries is often accomplished in one day. Believe me, if you consider your own reputation or the condition of the empire, you will realize that, as with your situation, ours does not brook delays. Is it not true that life is uncertain and fleeting, and though you may be at its peak, your life is still unstable and continuously flying and flowing away? Therefore, even though you may not sense it, each day thrusts you toward old age; and while you look about in hesitation, unexpected gray hairs secretly begin to appear. Or perhaps you hestitate lest you undertake too soon what you believe the longest life will scarcely suffice to accomplish? You must turn to matters that are neither simple nor ordinary. The Roman Empire,

*Charles of Bohemia was not officially crowned Emperor until 1355, although he had been proclaimed king of the Romans in Avignon in 1346 upon his father's abdication. This letter was written February 24, 1351, but the Emperor's response did not reach Petrarch until 1353, following his second appeal in *Fam.* XII, 1. Both appeals were written prior to Petrarch's personal acquaintance with the Emperor in 1354.

long buffeted by countless storms, has finally placed its often deluded, although at present hardly confident, hope of safety in your valor. After innumerable misfortunes it breathes in some fashion in the shadow of your name, but it cannot feed for long on hope alone. You understand the great and sacred weight of responsibilities you have assumed. We beg you to bring them to a conclusion, and to do so as soon as possible. Most precious, indeed inestimable, is time; in this alone does the authority of learned men recommend avarice. Cease all delay, therefore, and view each passing day as a great good, a most useful trait for those who attempt great deeds. Such an attitude will make you frugal with time; it will compel you to come to Italy and to reveal the desired light of your venerable face amidst the clouds of our adversities. Do not let your solicitude for transalpine affairs or the sweetness of your native soil detain you. Each time you view Germany, think of Italy. You were born there, but raised here. There you have a kingdom, here you have a kingdom and an empire; without offense to any nation or land, here you will find the very head of the monarchy whereas elsewhere you will only find its members. There is, therefore, no room for sloth so that all things may happen as you desire. It will be a great achievement to gather together so many scattered pieces. I understand indeed that every new idea is suspect, but you are not being drawn into any novelty since you know Italy as well as Germany. Sent to us by a propitious divinity, you followed from infancy the lofty path of your illustrious father; under his guidance you came to know the cities of Italy, the customs of its people, the location of its lands, and the beginnings of a glorious army. Even as a mere boy, in a kind of superhuman fashion, you often earned here remarkable victories. However great your other accomplishments, still greater ones were hidden in the mysterious expedition of your youth. Because of it, you as a man would not fear the land which offered you, while still a boy, the opportunity for countless victories; and because of it you were to find here in your first military campaign what you might expect as emperor. Add to this the fact that Italy never awaited with greater anticipation the arrival of any foreign prince, it never hoped for a remedy for its wounds from any other source; neither did it fear your yoke, although you were a foreigner. This is how extraordinarily your majesty is viewed among us in case you did not know; why then should I fear expressing to you my ideas about matters that can be put to the test with your personal judgment? Through a wonderful favor of God, indeed, in your person has been restored to us our ancestral rule and our

Augustus after so many centuries. The Germans may claim you as much as they please for themselves; we consider you Italian.

Make haste therefore, as I have said so often, and I must repeat still more often, make haste. I realize that you find pleasure in actions worthy of Caesars, nor can I blame you since you are Caesar. Yet that first framer of the Empire is said to have worked with such speed that he would often arrive before his emissaries. Do likewise, attempting to equal in deeds him whom you have equaled in title. Do not weary deserving Italy any longer with its desire to see you; do not extinguish our ardor with expectation and announcements. You alone do we desire, only your divine face do we wish to view. If you are a friend of virtue, if you are desirous of glory, "you will not deny"—to say about our Charles what Marcus Tullius said to Julius Caesar—"that, although you are wise, you are most eager for it." I beg you not to avoid the needed labor, for he who flees toil flees both glory and virtue which can be attained only over a steep, toilsome road. We urge you whom we know to be most desirous of noble toil and true fame to rise up, to act, and as a just distributor of heavy burdens, to assign the more weighty ones, whatever they may be, to someone of appropriate age with broader shoulders. Youth is more suited to toil, old age to repose. There is little question that, of all your most worthy and holy cares, none is more important than restoring a tranquil peace to Italy. That burden is equal to the powers of your present age, while all others are too insignificant to preoccupy such a great and noble mind. Do this first then; what remains will have its time, although once Italy has been fully pacified and restored, I believe there will remain hardly anything to do. Imagine now in your mind this cherished image of Rome; behold an old lady advanced in years but with few gray hairs, with her garments torn to shreds and a mournful pallor, yet unbroken and elevated in spirit, fully aware of her earlier majesty, who speaks to you in the following manner: "O Caesar, disdain not my age. Once I was powerful and accomplished much. I established laws, I assigned divisions to the year, I taught discipline to the military. After having spent five hundred years in Italy, during the following two hundred years—and there are many worthy witnesses of these events—I wandered throughout Asia, Africa, Europe, the entire world, fighting wars and earning victories, strengthening the foundations of the rising Empire with much perspiration, blood, and deliberation. I beheld our first founder of liberty, Brutus, when he obeyed me by killing his sons, dying from the wounds suffered in common with his arrogant enemy. I was astounded by an armed man and a helpless maiden swimming in the Tiber. I saw the generous exile of Camillus, the toilsome military service of Cursorius, the unkempt hair of Curius, elected consul while still working his plow, the farmer become dictator, the regal poverty of Fabritius, the famed funeral of Publicola, the strange burial of Curtius while he was still alive, the glorious prison of Atilius, the Decii devoted to death with a singular devotion, the memorable duel of Corvinus, Torquatus gentle with his father but demanding with his son, the blood of the Fabii shed together, the astonished Porsenna, and the generous, smoking hand of Mutius. I have suffered the flames of the Senones, the elephants of Pyrrhus, the wealth of Antiochus, Mithridates' obstinacy, the folly of Syphax, the troubles with the Ligurians, the Samnite Wars, Cimbrian uprisings, Macedonian threats, and Carthaginian deceits; I have seen Carrhae, Egypt, Persia, Arabia, Pontus, the two Armenias, Galatia, Cappadocia, Thrace, Moorish shores, and Ethiopian sands. I have seen the fields of Libya and Spain, the Sestian waters, the Ticino, the Trebbia, Lake Trasimeno, Cannae, and Thermopylae made famous with Persian blood. I have seen the Danube and the Rhine, the Indus and the Hydaspes, the Rhone and the Iber, the Euphrates and the Tigris, the Ganges, the Nile, the Hebrus, the Don, and the Aras. I have seen Taurus and Olympus, the Caucasus and Atlas. I have seen the Ionian and the Aegean, the Scythian and Carpathian seas, the Gulf of Hellespont and the narrows of Euboea, the Adriatic and Tyrrhenian seas. Finally I have seen the ocean subdued by our fleet, which I stained with the blood of my enemies and of my sons so that an eternal peace would follow a succession of wars, and so that through the labor of many the Empire, destined for you, would be established. Nor did my intention fail me, for with my prayers answered I saw the entire world at my feet. Then, slowly, in a manner unknown to me except that perhaps works of mortals are intended to be mortal, a strange sluggishness crept into my labors; not to tell a tearful story, you can see for yourself to what the situation has been reduced. You, destined by God to help me who am now so near to despair, why do you delay, why are you uncertain, why are you waiting? Never was I more in need of you, or were you more suited for rendering assistance; never was the Roman Pontiff more clement or the people's expectation greater, the good will of God and of men more propitious or an undertaking more illustrious. Do you delay? Delay has always been the enemy of great princes. Let your mind be moved by outstanding examples of men who, deferring nothing until old age, energetically seized the occasion as it presented itself. At your age, Alexander the Macedonian attacked the kingdoms of India after having wandered through the Orient in order to plunder others. Will you not enter Italy, which is devoted to you, to reclaim what is yours? At your age, Scipio Africanus crossed over into Africa, though against the better judgment of his elders, and extended his generous hand to aid the Empire which was already wavering and threatened by destruction. Through his singular virtue, the Carthaginian yoke was broken. It was a truly remarkable undertaking, memorable because of the unusual danger, to invade enemy territory while our own burned, and to lure from here in order to conquer with arms elsewhere that Hannibal who was then mulling in his arrogant mind control of the entire world after his conquests of Italy, France, and Spain. You will not have to cross any rivers, or defeat any Hannibal; the journey is easy, the road flat and open. Those roads that some men consider closed will open at the thunder of your approach. Unless it is not to your liking, an enormous arena for achieving new glory is open to you. Enter vigorously and undaunted! God, the defender of justice and the helper of princes, will assist you. Armed forces of good men, seeking once again their lost liberty under your leadership, will assist you. I could now incite you with contrasting examples of men incapable of bringing an undertaking to a successful conclusion after auspicious beginnings because of death or an extraordinary obstacle. If domestic examples suffice, there is no need to seek foreign ones. Therefore, one alone, quite near in time, and not to be found in the chronicles, will suffice for all. I am referring to your grandfather, Henry, that outstanding man of eternal memory. Had he lived sufficiently long to bring to a conclusion what he had conceived in his holy mind, the flow of events would have been altered; he would have shattered the enemy, leaving the people completely free and exceedingly happy under my rule. Now, as an eternal inhabitant of heaven, he looks down upon us, counting the days and the hours, and together with me he rebukes you by saying: 'Dearest grandson, in whom neither the hope of good men nor I perished entirely, cherish our Rome, her tears and her prayers, and pursue determinedly the reformation of the republic which my death, more harmful to the world than to me, halted; pursue with equal conviction but more happily and successfully that zeal of spirit which was futile to me. Begin, hesitate not, and, mindful of me, know that you are mortal. Move rapidly and cross the Alpine passes amidst the inhabitants' rejoicing. Rome summons her bridegroom, Italy summons her deliverer and desires to be trampled by your feet. The joyful hills and rivers await you, the cities and towns await you, bands of good men await you. If nothing else urges you on, then let the knowledge that for evil men your delay will never seem sufficiently long, while for good men your haste will never be sufficiently fast, provide cause enough for hastening to bring joy to the good and punishment to the wicked or, if they prefer to repent, forgiveness. For you alone did Almighty God reserve the glory of my interrupted plan.' "

24 February, from Padua.

Fam. X, 2.

To his Socrates, freindly concern about his condition.*

The absence of friends always produces fear, while their presence causes apprehension; we are displeased by things of slight importance and we fear things of the slightest importance. And so I wish that my present fears be founded not on things of slight importance but on those that are altogether false. I confess that, fluctuating between uncertain reports about your condition, I incline toward the worst, although what is best or worst for man only God knows, not any individual. But I am speaking as mortals do who call what they cannot avoid the worst lot, while as wise men know, nothing is better, nothing is more just than death, which liberates us fully from these bonds and offers us eternal freedom. Because the matter is very ambiguous and, as I believe, known only to God—and while in our general discussions on the soul's state I do not fear to assert what prejudiced reason will suggest—I consider it more prudent to suspend judgment whenever ultimate certainty is involved. With the obstacle of that difficulty now overcome, I shall proceed; nor is there need for long discussion. I cannot be convinced that, if you were still alive, you would leave unanswered so many of my letters. On the other hand, it occurs to me that the death of such a close friend, if it were true, could not be hidden from me for long, especially by certain surviving friends who still hold us dear. But a new fear once again banishes that hope. There are those who do not inform friends because of their soft and effeminate compassion about troublesome matters, prolonging and concealing them in order not to appear the authors of affliction—as though anything is more wretched than to be wretched without being aware of it. I find myself at this crossroads, not knowing where to turn. While I know what I desire, I do not know what to hope for, thus resulting in a crowd of conflicting thoughts in my mind. Your life or death is not of light moment within the total measure of my life. Your age, your moderation, and your state of health afford me hope that you are alive, but the contagiousness of the recurring plague as well as the unhealthy air which, according to reports, once again rages over you, terrifies me. Free me from these fears as soon as possible by a letter from you, my dear brother, if you still live. Otherwise, if friendship or trust still exists anywhere, I beg whoever of our friends may read this to deliver me from such wretched uncertainties by writing openly

*See I, 1.

whatever may have happened. I expect nothing pleasant, accustomed as I now am to sorrowful news. This mental toil and vivid recollection of misfortunes, which are no greater for me than for the world, however, have brought before my eyes the image of Gherardo, my only brother and a Carthusian monk, in my opinion the happiest of men. Having overcome all these miseries with which we are constantly agitated, he has become for me also a source of perennial reproach as he holds fast to his port, watching me labor in these waters, and disdains from his lofty perch human tempests. I have therefore decided to write to him; you will take care that his letter reaches him. Farewell.

Carpi, 25 September.

Fam. X, 3.

To Gherardo, Carthusian monk, on his blessed state and the
wretchedness of the times, with an appeal to persevere in his purpose.*

I have made up my mind, O brother dearer to me than light, to
put an end to my long silence. But if by chance you believe that this
silence indicates a forgetful mind, you are mistaken; I would no
more forget you than I would forget myself. So far I feared to interrupt the silence of your novitiate; I knew that you were fleeing
tumult, that you loved silence, and indeed that once I began writing
I could scarcely stop. This then is an expression of my love for you
and my admiration for what you are doing. Therefore, from the two
extremes I chose, not what was more pleasing to me, but what
assured greater tranquillity for you. But now, to confess the truth, I
have decided to write you not in your interest but in mine. Have
you need for preachings from me when you have entered upon the
heavenly journey and constantly rejoice in angelic discussions? Happy
of mind, fortunate in purpose are you who were able to scorn the
world in the flower of your youth when it was most alluring to you,
and were able to cross over with closed ears amidst the siren songs.
So while I do speak to you I am thinking of myself in the hope that
perchance my worthless heart, sluggish and frozen by long inertia,
would be warmed by your holy ardor. Therefore, this clamoring,
though it be of no use to you, should inconvenience you minimally.
For you are now no longer a recruit but a soldier of Christ who has
proven himself by long military service, thanks to Him who deemed
you worthy of such an honor. As so often happens, He drew a noble
deserter to His banners from the battle lines of His enemies. At first,
I feared to address you with untimely words; but subsequently,
knowing that you were secure, I considered it safe to speak to you
this way. To beginners all things appear formidable; many things we
feared as youngsters make us laugh as adolescents; every sound terrifies the inexperienced soldier, but no noise upsets the soldier
hardened by battle. The new sailor is horrified by the first murmur
of the winds, but the experienced helmsman who has so often led his
battered and disarmed ship into port looks down haughtily at the
stormy waters. I trust in Him who from your mother's womb has

---

*Petrarch's brother, Gherardo, was born in 1307 and educated at Bologna.
After a carefree youth in Avignon, he entered the Carthusian Order in 1343 and
remained at the monastery of Montrieux, north of Toulon, for his entire life. His
decision had a profound effect upon Petrarch both personally and in his writings.

taken you on this journey, which is certainly laborious but also glorious, so that through various difficulties you could safely reach your homeland. Nothing can disturb you any longer: mourning or cares, illness or old age, fear or hunger or poverty, "terrible shadows, death and hardship," not even that enormous "guardian of Orcus lying on half-chewed bones in his bloody cavern," not anything else invented by poetic genius to terrify the hearts of mortals. Nor did Jupiter endow with greater courage against all terror his Hercules, fathered in adultery, than you were granted by the eternal Father of all, born of a Virgin, who recognizes and assists the upright wills of those who have faith in Him. Such being the case, you can listen to the voices of your dear ones and, should any free time become available amidst your holy occupations, you can briefly respond. Allow me, however, to use with you words from secular authorities cited abundantly by Ambrose and our Augustine and Jerome, which even the apostle Paul did not scorn to use. Do not close the door of your cell to words worthy of my mouth and not unworthy of your ears.

Pythagoras was a man of outstanding genius, yet his cleverness, separated by a wide margin from the truth, often penetrated no further than does the silliness of old maids; hence that ridiculous transmigration of souls into many and varied bodies and his rebirth as a philosopher from the warrior, Euphorbius, who had been in the Trojan War; hence that famous metempsychosis which I marvel could have been accepted by Plato or Aristotle. But I marvel still more at Origen, who seems to have embraced the same madness and therefore deserved the condemnation of Jerome, who admired and praised him, as well as of other followers of the truth. But lest this encounter with Pythagoras prompt me to digress, the fact remains that, whatever his intelligence, he did possess an exceedingly upright character; as a result, he was given the highest honors during his lifetime, while after his death he supposedly joined the council of the gods, and his home was considered a temple by posterity. What was the first precept of this man? That his disciples observe five years of silence. Very admirable indeed, for it is only a fool who speaks before he has learned. Thus, in order to remove the restraining bar from the mouth, though not the bit which should never be removed, he considered sufficient a period of five years. Yet if I calculate correctly, you have been silent for seven years in the service and in the school of Jesus Christ. The time has come when you ought to begin speaking, but if silence pleases you above all else, you may answer me even with silence. Remember, dear brother, what our situation once was, what a toilsome sweetness used to wrench our minds, interspersed as it often was with bitterness. You remember, I think, that you are now enjoying liberty while grieving for your brother's servitude which still holds me tightly in the usual chains, at times preparing a knife for my side and at others a noose for my neck. And it would have long ago completed its work, had the right hand of your Redeemer, which freed you from servitude, not defended me from destruction. Pray, dear brother, that He grant freedom to me too, that He may let us enjoy a like end because we emerged from a single womb, that I who ought to precede you shall not be ashamed to follow you. You will remember our vain desire for expensive clothes, which still entraps me today, I admit, but daily grows weaker; what trouble we used to take repeatedly putting on and taking off fancy clothes morning and evening; what fear we felt that a single hair might fall out of place or that a light breeze might spoil our elaborate coiffures; or how we tried to avoid animals coming from any direction so that any dirt they kicked up might not soil our perfumed, spotless clothes or so that in the encounter they might not crumple our pressed creases. O true vanity of men, especially of youth! To what purpose all that mental anxiety? Obviously so that we would please the eyes of others. And whose eyes, I might ask? Certainly of the many men who were displeasing to our own eyes. In a letter to Lucilius, Seneca says, "Who has ever worn fancy clothing without desiring to be seen?" It is indeed extraordinary idiocy to base our lives not on reason but on the multitude's folly, to allow our lives to be guided by those whose own lives we hold in contempt. No one chooses as his leader the man whose back is deeply scarred, and no one chooses as his helmsman the person noted for his shipwrecks. Instead we select those we admire, usually committing the direction of our lives to those who have been successful in directing their own. Therefore, to base your way of life on the mad multitude whose customs one derides and whose very opinion and life one disdains is more than ordinary madness. To continue my discourse, let all ambition cease and let the multitude keep its distance. How much more useful and appropriate for any occasion and how much more manageable is the dress of common people than of royalty! Nevertheless at that time we felt differently, in the manner of those whose energy and effort are spent on appearing conspicuous, "to be pointed out, and to have people say: there he goes," as that author once said. Quintus Hortensius was an outstanding orator, more effeminate than became a man, as careful with his appearance as with his eloquence. He never appeared in public without first consulting his mirror; he would comb and admire himself, arranging both his appearance and his clothes. Much has been said about his effeminacy, but one story in particular recounts his chance encounter in a narrow place with a colleague who brushed against him and ruffled the folds of his garment. With a totally feminine vanity, he tried to accuse him of injury as if it were a capital crime, when ordinary contact causes a carefully pressed garment to become wrinkled. Although we, dear brother, brought no judgment against anyone because of that kind of injustice, we were not much different at heart. But a sudden intervention by the hand of the Almighty led you out of those serious shadows of error. I am rising slowly and through many labors; I believe that the assistance of letters and works of talent are of no avail, but that all is the gift of God, who will perhaps offer His hand to me too when I humbly confess my weakness. Indeed if I were not persuaded of this by reason, I would be compelled by old age, which I feel approaching more surely each day and already riding into my territory. What shall I say about our shoes? How heavy and continual a battle did they wage against our feet, which they were intended to protect! I confess that my feet would have been rendered useless except that, warned by extreme necessity, I preferred to offend others' eyes a little rather than to destroy my nerves and my tendons.

What should I say about the curling irons and the care we took of our hair? How often did the resulting pain interrupt our sleep, which had been delayed by such activity! What pirate could have given us a more cruel torture than we inflicted upon ourselves with our own hands? What furrows caused by those nights were impressed upon our blushing foreheads as we looked in the mirror, so that we who wanted to show off our hair were compelled to cover our faces! These are things pleasing to those who undergo them, horrible to remember for those who have undergone them, incredible to those who have never experienced them. And in truth, how much does the recollection of those past activities now give you delight! Your wide shoe no longer is a chain on your feet, but a protection; your hair combed high and gathered together no longer interferes with your ears or your eyes. Now your dress is simpler, its purchase and care easy, no more laborious to put on than to take off, thus protecting your mind from folly as much as the body from coldness. Happy are you who had a good foretaste of bitter experiences in order to taste these more sweetly! But leaving these matters of little account, recall also the extent to which you owe due gratitude to God even more for having been freed of this Charybdis—the great trouble we took, the many sleepless nights we spent so as to make our madness widely known and be the talk of the town. How often did we give a fancy twist to our syllables or use fancy words! In sum, what did we not do so that love, which modesty at least required be kept hidden if we could not extinguish it, might be sung in a popular manner? We were praised for our learning and we greased our hair with the mad oil of sinners. But the ineffable mercy of God gradually directed your feet to the straight path; He punished your precipitous passion by allowing you your fill of fleeting pleasures so that, as a resident of both cities at different times in your life, you could learn by experience the difference between Babylon and Jerusalem. O merciful God, how silently You give advice, how secretly You intervene, how imperceptibly You heal! For indeed what else did we seek through so much toil, good Jesus, what else if not a mortal love, nay indeed a fatal love whose deceitful and truly dangerous sweetness You allowed us to taste to the bitter end so that it might not appear special to us neophytes? And so that it might not prove so powerful as to oppress us, You have mercifully caused those who were the object of our delight to be taken from our midst by plucking with Your right hand from the earth our hopes when they had barely taken root. In their youthful years You recalled them through death, which I hope was as beneficial to them as necessary for us. Thus have You removed the chains from our souls. But nevertheless—O blind mind of mortals—how often did we lament as if we were losing too early what we desired at the greatest risk to our lives, as if anything beneficial may be untimely! How many sighs, how many laments, how many tears did we cast to the breezes, and in the manner of madmen who insult their physician we refused Your hand as it tried to apply the greatest of all salves for our wounds! So now tell me, O dear man, now a friend of God though once His enemy and now a subject of God though once His opponent, do tell me, now that you have turned away from your former ways to new ones, what resemblance is there between those empty songs replete with false and foul praises of ordinary women, those open confessions of lust, and these hymns of praise, these sacred vigils when in the ranks of the soldiers of Christ along the ramparts and fortifications of the city of God you pass the night in constant vigilance against the perfidies of the ancient enemy? A happy and enviable militia, a great and burdensome labor, I admit, but brief and worthy of eternal reward.

There remains, however, my Lord, one thing that I would like to discuss with You if You would allow. Why is it, I ask, that although my brother and I were imprisoned by similar chains both of which were destroyed by Your hand, we have not been equally liberated? In fact, he flew off while I, though held by no chain, am still besmeared with the lime of an awful habit and cannot spread my wings. Where I had been bound, there I cling unbound. What other reason is there except that, though the chains were destroyed in a like manner, what followed was not at all similar, namely "our help in the name of the Lord"? Why then have we ended so discordantly this psalm of David which had begun so harmoniously? The will of God is never without cause; and indeed since everyone depends upon it, His will is the source of all causes. My brother, then, sang his song with his mind set upon heaven; I bent toward the earth, keeping in mind earthly things. Perhaps I did not recognize that liberating right hand, perhaps I hoped in my own strength. For this or some other reason I am not free, though my chains are broken. Have mercy, O Lord, so that I may merit still greater mercy; for without Your gratuitous mercy human misery can by no means deserve compassion.

Now I return to you, dear brother, and slowly proceed to more serious matters to show you how gradually you attained such happiness. Remember the swarm of people around us, the crowd of well-wishers and rush of visitors; or recall our great perspiration and labor to appear elegant and fancy to some group. O greatest Lord who makes the blind see, the lame walk, and the dead rise again, what ostentation that was! For when we are known in every nook and cranny and have attended every public affair, there still will remain the journey of our fathers and the frightening threshold of the grave that must be crossed with irretraceable steps. Add to this the well-known problems arising from entertainment and banqueting, which, as they say, cannot be avoided without grave risk to one's reputation, and the infinite storms that rage in a troubled stomach from such feasts. If we suffer all these inconveniences at the hands of friends, what can you expect from enemies? Many are the species of enemies, both external and internal, of which some remain hidden, others indicate open hostility, while still others battle you with their tongue or with deceit or even with the sword. I speak rather briefly of them since you are acquainted with all such types. In the same vein, how many attacks and insults did we not suffer at the hands of our servants? Using various arguments Seneca excuses them and places the entire blame on their masters, praising his Lucilius for living on such friendly terms with his servants. What can I say? I hesitate to criticize the opinion of such a great man, yet what prevents me from doing so? To me the situation seems otherwise.

Perhaps either prudence enabled those men to enjoy good servants or luck gave them assistance in finding reliable ones. Until the present, neither has happened to me, I confess, despite my earnest efforts. Therefore, let others judge as they will; I cannot praise what I do not know. For me the servant class is a most ungodly lot and that ancient proverb rejected by Seneca holds considerable truth for me: "Every servant is an enemy." But his letter speaks of good servants, for the author excludes wicked ones from association with masters. This I believe; thus his words do echo the truth and we do read in books many examples of good servants. Indeed I am not ignorant of this nor do I deny credence to the writers, but whether the change in the times, chance, or my own impatience is the cause, I must say I have never seen a good servant. I nevertheless continue searching; if by chance I were to meet one I would be as astounded as meeting a two-headed man. But lest anyone impute this attitude to my harshness or to my indecision, I have tried everything. I have lived with my servants no less intimately than Lucilius did. I have allowed them to assist with my plans, to participate in my conversations, to have meals with me; I entrusted my affairs to them in the belief that by so doing I might foster their faithfulness. But my attempts led to nothing. Indeed all my care led to the opposite result. None of my servants departed from conversations with me without being more impudent than previously, no one left my dinner table without being more insolent; just as familiarity bred contempt, so trust led to theft. As Seneca was allowed to do with his, so let me speak the truth about my servants and those of my friends—for nearly all are strangely alike. I even confess that I suffer nothing more annoying in this life than the obstinacy of my servants. Other wars may have truces, but with our hostile servants we battle without interruption although I am not unaware that I too must bear what even the greatest men endured. In the first age that is called heroic, illustrious writers said that even Ulysses, among the many labors he had to undergo, was afflicted by outrageous actions on the part of his servants and his maids. In more recent times, it is said that the Roman emperor Frederick, throughout his life and at the point of death, complained about the harm suffered at the hands of his servants. These incidental complaints about servants, however, were intended to demonstrate your good fortune in being free of servants' tyranny and in having bowed your neck under the most pleasant yoke of Christ.

What should I say about other evils, such as that poison of flattery hidden in seeming sweetness, smiling in one's presence but biting behind one's back? What should I say about the wounds against one's reputation unexpectedly inflicted from unknown sources, and about the darts secretly hurled in the midst of the rabble? What can be said about the folly of avarice which poisons minds, producing a destructive forgetfulness of all divine and human justice? This causes guardians to become thieves. But the worst type of evil is the mixture of poison with remedies. Choose a person with whose trust you may feel secure amidst human deceit and he is the first to deceive you. What can you gather from this advice? As the Satirist says, "Who will watch over one's keepers?" This bane has been haunting us from childhood; whether it was our luck or our naiveté, we were young, careless and alone, fitting preys for injustice. There is a time-worn proverb that says, "Circumstance makes the thief." It was this, dear brother, to clarify the issue once and for all, that caused us to go from wealth to poverty. Indeed, so as to recognize it as a gift of God, it changed us from being terribly busy to being idle, from being terribly enslaved to being liberated. One might add that all those who had burdened themselves with our spoils were soon victims of the same fate, and we saw them either destroyed by a sad death or languishing in extreme poverty or in a wretched old age; nor is revenge for injustice small consolation, especially when it is at the hands of the Lord. What shall I say about the storm of legal controversies that caused me to hate not only the court but the entire world? Or what could I say about the other dangers, considered the most serious next to death, of being captured or being enslaved that we once risked both on land and sea? The mere recollection renews my dismay and horror. We escaped, but that was not the result of any valor on our part but of divine mercy. We escaped, but we could have perished, and certainly would have, except that our compassionate Father watched over us with His life-giving eyes. We escaped, but our friends and colleagues perished in those very same dangers—by fire, sword, prison, shipwreck, and in innumerable other ways which would be bitter and sorrowful to relate because of the serious and recent misfortunes of our friends. We walked between such snares, we navigated among such reefs, my dear brother. But why do I speak as if our states were similar? I, a wretch, am constantly involved with them; you, thank God, have already arrived in port. Happy the hour in which you were born, happy all those dangers that led you through many trials of formidable events to a love of mental peace. I ask you now to compare your present condition with your previous one: your highly peaceful poverty with those turbulent riches, your sweet idleness with those bitter affairs, your dear brothers with those evil enemies, in short, your silence with those disputes, your solitude with those mobs, your groves with those cities, your fasting with those banquets, your nocturnal chants with those daily parties, finally your Carthusian monastery with Avignon, your heavenly peace with earthly perils, your friendship with the Lord with the subjection to the devil, your eternal life with perpetual death. You will have to admit that you are extremely happy. As Seneca says, "Persist in your resolve and complete what you have begun." May toil not frighten you; may the harsh life not crush you. In the words of Flaccus, "Life gives nothing to mortals without great toil." But if in this life about which he was speaking even the smallest things are gained only through the greatest toil, as we ourselves so often experienced by our vain striving, what toil will ever seem to us excessive in order to attain eternal blessedness? Away with sloth, down with sluggishness! When you are awakened at morning-tide, believe that you have been called forth to hold discourse with God. And alas, how often did we awaken to the command of a mortal lord, how often did such a command subject us to perils and labors! And what, I ask you, was the result? Clearly nothing more than human friendship, which is ambiguous, dangerous, and troublesome. Now you are offered divine friendship, which is certain, secure, and easily procured. Believe me, weariness will fall from the mind, and drowsiness from the eyes when you realize that God is calling you, and you will realize His privileged treatment of you, since you have been commanded to stand watch while the rabble around you is snoring. It is the custom of generals to entrust difficult assignments to proven soldiers. While cooks and millers and, to use the discourse of Horace, bands of harlots wander about the forum of vanities, those soldiers dwell amidst swords and weapons, finding consolation for serious dangers in a fleeting glory. When, however, you will have communication with God through prayer, joy will contend with reverence so that you can prove yourself sleepless and diligent in the eyes of such an observer. In histories you have read that the soldiers of Marcus Cato endured in his presence thirst, dust, heat, serpent bites, and died in his presence without a groan or lament. You have heard that Sceva, a man more powerful than just, wished not only to fight but to die under his leader's eyes. But if reverence for a mortal lord could have such influence, what ought the presence of Christ inspire? Indeed one must not wait for His coming, as did that unfortunate warrior for the coming of his Caesar; He must instead be welcomed and venerated. He is present in all places and in all ages, He sees our every act and listens to our thoughts, He is a tremendous strength to our minds if the sluggishness of evil habit does not interfere. There is a teaching of Epicurus that one must seek an imaginary witness of his life; in writing to a friend, he says, "Behave as if Epicurus looks upon everything you do." And in order to help shape the life of his Lucilius with examples of illustrious men, Seneca would suggest that he select Cato, Scipio, Lelius, or any other man he wished of proven reputation. Such a practice praised by great men cannot fail to be acceptable, for I note it pleased even Marcus Tullius, since he inserted it, although in different words, in a letter to his brother, Quintus Cicero. The advice of Epicurus, then, pleased those who transcribed it and gave it their approval. We have no need of this practice; we do not seek an imaginary witness when we have Christ alive and real and always present to us; for "if I ascend into heaven He is there, and if I descend into hell He is there." Let us, therefore, act not as if He were watching but as if He were truly present. And we will be ashamed both of our actions and of our hidden desires which not only the imaginary, but even the actual witness of Epicurus could not perceive. For He from whose eyes nothing is hidden knows them. Let us imagine Him standing before our eyes and crying out: "What are you doing, O blind and ungrateful ones? I willingly endured death for you, you deny Me simple toil; this is your piety, this is your acknowledgment for benefits received! I who govern with a nod the heavens and the earth and the seas, who hurl thunderbolts from the clouds, who alternately bring storms and clear skies, who adorn day and night with their lights, who measure out darkness and light with varying hours, who guide the sun's unending obedience through the twelve houses of the zodiac to the four seasons of the year, and who direct the cycling year in a pleasing and unceasing change of seasons in order to avoid monotony; I who formed for you not only the solid earth, the flowing water, and the breathable air but also the protection, delights, and ornaments of countless things, and finally who created you from nothing in My own image—notwithstanding the obstreperous denials of fools—and revealed to you the path over which I desire to be sought; I myself declare that, following the many favors intended to recall you who were rebellious and straying, I descended among you from on high disguising My majesty under a humble condition, and for your salvation did not fear hardships, betrayals, abuses, insults, imprisonment, scourgings, lashings, death, and the cross. What have you done in return, not to equal the many benefits which you are incapable of imagining, but at least as a sign of minds not ungrateful?" What, my dear brother, could we answer to all this? Is there anything ambiguous in these words? If we should truly wish to listen to the Lord speaking within our souls, let us cheerfully arise during the night—as I have been doing—so that we may sing the praises of Christ with greater devotion at the hour when, we recall, He suffered shame and insults in our behalf.

Because I already fear to have distracted you too long from the loftiness of your contemplation, dear brother, here is my conclusion. Christ, the eternal witness of your entire life, protects you. Look upon Him, therefore, if you wish never to be wearied by hardships and by sleeplessness. It was for this that the inaccessible and ineffable Trinity desired that the eternal, immortal, and omnipotent son of God assume the cloak of our mortality. As a result, there being no analogy between God and man, He became their mediator by uniting Himself perfectly to both natures in order to draw man to God and incline God toward man and in order to focus our mortal vision upon God dressed in mortal flesh. But if it is difficult for you to follow Him with your eyes and your mind as He ascends into the glory of His divinity after having reassumed His immortality, and if you wish the testimony of a mere man, choose for yourself from among the leaders of your persuasion: John the Baptist, Antonius, Macarius or, if these appear too rigid, Benedict; or choose those who rejected the errors of their centuries, Augustine and Arsenius, who I know have always pleased you. You have the lives of the Church Fathers; read them thoroughly as you indeed do; there you will find the friend whom you will not refuse as the witness of your secret thoughts. Being conscious of him, you will accordingly govern yourself and your life; without him you will do nothing and think nothing. Read the dialogue of Gregory, the soliloquies of Augustine and his *Confessions* bathed with tears, over which certain fools usually laugh. You will find in them no little consolation and comfort. As for the Psalms, undoubtedly you are following the advice of Jerome, that they never slip from your hands. Some time ago, as is my custom, I wrote something about this in poetic form since I felt you would like it. So that it would not be too great a burden you will receive it from a subsequent messenger. But, to come to a conclusion, divide all your life between contemplation and psalm singing and homilies and readings. Yield nothing to your body, that stubborn slave ever ready to rebel, except what you cannot deny it. Keep it in chains; it must be treated as a slave in order to understand whence it comes. A faithless enemy creates a suspicious peace. You know those men whose insidiousness you have suffered in this world, so always beware of them; it is imprudent to return to the good graces of untrustworthy enemies. In the meantime, rejoice and hope and sigh, serving the Lord in fear, exalting Him with trembling, and rendering Him gratitude because He gave you the wings of a dove that you might fly away and find rest. These you have used not sluggishly, but extended as you fled, so that in your retreat you would not experience the countless evils of the world which I, in my wretchedness, experience; by them I am beset and because of them I shudder as I look around. Thus far I am not fleeing Babylon, though its gates are open. But do not despair on my account, I beg you; rather pray that I might some day rise above it. I confess that the weight of my sins is great, but it is still finite, while the clemency of Him whose aid I await is infinite. I have written these things to you, dear and only brother of mine, not in my customary style but in a strange one that is almost monastic, in consideration of you rather than myself. You will read them as time allows, and if nothing of this contributes to your improvement, know that at least I gained considerable benefit in writing them, since a happy envy for your situation has meantime struck me as I meditated on my perils. Farewell, and remember me.

25 September, from the town of Carpi.

Fam. X, 4.

To the same correspondent,* concerning the style of the Church Fathers and the relationship between theology and poetry, with a brief exposition of the first eclogue of the "Bucolicum carmen" being sent to him.

If I know the fervor of your spirit, you will shudder at the poem enclosed with this letter as inharmonious with your profession and contrary to your goals. Do not judge rashly, for is there anything more foolish than to pass judgment on what is unknown? In truth, poetry is not in the least contrary to theology. Does this astonish you? I might almost say that theology is the poetry of God. What else is it if not poetry when Christ is called a lion or a lamb or a worm? In Sacred Scripture you will find thousands of such examples too numerous to pursue here. Indeed, what else do the parables of the Savior in the Gospels echo if not a discourse different from ordinary meaning or, to express it briefly, figurative speech, which we call allegory in ordinary language? Yet poetry is woven from this kind of discourse, but with another subject. Who denies it? That other discourse deals with God and divine things, this one with God and men; whence even Aristotle says that the first theologians were poets. That such was the case is indicated by the word itself. Research has been done on the origin of the word *poet*, and although opinions are varied, the most probable holds that men, once ignorant but desirous of the truth and especially knowledge of God—a desire natural to men—began believing in a certain superior power that governs mortal affairs. They considered it proper that this power be venerated with a submission more than human and a worship more than venerable. Thus they chose to build magnificent buildings called temples and to have consecrated ministers whom they named priests, as well as splendid statues and golden vases, marble altars and beautiful vestments. Furthermore, lest their praise remain mute, they determined to appease the divinity with high-sounding words and to bestow sacred flattery on the divinity in a style far removed from common and public speech. In addition they employed rhythmical measures in order to provide pleasure and banish tediousness. Indeed it had to be an uncommon form of speech and possess a certain artfulness, exquisiteness, and novelty. Since such language was called *poetes* in Greek, those who used it were called *poets*. You will say, "Who is the source of such ideas?"

*See preceding letter.

You could, dear brother, have confidence in me without the testimony of others. I perhaps deserve to be believed without need of witnesses when I recount the truth or anything resembling it. But if your mind moves rather cautiously, I shall provide witnesses who render the richest testimony and deserve the strongest faith. First there is Marcus Varro, most learned among the Romans; then there is Suetonius, a most diligent investigator of all matters; and I would not add the third except that he is, I believe, more familiar to you. Isidore, therefore, briefly citing Suetonius, makes mention of this in the eighth book of his *Etymologies*. But you will retort: "I can even believe a holy doctor of the Church, but the sweetness of your song does not behoove my rigorous life." Do not believe this, dear brother. Even the fathers of the Old Testament made use of heroic and other kinds of poetry: Moses, Job, David, Solomon, Jeremiah; the Psalms of David that you sing day and night possess poetic meter in Hebrew. For this reason I dare call him both deservedly and eloquently the poet of the Christians. This certainly is self-evident; and if you will believe nothing today without testimony, I note that Jerome felt similarly, although he proved incapable of translating into another tongue, while retaining its meaning and meter, that sacred poem which sings of the birth, death, descent into Hell, resurrection, and return of that blessed man, Christ. He therefore concentrated on reproducing its meaning, yet even now it possesses a metrical quality which causes us to call those lines of the Psalms verses. That suffices insofar as the ancients are concerned. You must know, however, that it is not difficult to demonstrate how recent authorities on the Scriptures such as Ambrose, Augustine, and Jerome made use of poetry and rhythm. In the case of Prudentius, Prosper, Sedulius, and others whom I shall not discuss, we have none of their prose and only a few works in verse. Do not therefore, my brother, be horrified by what you know pleased men who were most devoted and consecrated to Christ. Concentrate on the meaning; if it is true and wholesome, embrace it regardless of the style. To praise food served in an earthen vessel while feeling disgust at the same meal served on a golden platter is a sign either of madness or hypocrisy. To thirst for gold is a sign of greed; to be unable to tolerate it is a sign of the petty mind. A meal surely becomes neither better nor worse because of gold. I most certainly do not deny that, as with gold, poetry is more noble in its own class, just as lines drawn with a ruler are straighter than those drawn freehand. While I am not of the opinion that poetry is to be preferred, neither do I feel that it should be spurned. Let these points serve as premises in defense of style. Now I must turn to the main point of this letter.

Three summers ago while in France on business, the heat forced me to visit the source of the Sorgue, which as you know we once selected as our lifelong dwelling. But while a more secure and peaceful abode was being prepared for you by divine grace, I was destined not even to enjoy that place, since fortune was to drag me higher than I wished. Thus I found myself there in this state of mind: while not daring to undertake anything major because of my countless pressing matters, I nevertheless was incapable of doing absolutely nothing, since from childhood I was constantly taught to do something, if not always something good. Thus I chose a middle course; though delaying greater projects, I got involved in something to while away the time. The very nature of the region with its wooded groves, where the rising sun often drove me weighted with my cares and whence only the coming of night recalled me, persuaded me to sing something pastoral. I thus began to write what had been in my mind for some time—a bucolic poem divided into twelve eclogues. It is incredible how swiftly it was completed, so much did the atmosphere of the place stimulate my inspiration. Furthermore, because I had no subject of greater importance in mind, the first eclogue was written about the two of us. For that reason it also made great sense to send it to you without indeed knowing whether it would give you pleasure or impede your pleasure. But since its nature is such that it must be explained by the author himself to be understood, and in order not to weary you uselessly, I shall briefly explain, first what I say, and then what I mean.

Two shepherds are introduced; for since the style is pastoral, it thus involves shepherds. The names of the shepherds are Silvius and Monicus. Seeing Monicus alone and enjoying an enviable repose in a certain cavern, Silvius speaks admiringly of his good fortune. He laments his own misfortune because Monicus had found peace after deserting the countryside and his flock, while he himself still roamed the barren hills in great discomfort. What astonished him even more was the great difference in their fortunes since, as he points out, both had the same mother, which leads one to understand that the two young shepherds are brothers. Monicus responds to this by placing all the blame for his brother's hardship on Silvius himself, saying that with nothing restraining him he wanders of his own accord over the byways of forests and summits of mountains. Silvius responds that love, specifically love of the Muses, was the cause of his wanderings.

In order to clarify this, he begins a rather long tale of two shepherds who sang most sweetly; he remembers having heard of one in his boyhood and of the other later on. Captured by their charms, he neglected all else. While he eagerly followed them over the mountains, he had learned to sing so as to win praise from others, although he was not yet content with himself. He therefore determined to strive for the highest summit of perfection, and either to attain it or die in the attempt. Monicus tries to persuade Silvius to enter his cavern so that he might hear a sweeter song, but soon interrupts his unfinished discussion as if recognizing on Silvius's face the signs of a disturbed mind. The latter, however, begs forgiveness, and so Monicus completes what he started to say. Whereupon the marveling Silvius asks the identity of that shepherd who sings so sweetly, but whom he has just heard for the first time. With a shepherd's ignorance, Monicus gives, not his name, but a description of his fatherland. In the manner of peasants whose words often stray, he mentions two rivers flowing from a single source, and immediately corrects his words as if recognizing his error. Where he had begun speaking of two rivers, he now proceeds to speak of one flowing from two sources, both located in Asia. Silvius, however, says he knows that river and proves this to be true by recalling that a certain shaggy boy bathed Apollo in it. Monicus then mentions that his poet was born there. Upon hearing this, Silvius immediately recognizes the man and disparages his voice and style of song while exalting his own shepherds. Whereupon Monicus heaps deserved praise on his poet. Finally, seeming to acquiesce, Silvius says he will return another time to examine the sweetness of his song. Now, however, he has to make haste. Astonished at this, Monicus asks the cause of his haste and learns that Silvius is occupied with a song composed for an illustrious young man whose deeds he briefly narrates; and therefore he can undertake nothing else at present. Whereupon Monicus brings the conversation to a close, giving his farewell to Silvius and urging him to consider the dangers and risks of delay.

That is a summary of the story, but this is my intended meaning. We are the conversing shepherds, I Silvius and you Monicus. This is my explanation of the names. The first is called Silvius because he had spent his life in the woods, and because from an early age there had been planted in him a hatred of the city and a love of the forest. This is why many of our friends generally call me Silvanus rather than Franciscus. For the second shepherd, on the other hand, the name is appropriate since one of the Cyclops is named Monicus, as if he were one-eyed. Such a name seemed in a certain respect fitting for you since of the two eyes that we mortals usually use, one to gaze upon heavenly things and the other upon earthly ones, you renounced the one that beholds earthly things, being content with the better eye. The cavern where Monicus dwells in solitude is Montrieux where you now lead a monastic life amidst grottoes and groves, or else that grotto near your monastery where Mary Magdalene lived as a penitent. There, in fact, with the aid of God who raised your uncertain heart, you strengthened this sacred purpose about which you had previously spoken to me many times. Interpret the countryside and the flocks—for which it is said you did not care—as the city and mankind that you relinquished in fleeing into solitude. That there was one mother for both is not allegory but the naked truth, just as there was one father for both. The grave is to be understood as our last abode, which for you will be heaven and for me will continue to be hell unless mercy intervenes. Or else its meaning could be more simply understood as follows: you already possess a secure abode and thus a surer hope for your grave, while there is nothing for me thus far but extensive wandering and an uncertainty about all things. The inaccessible mountain peak that Monicus accuses Silvius of seeking with great toil is the summit of that rare fame attained by few men. The deserts through which Silvius is said to wander are his studies, which are truly deserted today, abandoned because of a desire for profit or hopeless because of a sluggishness of talent. The mossy cliffs are the powerful and the wealthy covered with their patrimony as though it were moss. The resounding springs can be called men of letters and men of eloquence, from whose profound genius emerge rivers of learning with a delightful sound. The oath that Silvius takes in the name of Pales is a pastoral vow, for Pales is the goddess of shepherds; for us she might be understood as Mary, not a goddess but the mother of God. Parthenias is Virgil himself; this name was not recently invented by me, for in his life we read that he deserved to be called Parthenias as if he had proved it by his manner of living. So that a reader might understand this, I add a passage revealing that Lake Garda in Cisalpine Gaul begets a son closely resembling herself. This son is the river Mincio, a river of Mantua, which is Virgil's homeland. The noble shepherd who had come from elsewhere is Homer, about whom nearly every word possesses a particular meaning. This is why the word *then*, that is *later*, is said somewhat mysteriously since I came across Virgil while still a boy, though no longer an infant, and only later did I come to know Homer; you should understand that he who is called Homer by the multitude is in a small book by a scholar unknown to me, but containing a summary of Homer's *Iliad.* He is said to be from foreign shores, signifying that he is not Italian and knows no Latin whatsoever. Thus I say that he does not sing in our strain, since he sings in Greek. Truly he deserves the epithet of noble shepherd, for what is more noble than either the language or the genius of Homer? I know not, however, the valley where he was born, because of the varying opinions concerning his place of origin, which I cannot discuss here. When I finally indicate that Virgil drank from the Homeric spring, anyone engaged in poetic pursuits will understand me. The female friend of whom I say both are worthy is Fame, for which poets sing as lovers do for their female friends. The savage forests and lofty mountains that to Silvius's astonishment were not interested in the sweetness of poetry signify the uncultivated public and prominent rulers. The descent from the mountain's summit to the deepest valleys and the ascent from the deepest valleys up the mountains, to which Silvius refers in speaking of himself, represent the journey, alternating the height of theory with practical application and its converse because of the diversity of feelings. The spring that applauds the singer is the chorus of scholars, while the arid rocks are ignoramuses on whom, as an echo among rocks, the word resounds emptily without meaning. The nymphs, goddesses of springs, are the divine talents of scholarly men. The threshold that Monicus invites Silvius to cross is the Carthusian order, which no one enters by deception or against his will as in many other orders. The shepherd whose songs Monicus prefers to Homer and to Virgil is David himself, who is worthy of the verb *to sing psalms* because of the Psalms he composed. In the middle of the night, moreover, refers to psalm singing at matins, since especially at that hour they are heard in your churches. The two rivers from a single source concerning which Monicus commits his first error are the Tigris and Euphrates, well-known rivers of Armenia; the single river from a double source is the Jordan in Judea about which many authors, including Jerome, longtime inhabitant of those regions, speak. The Jor and the Dan are names of streams from which derive the river and its name; it descends into the Sea of the Sodomites where it is said fields are ashen because of the burning of the city. In this stream you will recall that Christ was baptized by John. Indeed the shaggy young man is John the Baptist; I call him a young man, virginal, pure, innocent, shaggy, uncultivated, dressed in rags, with uncombed hair and his face burned by the sun. Apollo, son of Jove, is called the god of intelligence, in whom I symbolize Jesus Christ, true God and true son of God; I call Apollo god of talent and of wisdom since, as theologians know, among the attributes of the most exalted indivisible trinity is that wisdom which belongs to the Son who Himself is the wisdom of the Father. David's voice is said to be hoarse, and reference is made to his unceasing tears and his constant repetition of the name of Jerusalem to suggest that at first sight his style appears rough and mournful, and that his psalms frequently mention that city either historically or allegorically. At this point the themes sung by Silvius's preferred poets are briefly indicated; a full explanation here would be too long, but all is clear and evident for those expert in such studies. Monicus objects, justifying David's hoarseness and reviewing in an equally brief fashion his poet's subjects. The young man concerning whom Silvius has begun to weave a song is Scipio Africanus, who overthrew on the African shore Polyphemus, namely Hannibal, commander of the Carthaginians. Just as Polyphemus had one eye, so did Hannibal after losing an eye in Italy. The Libyan lions that abound in Africa are the other Carthaginian leaders whom Hannibal exiled from the empire. The burning forests are the burning ships in which the Carthaginians had placed all their hopes; Roman history recounts that Scipio burned five hundred ships before their very eyes. This young man is called a celestial youth either because of his heroic virtue in which he so magnificently excelled that Virgil called him "glittering" and Lucan "fiery," or because of the Roman belief in his heavenly origin, which caused them to hold him in high esteem. The Italians are said to praise him from the opposite shore, for the Italian coast is opposed to the African not only because of differences in character but because of geographical location, Rome being directly opposite Carthage. Yet no one is celebrating this young man, so highly praised. This I say because, while every history may be filled with his praises and his achievements and while Ennius undoubtedly wrote a great deal about him in a "rough and unpolished form" as Valerius says, there still exists no work on his accomplishments written in a sufficiently cultivated meter. I therefore undertook to sing about him in some fashion, and thus my book entitled the *Africa* indeed deals with him. My desire is to bring to a happy conclusion what I began in my youth with great enthusiasm. There is no need to explain the final words of Monicus stressing how dangerous it has always been to defer salutary resolutions, and how changeable and unforeseeable are the vicissitudes of this life. The remainder you will understand through meditation. Farewell.

Padua, 2 December, in the evening.

Fam. X, 5.

To the same correspondent,* felicitations on his progress, and concerning the great variety and differences in mankind's inclinations and activities.

Yesterday at eventide, my dearest brother, I received with great joy the double gift of your free time—a boxwood case highly polished on a revolving lathe, work of your own hand, and an edifying letter abounding in many lessons from the Fathers, witness of your sacred learning. I must, however, confess that upon reading it I experienced such diverse feelings that I was at times struck by the ardor of a generous enthusiasm and at others by the numbness of an icy fear. So magnificently did you appear to inspire the desire and stimulus for a better life and to tighten the reins on my present backsliding that I saw more clearly than light where I am, where I ought to be going, how distant I am in my misery from your fatherland, Jerusalem, for which we yearn in our exile except for the distraction of this muddy and filthy prison. What more can I add? I offer my congratulations to you and to myself, to you for being as you are and to myself for having such a brother. Among these felicitations there is one thing for which I grieve, lament, and complain: namely, that though born of the same parents, we were not born under the same star. We are too dissimilar, O brother; our two births from a single uterus were too unlike for anyone to understand that we are the gift, not of mortal parents, but of the eternal Father. For what is a father if not vile semen? What is a mother if not a loathsome dwelling place? God gave us a soul, a life, a mind, desire for the good, and a free will. Whatever human nature possesses that is holy, religious, pious, and excellent, all derives from God. Thus to your letter which brought me both comfort and shame, and in which I rejoice seeing you and blush thinking of myself, I have nothing to respond except that all you say is excellent and wholesome; and though supported by sound witnesses, it is nonetheless very true even without them. To mention but one point, what is more certain than that idea, for which you cite Augustine as an authority, that the inclinations and feelings of men conflict? In this regard, I beg you to have patience while I disgress somewhat freely before coming to Augustine and say something of my own that will prove enjoyable to me, yet perhaps not irksome to you. Human inclinations conflict not only for man in general but also for the individual: this I confess

*See X, 3.

and cannot deny, since I know others and myself as well, and since I contemplate the human species in groups and singly. What in truth can I say about all men, or who could enumerate the infinite differences which so mark mortals that they seem to belong neither to a single species nor to a single type? Thus, philosophers laid aside those differences that cannot be identified and divided everything into three parts; each part in turn was divided into many smaller sections, which is believed to be the derivation of the word *sect*. We see some men dedicated to pleasure, and together they are a large and immeasurable group; good Lord, how great their diversity and their artfulness, how many different tastes and opinions! What pleases one displeases another, what one considers wretched another considers most fortunate. We observe many engaged in undertakings pertaining to the active life—the pursuit of wealth, honors, and power. Some of these men strive to achieve their goal through war, others through peace, others on land, still others on the sea, others by the use of their hands and countless others by the use of their minds. Here too, what a variety of human skills, what diversity of objects, what varied dedication! In these two ways of life are involved all those skills which are called mechanical, serving the needs of the body. When they finally became part of the other arts, in the judgment of many they deserved last place in philosophy, but now is not the place to treat this in great depth. Let us proceed then to the variety of human activities. Certainly more often than we see them, we hear about a few men dedicated to knowledge and meditation. Our age moves along the first two of the above paths, but along the third no one proceeds, or so few that it bears almost no recent footprint. There is no doubt that the only true knowledge is to know and to honor God, whence it is written: "Piety is wisdom." This most noble and sacred study of all had been given man in order to achieve such wisdom, if only our corrupt vanity had not transformed theology into dialectics. We must nonetheless deal with what the rabble calls wisdom and I would more accurately call knowledge. What great disagreement there is in this matter! Some weave grammatical rules, others are enraptured by ornamentation and color, others meditate on sophisms or on numbers, still others join numbers to sounds; some take measure of the earth and others gaze at nothing but the heavens and the stars; happy would they be if they gazed instead upon the creator of the heavens. These are the arts which are called liberal, but there are others. There is the art which investigates the nature of all things, a magnificent practice provided the Lord of nature is not overlooked, as nearly always happens. Just as medicine gives health to the body, so there is an art that assures health to sick minds, a most useful art, if it delivered what it promised and if it sought divine aid without which nothing can be done. This is indispensable to all the arts, but especially the last two. Although the potency of herbs growing in the soil is useful for a sick body, and although many have composed and collected medications made of words for a sick and weak mind, nevertheless true health of both parts of man derive from God. Among those who heal minds, some provide cures for the individual, others for the family, still others for the state. The first is the responsibility of ethics and the second of economics, while the third involves teachers of politics and legislators. Along all the byways of the third path, there are those who proceed openly and those who proceed slowly. Avoiding the open, the latter delight in the shadows, wishing not to be faulted or disdained because of excessive familiarity but to be seen by a few and sought with difficulty. These are the poets, a rare species particularly in our age, and even among these men not everyone seeks the same goals or the same paths. As a result, it is not surprising that, although this manly and magnificent species of poets was always held in great esteem, the other species, which is more shallow and weak in style, is despised by demanding critics.

There you now have, my dear brother, as much as was possible in so little time and so few words, the three famous paths over which human curiosity proceeds in various directions and with different strides, manifesting an infinite disparity of intentions. These three paths, however, which are indicated by Aristotle and many other philosophers, you know are not unknown to poets, although in designating them they express it, as is their custom, more obscurely. Indeed, this is the implied meaning in the contest of the three goddesses in which a sensual man chosen as judge preferred, according to the false but widespread opinion of the rabble, Venus to Juno and Minerva. And the prize was worthy of the judge, an enticing yet brief passion, at first sweet but ultimately bitter. Nothing surprises me about the first two paths; but I cannot help wondering why almost innumerable schools of thought exist among the group pursuing a single path which is so secure and in which they boast of one name, that of philosopher. These I know but shall not mention, because of their great number and their careful identification by Marcus Varro, and after him by Augustine. I shall not, however, omit the fact that there is such disagreement among a variety of talents and of serious men that they scorn and deride one another.

Although I could cite many examples of this, I shall mention only one. Socrates—the first to bring philosophy, as it were, from heaven to earth, to compel her to dwell among men, after having led her from the stars, and to deal with their customs and their lives—is scorned by Aristotle, who considers him a practitioner of vile things, a mercenary dealer in morals, and an ignoramus concerning nature. So you doubt not that contempt, Cicero in his *De officiis* writes as follows: "I judge Aristotle and Socrates in like manner; each concentrated on his own specialty and disdained the other." This then makes me marvel greatly, and even more so when I consider that aspirations are at variance even within a single individual. Who among us, I ask, desires the same thing in his old age as in his youth? I shall take an even simpler example: Who of us wishes the same thing in the winter as in the summer? Still I have not expressed what I intended: Who of us really wishes today what we wished yesterday or, even more, wishes in the evening what we wished in the morning? Divide the day into hours, and the hours into minutes, and you will find the desires of a single man more numerous than the number of minutes. It is this in particular that surprises me; I find still more incredible the fact that all men are not equally surprised. But I have digressed enough; now I shall return to you, dear brother, and to your Augustine. I am especially astonished at your words, which give him as the source. Though not in these exact words, you clearly suggested the following: an individual can be at variance with himself concerning one and the same matter and at the same moment in time. It is common madness for us to desire to proceed without ever arriving, since it simply reflects simultaneous desires to go and to stand still. This means to wish to live and to refuse to die, even though it is written in the Psalms: "Who is the man who lives and will not see death?" And yet that is the way matters stand; this we desire, we are of this mind, so great is our blindness, our perverseness, and our madness. We wish for this life, we curse death, which is the end of this life. There you have our truly conflicting desires, our inclinations battling within us, not only because death necessarily follows upon life, but because what we call our life is death according to Cicero, whom I almost trust more regarding this matter than the majority of Catholic writers. Whence it happens that we hate and love death more than anything else, deserving to have said about us what the Comic once said: "I want and I do not want; I do not want and I want." But laying aside this perhaps displeasing, but true, philosophy and speaking in the manner of the multitude, to view this as the life that the common people call life and guard so carefully, how long is this life, I ask, even though it were to begin today? Anyone who recalls the past years of his life can easily apply, if he is able, the same measure to the future as he does remembering the past, even so far as to wish to stretch his hopes and cares to the hundredth year. With so many years already passed, how few remain, I ask! For whatever is behind us was snatched away by a certain death; whatever remains before us promises a brief life, swift and uncertain. Even if this promise were fulfilled, the fact still remains that, though the years be of like number, for unknown reasons those of old age are briefer than those of youth. Who will doubt that what you say is true of all things—that we here on earth are continually and enthusiastically seeking joy and happy days when there exist no happy days, no joy, no repose, no salvation, no life, nothing but a rough and difficult road to eternal life if we do not reject it, or to eternal death if we neglect it? Only there, where all is excellent and perfect, ought we to search for happy days while there is time. I shall not speak of all the other subjects you treated so eloquently in the same letter, because you thoroughly dealt with them and because devout discourse in a sinner's mouth does not have similar authority. In silence I admire the steadfastness of your mind and the strength of your style, from which I note that you have had a different type of preceptor in the monastery than in the world. He who taught you how to behave certainly taught you how to express yourself, for your discourse is very similar to your mind and your actions. In a brief period of time you have greatly changed, both inwardly and outwardly. I would marvel even more, had I not learned how skillful is the hand of the Almighty in bringing about change, it being the simplest matter for Him to change not only a single mind but the entire human race, the entire world, in short, the entire nature of things. You gathered for me such a wealth of sayings from the Church Fathers, connecting them with such skill, that I feel compelled to praise your ability to integrate them no less than the ideas contained therein. Such skillful juxtaposition of others' words and concepts often makes them ours; we read about its great power as not among the least precepts of the *Ars poetica*. I only wish you to be indulgent of your modest shyness and for a while loosen the reins of your shy modesty, so that you would not fear being included among the names of major writers. In writing under the same Spirit that made them eloquent, concerning which it is written, "It is not you who speak but the spirit of my Father who speaks through you,"

you would not despair of your ability to say something of your own, indeed much that would benefit you and others.

Finally, so that you may have reasonable hope for me, not to say peace of mind, since your brotherly love is so preoccupied about me—not without reason admidst my many and various tempests—please rest assured that I have not forgotten your advice at our last parting. I would not dare assert that I have thus far been resting safely in port. I have done, however, what sailors are wont to do when a storm strikes them on the high seas; I have sought refuge from the winds and the waves on one side of an island, so to speak. There I am in hiding until a safer port appears. You may say, "And in what manner?" With the aid of Jesus Christ, know that I have done the three things you advised, and daily expend the greatest effort attempting to perform them even more perfectly. I say this not for my own glory, since I continue to remain amidst many evils and miseries, suffering as I do great sorrow for the past, hardship for the present, and fear for the future; I say it as a source of joy for you, so that with your greater hope in me you might begin praying more fervently in my behalf. These are the three ways in which I obeyed you. First of all, I revealed with the help of a salutary confession the base ugliness of my sins, which had rotted in fatal sluggishness and long silence; having done so quite often, I pursued the habit of revealing the blind wounds of my soul to the almighty Healer. Then according to His counsel I became so solicitous in singing Christ's praises not only by day, but at night, that not even during these very brief nights, however great my weariness from long wakefulness, did dawn ever catch me sleeping or silent. I found so pleasing that saying of the Psalmist, "Seven times in one day I sang your praises," that once this habit was acquired, no other activity ever distracted me. And I have so liked that other saying by the same Psalmist, "I would rise in the midst of the night to confess to you," that every day at that hour I feel someone who comes to rouse me, preventing me from sleeping even while weighed down with deep slumber. Thirdly, I now fear more than death the company of women, without which I once thought I could not live. Although I am often disturbed by strong temptations, nevertheless upon recalling woman's nature, I feel every temptation immediately disappear and I return to my freedom and my peace.

In all this, dearest brother, I believe I have been aided by your prayers, and I hope to be always so aided; I implore this through the mercy of Him who deigned to summon you, wandering in the region of confusion, from your shadows into His light. In Him, may you live in true happiness, constantly scorning false and transitory happiness, and remembering me in your prayers. Enjoy good health and farewell, my dearest brother.

11 June, in solitude.

Fam. X, 6.

To Jan, Bishop-elect of Naumburg, Chancellor of the Imperial Court,* a friendly reply.

You cannot imagine how much I enjoyed reading your letter and how much more than usual I was flattered. I gathered that my name, however obscure it may be, has now traversed the summits of the stormy Alps and under a German sky is flying about on the lips of learned men. I did not deserve it, I confess; but many things both good and bad certainly occur that one does not deserve. While glory may be empty and similar to the wind, there is something truly sweet about it that can entice even great minds. I therefore embrace my destiny and accept with exultation the kindness extended by such a man. Although born far from the Roman world, you were nonetheless nourished on Roman eloquence, displaying for me the shining splendor and vigorous strength of the Latin language. However much you judge yourself inferior, so much the more do you appear superior in those eyes that see the truth. Your actions are such that what has been said of Italy now may be clearly said of Germany: it will not be more powerful in virtue and in arms than in its language, provided men of talent do not lack good will. For me your pen is an authoritative witness of transalpine eloquence. But I shall say no more lest you think that I am now repaying you in turn for your praises bestowed on me in which, most eloquent friend, you indulge so exquisitely and so seriously that I only wish they were deserved. Because of them, I feel a mixture of shame and delight; in fact it flattered me to appear of some worth to you, but it shames me not to be what I appear. I understand, of course; that excellent man has deceived you. Henceforth know that you should trust him in everything except matters regarding me, for he loves me. Thus you understand the blindness of his judgment; he speaks of me as he would have me be. Live happily and farewell.

---

*Jan ze Středa (Johann von Neumarkt), a Bohemian humanist, was elected Bishop of Naumburg in 1352 and later Bishop of Olmütz. He entered the Imperial Chancelry in 1347, and later became prothonotary and chancellor. Through his efforts Petrarch's works were circulated widely in imperial circles and throughout Bohemia.

Fam. XI, 1.

To Giovanni Boccaccio,* concerning his pilgrimage to the city of Rome in the year of the Jubilee.

I used to hope that fortune could be changed by changing one's location and ideas, but I see that I was wrong. Wherever I flee, ill fortune follows me. Whether on a speedy chariot or on a snorting horse, on a swift ship or on the wings of Daedalus, grim fortune precedes my flight. All in vain, however, for though she may be able to taunt me and goad me, she cannot lay me low while the good Lord offers me support. As with Democritus, I have learned how to tell her to go hang herself when she threatens me and how to give her my middle finger in indignation. She nonetheless continues to attack me with her tricks, intent now that I have reached a sober and tranquil age, on overcoming the one who had often conquered her during his younger years. As if it were easier to do battle with an elderly person! As if the mind's strength decreased during a long life along with the body's vigor! Had this not in fact increased, I would believe I have lived in vain. Not to keep you any longer in suspense, I shall now tell you about the recent traps she set for me. As you know, after having taken my leave of you, I left for Rome where this year, so eagerly awaited by all us sinners, nearly all of Christendom is gathering. So as not to suffer the tediousness of a solitary pilgrim, I brought with me several traveling companions; the oldest was included because of his religious seriousness and his advanced age, another because of his knowledge and eloquence. The others because of their worldly experience seemed able to alleviate with amiability any journey, however demanding. Thus had I provided myself with a plan that events proved to be prudent rather than wise. With fervent determination I had now at length undertaken the journey in order to put an end to my sins; for as Horace says, "I was not so ashamed to have played the game as not to have withdrawn." I hope fortune has not, and will not, make me stray from my purpose. However much she may dash and batter this insignificant body of mine against the rocks, splattering them with my blood and

---

*Giovanni Boccaccio (1313–75) became an ardent admirer of Petrarch following the latter's examination by King Robert for the laurel crown in 1341 (which Boccaccio may have attended), but they did not personally meet until 1350 when Boccaccio hosted Petrarch in Florence. Boccaccio was instrumental in having the Florentines return Petrarch's patrimony and in their offer to have Petrarch settle there. Aside from Nelli, he is Petrarch's chief correspondent, with thirty-two prose letters and one metrical letter addressed to him.

brains, she will in all probability snatch at, but never crush, my spirit contemptuous of her and her affairs. She may quite frequently cause my limbs to weaken, but she will never make my mind succumb. Not to tire you with excessive anticipation, what she recently did to my body was certainly of no little consequence. Having left Bolsena, at present a small and nondescript town but once among the most important in Etruria, I was hastening cheerfully along in order to see the holy city for the fifth time. In my mind I was reviewing thoughts such as these: "Behold how swiftly life slips by, behold how the affairs and opinions of men are rapidly changing, behold the truth of what I wrote in the *Bucolics*: 'the enthusiasm of youth displeases old age and mens' concerns seem to vary with the color of their hair.' It is exactly fourteen years since my first visit to Rome, attracted as I was by its wonders and my desire to see it. A few years later I was drawn here a second time by a perhaps untimely, but sweet, love for the laurel crown. The reason for the third and fourth journeys was compassion for some famous friends whose downcast and wretched fortunes I did not fear to assume on my weak shoulders. This is now my fifth voyage to Rome; who knows whether it will be my last? It is truly all the more happy than the others because it is more noble to be concerned about the soul rather than the body, all the more desirable to be concerned about eternal salvation rather than mortal glory." As I was pondering such things and rendering silent thanks to God, the horse of the religious, the aged abbot mentioned above, was traveling on my left but was to cause something even more sinister; in an apparent attempt to strike my horse he struck me instead at the juncture of the knee and shinbone. He did so with such force that the loud cracking sound of many bones fracturing caused many men accompanying me to gather around to see what had happened. Because of the incredible pain, at first I considered stopping; but the place itself frightened me and necessity became a virtue. Later that day I arrived in Viterbo and some three days later in Rome. When doctors had been summoned, the bone was exposed, revealing a dreadful whiteness. They expressed uncertainty as to a fracture, but they did find clear markings of the horseshoe. So troublesome was the odor from the neglected wound that often I would turn away violently, with an incredible inability to tolerate it. While it may be true that innate intimacy with our own bodies will cause most of us to bear more readily what would be disgusting in the bodies of others, I have rarely recognized in any corpse as I now do in my own flesh what an insignificant, indeed what a wretched and vile animal man is, unless he redeems the worthlessness of his body by the nobility of his spirit. What more can I say? I have now lain in Rome for fourteen days in the hands of doctors, between fear and hope, doubtful of my health. Were these days converted into years, they would be in my judgment no longer, no more annoying. This then is the condition in which I find myself—a condition that would have been very painful and inconvenient anywhere because forced inertia and repose numb the powers of my mind, however small; whereas moderate activity quickens them. This is particularly inconvenient and troublesome now because of my insatiable desire to see the queen of cities; for the more I see her, the more I marvel at her, and the more I am led to believe whatever we have read about her. I take comfort, however, in my situation and in my pain with the thought that it is heaven's will and that, since my confessor seemed to have been too indulgent toward me, another would compensate for it. I confess to believing at times that it might be God's will to raise with His own hands a person whose spirit had long been limping, by causing his body to limp. This exchange was hardly to be considered sad or unhappy, thanks to Him who renewed my hope of seeing you again soon, once I have recovered in both soul and body. You can tell from the form of this letter, dear friend, that I am writing you from my couch, not to make you feel badly that this has happened to me, but to make you rejoice that I have patiently borne all these misfortunes and would bear much more serious ones if they should befall me. Meanwhile live happily and farewell, and remember me.

Rome, 2 November, in the dead silence of the night.

Fam. XI, 2.

To the same correspondent,* a lament over his own condition and over the wretched and undeserved death of Jacopo da Carrara the Younger.

Much time has elapsed since the arrival of your poem filled with laments. The most serious, as I recall, was that a number of my creative writings have fallen into the hands of both the general public and evil men, while you alone, whose appetite for my labors exceeds all others' and whose enjoyment would exceed all others', continue to have trouble acquiring them. Whereupon with a truly hasty pen I composed in reply a number of verses, the reason being my fear that you might believe that I had overlooked your complaint. Unfortunately I had scarcely carried them to the door than I lost them among confused heaps of other writings. Despite many careful searches they were subsequently never seen again until today when, unexpectedly and beyond all hope, they appeared while I was occupied with other matters. At first it seemed improper to send them to you, but since, as I realize and as the final verses attest, I am confident that all my writings would be pleasing to you, I gladly changed my mind so that you would know that I had not been telling untruths in saying that they were lost. After such an interval of time I feel that one thing at least must be added so as to conceal nothing from you. If the poem, written then for you and finally reaching your hands now, depicted me battling on equal terms with fortune, as if fighting in a battle line, it was nevertheless not without great hope of victory. At present, unless I am mistaken, the passing of time has indisputably made me the victor. By living I have learned to deal with the battles of life: now I confront fortune's blows not with the laments and groans of yesteryear, but with the thick skin of a hardened spirit; and though once accustomed to faltering, I now stand firm. Therefore, indignant at my failing to fall beneath such a cloud of arrows and distrustful of smaller weapons, she recently struck me in the chest with a huge firebrand. After stripping me bare through the recent deaths of so many friends, after making me lose so many supports of my life, she recently snatched away my best and dearest and sweetest comfort and support by a sudden, horrendous, and truly undeserved death. Worthy of every praise and distinguished by a uniquely angelic sweetness of manners, he was a man I

---

*See preceding letter.

wish you and posterity to know, Jacopo da Carrara, second in line by birth but first by far for excellence and glory, the lord and father of Padua. To the best of my knowledge, following the death of the King of Sicily, he alone remained in all the world as the great friend of learning, the cultivator and just critic of talents. As long as I live, it will be pleasing to sing his praises and remember him. But to return to what I started to write, he was, I confess, a man to whom I owed everything and on whom I depended completely. Fortune has snatched him from me—alas, how fiercely and suddenly!—so that having once and for all removed the only foundation of my hope she might destroy me too, which seemed very likely. I stood firm, nonetheless, very sad indeed, I will not deny, but erect, undaunted, and more secure because I can scarcely expect a greater wound. Henceforth I shall always detest and curse that dreadful monster, but I shall not fear her. Farewell.

Padua, 7 January, in haste, with the messenger pressing.

Fam. XI, 3.

To Giovanni Aretino, Chancellor of the Lords of Mantua,* concerning the same matter but on a broader scale.

As one sharing my love and grief, you ask, indeed you remind me of my obligation to write something in artistic form encompassing the honors and vicissitudes of Jacopo da Carrara, the younger, an excellent man especially worthy of my praise. I refer to the man recently proclaimed Lord of Padua, who was truly nothing less than its master, nothing more than the real father of his country. Your request is indeed a small matter if superficially considered, but upon deeper examination it is perhaps more demanding than you think since his virtue demands a panegyric and his death a tragedy, two of the most distinguished poetic labors. You thus offer a vast and fertile subject for my pen but one in which the eloquence of the matter deserves greater praise than my talent. What did he lack that might be unworthy of high praise or of our sorrow or our grief? Sorrow is eloquent by nature, and grief is kindled by the power of mutual respect. It is easy then to write you about him, not fearing excessively either one of the two extreme styles. It is also easy to praise for your friendly ears the man you loved so much, knowing that all of Italy will applaud and that there will be general agreement among good men except for the obstreperous clamor of evil ones. Also contributing would be the unworthy and unusual nature of his death, which very clearly supports the common proverb that he who disdains his own life becomes lord of another's. For unexpectedly, in the very midst of his venerable home, teeming with dignitaries and noble friends, surrounded by hordes of bodyguards, in broad daylight on a feast day while he was carefree and secure, he was struck down by the rage and bloody blows of a foul and desperate dog. Not to omit anything about the monstrous crime, that same dog had dined at his table that very day, indeed had often dined there. I believe a more shameful spectacle never defiled human eyes. If we who only heard about the crime were so horrified, how wretched are they who happened to see that gentle man worthy of another kind of death and that wild and infamous beast both sink to the ground at the same time, as if felled by the same blow. So quick and so unexpected was the ugly deed, so extraordinary the bystanders' stupor that his faithful followers, who would have calmly suffered death for their beloved leader, were able to offer no appropriate

*See VII, 8; also known as Giovanni Aghinolfi.

assistance to the dying man; one group lifted him in their arms and another group with a thousand blows slew the perpetrator of the shocking crime. Alas, how could two such unequal spirits, worthy of such unequal ends, have suffered similar fates! Though it happened thus, I have nonetheless resisted your request until the present, not to escape toil or more involvements, although both these factors may enter somewhat, but because my spirit became chilled once it was wounded by grief. It delights in the recollection of such a friend and welcomes this occasion for endless tears, but it fears exhausting its eyes and daily keeps something in reserve—O lamentable economy—in order to speak of him, remember him, and weep over him. Finally, my spirit hopes to have always before its eyes the face of that illustrious man and his ways, his virtue and his fate. All things considered, it can lament nothing about him except his death, although I do not deny that such lamentation proceeds from philosophical, and not human, concerns. Often with the steps of reason I ascend that loftiest summit of pure intellect from which, as from the highest summits of Mount Olympus, the clouds may be perceived beneath our feet. From that vantage point, I perceive the mist of human affairs, the cloud of errors with which we are so sur- rounded, the many shadows in which we walk. I see that whatever we generally enjoy or lament in this life is nothing, that what we either greatly desire or fear is nothing, that what distresses us are mere trifles, what terrifies us as children and adults are specters, and what casts us down or raises us up is but the gentlest breeze. I see that even what is called life is but a shadow of a fleeting cloud, or smoke wafted by the winds, or finally troubled sleep or an unfin- ished tale or anything else conceivably more empty. I see that nothing but virtue can be considered constant in mortal affairs, that she alone can make blessed those who embrace her and wretched those who forsake her. I fully adhere, as they say, to the opinion of the Stoics, to the point of preferring their definition above all others; it defines virtue as feeling rightly about God and acting rightly among men. Indeed whosoever lives by such a definition will never suffer a deplorable fate, but a desirable and enviable happiness. Yet we, feeble and mortal species that we are, humans living in the lowest of valleys, weighed down by heavy burdens, rarely ascend to the higher elevations and therefore speak in ways more befitting the rabble than the truth. This is the source of my complaint and those of many others concerning matters which are sometimes frivolous, sometimes empty and sometimes even happy; such is the perversity of our desires, such is the blindness of our hearts. But now we have slowly wandered from the main point, so let us return to the beginning.

I have, then, not yet dared to write anything of sustained inspiration on the proposed subject, and you have heard the reason. Furthermore, subject as I am even now to human ills, every day provides new reasons for grieving over his death. Were I to include them all in a letter, I would be doing practically nothing else, and would thus be better advised to commit such thoughts to the winds. But sometimes it is better to commit them to letters, as in the case of what happened to me the day before yesterday. I remembered as I was about to leave for Padua that I had been asked to compose an epitaph for those dear and beloved ashes—something I should do without being begged. But as one day led to another and I did nothing, I grieved and blushed that I could postpone for any reason such a pious and worthy act of respect. When a number of visitors subsequently urged me on, reminding me of my early promise, which my shame did not allow me to deny, nor time to accomplish, what could I do? I thereupon sought ways and means of spurring the Muses; I proceeded with a few friends to his tomb as if to request permission from the dead man as I customarily did when he was alive. Being an inconvenient hour of the day, the gates of the church were barred, and I was admitted only with great difficulty after awakening the sacristans from their siesta. Having asked my companions to wait for me, I went alone to the tomb and addressed, while sitting by it, many words to those silent remains. After a brief stay, as time allowed, I tearfully composed sixteen elegiac verses, inspired more by my spirit than by study or by art, and handed them still in rough draft to my waiting friends. I departed, urging them to select whichever ones most pleased them—if nothing better occurred either to them or to me in the meantime—to be engraved on the tombstone which illustrious sculptors were already hard at work decorating. I am appending those verses to this letter to make you aware of whatever I am composing, whether it be done seriously or hastily or extemporaneously. Farewell.

12 May, from Leonico.

Alas, O abode so confined for so great a soul!
Here, under a small marble slab, lies the father, the hope and
*   salvation of his country.*
Whoever you may be, O reader, who turn your eyes to this stone,

In reading about the public ills add prayers to your tears.
It is wrong to mourn over him whose virtue bore him to the
*   heavens,*
If there be any recompense for human merit,
But mourn instead the grave misfortune befallen the fatherland
And the crushed hope of good men and the groaning caused by
*   unexpected evils.*
The leader whom native Carrara recently gave to the people and
*   to the fathers*
A hostile death has born away in Padua.
No one cultivated friendships with such sweetness
While being a terror to his enemies.
An excellent man, always eager to serve good men,
He was ignorant of envy and distinguished in loyalty.
Therefore mindful of Jacopo, confidently inscribe his splendid
*   name among the rarest names of all ages, O posterity.*

Fam. XI, 4.

To Philippe, Bishop of Cavaillon, * *a friendly letter.*

Long has my mind, anxious and desirous of conversing with you, had many things reserved for you; but the lack of time and of energy compel me to hasten toward the conclusion which, as philosophers believe, is first in our thoughts but last in application. You will realize the nature of what I propose and strongly desire for myself without the many details needed for its achievement, which my surroundings, the place and time, the messenger's eagerness, and my comrades' clamor do not permit me to include. This goal I have not set forth in free prose but, knowing that poetry is a friend of brevity, I have compressed as much into eight verses as chance allowed a busy mind amidst its urban cares and wooded thickets. If you will keep their writer before your eyes while reading, you will understand, I hope, the desires and state of a weary mind, heavily burdened. Farewell.

> No place in the whole world is dearer to me than the
> Vale Enclosed, and none more favorable for my toils.
>   In my boyhood I visited the Vale Enclosed, and in my youth,
> when I returned, the lovely valley cherished me in its sunny bosom.
>   In my manhood I spent my best years sweetly in the
> Vale Enclosed, while the threads of my life were white.
>   In my old age I desire to live out in the Vale Enclosed
> my allotted time, and in the Enclosed Vale, under thy guidance, to die.
>   (Trans. E. H. Wilkins, *Petrarch at Vaucluse*, p.80)

*See II, 1.

Fam. XI, 5.

To the Florentines, * *an expression of gratitude for the restitution, or better, the gift of his estate.*

I believe that now I have lived long enough, excellent citizens, and I seem to hear the voice of a wise friend: "Die while you are joyful, for you are not about to ascend into heaven." A most remarkable observation indeed! Where does one get this insatiable desire for living? Happiness must be measured by the valor of one's spirit, not by the number of years; and when the goal is reached, it is fitting to stop. I shall venture to boast frankly to you all the more confidently because, however minimal my glory may be or may appear to be, it will be an ever so slight addition to your sublime glory. I have never desired wealth or power, which I was at least allowed to aspire to, though not perchance to attain. From my earliest years I considered inconsequential what seemed of great importance to many men. I know not how I became that way, but my life, as well as my words and my spirit, are proof that I speak the truth. I have concentrated all my preoccupations and all my waking hours on the search for whatever might assist me in becoming good, or at least not unworthy of the love of good men. I regret that I have not as yet achieved the first. How fully and beyond all expectation I am achieving the second is due to your kindness, as revealed in your letter from which, I confess, I derived as much astonishment as delight. I truly rejoice, and as Plutarch said to the Emperor Trajan, I rejoice both for your kindness and for my good fortune. Yet I am astounded beyond belief that in this age of ours, which I considered so barren of any good, and, even more miraculously, that in so many minds there still exists such a popular and, so to speak, public generosity. From this can be understood, to use Cicero's words, "how praiseworthy is giving when the glory of receiving is so great." Indeed I ask you, what could I, were I there with you, have requested or desired that is more remarkable or important than what you have recently offered me, though absent and silent, O distinguished and illustrious fellow men? Was there ever a country that showed such generosity and liberality toward a worthy citizen? Search throughout antiquity, read through histories. Rome recalled her Cicero as well as Rutilius and Metellus from exile, but it was from an exile to which she had sent them; she also recalled Camillus, but only after grave misfortunes

*Through the intervention of Boccaccio, the Florentines also offered Petrarch a professorship at the newly organized University in Florence, which Petrarch refused.

compelled her. The banishment of these men was as unjust as their recall was just; indeed the recall of Camillus was necessary and almost compulsory. Athens recalled Alcibiades, but under similar conditions and with a similar public need. But when was a citizen, absent by choice, ever recalled by plebiscite or by senate decree when a country was not in danger. Caesar Augustus returned Virgil's lands to him, but it was he who had deprived him of them. Still, what son ever had his land, lost by his father or by his ancestors, restored by public decree? These are rare examples of piety and generosity, and since rarity brings renown, your unique kindness will shine ever so brightly! I am summoned; but who, I ask, summons me? By whom am I summoned? And with what powerful entreaties, with what imperious flattery, with what expectation? My ancestral land is being returned to me after its redemption from private hands at public expense. What a hoe of eloquence cultivates it, what flowers of words adorn it, what praises of me it exudes, how fertile it is with the rich harvest of your virtues! Your diligence indeed overcomes the natural sterility of the soil so that I bear no envy for the fruits of Africa or of Sicily. From my most productive and pleasing country place, I scornfully observe the battle in Campania between Bacchus and Ceres, feeling in my heart wealthier than any king. May I one day deserve this great favor of your republic, which is now owed exclusively to your generosity, as I place greater value on your opinion of me and the flattering praise accompanying your gift than on the land itself, which was not returned but donated to me, and on whatever can be sown or grown upon it. I do not believe it would be difficult to convince anyone of this who has any knowledge of my affairs. What will this infinite thirst for riches avail me, or this anxious and toilsome extension of holdings? There is little doubt that the further I set my goal and the further I proceed, the more I realize how much remains, and the more clearly I recognize the smallness of my increased holdings and my poverty. O useless toil, since nothing ever satisfies greed! How much is sufficient for human nature? Enough for a burial place. A small urn contains those dissatisfied with the limits of their kingdoms; and even without this, one can live well and die happily. Indeed, O illustrious fellow citizens, just as this generosity of yours has acquired eternal praise for you, so has it given me no little consolation to have that sweet and delightful dwelling returned to me where lived my father, my grandfather and my great-grandfather, a man rich in genius but inept in letters. In short, it is a dwelling in which grew old a long line of other ancestors, conspicuous not so much for their smoky portraits as for their shining faith. I, however, decided to fly far away on wings forged either by nature or by fortune. Now, thanks to your initiative, you offer me the nest of my youth to which I may fly back, weary at length of my long wanderings. I do not deny that yours is a great gesture, yet it becomes still greater because your public gift is adorned with great praise, which I wish were merited, with such warm prayers and flattering words that, unless I am made of stone, your kindness will provide me with an eternal beacon of glory and a spur to virtue. If I express my gratitude in a manner unequal to your actions, the reason is not an ungrateful spirit but the magnitude of your generosity. I shall express my gratitude, therefore, as I can, for it is certainly great; but, as Cicero says, I feel still more gratitude, which requires a more accurate style and a richer eloquence. Thus I am so overwhelmed and overcome by your kindness that whatever I may have said is less than what I would like to have said. Finally there is one thing I should not like to overlook, which I recall having said last year upon my return from Rome to the outstanding men then governing your city. The kindness of my fatherland so exalts me that I, insignificant little man that I am, do not fear to avail myself, in exchange for substantial honors both material and verbal, of that brief and tearful response of the Emperor Augustus to the senate, expressing his joy over the new title of emperor. He said, "Illustrious senators, with this answer to my prayers, how else could I pray to the immortal God than that He allow this unanimous decision of yours to endure to the end of my life?" Similarly, what I have in mind concerning my return if God so wishes, indeed how much I wish to comply with your commands, I would rather not put entirely in writing; a portion will be delivered verbally through your emissary, the distinguished Giovanni Boccaccio, through whom I have received your letter, your wishes, and your commands. Just as he will faithfully deliver this letter, so will he eloquently convey my affection for you; and listening to him, rest assured that he speaks for me. Wishing you the very best within your ever-flourishing republic, I bid you farewell.

6 April.

Fam. XI, 6.

To Giovanni Boccaccio, concerning the writer's intention to cross the Alps.*

What we read in fables I now consider nearer the truth: the virgin loved by Apollo felt herself stiffen in mid-flight and become suddenly enmeshed in roots, while thinking that she was touching the earth with her feet. Indeed I too, for reasons of which I am unaware, at times possess tenacious roots in place of obedient and mobile feet. I had promised you that my departure from Padua would be on 18 April; I barely departed thence, indeed I was, to be more exact, torn from there on 3 May. I had decided to spend two or three days in Verona, yet here too nearly a month has elapsed in procrastination. Although the city is particularly attractive at this time of the year, my sojourn has not been without tedium, desirous as I was to make haste. But so far I have been incapable of freeing myself from the sweet chains of an indulgent friend, which daily closely resemble an actual prison. Though I neither consider nor desire anything more pleasant than the affection and devotion of friends, still I must complain, and I shall continue complaining as long as I live, that I am loved more than befits my leisure time. Upon my departure from here today, I am setting out for Mantua, the illustrious birthplace of our Virgil. There I shall find a similar set of chains but more easily undone, unless I am mistaken. In Parma, I expect no delay caused by some important friend, so great has been the change there in a brief time, and in the remaining towns and cities on my itinerary I have no official business. Therefore, if my health allows, I shall write you soon from my transalpine abode; do not expect any letter then before the one announcing my arrival. How long shall I remain there? Let fortune decide since she rotates our affairs and our plans. As for me, to repeat something well known not only to you as a special friend but also to the public, I would choose to spend the remainder of my life on those lands, if it were granted from above, since I have considered and rejected all other possibilities. Though it does not possess many of the delights with which cities abound, it still has much that a city lacks and that I myself find most pleasurable— freedom, leisure, silence, solitude. I confess that two things about it do not sit well with me: first, the distance from Italy, to which I am naturally attracted; secondly, the nearness of the Babylon of the West, the worst of places and most similar to hell, which my nature also abhors and flees. I would, however, accept both shortcomings,

*See XI, 1.

mitigating the bitter with the sweet, except for other reasons that cannot be included here. Because of them, I certainly hope that my sojourn there will be extremely brief, unless something unexpected happens which I cannot even begin to foresee. This I know, that there is almost nothing that cannot happen to man, being so utterly frail and mortal yet so haughty amidst affliction. What will happen, therefore, lies hidden, but my present intentions, which I do not wish to conceal from you and our friends, are not. To be sure, the Roman pontiff, whom our fathers used to seek on the banks of the Tiber, we seek on the banks of the Rhone. Our grandchildren will perhaps seek him on the banks of the Tagus, there being evidently nothing that a long day may not confuse and alter, since clearly all things hasten toward sunset. Let this be taken care of by the holy and austere fisherman who, although knowing the Rhone and by no means ignorant of the Tagus or of the Seine, still moored his little ship and his nets in the Tiber's waters. Let him see to it, I say, whose small boat is now buffeted by storms and whose dockyards are deserted. Let those provide who are seated at the rudder; we are simple passengers snatched by the tides, partners in fortune but not in blame. Since I cannot find him where I wish, I intend to seek him, as well as my dear and widely scattered friends who remain, wherever I can. After my expression of farewell to all, I hope to flee those cruel lands and greedy shores for my previously mentioned dwelling about fifteen miles distant at the clear and sonorous source of the Sorgue. There amidst forest and rivers, there amidst my various books, which for four years bound and silent have been awaiting me under a rustic's guardianship, I shall spend what remains of the summer in solitary retirement. Were I once again to resume my travels, soon my poor body, though accustomed to continuous toil since childhood, would perhaps be overcome by the excessive heat. I am careful with it only because I have been tiring and twisting it too long. In the autumn I hope to return with the books that I decided to include in my Italian library. You now know the reasons for my past slowness and the summary of my future plans. As a result, neither astonishment nor ambiguity may take you by surprise. There remains my request that you render my sincere homage to our senate, to which I am greatly indebted, as you know, Furthermore, give my personal greetings to our three fellow citizens, truly excellent and honorable friends whose faces and words I carry with me wherever I go, and who without realizing it accompany me on my longest journeys. Farewell.

1 June, from Verona.

Fam. XI, 7.

To his Socrates, * *concerning the earthquake in Rome and his subsequent foreboding.*

What should I do first, lament or be frightened? Everywhere there is cause for fear, everywhere reason for grief; nor does any present evil not forebode a more serious tragedy in the future, although I can barely perceive what to expect of a more serious nature. The world is consumed and emptied by man's madness on the one hand and by the avenging hand of God on the other. Misery has reached such an intensity that new forms of evil are inconceivable. Indeed whoever relates this state of human affairs to posterity, if there be any, will seem to be telling tales; nor should we be indignant that others would not believe from us what we would in no way believe from others. I confess that present events have disposed me to believe a great deal, since every kind of evil has been experienced by the human race. I shall not speak of the floods, the storms, and the fires by which entire cities have recently perished, of the wars raging throughout the world that are causing great slaughter of people, or of the plague from heaven that is unequaled through the ages. These are matters known to everyone, witnessed by vacant cities and fields without farmers, mourned by an afflicted and nearly deserted world and by the tearful face, so to speak, of nature herself. To pass over these matters, I say, as well known in the west as in the east and in the north as in the south, for some time now the Alps have been shaken to their roots in many places, as you know. In an unusual and violent foreshadowing of the future, a large section of Italy shook simultaneously with a considerable area of Germany. There soon followed misfortunes we can neither recall without tears nor have the strength to enumerate. Lastly, when we few who seemed to have avoided the public calamity had surrendered to the hope that death was weary and the Lord's anger appeased, an unusual tremor about which you probably still do not know shook Rome itself. It was so strong that nothing similar had occurred since the city's founding over two thousand years ago. Massive ancient buildings, neglected by the citizenry but admired by foreigners, fell; that tower truly unique in the world, called the Tower of the Counts, weakened by huge cracks, crumbled and now looks down upon its head, once the proud decoration of its summit, which has tumbled to the ground. Finally, to cite still more testimony of divine wrath, the beauty of many churches was

---

*See I, 1.

destroyed; in particular, the one dedicated to the apostle Paul had a good portion of its sanctuary tumble to the ground, and the top of St. John Lateran has crumbled. Such calamities have saddened the Jubilee's ardor with an icy terror, although the damage to St. Peter's has been less extensive. The event had indeed been without precedent, justifiably causing many hearts to become dejected. For if the quaking of so many members portends such great calamity, what does the trembling of the head foreshadow? Let those who think they know all become indignant and murmur unhappily, but the fact remains that Rome is the head of the world; though exhausted and unkempt, Rome is without doubt the head of the entire world. If it could speak with one voice, the world itself would not deny this; anyone not wishing to recognize this in good faith must be convinced with proofs and documents. Lest you believe that I am making the most dire predictions by creating them from nothing, I shall justify them with recent examples of misfortune and with the authority of Pliny, an unquestionably outstanding writer. To avoid the accusation of changing his meaning, I cite his own words on the subject. "There is no absolute evil or danger in the quake itself; there is just as much, or more, in what it portends because Rome never quaked but that it foretold some future happening." So wrote Pliny. Now indeed, what shall I withold or what shall I say? Therefore I am addressing you as one of our own who deeply love the republic. What difference does it make whence the roots of your origin? I focus rather on your mind, which our friendship has made distinctly Italian. Wherefore lend your ear, my Socrates: I am deeply distressed concerning the ultimate condition of the republic, and the earthquake stirs within me gloomy presentiments not only about Rome but all of Italy, not only about the quaking of land but its effect on minds. Among the many things that terrify me is that prophecy written long before the founding of Rome, found not in secular writings but in Sacred Scriptures. When I first read it I confess that, though familiar with secular works and ignorant of the others, I shuddered and my blood froze around my heart. It is found among the final words of Balaam's last prophecy, which I include in this letter to help you avoid a laborious perusal of the book of Numbers. There it is written: "They shall come in triremes from Italy, they will overcome the Assyrians and they will ravage the Hebrews, and finally they themselves shall perish." Although this prophecy may seem fulfilled in the ruins of the Roman Empire, would that the city's quaking is not announcing another destruction of peace and liberty! Meanwhile submit your vacillating mind to the support of virtue and constancy so that, even if the earth quakes, your mind may have a stable abode. Indeed as Horace says, "If the world were to crumble, let the mind fearlessly suffer the ruins." This letter written to you some time ago at Padua, has been long delayed for lack of a messenger. I have decided to send it from here to please our common friend who refused to visit you without a letter from me. In fact, there was no need for a messenger or a letter since I am about to follow in his footsteps. Therefore when you read this letter, know that I am already near. Indeed it will be a good idea if you come to meet me at the source of the Sorgue. Farewell, enjoy good health and remember me.

11 June, from Piacenza.

Fam. XI, 8.

To Andrea Dandolo, Doge of Venice,* an appeal for peace with Genoa.

On the one hand, my faith and your kindness suggest that I write you, O illustrious doge; on the other, the state of present affairs and the times compel me to do so. The first indeed urges me to speak, the second dares me to do so, while the third makes it impossible for me to remain silent. For who would expect silence from a loving friend? The freedom of love is not bridled by modesty. Were the hand of reason to close one's mouth, and were the mind, recognizing itself unequal to the magnitude of affairs, unwilling to lie down or remain silent, the uneasy heart nevertheless breaks out in cries, seeking not unfamiliar thoughts or words, but speaking whatever comes to mind, whatever sorrow and apprehension urge it to express. Its speech is hasty, agitated, tumultuous, and very similar, as is natural, to the mind's fluctuations. Please know that this is truly happening to me now as never before. I am moved indeed, O illustrious doge, deeply and intensely moved. If you really wish to know the cause of my anxiety, it is that I am disturbed by the storms roaring about us and by the upheavals that we see everywhere. But to leave aside my laments for the entire human race, as an Italian I shall limit myself to my fears for Italy. At present two powerful peoples are taking up arms, two flourishing cities or, to put it briefly, two bright lights of Italy, which it seems to me Mother Nature has so strategically located on opposite sides of the approaches to the Ausonian land so that, with you in the north and east controlling the Adriatic and with them in the south and west controlling the Tyrrhenian, the four corners of the earth would realize that Italy still is queen, even after the weakening and decline, or rather the prostration and destruction, of the Roman Empire. While the pride of certain peoples may make them seriously question this, surely no one would have the audacity to dispute your supremacy on the sea. If, as I shudder to contemplate, much less to predict, you now turn your victorious arms against one another, we shall without doubt perish of self-inflicted wounds. Plundered by our own hands, we shall lose not only our fame but our domination of the seas acquired through so much labor,

---

*Andrea Dandolo became Doge of Venice in 1343 at the age of thirty-six. His learning and skills were responsible for raising Venetian commerce to unprecedented levels. The intense commercial competition with Genoa provoked many naval battles between the two countries throughout much of the Trecento.

without however losing that comfort in misfortunes that we have often experienced in other moments; for the enemy will be able to enjoy our calamities but not boast about them. Among my numerous apprehensions which distress or terrify me, I fear none more than the intractable minds and opinions of young people, for youth is an age of ignorance, inexperienced with fortune's fickleness and its power to overthrow empires once great. Young people promise themselves all they desire and consequently very often fail. Just as the words of a famous warrior in Livy are true, "He whom fortune has never deceived does not easily reflect on the uncertain nature of events," so what follows is similarly true, "Never does the outcome correspond less to one's expectation than in war." Unfortunately, those men must be deceived to whom fortune's face has always appeared serene and calm, for she is two-faced, considerably more violent than gentle. I was therefore pleased to hear that you had referred the uncertain state of affairs to a council of elders. This behooved your foresight and your character, whose seriousness and maturity made you leader of that group, although you still belong to the other because of your age. Arrogance is attributed to youth and prudence to old age; for this reason the masters of the Roman republic in antiquity, whose virtue found nothing impossible, whether called fathers out of respect or in recognition of their paternal solicitude, without doubt justly deserved to be called senators because of their age. Now that such responsibility has been given first to young people and more recently in our own age even to children, would that the height from which we have fallen were not so evident! But more about this at another time, for it is difficult for one afflicted with grief and fear to deplore the past and to foresee the future, to shed tears for misfortune and to seek a remedy for danger.

I shall therefore return to my fear tormenting me concerning the future. The condition of your country, I confess, worries and amazes me. What shall I say about you? It would behoove me little to rejoice at your glory and to feel compassion for your toils. I must pity your talent, for I feel the great distance between the clattering of arms and the restfulness of the Muses, the weak sounds of Apollo's lyre amidst the trumpets of Mars. You can really deny nothing to your fatherland, which was so worthy of you in peacetime that neither weariness of war nor fear of death made you forsake it. If, abandoning Helicon ever so briefly and sending your books on leave, you pursued the path of public service, you performed the office of a grateful citizen, of a good man, and of a distinguished leader. These duties you have discharged in such fashion, however, that, though armed, you think of love and peace, and are convinced that you can offer the fatherland no greater triumph and no finer spoils than peace. Whenever the subject of peace arises, I gladly make reference to that saying of Hannibal, because truth itself evidently seems to have wrenched from the mouth of that martial man words so opposed to his character. What then does he say according to Livy? "Better and safer is a certain peace than a coveted victory"; and this from a man who burned with a desire for victory and disturbed the peace of the entire world! What, therefore, should a friend of peace say? Should he not rather say, "Better and more sacred is certain peace than certain victory?" This is particularly true because peace is laden with repose and charity and grace, while victory is laden with toil and crimes and arrogance. Indeed what is more pleasant than peace, what is happier or sweeter? Without peace what is man's life except danger, perpetual fear, and a gloomy workshop of unending cares? I ask you, what pleasure can it be to pass the night under the heavens, to break one's sleep with a horn, to enclose the body in a breastplate, "to conceal gray hair with a helmet" in Maro's words, to die suddenly while still girt in iron, and to remain unburied, which is the greatest concern of brave men? It certainly must be pleasing to consume the wretched heart with stinging anxieties, fear, and hatred, and to waste the uncertain time of this fleeting life in such pursuits! What safety can there be in fighting simultaneously the sea and an enemy when this means battling a double death? I pray that no one will deceive you: you are waging war with a courageous, unconquered and, I must sadly add, Italian people. Would that your enemies were cities such as Damascus or Susa, Memphis or Smyrna, rather than Genoa! Would that you were fighting the Persians or Arabs, the Thracians or Illyrians! Now what are you really doing? If you still have any respect for the Latin name, consider that those you endeavor to destroy are your brothers. Alas, as in Thebes long ago, now throughout Italy battle lines of brothers are being drawn, a tearful spectacle for friends, a propitious one for enemies. What could possibly be the purpose of a war when, whether conquerors or conquered (for the game of fortune is uncertain), one of the two lights of Italy must be extinguished and the other dimmed? Decide for yourself whether the expectation of a bloodless victory over such an enemy may be a sign of absurd madness rather than of noble confidence. See for yourselves, O magnanimous men and most powerful peoples—what I say to one I mean to both, and if these words are sent primarily to you it is because of my respectful familiarity with your virtues and our proximity—consider for yourselves, I say, where to direct your minds and what may be the boundaries of your madness or of your hatred, consider your own security and finally the public welfare which in large measure depends on you. Bear in mind that, unless some spring of piety extinguishes the heat of this impending war, there will emerge from the wounds inflicted Italian blood, not Numantine or Carthaginian. And it will be the blood of men who, in case of unexpected violence or a foreign attack against our territories (which have sometimes been attempted but never with impunity), will be among the first to take up arms with you in defense of a common cause. It is they who will immediately expose their breasts to death and to enemy weapons, who will be protected by your shields and your bodies as they will protect you with theirs, who will take vengeance on the fleeing enemy once they have surrounded their fleet, and who will die, fight, and triumph along with you. I cannot understand the pleasure in attacking and destroying men such as these because of brief moments of anger, even though it may be done with impunity. Perhaps the angry minds of those who, in the fashion of women, delight in the punishment of friends and in vengeance for the least offense will better understand it! Certainly it is not useful or noble, and, ultimately, not even human. It is preferable to forget wrongs than to punish them, and to appease an enemy rather than to destroy him, particularly an enemy of great merit who can be counted upon once he returns to the fold. Though the toil may be similar for either goal, gentleness befits men while wrath befits beasts, and not all of these, but only the ignoble ones fashioned by the sinister hand of nature.

If therefore my words reach your advisers, whom I doubt not are many and eminent, not only will you not refuse the coming peace, but you will go to meet it and, embracing it eagerly, you will try to keep it with you eternally. This you will accomplish quite easily if, whatever happens, you call upon reasonable and respected old age to participate in your deliberations. Listen to men who have known the whims of fortune and have learned to love their land, for the sweetness of peace is more pleasing for those who have previously tasted the bitterness of war. Keep the others, as enemies of peace, away from your threshold. Nor would I admit those whose only indications of old age are wrinkles and white hair, baldness and curved backs, "running noses like children and trembling voice and limbs," as the Satirist says. Let them keep their certainly unenviable traits, for we do not seek men who are falling apart, but mature ones. Neither do I exclude those men, if there are any at all, who acquired maturity of judgment while still young; I do not scorn in others what I admire in you, provided a precocious wisdom shines forth. I realize how much assistance my young Africanus gave his distressed country, not only with deeds but with counsel, or how Papirius Pretextatus deceived his mother through jest in order to conceal a secret of the Senate; I know what Portius Cato said to his teacher, or how the young Alcibiades persuaded a wretched old man. But believe me, very rare are those men who possess wisdom while still in their youth. Whenever indeed you see such a youth who has progressed beyond his years—I do not deny that it could happen—enroll him in your group of elders. With such advisers, hasty opinions are not advanced, nor is falsehood hidden secretly under the mantle of truth. You who deserved to be a leading voice of the council and the head of state, bear constantly in mind that the major share of glory or of infamy will touch you; for that reason, though others may sleep, you alone must remain vigilant. Illustrious men have long believed that the labors of a general and of a soldier are not the same. He is more likely to act who is driven by greater hope of reward, and while the types of reward may be many and diverse, toward which we incline differently for a variety of reasons, there is still little doubt that for noble minds glory is the greatest spur after virtue. With this motivation, then, turn your mind to the most noble concerns, and according to Cicero, "the noblest cares relate to the well-being of the fatherland." With such concerns, you will prepare a path to heaven for yourself; rise and soar above yourself. Observe, heed, and contemplate all things; and compare successful outcomes of war with unsuccessful ones, destruction with comfort, joy with grief. And since, as I said, a most fitting witness in the cause of peace is Hannibal, take care, as he writes, "lest you risk the happiness of many years in a single hour." Consider the great toil with which your power was acquired; consider how many steps are required to reach this pinnacle of fortune! Should you not know it, the fame of your people is very ancient, something which a great number of people do not believe. I read that the reputation not only of the Venetians but, even more astonishing, the name of their leader, Venetus, was famous many years prior to the founding of Rome. You should carefully keep this in mind lest you subject proven valor and honor acquired through the counsel of so many years to the power of ravaging fortune. Since the reward of fame is virtue's greatest prize, as wise men have always realized, know that you will behave most properly in behalf of the republic if you provide for the public good when circumstances warrant, even at the loss of personal praise; if you give the grumbling crowd advice that is wise rather than specious, and useful rather than pleasing; if you prefer to be called procrastinating rather than precipitous, following the example of the commander Maximus, about whom Ennius says, "he did not place gossip before security"; and if you do not fear the resulting dishonor or the hatred of fools in your pursuit of virtue. As happened to that same leader, you too will enjoy not only greater glory but the love of the people amidst the admiration of all. Even were this hope not realized, still you know through experience and have learned from philosophers what we owe to virtue and what to glory.

With what grief, to be perfectly honest with you, do you think I heard of your recent alliance with the King of Aragon? Is assistance then being sought from foreign kings, so that Italians may be destroyed by Italians? Whence could unfortunate Italy expect aid if her sons not only tear to shreds their mother whom they should cherish, but also have foreigners attack her in public massacre? Someone will remark: "The same sort of evil was previously attempted by the enemy." I have already emphasized that, although I address one, I am reproving both of you. How much more proper it would have been to have the Venetians become one with the Genoese, once the rust of wrath had been cleansed, from which neither sincere friendship nor fraternal love nor even the devotion of parents and children is entirely immune, than to tear to pieces the beautiful body of Italy, with you imploring the aid of western tyrants and with them, I understand, imploring the aid of eastern tyrants to take part in this madness. O fatal and useless precautions, O ultimate form of malice, to substitute deputies for crimes which you cannot commit yourself and to seek those whom you could incite to do your work, thereby offering your neighbors reasons for hatred! The origins of our many afflictions flowed, in fact, from our strong admiration for external affairs while we shamefully considered our own with a strange loathing; we have long since, because of a fatal attitude of ours, neglected Italian loyalty in favor of foreign treachery. We must be insane to seek in venal minds the loyalty which we despair of finding in our own brothers. The result has been that we have most justly fallen into misfortunes that we now lament too late and in vain, since we opened to the Cimbrians, the Huns, the Pannonians, the Gauls, the Teutons, and the Spaniards, with the keys of spite and avarice and arrogance, the Alps and the seas with which Nature had protected us without need of fortifications. These were the gateways to our borders that had been erected and bolted by divine providence. How often have we tearfully recited that pastoral verse of Virgil: "Will an impious soldier possess this well-cultivated meadow, will a foreigner occupy these cornfields? Behold whither discord has led our wretched citizens!"

But to return to my point, I do not know what determinations you are about to make. This much I do know, that once in a similar situation but under dissimilar conditions the occasion arose for the Spartans to destroy the troublesome capital of the Athenians, but they decided against destroying one of the two glories of Greece because the matter had become one of convenience rather than capability. Certainly a remarkable decision, most worthy of the venerable discipline of the Spartans! If that emerged from the mouths of men whom Plato considers hungry for conquest and power, what should I expect of such gentle and modest men as yourselves? The fact is that I am losing peace of mind, being incapable of remaining unmoved by great upheavals and by conflicting feelings such as love, fear, and hope, which simultaneously oppress my heart and struggle among themselves. I believed myself to be immune from any just reproach if, while some men transform forests into fleets, others sharpen swords and arrows, and still others fortify embattlements and shipyards, I had recourse to the pen, my sole weapon, not as an agent of war but as an emissary of peace. I have for some time thought of concluding this letter, aware of the appropriateness of keeping one's words to a minimum when speaking to superiors; but no one is superior in love. That will compel you to forgive me as it has compelled me to verbosity. Finally, prostrate and tearful before the leaders of two peoples, I implore one thing: cast off your murderous weapons, shake hands, exchange kisses of peace, and join your minds as well as your banners. Thus, the ocean and the gates of the Black Sea will lie open to your fleets, and all rulers and peoples will respectfully run to welcome you. The Scythians, the British, and the Africans will fear you; and your sailors will safely navigate the shores of Egypt, Tyre, Armenia, and the once feared ports of Cilicia and Rhodes, at one time mistress of the sea; and toward the Sicilian mountains and its sea monsters; and along the Balearic Islands, infamous for piracy in ancient and modern times; and finally toward the Fortunate Isles, the Orkneys, the famous but unknown island of Thule, and all the southern and northern shores. Once you are at peace with each other, there is nothing to fear from any other source. Farewell, greatest of leaders and of men.

Fam. XI, 9.

To Giovanni Aretino, * *in transit.*

The Po has carried away my anticipated comfort. There was nothing humorous for me to write unless my anxious search for something laughable is perhaps itself worthy of laughter. Antiquity was much more serious and our age more humorous, it seems to me, since it is in the nature of things that during troubled times we be moved by serious matters and in lighter moments by foolish ones. Believe me, Crassus the elder would have laughed more than once had he lived in our day; and Democritus would not have denied, in comparing the two ages, that his laughter was premature. Today silly old men and crazy old ladies are so prevalent that I need not refer to worthless and absurd young people. But all this will be more pleasant to discuss in person. I am writing this to you while crossing the Alps, so do not wonder at my alpine handwriting and at my letter which has had to adapt to the lack of space and time. I urge you to follow me without delay, and I know that you will oblige me. I would prefer that you had accompanied me as you have often done on other journeys, but no delight is perpetual in this world. I shall wait for you at the source of the Sorgue, a place always wonderful and attractive, but during the summer very like the Elysian Fields. There we shall breathe a bit before we step over the Tartarean threshold of nearby Babylon. Farewell.

20 June, from the summit of Mont Genèvre.

*See VII, 8.

Fam. XI, 10.

To Philippe, Bishop of Cavaillon.*

Incapable of resisting my desire, which long absence had produced in me, eager above all to see your venerable and dear face once again and then afterwards the scattered and decimated remnants of our friends, I have completed the long and arduous journey during this unfavorable season of the year by means of my spirit's support of my body, so that you might think the poet's words quite applicable to me: "Devotion overcame the difficult road." At the source of the Sorgue in the tranquillity of your countryside I am now resting myself and my limbs, weary from the journey. From here then I am hastily writing this letter to you lest you hear of my arrival from someone else first and accuse me of laziness. The remainder I shall tell you very shortly in person. I shall come as soon as I have cleansed myself of the dirt and of the summer dust, with the aid of this clear spring. Farewell.

27 June.

*See II, 1.

Fam. XI, 11.

To the same correspondent. *

I have carefully read, dear father, what you wrote concerning me to those two great oarsmen of the apostolic vessel. The truth of your words must be judged by the writer and by the reader. As for me, the better I know you and your feelings, the more I believe that old familiar saying that "the judgment of lovers is blind." I am happy that it is so, however, and I wish you to be so persuasive that, once they have begun to share your sentiments because of your authority, they will feel as you do and become partners in your error and in your love; and I shall remain unknown and beloved by both sides. Farewell.

29 June, at the source of the Sorgue.

*See II, 1.

Fam. XI, 12.

To Olimpio,* on the mutability of intentions.

From me you may learn how unstable and varied are the wishes of mortals and how constantly uncertain their plans for the future, especially the plans of men far removed from wisdom. I was suddenly seized with the longing to see once again the hills and caves, the groves and stones covered with green moss that echo continuously at the source of the Sorgue. Where I had been once as a boy, then as a youth and once again as a grown man, I have now returned on the threshold of old age, although I had determined never to return again, as you know. A certain sweetness about the place inspired me, secretly motivating my spirit so that reason was unable to restrain it. No hope drew me here, no need or pleasure except the austere and rustic kind, indeed not even my love of friends which is one of the most honored of earthly reasons. What friends could I have here where no one understands the meaning of friendship? The common people, intent as they are on working their sterile clods, their flourishing vineyards and olive trees, or their lines and nets in the river, can have no kind of fellowship in my life and in my conversations. I was not attracted here, however, in ignorance of the situation or strictly by chance. Indeed only after careful consideration have I returned where I remember spending a good portion of my life, being fully aware and knowledgeable of what I was leaving and what I was choosing. If any justification can be found in my change of intention, it is my love for nothing else but solitude and tranquillity. Being too well known in my own country and fleeing the resulting boredom, I seek a place to hide, alone, unknown, and inglorious; a strange desire indeed, especially among the many followers of vainglory! But so it is, I do seek this, I do desire this. The dazzle of fame, once so enticing to me, and the attraction of a life of glory will not tempt me to depart, nor will all the obstacles and even the austerity of rural living frighten me. So that you may know the great value I place on my leisure, there is nothing in my possession that I would wish to exchange for it. As I said, the memory of this secluded and silent countryside that I have frequented since my early years moved my spirit with a certain kind of appeal. I have less reason to wonder

*Luca Cristiani (Olimpius) was one of Petrarch's most intimate friends, dating back to his days in Bologna and their service under Cardinal Giovanni Colonna in Avignon. He was provost of Sant'Antonino in Piacenza. In the note to VIII, 2 (vol. 1 of this series) Olimpio is wrongly identified as Mainardo Accursio.

that the great Camillus as an exile from his native land could have felt the desire and attraction of his Roman soil when I, Italian-born on the banks of the Arno, have felt the sweetness of a transalpine home. Indeed a rather strong habit becomes second nature; for this reason, let no one be astonished as to why I dwell so eagerly in foreign lands. By now, through custom, I have become an inhabitant of this country retreat; in coming here I seem to be entering my native land. Nothing moved me more deeply, however, than my great aspiration of putting the finishing touches on certain works of mine so that, even as they were begun here under the protection of God, they may be completed here with the same guidance. If you were to ask the length of my stay here, I must answer that it remains uncertain, as do all future events. While in transit, indeed before leaving Italy, I wrote certain friends about my departure and my plans for return, saying that I would be back next autumn. This was my belief at that time, but one ought not to make plans too far in advance. An ancient proverb says that "a gladiator makes up his mind in the arena"; the present, then, is much more appropriate for deliberation. Often temporal conditions, the appearance of places, and conversations with friends alter many factors relating to human decisions. Therefore, to the degree that I can judge the future by the past, two years will suffice for what I expect to undertake. Generally, after such an interval, I customarily alternate my residence between Italy and France, although I am aware that such projections are uncertain even for one day, let alone for two years. I have always liked the reply by an old monk who, as the story goes, after his king's invitation to a late dinner on the morrow, answered that there was no tomorrow for him. That was surely an admirable and serious response, revealing that he did not deceive himself as do the majority of men who let the present day vanish in the hope of tomorrow. As his words implied, that monk, gathering his little bundle, lived each day as his last; and so that his response might be corroborated by events, they say that on that very night the old man died. It is habitual for us to lose the present in expectation of the future, but I lay aside such matters, in which nearly everyone equally errs, in order to return to my point. If I have done anything contrary to the promise I once made you, you must forgive me. Let the diversity of human judgment, inherent even in the more learned, also be a justification, for such diversity is almost never avoidable except by perfect people devoted to the greatest good. Let my further excuse be that uniformity, the mother of boredom, can only be eluded by a change of location, a subject about which I have previously said a great deal. Finally, I beg you, allow me to see once again my small gardens planted with my own hands, or whether there is anything superfluous or unbecoming in my possessions that are here. In any event, allow me to view once again the hills and fountains and woods so dear to my studies. Let me restore to the light my books, which are here in considerable and pleasing abundance, for they have long been hidden away, enclosed in chests under lock and key. Let me return their eyes to them and them to my eyes. If nothing else, let me at least brush the worms and dust from their ancient parchments. But I do hope more will be granted me. As I have said, two years would suffice to complete those works already begun or pending. If I be allowed to finish them, I shall enjoy another way of life for which I long and yearn with great desire, except when I am weighed down by my burdens. Farewell.

At the source of the Sorgue, 19 July.

Fam. XI, 13.

To Niccolò Acciaiuoli, Grand Seneschal of the Kingdom of Sicily.*

I cannot, illustrious sir, defend this tardy response with the shield used by a great number of lazy writers, namely, that I had nothing to write. Recently your accomplishments afforded me an extensive field for writing not only friendly letters but entire books. I see you battling fortune with such a great and invincible spirit that often I have been moved to compose a rather grandiose work about you, worthy of you and me, and not unworthy of our common fatherland, which gave birth to us under very different stars, you for splendid and glorious actions and me for stringing words as best I can. The recent good fortune of the king, supported by your wise counsel, has provided still more fertile matter for my pen. It has restored to me the welcome hope that, while he lives, foreigners will never control Italy. Your deeds, then, offer sufficient subject matter to writers of history or poetry, not to mention fitting themes for lyrical poetry implicit in your life of serenity and in the sweetness of your ways, in the tranquillity and gentleness of your noble mind. Still this pen, conscious of its strengths and now quite weary from its preceding labors, fears to undertake new subjects. This is the true reason for my silence. I do have, I confess, subjects on which to write, and even if I had no others, you would provide them in abundance. Would that you could also provide me with time! That is something I certainly do not possess, beset as I am with my concerns which benefit and occupy my mind when moderate, but oppress and weaken it when excessive. The fault therefore lies with chance, but I beg you, excellent sir, to accept with generosity my affection, though it has been unproductive, remembering that I am yours even in silence. And if, as I hope and indeed pray, divine favor supports your lofty undertakings so that I might see Italy's body cleansed to its marrow of the foreign plague—it is said you are making preparations pleasing to our people though disturbing to the enemy—I will no longer feel able to resist my desire to cast aside the nets of my affairs and to return to those

---

*Niccolò Acciaiuoli (1310–65) went to Naples in 1331 to represent his father's business interests, but he soon became a favorite of King Robert and served as Grand Seneschal of the kingdom. Petrarch had great admiration for his diplomatic skills, especially during the unstable period following the king's death when Acciaiuoli acted as guardian and adviser to Luigi da Taranto, Robert's nephew.

shores which writers in Italy and throughout the world consider the most beautiful, and to see you in person and Naples once again. Farewell, and enjoy good health, O you who are the glory of our age.

29 August, from Avignon.

Fam. XI, 14.

To Philippe de Vitry, Bishop-elect of Meaux, * his uncertainty as to whether to congratulate or pity him.*

Should I congratulate you or feel pity for you, dearest and illustrious father? For I see the greatest toil imposed upon you when you most needed repose, and the weighty responsibilities and anxieties of the bishopric following upon your sweet concerns for study and your pleasant leisure. Alas, how often did Caesar Augustus, to limit myself to a single yet noble example, at your very age consider renouncing the empire in order to diminish his labor! This is attested by his letter addressed to the Senate in which he pleads for permission to spend a private and tranquil old age; this he did not doubt could be honorably spent far from that lofty responsibility. Though honored, tranquil, and freer than anyone I know, you willingly submitted to toil and voluntary servitude in accepting an episcopate full of knotty and entangled cares that grow incessantly beneath the scythe. Because of your great and noble spirit, you have put the public welfare ahead of your own peace and pleasure, which were truly deserved. I therefore applaud your decision and sympathize with your fate. Above all, I urge you to pursue with tireless persistence what you have reluctantly assumed, so as to earn glory on earth but a more enduring reward in heaven. With nothing more to say, I decided to write you this in haste while the messenger waits, especially so that you might know my whereabouts. My fate has forced me to return to the shores of the Rhone, and I wish to see you before I begin once again to roam. Live happily and farewell, and remember me.

Avignon, 23 October.

*See IX, 13.

Fam. XI, 15.

To Philippe, Bishop of Cavaillon, * *on the pursuit of tranquillity and the avoidance of toil.*

I am happy to hear that you have returned from your long journey. With my palms turned heavenward I exclaim with Anchises: "So you come at last . . . over what lands, what wide, wide seas you have made your journey, and now you are here with me!" But how could I not greatly rejoice at the safe return of a father so dear and deserving of my love? With me rejoices the entire church which you left leaderless for two months that seemed longer than two years. All of your devoted flock applauds the awaited return of its shepherd, perceiving his face, ever serene and gentle, hearing the sound of his persuasive and salutary voice calling them to joyful pastures, and recognizing in this a light yoke and a pleasant pastoral sceptre. The very hills and vales, the very walls of your city truly seem to me to rejoice even in their silence at the return of their sun. Absence is always unpleasant for those who love, but it is sometimes useful for arousing affection. I believe that many people have learned from your absence with what veneration they ought to cherish you. Just as it is good for a field to lie fallow, so it is with personal relations; and just as a temporary interruption improves crops, so does it produce a more abundant harvest of pleasure for the spirit. In truth this agricultural law applies to barren lands as the rule on friendship does to tepid spirits. Just as those who cultivate their fields with some success have no need for such absences, neither do I nor do all those whose spirit burns with love for you. Rather we desire and seek that you always be present, if possible, and never absent from our sight. But let me offer you as well as myself my customary and practical advice: it is now time for us to turn our prows toward the shore in search of the closest port where we may find some repose after casting our anchors, leaving to others the boundaries of the earth and the sea full of countless difficulties and risks. We have experienced sufficiently, even excessively, unless I err, how wrenching are nightlong anxieties, how wearying daily business, what panting and sweating is experienced in a mountain's ascent or its descent, what boundless tediousness results from endless plains, what terror the raging waves of an angry sea bring in the shadows of a stormy night and the sound of a ship crumbling on a reef intermingled with the sailors' screams. We have passed through mud and dust, over

*See II, 1.

snow, ice and stones; we have suffered through hail and storms, winds and rain, as well as fire and cold, bandit ambushes and attacks by wild beasts. We have not left untried nearly every kind of misfortune. Just as we experienced such misfortunes in our youth and afterward remembered them as pleasant, so it would be unpleasant never to be able to free ourselves of them. Let us therefore leave them to others who are inexperienced or who can experience them more happily. Even what we learned at our risk, let them learn in the same manner. Let them proceed with their own armor, which is appropriate and suitable for us to discard. There are those men who view unending toil and continuous danger with pleasure; for us, mindful of our situation and of our affairs, repose is appealing, security desirable. We have wandered far and wide, the time has come to make a halt; for, dear father, evening approaches and before nightfall a resting place must be found. I have sent you this short letter to meet you en route, and I am about to follow it on foot. Live happily and farewell, O you who are a glory of our age.

25 October, from Avignon.

Fam. XI, 16.

To the four cardinals chosen to reform the government of the Roman Republic. *

A great burden is placed upon my weak shoulders by and for that person to whom I have never been able to deny anything; love, the master of my soul, has ordered me not to reject it. The welfare of our common homeland, mother of us all, hangs in balance. No son remains untouched by a wrong that befalls his devoted mother. To the debt that the entire human race owes to Rome, I add my own—she has bestowed upon me the remarkable privilege of being called a citizen, perhaps hoping that I would not be the last defender of her name and of her diminishing fame in these times. In short, she has always been deserving of the following consideration from me: when her welfare is involved, it is not only shameful, but inhuman and ungrateful, for me to remain silent. I decided to preface these thoughts so that no one would think me insane or forgetful of myself in attempting something beyond my strength, or against the advice of the wise man in seeking goals that are too lofty or matters that are too difficult; and also so that no one would become angry upon hearing that the liberty of Rome is being defended with praise that is reverent but excessively humble, even contrived, pedestrian, and perhaps inappropriate. It is a grave matter, I confess, to be discussed in the presence of great men and to be referred to the greatest of them. In truth I am conscious of my insignificance, but an inborn allegiance gives me the courage to speak. Therefore, O illustrious fathers, you who have been entrusted with such a burden, if my independence has so far been judged favorable, as I hope, I beg you to lend your pious ears to my respectful words, considering not who I am but what I say, and indeed not even what I say but what I may wish to say and what can be said concerning such serious matters.

First of all I believe that the following truth is implanted in your minds, namely, no name in human affairs is more resounding than that of the Roman Republic. No region, no people, no foreigners will deny this; but the entire world, if it could speak, would admit it with a single voice and would frankly recognize Rome as its head, though it be admittedly disheveled, miserably neglected, and untidy.

---

*The four cardinals—Bertrand de Déaulx, Gui de Boulogne (see XIII, 1), Bertrand du Puget or Guillaume Court, Niccola Capocci—were chosen in November of 1351 by Pope Clement VI to reform the Roman government so as to prevent further political deterioration.

Wherefore even if Rome were nothing more than a name, it is still the name of a city that was once a queen and in my opinion ought to be treated with a certain reverence. I refer to the city which almighty God had adorned with so many great signs of temporal and spiritual prerogatives, decreeing it to be the see of the true faith, the foundation of the church and the supreme empire of the world. Now indeed Rome is something more than a name, something that can inspire hope or fear. It must occur to reasonable men that it was neither by chance nor without reason, but by divine decree that the Roman pontiff assigned to you from among the cardinals of the Sacred College this glorious and meritorious burden, although in balance not too weighty. In addition to your profound wisdom and abundant learning, experience has taught three of you knowledge of Roman affairs. The fourth is indeed not only of Roman origin but, as some believe, a descendant of the noble and ancient family nelia, and yet—O genuine piety, O sweet love of the fatherland!—also a powerful defender of the common people against the proud nobility and a champion of suppressed liberties. Thus, having been chosen by God as judges in this sacred cause, leave no room for indolence, for human requests or favors. But to summarize briefly the heart of my doubts and thought, I believe that an ancient controversy is being repeated, and I pray that none of the ancient arrogance will be added to the new tyranny. Cowardly and self-indulgent without reason and scornful of all things, the nobility is abusing the excessive submissiveness of the Roman commoners, shamefully dragging them in a triumph as if they were captured Carthaginians or Cimbrians condemned to the yoke. And yet, no law prescribes, no custom allows, and no words have ever proclaimed that one may triumph over conquered fellow citizens. At this point, so that not even a single doubt interfere and so that no suspicion arise that my words be touched with even the slightest animosity, let me say that of the two families involved in controversy I have never disliked the one; as for the other, as everyone knows, not only do I love it, but I have always cherished it with intimate devotion, for no princely family is dearer to me in the entire world. The Republic, however, is still dearer to me, as is Rome, Italy, and the peace and security of good citizens. Therefore, to speak with the leave of the living and the dead, unless I am mistaken, this was the reason why God, valor, toil, and fortune equally concurred in having one city attain such magnitude: to become head of the church and of the empire, and not a kingdom of a few citizens or even—if the indulgence I have sought will allow me to speak the truth—of Roman citizens and lovers of the Roman name. I shall not review the origin of both families, for that is well known in the Rhine valleys and celebrated even by the shepherds of Spoleto. Thus the mistress of peoples, fallen into all kinds of wretchedness and mourned by no one, torn not by her own hands, as was once the case, but by foreigners, has lost the ancient solace for her misfortunes: "To admit no kings but to serve its subjects." And yet one hesitates to oppose this kind of harm, and overlooks a question worthy of consideration before all others, namely, what types of appropriate punishments should be used against such public plunderers, or at least how distant from public office in a free state should these enemies of freedom be kept? Surprisingly this alone is the question to be resolved: whether the Roman people, once rulers of all peoples, ought to reacquire as much liberty as will allow it today to participate with local tyrants in its own governance on its own Capitoline, whence she drove the flaming arms of the Senones, where she viewed captured kings marching before the triumphal chariots, where she heard supplications by foreign ambassadors, where she cut off and made roll the proud heads of citizens and enemies. O good Jesus, among what kind of people are we living? Do you observe this, O Savior, or offended by our sins do you avoid looking upon it with your customary mercy? Have compassion now and wipe away the stains of this great disgrace. Have we then sunk so low, was this the goal of our tribulations, that in public or, what is more than public, in the presence of the Vicar of Christ and of the apostles' successors, we must ask whether a Roman citizen may be elected to the senate, when we have long seen the rule of foreigners and of many Tarquinii Superbi on the Capitoline?

This is the matter whose resolution requires the labor of four cardinals of heaven. If consulted, I would not hesitate to respond that the Roman senate according to Roman tradition consist only of Roman citizens with all foreigners necessarily excluded, not only those from distant lands, but even the Latins, a neighboring people contiguous to the Romans and indeed almost one in body with them. All of them must be excluded, not only with spoken words or with the pen, but if possible even with the sword. An example of this was Aulus Manlius Torquatus, who, at the Latins' request that another consul and half the Senate be elected from their numbers, was so overcome with anger that he swore to come to the Curia wearing his sword, and if he saw any Latins there he would slay them with his own hand. With what kind of spirit would he have regarded an entire senate composed of people from the banks of the

Rhine or from Umbria when he bore with such indignation the mere mention of a senate half composed of Latins? Our present foreigners, however, so as not to seem infuriated without cause, advance as their reason for usurping the senate their greater power to bear the burden of this great office. What is this power that is known only for its harm to the state? Whence indeed does it derive, however small it is, if not from the blood of the people and from the bowels of the state? Were it even a great and just power, to what does it avail? When the above-mentioned embassy of Latins came to Rome, Latium was described as glittering with arms, men and wealth. Their request was rejected, nonetheless, because they aspired to an undeserved honor on the strength of their power, and thus the rewards of virtue were not granted to an undeserving demand. Surely if the senatorial dignity of Rome is handed to naked power without respect either for origin or virtue, then Macedonia and Carthage in those times, and at present peoples with great power throughout the world, could claim the same right and privilege. But they will reply: "We too are Romans and have inherited the rights of Roman citizens by our long tenure in office and oppression of liberty." I would think considerable progress had been made, had I persuaded those proud spirits to be citizens and not oppressors of citizens, nor would I then expel them from the ranks of office with the rigor of a Manlius. But in the name of God who has compassion for human affairs, O most gentle fathers, if you have any feeling for the Roman name, I ask you to consider whether they have seized the Roman Republic for the sake of giving succor with their own wealth to public poverty. Would that they did have this in mind! I could then grant pardon to their bountiful ambition and admit them to candidacy regardless of their place of origin. But believe me, they are contemplating the opposite course; they doubtless enkindle, more than they appease, the insatiable hunger of their avarice with the remains of a devastated city. But they will perhaps try to deny this and conceal with the impudence of a single word the vicissitudes of an entire life, which are known to all, wishing to appear as Roman citizens and lovers of their native land. It is not so. Indeed it is a capital offense for them to be called citizens or men rather than princes or lords. Because we are really discussing an unusual matter, although before fair judges, let it be granted for the sake of harmony what would be very easy to deny, namely, that they are citizens and indeed peaceful citizens. Let them inherit their honors unworthily provided they do not exclude those who are truly deserving. For if foreigners can presently litigate as equals with Romans, with everyone being considered under the single name of Roman, why is it that only those should be so honored who possess this purchased title? Indeed why should preference by given in any matter to their supporters? Is it because of their nobility? But the nature of true nobility is no small subject for debate. Only then will they understand how noble they may be when they have begun to understand how virtuous they are. Is it because of their wealth? I do not now wish my words to disparage it, but I am giving warning that they should not disdain the less wealthy. Moreover, they should know that wealth contributes nothing to good character. As for the wealth that they sucked from the fertile breasts of Mother Church, let them use it with moderation and for transitory things. Or if they please—for sluggish spirits do not rise toward greater goals—let them enjoy it for eternal things provided they fulfill their responsibility not to convert into public ruin the wealth acquired from public generosity. If they do believe that private wealth is necessary for government, I would like them to tell me how rich was Valerius Publicola when he assisted Brutus in overthrowing the arrogant kings, when he triumphed over the Etruscans during his first consulship and over the Sabines during his third. Yet he was a man who had to be buried at public expense. Or how wealthy was Menenius Agrippa when he healed the discordant and divided republic with his divine eloquence. Or how rich was Quintus Cincinnatus when he left his rural abode to liberate Rome from fear and helplessness, as well as to deliver the Roman consul and army from a siege. How rich was Curius or Fabritius when they overthrew the forces of King Pyrrhus and the Samnites. How rich was Atilius Regulus when he scattered the Carthaginian legions; how wealthy Appius Claudius when he governed the state with wisdom though deprived of his sight. It would require much labor to gather all the examples of illustrious poverty. Indeed I dare affirm, despite the mob's protestations, that there is no greater obstacle to virtue than excessive wealth. Without attempting to overturn the deep-seated opinion held by other nations, I also dare express what writers on the subject have affirmed, namely, that wealth conquered Rome, once the conqueror of nations. Nor is there any doubt that, on the same road that poverty left Rome, the shameful acts of foreigners entered. Thus, what is most harmful to rulers of cities is what they themselves believe most useful, or to put it in other words what they pretend to believe. There now remains for us to inquire into the true cause of their desire for power. One need not dig too deeply for an answer. I shall leave aside avarice which, although obviously suspect, seems to me indeed unworthy of mention in this discussion because of a certain kind of propriety, for what dwells most shamefully in noble minds remains distant from them; but at present I am speaking of ordinary nobility. I am thus speaking only of pride, "the common evil of nobility" as Sallust writes, certainly not a new plague in the Republic since it affected even those true Romans of antiquity. Its livid swelling stole upon the greatest virtues, but was constantly checked, however, by the weight of humility even as, I hope, it must now be checked by your judgment, O most illustrious fathers. Perhaps an example is needed.

From the very beginning the Roman people, vexed by inhuman wrongs, sought in their officials protectors and avengers of their insecure freedom. The nobility opposed them in a bitter struggle, thus causing the first secession on Monte Sacro. Plebeian justice finally conquered the arrogance of the nobility. In spite of the useless protestations by patricians, there then arose the first, and only, spur and check against their violence, the creation of a plebeian tribune. A serious dispute arose about this as well, the commoners insisting that the new official be elected by its own tribunal assemblies. From this too, the people emerged victorious, notwithstanding the obstinate opposition of Appius Claudius, an extremely violent man. Then another dispute arose because the nobles arrogantly denied intermarriage between commoners and nobility. With the most sacred bond of the human race thus severed, the city was once again divided into two parties. The indignant populace resisted; despite all opposition the law was broadened to allow intermarriage once again. The decemvirate on sacred matters, the quaestorship, and the curule aedile were restricted to the nobility. Once the people realized that they were being held up to ridicule, they struggled to win a share in these offices as well. Here reference should be made to what seems a small item related by Titus Livy, but it provides clear evidence of the nobility's arrogance and the people's independence. Gneus Flavius, a scribe's son, very humble in origin but otherwise sagacious and eloquent, was made curule aedile. That so upset the horrified nobility because of its novelty that, for the occasion, many of them removed their golden rings and other ornaments as though in mourning. Unperturbed, he calmly opposed his unshakable perseverance to their arrogance. Thus, during his visit to a sick colleague, some young nobles who happened to be present when he entered the bedroom did not stand, out of contempt. He had his curule chair brought at once, and having thereby become a more noble despiser than his despising young nobles, he disdainfully looked down upon them in their envy from the seat of public office and not from an ordinary chair. This single act of independence indeed makes him for me most worthy not only of the aedileship but even of the consulship. I have purposely left this discussion to the end because the two senators who still remain from the great number of conscript fathers can surely be viewed as successors to the two consuls. Just as that magistracy had a limited term, so does this one, whereas the senatorial office did not. If I were to begin narrating how often men ruthlessly struggled for this consulship, I would stray from the central purpose of my letter, to which I now hasten. Let it suffice to say that, when the common people of Rome demanded a share even in the highest office, the nobility considered it a terrible disgrace and resisted them with all its strength. In this area as well it finally had to succumb to defeat. Following much violent struggle, they first arrived at a compromise to create four military tribunes with consular powers rather than additional consuls. Not even this satisfied the wishes of the common people, and what they had long been denied because of puffed-up arrogance was obtained through the power of justice. Thus, a plebeian consul sat next to a patrician one; and both ruled a single fatherland, and the empire acquired through their common effort an equal majesty.

If all this is true and well known to the most illustrious historians, why do we hesitate so long, O most prudent fathers? Why do we need more urging? If you have compassion on the misfortune of the Romans, if you have devotedly determined to assume the responsibility of righting its enormous downfall, follow the exempla of that era when this city rose from nothing to the stars, and not of this era when it has been reduced almost to nothing from fortune's great heights. I believe there is no doubt that Rome has many men more noble and upright than these few who scorn heaven and earth by vaunting their aristocratic titles. If they are good I shall not deny that they are noble, but certainly not only I, but even Rome herself, will deny that they are Romans. But let it be so, and let them be nobles and Romans. Yet should they be preferred to our great men of the past, those cultivators of justice, protectors of the weak, conquerors of the proud, and founders of the empire? However great their impudence they will not dare maintain this. And if those men yielded, let these too be unashamed of yielding to the worthy demands of the common people who simply wish not to be exiled from their own city or banished from public office as if a source of infection. It would be well to recall Aristotle's teaching on the way to straighten crooked wood: you may thereby force the nobles not only to share senatorial powers and other offices with others, but also to stay away for some time from such positions, usurped only through their arrogance and through the patience of the common people, until the republic changes direction and slowly reverts to a just equality. This is my opinion, this I humbly beg, this an aging Rome tearfully implores; but if you delay in restoring her freedom she will call you to the tribunal of the fearsome judge. This Christ commands. He will be in your midst during your deliberations so that until the end He may watch over those whom He elected from the beginning. This is demanded by the apostles Peter and Paul, who inspired the Roman pontiff to entrust the responsibility to no one but you. If you desire to listen to their silent and secret prayers, you will scorn with great ease any contrary demands and favors, calling to mind not what pleases the arrogance of others, but what befits your reputation and benefits the city, Italy, and the world.

18 November.

Fam. XI, 17.

To the same correspondents. *

O illustrious fathers and lovers of virtue, I know that you, as elected judges between reasonable humility and unbridled pride, have no need for the advice of an insignificant man to render a just decision. But I should like to suggest something about a matter relating to our common fatherland and to express courageously at least some ideas in an area affecting me, since I cannot act with deeds to assist freedom. I shall therefore speak out of sincerity, serving my conscience rather than glory, not from the desire that my words be praised but that my silence not be blamed. Nor will it greatly matter whom my words offend as long as they do not offend justice. It is certainly difficult to attack the powerful, particularly if they are dear friends, but that man is a friend of truth who places it before friends and all other matters. Therefore, I lay aside my feelings to question these foreign tyrants, though they be very dear to me and close friends of long standing. I ask them the reason for their consummate arrogance in a city which is not theirs. Three of you perhaps will be astonished; the fourth without doubt understands what I say. If perhaps they make light of this in the hope that time's passage may have erased the origin of the two families, the fact remains that either Rome or Italy will provide testimony. Theirs is a truly astonishing and intolerable arrogance! Treated as guests in exile, they banished venerable citizens from participation in public offices, and they will forever do so unless prevented through the intervention of the supreme pontiff and through your deliberation. Because of our sins we perhaps do not deserve your assistance, but certainly the home of the apostles deserves to be set free from the violence of tyrants, sacred churches deserve to be delivered from the hands of thieves, and the land adorned with the tombs of martyrs deserves not to be defiled by its people's blood. Without your bridling this tyrannical madness, there will be no timely remedy for the wretchedness of the masses, and all this cannot be realized. Although some men may succeed in putting an end to their sinful ways, returning through a late repentance to the straight path, others never return unless compelled. It is well to handle with force those who are thus disposed. It is a wonderful thing for a man voluntarily to cherish virtue and abandon vice, but the next best thing

*See preceding letter.

128 / FAM. XI, 17.

is to compel him to do so. Compel them, therefore, though they are unwilling, to extinguish that tyrannical plague even if they protest. Do not allow only the Roman people to participate in public offices, but forbid undeserving men to occupy a senate seat, since it has been so poorly administered. If they be upright citizens, they still should have a right to no more than half. As matters now stand, they are behaving in a manner that makes them unworthy of a city which they are destroying and of the rights of citizens whom they are oppressing, let alone of the highest offices. It would require many more words to express how truly frivolous is their boasting about nobility and wealth in which they abound, extolling such things despite their lack of any virtuous foundation, or to express the reasons why the ancient Romans, who possessed extraordinary and outstanding virtue, nonetheless were unable to exclude the common people from public office. If I wished to develop such details at this point, it would become tedious. Suffice it to recall that nearly every time a dispute arose concerning public office, the arrogant nobility was always defeated by the humble public. I have covered this subject at great length and in greater detail in the letter recently sent to you. If you will deem worthy to devote even one hour to the letter while your minds are not engaged, I hope that, following in the footsteps of your ancestors, you will succeed in saving the republic and the very precious sheepfold of Jesus Christ, to the care of which He assigned His best shepherds. Seeing them frightened by the wolves' ferocity, He Himself, as you know, hastened to go in person without fear of a second cross.

24 November.

Fam. XII, 1.

To Charles IV,* a second appeal to cross into Italy.

Some time ago, O illustrious prince, with a friendly confidence resulting from your reputation rather than my inspiration, I wrote you in a letter what seemed to befit your fame and the public good. Then upon pondering the many and varied difficulties which powerful fortune, ruler of all empires, as they say, opposes to the public will, and yet with no doubt that everything humanly possible was being done by you and by your councils, I gave respite for more than a year to your eyes and to my pen. This I did although with grieving spirit I perceived the passage of time and the deferral in the meantime through delay and procrastination of peace for many people. But I excused your slowness, as I said, because of difficulties that bordered on the impossible. Now, however, that divine providence has prepared your paths and has mercifully arranged for the welfare of His faithful people, the condition of your Italy has been so fashioned and her expectation so fervent that I ascribe the very delay that interfered with your first glorious undertaking to providence rather than to fortune—since evidently the short delay of their beloved prince aroused tremendous public enthusiasm. Consequently I hope to persuade you that the minds of good men could not be more glowing and that there is the danger, as happens naturally, that lukewarmness will gradually replace ardor, unless by your presence you offer nourishment to the noble flames enkindled by your name. I believe no one realizes better than you that the matter has reached this point: Your Majesty cannot defer an imperial visit without diminishing your fame, and my devotion can no longer remain silent without impairing my beliefs. I thus once again address my lord, and unless it is displeasing, I am speaking to the lord of all with the greatest simplicity yet with the purest faith; I speak of nothing new, but of what is well known to you, and of what I know is believed or will be believed by all friends of the Roman Empire. Indeed I am doing this not to instruct, but to perform my duty in accordance with my conviction, and thus I do not seek to adorn my subject with colors, knowing that lying takes delight in colors and fiction, as truth does in openness and simplicity. With simplicity and frankness, then, I beg and pray and implore you, prostrate at your feet and from the depth of my being, in behalf of the honor of the Empire, in behalf of the welfare of Italy, for the consolation of the city of Rome your desolate bride, for the delight of friends,

*See X, 1.

for the convenience of your subjects, for the tranquillity of troubled Christians, for the acceleration of matters in the Holy Land, for the attainment on earth of a splendid and immortal glory, for eternal blessedness well deserved after the miseries of this terribly swift life, that you seize without delay this opportunity offered by heaven to accomplish great and magnificent deeds. Lay aside all cares that prevent you from such a pious journey, avoid all postponement which always does damage to brilliant undertakings, and determine as soon as possible to visit Italy, which so badly needs you. If greatly desired, all things can go well. Do not fail fortune, because if you do you will procure for yourself the profound hatred of posterity and no less an infamy. A more favorable pathway to one's destiny, in fact, could scarcely be desired or expressed in words. Do you perchance believe such favor eternal? Destiny is as powerful as it is changeable, proceeding not according to human ability but its own will. No condition or appearance of things endures; you yourself will not always be what you are nor will you always have this opportunity. You understand, O most prudent prince, not so much what I am saying but what I am thinking. You see the present state of Tuscany. Where once there was strong rebellion against your grandfather and other princes preceding him, now there will be strong allegiance to you. Profit from this fortunate change of circumstances and do not overlook your destiny; keep before your eyes the brevity and transitoriness of mortal life, the instability of things, and the power of fortune. Her nature is to favor those who are audacious and active, while rejecting those who are timid and sluggish. As learned men like to say, she is hairy in the front and bald in the rear. I previously wrote you more extensively and would now write more except that even a few things suffice for your understanding and my brief words have in some fashion satisfied my devotion. Farewell, O magnanimous Caesar, and make haste.

Fam. XII, 2.

To Niccolò Acciaiuoli, Grand Seneschal of the Kingdom of Sicily, * on the education of a prince.

At length, O illustrious sir, faith conquers treachery, liberality greed, humility pride. Now hatred yields to charity, despair to hope, distress to persistence. Now torn asunder on the anvil of truth are the obstinacy of liars and the lying obstinacy of men who oppose your wishes. Eternal is the war between envy and glory, between evil and virtue, thanks to Him who is the lord of virtue and the king of glory, for under His leadership the worst side has been conquered in the present conflict and the best side has triumphed, contrary to what we so often see. Now your one care, that most glorious successor of the Sicilian king, will receive the honors denied him despite all envy. Evil men will look on and be enraged; they will growl through their teeth and be consumed. Sitting upon the ancestral throne more venerable and more serene than usual, having successfully removed the clouds of gloom and dissipated the shower of tears from Latium, he will once again with his heavenly brow and star-clustered crown bring light to our land, restoring desired tranquillity to the ravished kingdom and to the people. As you have done thus far in this matter, you will demonstrate to the world your well-known talent by revealing yourself all the more vigilant, since to rule a kingdom with just moderation deserves greater praise than to obtain it through good fortune. Now indeed is the time to collect all the strength of your mind and to arm yourself properly for vast undertakings. If you have any qualities of a Caesar, your accomplishments are as yet nothing, inasmuch as many things remain to be done and your celebrated glory requires a crowning touch. We saw you offering magnificent resistance to adverse fortune; today we see you the victor. Yet, take care since fortune, though conquered, so often returns with a milder mien, more appealing, as it were, with her shining golden helmet. You conquered her as an enemy; she now returns to the fray as a friend. What do you think of that? The weapons have changed, but not the enemy, and you need for yourself too a new kind of armor. I do not want you to believe that the undertaking is of less consequence because your enemy is more flattering. No war is more deceitful than the one in which credulity is attacked by flattery. You have indeed brilliantly succeeded in confined quarters; we are waiting to see how you fare in the open. Fighting in the open field has wearied many men

*See XI, 13.

who had been untiring in narrow quarters; a more favorable turn of events overthrew many men who had exhibited great strength in adversity. Hannibal, victor at Cannae, was defeated at Capua; his enthusiasm, which had been enkindled by frozen Trebbia, was extinguished by warm Baiae. Often peace has proven more dangerous than war, while the lack of an adversary has done great harm to many men. For some, their virtue was concealed by their idleness; for others, it completely withered away and dissipation took the place of the departed enemy. For man, there is no more obstinate contention than his battle with his own mind and with his personal conduct. In nothing else is there less truce, since the battle is fought within the walls. We are now confronting the kind of enemy who is sluggish during wartime yet zealous during peacetime, who is more daring in a toga than in a helmet. In the case of the Romans, to limit ourselves to one example, they were subdued by a calm peace after being indomitable in war and victorious over all other nations. As certain writers of that age lamented most elegantly, following their conquests the triumphant dissipation of the victors avenged the defeated world. This seems to have been foreseen by Scipio, esteemed above all others by the Senate, when he so strenuously opposed the recommendation of Cato, very wise and much older, that Carthage be destroyed. He did so not because he hated Carthage any less, but as Florus asserts, "lest the happiness of our city should begin to dissipate with its fear of the rival city removed." Would that his advice had prevailed and that our battle had continued against the enemy and Carthage rather than against our vices and pleasures! Our affairs would be in better condition, I believe, and wars would be fought more rarely with more frequent triumphs. "What is the point of all this?" perhaps you ask. The point is that I honestly feel that probably for many men it will seem that the time has now come for you to rest. I disagree very strongly with this position. If you wish to listen to me, you must know that toil and life have one and the same end, and that as all other outstanding men you will have to struggle until your last breath against visible or invisible enemies. But indeed—to prove how greatly I dissent from the common view—you will feel your labor doubling, yet you will enjoy it. At no other time have you had to confront such a great struggle; never was your mind so much in need of rising above itself. You have now joined your greatest battle, one allowing the entire world to realize what is your stature and worth as a man confronting both kinds of fortune, indeed not yours alone but theirs who heed your advice as well.

You have a king wise in his thinking but young in years, with whom you have been tossed about on land and sea. You have aided him through many dangers to the highest reaches of the human condition, with destiny's assistance. Show him the steps with which he has achieved this summit of fortune, the skills with which he must solidify it; show him that from now on, instead of attempting to climb higher, he must prove himself not unworthy of the ascent and worthy of the royal sceptre for his virtue as well as his blood. A crown does not make a man but rather exposes him, and honors do not change conduct and spirit but rather reveal them. Convince him that it means less to be born a king than to become a king through election; the former results from chance, the latter from merit. Teach him to glorify God, to love his country, to serve justice, without which a kingdom cannot stand though it be wealthy and strong. Let him learn that nothing violent endures, that to be loved is much more secure than to be feared. Let him acquire the habit of preferring nothing on earth but a good conscience, to hope for nothing but a good reputation, and to fear nothing but dishonor; let him realize that the higher his station, the more clearly he can be seen, and for that reason the less his deeds can be hidden, indeed the greater his power, the less his freedom for license. Let him realize that a king differs from the general public no more by his vestments than by his conduct. Let him equally strive to avoid extremes and to follow virtue located in the middle. Let him stop wastefulness and do away with greed, for the former empties one's resources while the latter empties one's glory. Let him by all means be tenacious with his own fame, let him be moderate with his honors, let him be greedy with his time, let him be liberal with his wealth, and let that most modest and spirited response of the Roman leader always ring out in his ears, namely, not to rule over gold but over those who possess gold. Let him prefer to have his subjects abound in riches rather than his treasury, in the conviction that the lord of a wealthy people cannot be poor. Let him always remember the calamity and the labors which the calamitous Land of Labor has endured in these times. He will be able to fulfill his vows and consider himself a truly happy king only when he has removed with his virtue the wretchedness caused by others' crimes, when he has made restitution for damages, repaired ruins, reinstated peace, suppressed tyranny, and restored freedom. Let him determine to love those he governs, since love begets love, since no kingdom is more secure than the one that governs willing subjects. Let that regal tenet of Sallust never depart from your king's mind: neither an army nor a treasure form a kingdom's defense, but its friends, those whose obedience depends not upon arms or money but rather on kindness and trust.

Furthermore, let him keep in mind what follows: he must live harmoniously with his subjects, for harmony causes little things to blossom, while discord causes the greatest things to dissolve. Let him pay particular heed to this opinion by considering the example of Menenius Agrippa; by following it he will become a good brother, colleague, friend, and king. After God and after virtue let him hold nothing dearer than friendships. Let him retain as an integral part of his trust any man whom friendship has once declared worthy; following the advice of Seneca, "Let him deliberate all things with his friend but only after judging him." Let him have great trust, but not in many people, and let him have the persistence to discern a true friend from a flattering enemy. Let him accept genuine praises as stimuli to virtue, yet let him fear flattery like poison; let him enter friendship slowly, let him forsake friendship still more slowly—if at all possible, never—and let him do so gradually, not precipitously. As the ancient proverb states, let him unstitch his friendships and not cut them. Let him hope for the same spirit in others as he displays in himself, and let him not deign to be esteemed by anyone whom he himself does not esteem. That is a common error among the powerful. Affections are, however, unrestrained; they do not bear any yoke nor recognize any master. Never is love driven except through love, never can it avoid being so driven. Indeed, let him think no evil about his friends, and let him not believe rashly anything of anyone. Let him banish suspicion, and deny his ear to all accusers; let him argue firmly if they become insistent and punish those who do not desist. There is an imperial saying that states: "The ruler who does not punish his accusers incites them." Alexander the Macedonian, though certainly a very impetuous youth, nevertheless challenged his accuser with exemplary confidence so that events turned out happily, as they should have. When he was about to take a drug for the disease from which he suffered, there arrived a letter from Parmenion warning him that Philippus the physician, corrupted by Darius's gifts, had promised his death to the enemy; thus he was to be on guard against the plot as well as the fatal potion. After reading the letter, he hid it until the doctor had entered; whereupon he drank the potion and at last, staring at him, revealed the accusation. His action was certainly too late and useless, had it been true, but it was very dramatic and appropriate since it was false. So let him despise his detractors with a lofty mind by living in such a way that he either refutes them in silence or proves their lies. Let him recall the response of Augustus to Tiberius that he must not be indignant should anyone speak ill of him. He said, "It would be sufficient if we could reach that point where no one can do us evil." A true statement indeed, otherwise man would possess more than God, who may be immune to insults but is still often assailed by human censors. Let your king, then, engage his mind and his ears in this matter where the patience not only of the greatest and most modest prince, previously mentioned, serves as example, but of three other great rulers as well—Pompey the Great, that magnificent citizen, King Pyrrhus, and Pisistratus, the tyrant of Athens. Let him bear with equanimity other men meddling in his affairs, and let him refrain from scrutinizing to any great extent those of others. It is the sign of a great mind not to be troubled by such matters; on the contrary, to be troubled by them is a sign of diffidence for both kinds of conduct.

Let him therefore behave as he wishes to appear. In this fashion he will eventually not want to conceal anything and will fear the eye of any enemy no more than that of a friend. Nor will he take into account his rivals' advice any more than their testimony. It was with just such confidence that Scipio led both the Roman and Carthaginian scouts throughout his camps. With like magnanimity did Julius Caesar release the captured Domitius, scorn the deserter Labienus, who was indeed aware of his plans, and proceed to burn more than once his enemies' secret documents after their discovery without ever having read them. For these reasons he should neither fear nor believe that the title of Most Serene was imposed upon him fortuitously, but in order that no cloud of grief, no blast of exulting joyfulness, no icy fear or mist or earthly appetite might becloud his mind, which is close to God and above human passion. Let him realize that wrath is most shameful in a prince, that even the mention of cruelty is an abomination, and all the more fatal because of the power he possesses over the many instruments for doing harm. Let him realize the truth in what the Tragedian once said: "Every kingdom is subject to a greater kingdom." Laying aside all threats and pride, let him reveal himself the equal of his subjects, for whatever he may decide to do against them he may expect to be done unto him by a superior hand. Let him believe that pride, no less than envy, is an evil worthy of the rabble, not of a king. For how does it behoove a king to be proud if he is a debtor for countless gifts and liable indeed to such a great creditor? Or indeed why be envious, when he sees no one above him and so many below him? Let him not doubt that truth is the foundation of all trust and that through falsehood one may prevent speakers of the truth from being believed, for a small sprinkling of falsehood upon even the greatest truths obfuscates them. Thus if he wishes whatever he says to be believed, let him become accustomed to speaking the entire truth, and regulating his speech so that it knows not how to lie. For what is more ridiculous, not to say more dangerous, than an untruthful king under whom the state must vacillate, uncertain and fearful? His word must be entirely steady and firm, since the hope and tranquillity of many people depend upon it. Indeed, why allow himself to lie when it is absolutely to his advantage that no one ever lie, if possible? Why be a flatterer when he fears and desires nothing? Such qualities I would say are more properly spurs for flatterers. Furthermore, why boast when it behooves him to be praised with deeds, not with words? Why appear threatening when his mere presence creates terror? Why become enraged against anyone when he could actually punish calmly and exercise the most noble form of vengeance—pardon? Moreover, let him avoid excessive rejoicing by taking note of immortal concerns. Let him avoid sadness by recognizing his honors and God's generosity toward him; let him never dare to refuse aid to anyone, since he was born not for himself alone but for the state; let him realize that as often as he offers assistance to his subjects he offers assistance to himself. Let his rigor be tempered by justice and his sternness mingled with clemency; let joy be part of his prudence, mature judgment part of his aggressiveness, caution part of his composure, a sense of humor part of his moderation, authority part of his gentleness. Let elegance be contained in his actions, moderation in his collegiality, pleasantness in his discourse, charity in his censure, trust in his counsel, freedom in his judgment, hesitation in his laughter, measure in his repose, seriousness in his comportment. Let him possess a desire for rewarding and a reluctance to punish, approaching the former with eagerness and the latter with hesitancy. Let him strike his haughty enemy with one mien and the guilty citizen with another; let him exult over the former and grieve over the latter. Following the example of an illustrious leader when he dealt with the sins of his own people, "Let him deal with them as unwillingly as if they were wounds unable to be healed unless touched and treated," to cite Livy, and let him excise them with sighs and tears as if they were his own flesh. Let him impress upon his mind that through mercy a ruler becomes very similar to God and that those philosophers who condemned mercy erred seriously; and let him also keep fixed in his mind that the virtue peculiar to kings is magnanimity, without which they deserve neither a kingdom nor a royal name. Let him hold the conviction that kindness is not one of man's virtues but rather part of his very nature. If such kindness is absent, a man is monstrous rather than corrupt; for that reason it is more essential for a ruler, who must surpass all other men, who holds the highest position among them. Let him realize that chastity, the quality which appears beautiful in everyone, appears most beautiful in a ruler; there is nothing more beautiful than a chaste ruler, nothing more repulsive than an unchaste one. He must understand that when gratitude, observed even by dumb animals, is lacking in human hearts it is a shameful spectacle; if it appears as ornamentation in others, for a king it will even serve as protection. Ingratitude destroys the very sinew and strength of a state, for it displeases anyone to obey an unappreciative ruler and to throw perishable gifts into the bottomless pit of an ungrateful mind. Finally let him realize that he is weighed down by a burdensome esteem and by an esteemed burden, and that one who becomes a ruler, though he may have previously been unimpeded and free, inherits with the office a noble yet laborious and exhausting servitude, which forms the very mainstay of the state's liberty. Let him realize that thereafter he must live in an exemplary manner, for kingdoms are fashioned after the image of kings, and the shortcomings of the public are usually laid upon the rulers' shoulders. Let him desire nothing for himself except the sceptre and the crown, in addition to whatever naturally proceeds from these, namely, the personal concern for the welfare of all, a glorious but difficult responsibility having many ramifications, which resemble the constantly reappearing heads of the hydra. Let him give due merit to talent, respect to old age, virtue to his progeny, and majesty to his rule; let him scorn elaborate dress, disdain precious stones, despise pleasures, and reject all temporal things, pursuing and admiring only eternal ones. Let arms, horses, and letters be his royal furnishings, and let peace and war be his activities; let him practice both with Roman art, which Virgil reminds us is "to impose the laws of peace, to pardon the conquered and to subdue the arrogant." Finally let him realize that this life is a game of grave import to be played not for sport or enjoyment, not for lazy idleness, not for degenerate extravagance; it is ultimately given to man for no other reason than to allow him access to eternity through the merit of a brief life and to disclose the substance of everlasting glory. Therefore, let him prove himself a follower of the good, let him eagerly read and listen to the deeds of our great ancestors, and let him be a solicitous investigator of outstanding exemplars as well as their fervid imitator. Let him practice in his domicile what was once practiced in the Numantine army by the famous destroyer of enemy cities, who was subsequently to serve as an example of discipline to many Roman leaders. What that great general accomplished in his military camp, let him accomplish in his cities and in his kingdom, namely, the expulsion of all means of dissipation, in addition to the correction of all conduct that might become perverted through long license. Without such qualities there is no hope either for public welfare or, I would say, for victory. Let him borrow this quality, discipline, from that great leader, and additional ones from other men, so that by culling from all of them he may fashion a truly distinctive man. However many outstanding men preceded him, let him consider them all his teachers of life, his leaders toward glory. Examples enkindle noble minds no less than rewards, nor do words less than statues. It is of benefit to compare oneself to exemplary men who are highly praised, for beautiful is that imitation inspired by virtue. So that time is not wasted in detailed inquiry, let your king keep before his eyes a suitable exemplar, not one foreign or ancient in origin, but a local and contemporary one—unless, of course, love makes me blind. I speak of his illustrious and divine uncle, Robert, whose sorrowful death demonstrated how useful his life was to his kingdom. Let him contemplate that great man. Let him conform to his pattern of life; let him look upon him as though he were seeing him in a flawless mirror. He was wise, he was kind, he was high-minded and gentle, he was the king of kings. Let him follow him in mind and conduct just as he has in time and progeny. In fact, it often happens that imitation especially of character has been as helpful as other kinds, for the person who attempts to resemble a good person can already be considered good.

I have said much, but it is really little in comparison to the magnitude of the matter, and indeed there is much more to be said. Meanwhile you feel, O remarkable man, all things beginning to descend upon your shoulders. Nothing however is difficult or arduous to a great love, nothing painful except not being loved. As guide and pilot of his deliberations, you cannot doubt this, being so certain about your pupil's love and esteem. Chiron was not more grateful to Achilles, nor was Palinurus to Aeneas, nor Philoctetes to Hercules, nor Lelius to Africanus. Proceed then and complete what you have begun. Charity bears all things, "love conquers all." Indeed you know that whoever seeks any portion of glory must of necessity bear his portion of labor. One digs deeply for gold; spices are brought from great distances; incense is extracted from the trees of Saba, Sidon supplies the purple fish and India our ivory; the ocean releases pearls. All that is precious is difficult to provide; it is not easy to search for that most precious of all things, virtue. Fame is more brilliant than gold; it is sought with great toil, maintained with great effort, kept with great diligence. The rose dwells amidst thorns, vir-

tue amidst difficulties, glory amidst cares; the first requires risk to the
fingers, the others to the spirit. Prepare yourself therefore for a most
glorious beginning. Bear in mind that when you believe you have
finished, then will you be starting. Engage your prince in the greatest
concerns of a ruler and of the state, for when he has been stirred by
such cares he will live more happily here and will eventually depart
happily and will, as Cicero supposes, but we know, return more
swiftly to the heavenly abodes. Farewell, O you who honor our
fatherland and me!

20 February, from Avignon.

Fam. XII, 3.

To Zanobi, Florentine grammarian,* a suggestion that he abandon the teaching of grammar and aspire to greater heights.

That illustrious man whom Florence boasts of begetting and Naples of possessing, whose shoulders support in glory the full weight of the Kingdom of Sicily as Hercules or Atlas once did the weight of the heavens, but not as punishment as with the Giants under the weight of Etna, that man, I say, wrote me a letter in his own hand. Filled with an extraordinary tone of humility and humanity, its first section had almost touched upon the same subject as this letter. After a very flattering salutation, he turned to his failure to respond to my letter, courteously offering the excuse that all blame belonged to Nicola d'Alife and to my Barbato, who had often denied his request for the assistance of their pens. Yet I really do not expect lengthy letters from a man dedicated to such important matters, but I do know that, though he may consider himself a humble man, he needs no assistance if he wishes to respond. I confess that it would please me more if he were to remain silent as he customarily does, letting the facts speak for themselves and the glory of his outstanding achievements answer me despite his silent pen. Indeed I had written him what I did to stimulate not his eloquence but rather his noble pursuits. In another section of his letter, he asked me to urge you to abandon, at length, your school of grammar in order not to waste your entire life on the hooves of Donatus, to use his very words. Thus, I read in the letter of my great friend those two subjects: one pertained to me, while the other was to be conveyed to you by my pen, in which he placed much trust in dealing with the present matter. Although I realize that nothing is more difficult in human affairs than to have to divest oneself of a deep-rooted habit, nevertheless please give some consideration to my advice, which you can use as you like. You do feel, O wise friend of mine—who indeed does not feel what continually besets him?—you do feel the great danger and heavy burdens obstructing the pathway of those who enter upon life. The road is long and arduous, time is brief and unfavorable; the path lying on the right is difficult, narrow, thorny, rough, and the one that for us leads to the true life. "But the one on

---

*Zanobi Mazzuoli da Strada (1315–62) was one of the Florentines whom Petrarch met in Florence in 1350. A grammarian, he took over his father's school, but his literary ability and erudition led him to become royal secretary at the court of Naples and eventually papal secretary under Innocent VI.

the left administers the punishment of evil men, sending them to the ungodly infernal regions." This is known to our Virgil and to Pythagoras, who, following in the footsteps of Cadmus, forged with the anvil of his genius a new letter of the alphabet, which is useless in writing but useful in life. This letter, a two-horned symbol, points to the heavens with its narrower right horn, while with its broader left horn it seems to curve toward the earth. The left horn, as they say, represents the path to hell, and while indeed the approach is rather pleasant, the destination is very sad and bitter, so miserable that it could not be more so. For those who enter the path on the right, the rewards are as great as the toil required. Rarely can anyone ever be sufficiently on guard, cautious, or diligent, to compensate for the nature of the dangers involved. Everywhere there are so many dreadful dangers and complications, so many slippery passes and appearances that dissuade or delay or draw one back. Would that in this very brief time we may succeed in removing all the useless burdens that beset us and, naked and unimpeded, we may achieve among the many adversities the goal we have chosen! You may wonder why I wish to frighten you so by exaggerating well-known dangers. I indeed want to keep all fears as distant as possible from myself and from the hearts of my dear ones. I do this in every conceivable manner, and consequently love philosophy above all else; not that loquacious, scholastic kind with which our men of letters ridiculously pride themselves, but the true one which dwells more in minds than in books and deals with facts and not with words. Its main office, I believe, is revealed in the *Tusculan Disputations* where it is stated that "it heals minds, it removes empty cares, it delivers from the passions and banishes fears." What then? Fear must be expelled so as not to eliminate caution, for, just as to be fearful is a sign of cowardice, so to be incautious is a sign of madness. Moreover, do you think it permissible along this journey to stop or wander or turn off, to expend the time that barely suffices for your own uses on ungrateful boys?

You are dedicated to an occupation as burdensome as it is endless. When you have educated them, others will come forth. Never will there be an end, particularly in our city so full of both sexes and all ages, and most particularly of boys, that it could be said that they were begotten by stones or by trees or by the wind, or that Italians are Myrmidons. Believe me, you were born for other callings unless you wish to fool yourself, for you ought to be doing something more important and distinguished. Your fate indeed might have been to teach boys, but nature certainly had something else in mind when it brought you to light. She must be obeyed as a guide and the greatest of mothers; fortune must be resisted with persevering opposition as an enemy. Someone might observe: "You are behaving like an ingrate since you would deny transmitting to posterity that learning inherited from our ancestors. When it is impossible to express one's gratitude to those men, we must express our gratitude by benefiting the human race." I believe nothing is less worthy of man than to forget love or kindness and not to return such benefits when you can. But I urge you to aspire higher as one of those inspired from above. You have been exposed in books to the genius of the masters, and you have conceived a poetic flame from their fervor. Reveal yourself in turn to posterity and enkindle them. This is what your talents demand; this is what you must do. Let those men teach boys who can do nothing greater, whose qualities are a plodding diligence, a rather dull mind, a muddled intellect, ordinary talent, cold-bloodedness, a body tolerant of labor, and a mind contemptuous of glory, desirous of petty gains, and indifferent to boredom. You see how different these qualities are from yours. Let them watch boys' fidgety hands, their roving eyes and confused whispering, since they derive pleasure from such labor as well as from the dust, clatter, and outcry, mingled with entreaties and tears of those punished by the rod. Finding it pleasant to become young once again, such types are shy to deal with men and displeased at living among equals; they enjoy presiding over inferiors and always having someone to terrify, to torment, to strike, to rule, and to hate them since they are feared. This is a tyrannical pleasure such as soothed the fierce spirit of the old man of Syracuse, it is said, as an unworthy consolation during his well-deserved exile. But you, O most unassuming man, devote yourself to more useful concerns, and let those men who resemble the teachers of our early years instruct youth; just as were those writers who elevated our minds at an early age with their beautiful works, so let us be toward our posterity. Or perhaps you prefer to be a follower of the flogging master, Orbilius, when you can follow Cicero and Virgil, masters of Roman eloquence? What is more, neither grammar nor any of the seven liberal arts deserves the entire lifetime of a noble talent, for they are transitory, not ends in themselves. The roughness of the road does not frighten the seasoned traveler nor does its pleasantness attract him; in crossing rugged mountains and green meadow he is completely engrossed in arriving at his journey's end. A bright youth is a beautiful spectacle, yet nothing is more unsightly than an old schoolmaster, as learned elders are wont to say. You excelled in the first, avoid the latter lest you should excel there as well. It is better to die as a child than to grow old amidst childishness. Indeed I would feel pity for you, but there is no need. Since you are still young in age, there is still time to change your mind. I inconsolably pity those who wasted nearly all their lives in public school, as did my two friends in Cisalpine Gaul, both outstanding men yet always burdened by such obscure activity. I even congratulate you on attracting the favorable attention of that great luminary of our fatherland, for he is the only person who wishes, and may be able, to bring your inglorious toil to an end. Arise, he summons you; arise, look about you, begin to know yourself and to assume responsibilities equal to your powers. What then do you think you are doing, I ask you? You teach children; you perform a task for the state. That may be, but those who are similar to children will teach them more properly and usefully than you. Indeed as you grammarians have often said, communication is simple and effective among equals. Do what behooves a man rather than what children admire. Why do you confuse talents that nature made distinct? We are well advised by that Greek saying, "Let each man practice the art he knows." To this I might add that whoever knows several arts should prefer the one that offers the promise of greater glory. Farewell.

1 April, from Avignon.

Fam. XII, 4.

To Francesco, Prior of the Church of the Holy Apostles in Florence, *
*concerning the dissimilar responsibilities of the soldier and the
commander.*

Your eloquence soothes my spirit in wonderful ways. I would say
that an indication of that happiness, long anticipated, which we expect after the termination of these miseries is to be found in the joy
experienced in the mutual affection of friends and the pleasure of a
long-coveted intimacy with them. If we take such great delight in
hearing or seeing a friend, what do you think it will be when we see
Him who created us, our friends, and the very name of friendship? If
everyone loves himself as well as others so deeply, if he enjoys so
much those who are transient, how much is He to be loved who
gave to us all the wherewithal and the capacity to love, who gave to
each of us Himself and a soul to enjoy? But this is an ineffable and infinite subject, singularly difficult to ponder. And so I turn to the matter at hand. In answer to your inquiry, still pending is the affair of
my friend whom you deigned to make yours. Indeed that person
from whom aid was expected, perhaps even owed if every honest
promise is a debt (of course I speak of the abbot of Vallombrosa),
seems to me not to have observed what befits his own dignity and
reputation because of his misty blindness and tasteless simplicity; let
this be said without offending the sanctity of the man. For the duties
of a soldier and a commander are not the same; often the person
most valorous in warfare has proven indiscreet as a leader. A famous
commander has stated that "I was born a commander, not a
soldier." I had heard that he was a devout monk, but now I view
him as a lukewarm abbot; in any case that is his own affair. As for
me, except for some annoyance, I neither seek nor expect anything.
Perhaps the letters that your charity recently succeeded in obtaining
from him will be of some benefit, but the matter still remains in fortune's hands, as do most human affairs. Our excellent and courteous
patron is granting us much assistance, and bids us to have good
hope; he thus shows, I believe, more faith in me than in the above-
mentioned abbot, who perhaps is so saintly that he considers other
men wicked. Such is the status of the affair, in answer to your in-

---

*Francesco Nelli (Simonides), prior of the church of the Holy Apostles in
Florence, met Petrarch in 1350. Later he served the kingdom of Naples as royal
secretary. He was Petrarch's principal correspondent, and it is to him that the
Seniles are dedicated. He died in 1363.

quiry. It would have been decided long ago in some fashion or other, but for the interference of the Holy Father's prolonged and serious illness. This, as you can see, is delaying all royal and imperial matters. I am therefore somewhat less upset that even from this direction fortune has created reasons for greater delay, but I am nonetheless troubled. I recently wrote you a brief poem on this, which I am not sending yet because, in order to list in due order this prison without escape, I first refer to the four ancient labyrinths and I have doubts about their order. Moreover, I possess no means of consulting the appropriate books and lack sufficient confidence in my memory. You give me great pleasure when you write so appealingly about your friendship, with which you ardently embrace not only myself but all those who are dear to me or to whom I am dear, although I already knew it without your saying so. It also pleased me to learn of your hearing and seeing me as if you were actually present beyond the Alps and the seas, with your eyes sharper than a lynx's and your ears keener than a boar's, that remarkable and common privilege of lovers, who can see one another even in absence. I believe that a considerable portion of my good fortune befell me from the day you brought yourself to love me as you do. At the end of your letter you wrote with modest seriousness that the public would consider you of little worth if it knew how much pleasure you derive from reading and knowing the poets, whereas you silently feel greater self-esteem for this. For these two reasons I praise you, because you know the people's follies and you scorn them; the former reveals the sagacity of your mind, the latter its nobility. But even this subject is too vast to be treated in passing and ought to be covered, unless I am mistaken, with modest silence so that we seem neither to be wasting our leisure time nor insulting the ignorant. There remains my request to give my best to our friends who need not be named. You know where my heart resides; it has few guests, but faithful ones. Farewell and be happy, and scorn the multitude.

13 January, on the banks of the rivers of Babylon.

Fam. XII, 5.

To the same correspondent, * *a friendly letter.*

I was already hastily closing my letter after posting the date when another messenger suddenly arrived with your latest letter. It is so much more pleasant and agreeable than your earlier one because my love grows with time and knows no rest, no more than does the soul, love's dwelling place, which is in perpetual motion, according to the Platonists. What shall I say to this? The mind suggests much for which even the most eloquent tongue does not suffice. The eloquence of Cicero, in my opinion, was clearer in his mind than in the ears of his listeners, while the Muse was far more lofty in the inspiration of the Mantuan poet than in his writings. I consider it a great accomplishment to express great concepts with words and to reveal with artistically combined words the beauty hidden in the mind. If I am not mistaken, that is precisely the highest purpose of eloquence. Though the human spirit aspires toward it, often it halts overwhelmed in the middle of the road. I would now like to tell you something that will impress you; the concept is clearly in my mind, yet I am incapable of expressing what I wish to convey to you. How astonishingly feeble is the language of mortals! But so be it, for you can see inside my soul, read what is written therein, hear the words and ideas even if they be silent. Furthermore, whatever I say to you is not for your instruction but for the solace of my mind, something that I expect from few others, and that can obviously be accomplished with any style. Therefore, let me say the following, not for you, but for myself and for others: the more I observe you, the more I admire, embrace, and love you, the more I enjoy being loved by you. Because of your feeling toward me, I feel more self-esteem and more indulgence for my defects, as if I could not be so dear to a man such as yourself unless you were to see some kind of spark in my soul which I, being too close, admittedly do not see. It would not appear so to you, I believe, if you were to look more deeply, unless its basis were that true saying, "those who love, fashion dreams for themselves," to contrast Maro to Virgil and pastoral poetry to bucolic poetry. What do you expect? I am happy over your mistaken view of me, which is my fate with nearly all my friends. Nevertheless no error pleases my mind more than yours; I desire none to remain more eternal than yours, just as I wish our friendship to be eternal. I have no doubt that your love and talent will grant

*See preceding letter.

this to me; I shall make use of fortune, and I shall strive my utmost never to let that cloud vanish in which I appeared to you in the midst of the forest. Let this suffice for now. With open arms, as you wish, I shall receive your Forese, indeed mine and ours as he himself says, so worthy of being loved for his own sake. Would that some opportunity might finally be granted whereby I can reveal my mind to you, other than through words! Or if destiny denies this, would that he, like you, might understand the spirit of my silence! I hope it will be so. As for those modest verses addressed to you which you so insistently request, please be informed that they need some verification from Pliny the Younger, whom I left upon my departure from Italy in his native land, Verona, surrounded by an enormous company of illustrious men. Here there is no Pliny nor any other writer as far as I know, except at the Roman pontiff's. As you have heard, however, he is now slowly returning from the threshold of death which he had not long ago swiftly approached. When he regains his health, although for the elderly the ultimate hope for bodily health lies in death, when he is a little better—which would already be so in my opinion but for the mob of loquacious doctors, a truly enormous curse for the wealthy—at that time I shall inspect his Pliny at leisure. Then without delay your desire will be satisfied. You will receive my poem, long requested and promised. As in other instances pertaining to me you have been deceiving yourself in your hope and in your opinion, and will thus say, "What I had heard is really true; one's expectations are much greater than reality." Farewell, and remember me.

18 January.

Fam. XII, 6.

To Philippe, Bishop of Cavaillon,* a friendly letter.

Were you really able to come to our transalpine Helicon at the source of the Sorgue, sacred to our aging Muses, and spend five days there without me? Did it not occur to you, most loving father, that with me absent something was missing either in those pleasant places or at least in your spirit, well disposed as it is toward me, something that could easily have been supplied since I was so near at hand that I could almost be called. What then was the matter? Was it that you wished to deprive me, amidst the pressures of my innumerable cares, of the brief enjoyment of the country and of yourself? Yet your reproachless virtue would prohibit such conjecture. Was it that you considered me unworthy? This is unthinkable because of your remarkable love and well-known opinion of me, which I wish were as true as they are kind and flattering. Or did you think that I would not come, were you to call? But when, tell me, have I ever been so suspected of pride? Was it that you did not wish to interfere with my work or my affairs? If so, you consider me too slothful, too excessively attached to earthly things. Let me say without offense that wherever I turn I feel compelled to marvel at your behavior. I would thus complain about you and with you except that you sweetly assuaged my hurt with my books that are there, as your letter states. With them you passed all your days and nights on friendly terms. What I found astounding was that, while you did turn to the works of saints and historians, philosophers and poets, you satisfied in particular your desire—such is the power of love—for my modest works or, to speak more truthfully, my trifles. It is truly nature's doing that we love our own ugly children more ardently that the handsome ones of others. Nor did an obscure poet put this ineptly: "To each his own bride, to me my own; to each his own love, to me my own." Now you also, dearest father, consider when judging my circumstances, not who I may be, but how devoted I am to you. Certainly if, as my steward reports, you desired to take some works but not without my permission, that indicates a certain lukewarmness in your love for me. I ask you to use, as you please, whatever I possess, whether myself or my trifling possessions. Finally you should know that I have approached our common patron, the cardinal of Albano with your letter. He expressed his pleasure at what you wrote, but has decided never to weary the Roman pontiff with his own prob-

*See II, 1.

lems. It seems to me that having gone beyond human passions he has placed a boundary to his desires, and ought to be congratulated as much for his spirit as for his good fortune. You know the other news: the Sicilian king has finally received the crown, and a peace that hopefully will be eternal is being arranged between him and the king of Hungary; our Pope has returned from the threshold of death although he may soon return there; while I am writing this letter to you, the cardinal of Ostia is on the verge of death. By the time you read this, he will have expired; in my opinion he will surrender to a death that will be ripe for him and for nature but unfortunate for the state. Farewell, O illustrious patron.

Avignon, 1 February.

Fam. XII, 7.

To Barbato da Sulmona,* a complaint that he had not seen him in Rome during the year of the Jubilee.

Dearest Barbato who are so much a part of me, nearly an entire year elapsed during which your letter sought the road to me with its many pathways, following me throughout Italy to France where I was hidden. We are thus deprived of the consolation not only of hearing each other's voice, but even of silent letters. Fortune has held this sway over our lives from the day hostile death left us untouched while snatching from us our most delightful and sweetest bond, the king of Sicily, the greatest and most illustrious man our age had produced. With his death, he who had united our spirits in life separated our bodies, thus changing with this sad turn of events the entire purpose of our lives. Let us, however, not discuss what the inexorable laws of nature forbid us to reconsider; let us bear with silent patience what becomes more painful through laments. Our king was worthy of heaven, this world was unworthy of such a king. He deserved repose after toil, we deserved tears after laughter and pain after joy. A single event joined him to his Lord and separated us from ours. I have recently lamented this in a brief poem, which has taken its place among those dedicated to you. For the same reason I do not respond to that section of your letter deploring with fitting words, compassionately and mournfully, our country's condition and wretchedness, for I have nothing to add to your complaints. Moreover I fear that any rubbing might prove troublesome to your eyes reddened by weeping, and that once I began I would never stop. As for your including among your principal misfortunes the fact that you did not see me in Rome, that is in my opinion the hand of God. Had we been able to meet, we would have visited with poetic curiosity various places in the city, and without Christian devotion the churches of God, acting for the sake of scholarship and not our souls. Though certainly a very pleasant nourishment for the mind, scholarship is limitless and vain unless directed toward a single true purpose. Besides, had you remembered my natural slowness, you surely could have predicted that the end of the Jubilee year, and not the beginning, would bring me to Rome. Let this also be the answer to your request so that you may know that my plans remain unchanged about my *Africa*, about which you justly inquire. If it ever does see the light, do rest assured that I will keep my promise to

*See IV, 8.

have you read it before anyone else. In truth it is being delayed by its owner's laziness and by fortune's countless obstacles. Even if these were all to cease, it still seems preferable for the *Africa* to remain at home in order to ripen and mature with age. If it were to go forth prematurely it would appear, as do apples plucked unripe from the branch, bitter and immature, especially since it could not be retrieved once it has made a public appearance and since my judgment daily undergoes extraordinary change. Perhaps henceforth I shall feel differently and submit it to a final polishing, for many of the obstacles causing delay have been removed, and unless I am mistaken I have now become whatever was destined for me from above, although until the last day of my life I shall not desist from pressing forward as much as I am able. Nor will I despair of becoming better and more learned even under the tutelage of a sluggish old age, learning something every day, if perchance I succeed with some effort in applying to myself what that very wise old man once took pride in saying about himself. I shall certainly strive to do so, and I hope to succeed more readily and more happily when my passions, all completely withered, have been uprooted from my spirit, since thanks to God they now minimally disturb me. My last hope is that we will be able to see each other in the heavenly Jerusalem, if not sooner, since it was not allowed in the earthly city. Farewell.

20 February, on the banks of the rivers of Babylon.

Fam. XII, 8.

To Jacopo Fiorentino,* on Cicero and his works.

As is my custom, I recently withdrew to my transalpine Helicon in order to escape the pressures of that detestable city. I brought with me your Cicero who, astonished by the novelty of the place, confessed that he was never surrounded, to use his words, by icier waters in his Arpino than he was with me at the source of the Sorgue. I believe that while going to Narbonne he had failed to visit this area, although if we are to put faith in Pliny, it was then in the province of Narbonne, not in that of Arles as it is today. Whatever may be the provincial division, this famous spring, which yields in my opinion neither to the Campanian nymphs nor to Sicilian Arethusa, the delightful silence, and the exceedingly pleasant solitude of my isolated estate are to be found along the public road, on the right for those going and on the left for those returning. Because of what I have said, then, it should not surprise you if Cicero the traveler did not see the area, even though it was so attractive. In fact without definite purpose or knowledge of the place, no one passing through discovers it unless attracted by the spring's site or intending to devote himself to study or leisure. You will understand the rarity of such a happening if you consider the scarcity of poets or of men strongly dedicated to honored studies. This is why your Cicero seemed delighted and gladly remained with me. We spent ten thoroughly peaceful and tranquil days there together, for I seem able to breathe here as nowhere else outside of Italy. This is its peculiar virtue: it satisfies both the desire for solitude and the aversion for crowds, and it is able to provide an unusual peacefulness in place of the dense crowds, and a throng of noble cares and swarms of illustrious companions in place of the deserted forests. My guest was surrounded by countless illustrious and distinguished men who, aside from the Greeks, included our Romans, Brutus, Atticus, Herennius, all of them celebrated by Cicero. There was Marcus Varro, learned above all men, with whom Cicero himself delighted to wander through his academic groves. Then there were Cotta and Velleius and Lucilius Balbus with whom he used to indulge in penetrating studies on the nature of the gods. There were Nigidius and Cratippus with whom he would examine secrets of nature and the origin and essence of this world. There was his brother, Quintus Cicero, with whom he would discuss divination and law; his son,

*See VII, 8; also known as Lapo da Castiglionchio.

Marcus Cicero, still unperverted, to whom he dictated his *Offices* concerning the good and the useful, and the differences between them; there were also those very eloquent men, Sulpitius and Crassus and Antonius, with whom he explored the secrets of the art of oratory; Cato the Censor, that elder whose old age he would use as example; Lucius Torquatus and Marcus Cato of Utica and Marcus Piso, with whom he would prove through painstaking argumentation the purpose of the good; the orator Hortensius and Epicurus, against the former of whom he directed his praise of philosophy and against the latter his attack on pleasure; there were Lelius and Scipio with whom he gave shape both to ideal friendship and to the ideal republic. But to avoid continuing indefinitely, there were foreign rulers intermingled with Roman subjects whom Cicero personally had defended with truly divine eloquence in the most important legal cases. To mention something, however, which expressly pertains to your little book, dear friend, also present were Milo, whom he defended, Laterensis, whom he accused, Sulla, whom he absolved, and Pompey, whom he praised. With these and other such companions my rural sojourn was certainly peaceful, pleasant, and happy. I only wish that it had been longer! For soon the Babylonian net was again hurled at me and I find myself drawn once more unwillingly into the hell from which I now write this letter to you. A number of commitments has made it impossible either to have my young man transcribe a copy of your little book or to have him bring it back to you during this interval. Nor do I have any hope that such an opportunity will arise before we both return to Italy. I assure you that day will be near once I bring to my previously mentioned Helicon our Forese, should I perchance come upon him idle and free in these parts. If ever, then, because of fate or restlessness or boredom, I should later return to Vaucluse and not here to Avignon—where I shall never come willingly—I shall seem to my friends more deserving of pardon by producing him as a witness to its charms. Farewell, O you who are fortunate not to have seen this western Babylon.

1 April.

Fam. XII, 9.

To Francesco, of the Church of the Holy Apostles, * *a friendly letter.*

Never have I been so subject to an obstinate silence that your sweet voice would not easily rouse my own; and today, as so often in the past, this has happened to me. Overwhelmed by tedium, I was particularly weary of the affairs of the Curia. In addition there were letters to friends and fellow citizens, and several to my foreign friends; for I do devote to them, although reluctantly, considerable time stolen from more important matters. I am prompted in this by a sense of shame that I may seem not to share my leisure with my friends, which Cato advised, as you know, or that I may seem to spurn altogether those who do not spurn me. After spending a large portion of the day on these matters, I had risen with the intention of doing nothing until evening when suddenly your delightful letter took me, as it were, by the hand, led me back to my pen, and ordered me to write whatever came to mind. I noticed that it required no particular response, but it did help in our communicating and conversing together for an hour. Moreover it is filled with love, charity, faith, refinement, and charm; it contains many things better answered with silence. To concentrate on one point, what answer can I possibly give to the one section where you call yourself fortunate for living in my lifetime? What can one say that is more pleasing and friendly? That indeed is what they say Plato used to remark about his Socrates. Just as Socrates was much more fortunate because of his intimacy with Plato than Plato with Socrates, so am I more fortunate because of your friendship than you because of mine. But I pass over these things which no one but you would contradict. To come to the heart of the matter, I must confess to a feeling of vivid sweetness at the arrival of your letter, as if it were you who had come. Nothing could please me more than this, unless I were so self-centered or inconsiderate as to expect from you what they say Aeneas did for love of country, Orpheus for love of his wife, and Theseus for friendship, namely, that you should follow me to Hades and, as it is written, descend alive into hell. May the gods wish more propitious things for you! I prefer that your prayers ascend to heaven; when, as is your custom, you converse personally with God, who has considered you worthy of His table, I beg you to

*See XII, 4.

pray for my deliverance from here, if any way exists to return to the living. Regardless of my fate, my wish is that you, who are the best part of me, my dearest friend, remain where you are and live happily under your native heaven.

1 April.

Fam. XII, 10.

To Giovanni Boccaccio,* that there is nothing to write.

Lest you think you were overlooked, I did everything in my power to send you too something with this messenger, but because of lack of time or subjects, or because of numerous concerns with which I am now more than usually pressed, or even my sweet hope of conversing with you personally and my resolve of seeing you again soon, I found nothing worth writing, however much I tried, except the following: there was nothing new for me to write. For if I were to describe the happenings in this Babylon in which I am constantly involved, it would be pointless. I have already included much of it in letters to friends, and my pen would be insufficient if I were to write what my mind dictates; if I were to turn to my affairs my language would falter. Indeed what is there that I consider certain except that I must assuredly die? Let Seneca censure me as he censured Cicero in similar circumstances. I find myself in that group known as freemen, being neither alive nor strong nor dying nor ill. Only when I find an exit from this labyrinth shall I begin living and feel well. This is how I am living; this is all I do. Farewell, and consider pleasant whatever may be troubling you in comparison to this exile.

1 April.

*See XI, 1.

Fam. XII, 11.

To Brother Bartolomeo,* Bishop of Chieti.

The fact that springtime, which is by nature stormy, has proven peaceful for you, my dearest father, should make you realize that it was not because of Aeolus, who, as Maro says, "keeps curbed and stalled, chained up in durance to his own will, the heaving winds and far-reverberating trumpets," nor because of Neptune, whose allotment of fortune deluded antiquity thought was "the stern trident, (and) dominion over the seas," but because of Christ's grace, to whom indeed "the King of gods and men has granted . . . the rule of the winds, to lull the waves or lift them." Indeed, "with His words He quickly calms the swollen waters, rules not only the waters but the heavens and the earth, and by His nod alone quells storms in disturbed hearts which are the most serious kind; after banishing passions and restoring peace, He justly, as the poet says, causes 'the mob of clouds dispersed and the sunlight restored to power.' " To Him you are indebted for many things, among which I would certainly include your extreme modesty as reflected in your letter, which produced great joy in me. You solemnly declare in it satisfaction with your bishopric; you added toward the end with a truly lofty spirit something which, unless I am mistaken, is as true as it is in harmony with my feelings, that nowhere are you likely to live more happily than far from Babylon. An excellent and splendid attitude, indeed, for whoever is not satisfied with moderation, greatest of all qualities, will never find sufficient wealth. Whoever has once experienced disgust for this accursed city will find nowhere in the entire world a disagreeable place, unless perhaps the Babylonian poison has permeated to his very marrow through long habit—you understand those to whom I refer with this exception. I have often spoken thus; I would say even more if I did not fear offending, not so much the occupants of this swamp, powerful and fortunate in the multitude's estimation yet extremely miserable and insignificant in mine, but myself, since I irritate my indignant stomach with the painful recollection of indigestible names. I should not fail to mention that it was a clear sign of divine grace, should you not realize it, that you did not advance higher in this Babylon. For you would surely have advanced except that you seemed dissimilar in character to those in

---

*Bartolomeo Carbone dei Papazurri, Roman churchman, was named Bishop of Teano in 1349 by Clement VI and Bishop of Chieti in 1353 by Innocent VI. In Chieti he had to deal with a tyrannical ruler and unsettled conditions.

power, something that I consider very fortunate. If then you value your salvation, you will gladly depart from this place or, better still, you will voluntarily return to your native land from this exile. Whoever aspires to the celestial Jerusalem, while a prisoner by the rivers of Babylon, sits and weeps, hanging his lyre on the bitter willows and recalling with longing Mount Sion. But if the opportunity arises, he eagerly breaks away to return to the place for which he yearns. As for the rest, what else can I say except that I too sigh silently with you? For you desire to see all of us delivered from this prison and in Italy. If Christ were to grant me my desire, I would certainly live and die in Italy; but at the moment I know not what the future holds for me. He alone sees what I wish, what can set me free; He alone is powerful enough to grant both of them. To Him I entrust my affairs and my future. I realize that you are aware of the fact that it is bad for me to be here. But once again, what can I do? As you see, great upheavals are now being planned in Italy, but it is nevertheless also true that I would prefer to suffer there rather than remain silent where I am. Those successors of Arsaces, to whom I cannot deny indebtedness because of past kindnesses, are contriving at all costs to keep me here in Babylon or in Parthia. I have been resisting, but as of the moment the result is in doubt. Should I win, you will not hear of my return until it happens; if I fail, which I believe can happen only because of my shame at refusing them, I shall still remain outside the walls of Semiramis. You say, "Where will you go?" There is no need for a map: you know my refuge, you know where I usually spend my French summers, where I find consolation for my transalpine longing. Finally, whose mind would not be delighted and charmed by the splendid construction being erected on the shore of the Bay of Naples by the man who bears the surname, great, but who in my opinion should be called the greatest? I first learned about it from his letters and now from yours too. I am not surprised that, as you have written, you have enjoyed his favor through my intercession. I knew that it could not be otherwise. Though I do not personally know him, I do know his mind. I certainly rejoice over it; I shall express my gratitude to him either in writing or orally through the Florentine prelate who has recently been freed of these chains and returned to Italy. He has, however, first gone to the shrine of St. Anthony of Egypt in Vienne; then our agreement was for him to come and see my modest country retreat on his return. Tomorrow therefore, as promised, he will partake of a poetic repast with me at the source of the Sorgue. Farewell.

21 May, at dawn.

Fam. XII, 12.

To Francesco, of the Church of the Holy Apostles. *

"Nowhere are pledges secure," says Maro. The more I consider these words, the more I understand them; the older I become, the more I find them to be true. Someone has deceived me whom I would never have suspected would do so, namely, the bishop of Florence who is the most sincere person under the sun. But this seems my lot: there is no one really incapable of deceiving me. He had said that he would be coming to the source of the Sorgue to behold this region, a marvel throughout the world, as well as me and my way of life in this rural retreat. Our agreement was for him to visit me at my home upon his return from the sanctuary of St. Anthony. Knowing that he would be hard pressed for time, I sought before his arrival and contrary to my custom, the best produce available here in the country so as to receive him in a grander fashion than I usually do friends of lesser dignity. But why delay any longer? Perhaps he dreaded the poetic repast, forgetful of the poetic saying, "Have the courage, my guest, to despise pomp: train yourself to be worthy of godhead, and be not scornful of our humble fare"; or perhaps he did not deem worthy a visit to places once visited by King Robert of Sicily, the glory of our age, and after him by a number of Roman cardinals and earthly princes who at times did me the honor of visiting the spring and at others of visiting me—I have no shame in boasting of this to you. Or perhaps, and this I would prefer not to believe, neither I who am not the least of mortals nor the spring which is among the finest, unless I am mistaken, deserved his visit because it required a slight detour in his journey of some three miles. At any rate, though I may have been unworthy of such a noble guest, it still was fitting for him to keep his word.

When I had reached this point and was about to continue writing, there was a loud noise at my gates announcing the bishop's arrival. Thus I learn each day through the teachings of experience that the cares and laments of men are in vain. So that you too may realize this, I still am sending this short letter to you, though to no purpose. Farewell.

At the source of the Sorgue, 24 May, at the ninth hour.

*See XII, 4.

Fam. XII, 13.

*To the same correspondent.**

Having endeavored with the power of prayer to untangle the ridiculous and loathsome snarl which the abbot of Vallombrosa caused me with his constantly changing promises—I have often complained of this to you, if you recall—I acted in another's behalf as I had never done for myself: I was ambitious, assiduous, and importunate. You would have beheld a laughable and pitiful spectacle had you seen me, so desirous of solitude and idleness, so accustomed to wandering through the forest, suddenly shifting my interests in order to flit for days at a time with the huge crowd in the Curia along the fancy halls of the pontiff, all to the amazement of my friends and the disdain of the Muses. What more can I say? Finally my perservering labor has conquered the obstinate resistance. On 30 April, with the pope sitting on the throne of the fisherman, as is customary, and with the cardinals in full consistory, our friend finally had his wishes granted under the sponsorship of my name, which was continually uttered and repeated by the greatest men present and honored with many praises, which I wish were true. In this affair, both friendship and merit were advantageous to him, but nothing proved of greater assistance than the inexorable and greedy arrogance of his enemies and my own indignation, which made me vigilant rather than slothful. I simply could not allow the truth to be trampled so openly by falsehood. I wished to let you know this so that you might rejoice and so that I might express my gratitude because you offered so faithfully whatever you could. Farewell.

24 May, at the source of the Sorgue.

*See XII, 4.

Fam. XII, 14.

To Giovanni Barrili, Neapolitan soldier, an appeal to further the cause of peace.*

Incredible as it may seem, nothing is more important or more worthy of giving than what I am about to request of you today; it is, O illustrious sir, that you subject your mind to your reason or, to express it differently, you to yourself by compelling your worst qualities to obey your best ones. Magnificently indeed, carefully imitating nature herself, Plato discovered the threefold seat of the soul. What seemed muddled, he made clear with his divine talent. Having thus distinctly located anger in the breast and lust in the region of the heart, he placed reason in the head as in a fortress, so that its very location would reveal it as the controller and mistress of the passions. I do not believe that our own poets were ignorant of this, although they pursued the subject more obscurely, as is their custom. If I were to express all that is in my mind concerning this, a tremendous string of ideas would surge in me for which this is neither the time nor the place. Moreover, any attempt at describing anger will probably be superfluous here, since its sad results are known even to the multitude, and indeed fill entire volumes by philosophers, especially Plutarch and Seneca. I believe you should be briefly reminded about what every learned person knows, namely, that where passions dwell, there too reside the hideous clouds and dreadful darkness of the soul, and, to put it clearly, the total eclipse of reason. I believe this may truly be said not only of all the passions but in particular of anger. Nothing disturbs peace and serenity as much, nothing gives more evidence of a troubled mind: a pale face, a choking voice, shaking limbs, a wrinkled brow, raised eyebrows, burning eyes, and rapid breathing. To onlookers, these symptoms reveal, and visibly display, anger dwelling in the soul, like Cacus brought forth from hiding. On the other hand, when the mind is subject to reason and liberated from the passions, there reign undisturbed tranquillity, pleasant serenity and, ultimately, human happiness. Therefore it is necessary, if we wish to be happy with that happiness which may be enjoyed in this mortal life—although through it we aspire to another—it is necessary, I say, for it to partake significantly of the divine mind so that, as is said about Olympus's loftiest peak, no mists of passion

---

*Giovanni Barrili from Capua, magistrate and soldier in the service of Naples, also served as seneschal of Provence. Petrarch met him in 1341 while in Naples for his "examination" by King Robert, and remained his friend for life.

may touch it. I doubt not that your mind is of such bent, for I am very familiar with your nature and your ways. I believe the same about you as others believe about the grand seneschal of the kingdom. Him I know by reputation, but you through personal experience. Upon hearing that the friendship between you two had not really been broken, but somewhat unstitched, I determined to repair it with the needle of firm devotion and with a thin thread of words. With great confidence and trust I wrote to both of you at the same time, hoping not in the power of my eloquence but in the assistance of God and in your character. If I dared to do this with him, what would hinder me from daring it with you? Therefore I ask one thing of both of you, that you approach reading the letter sent to you both with well-disposed minds, weighing the kernel of my request and conveying it to that part of the mind which, as I have said, lies beyond all the mists of human passions. I hope this finds you well.

At the source of the Sorgue, 24 May.

Fam. XII, 15.

To Niccolò Acciaiuoli, Grand Seneschal of the Kingdom of Sicily,* on the same matter.

Your excuse for a tardy response so sweetly surprised my senses, O magnanimous sir, that I would not have wished it to arrive any sooner, since it came bearing a high and welcome rate of interest. I recognized in it at once your talent and the resonant pen of our Barbato, which proved a double delight and consolation for my spirit, although I do confess that your heroic actions, despite your silence, were sufficient response for me. For I do not speak to you to elicit a response, as orators and poets customarily do, but to add flames to your fiery virtue and even to your glowing spirit, if this be within my power. It is undeniable that I would deserve reproof from your republic if I were to draw you from your lofty and useful concerns to more humble matters, and indeed a generous effort of the mind is expressed more gloriously in action than in words. Do, then, as you are accustomed; express in deeds what you mulled over in your mind following in this matter as you have in others the venerable customs of the Romans. For among them, as the poet says, "everyone preferred to do rather than to say," although many of them were both active and eloquent. Consequently, the praise with which Statius Pampinius flatters Prince Domitian may apply to many others, namely, that we may see the same leaves decorating heads of military leaders and prophets, that we may marvel to find the Muses dwelling with dictators, consuls, and empires, and victorious laurels present in literary pursuits. If ever, then, there is sufficient time for you to mingle, as you recently did, glorious words equally with glorious actions, you will deserve the double honor enjoyed by Caesar. Just as we know you to be most distinguished in strength of spirit, so may we recognize you to be not only militarily inspired but artfully eloquent, incapable of dealing with insignificant matters. Both qualities were deemed peculiar to Julius Caesar by historians. Though you yourself may not be Caesar, who impedes you from possessing the spirit of a Caesar, or imitating his character and industry? Indeed those expressions of gratitude which you sent me for my arid and barren words, I return to you as more worthy of your richly written letter. In particular I thank you for your final words where you proposed to establish a new Parnassus bearing my name between Vesuvius and the Falernian countryside, which

*See XI, 13.

would even benefit posterity! May fortune gaze favorably upon such a noble project, be forgetful of her ways for a little while, and cease envying famous rulers. For such an undertaking, scholars of the present and future, as well as myself, render thanks to you. As for me, although glorying in the possession of two Parnassi, I would still not refuse a third, resounding with your Apollo, inhabited by your Muses, green with your laurels, and finally consecrated under your auspices. What more can I say? What you do is magnificent, what you say is magnificent; but that action would be the most magnificent, unmatched and worthy of Caesar, were you now to conquer yourself with that same magnanimity with which you often conquered others, were you to compel your perhaps reluctant spirit to comply with the heartfelt advice contained in my common letter to you and to the distinguished Giovanni Barrili, thereby returning to the yoke of your old friendship. While this may appear excessive to an angry mind, I nevertheless hope to accomplish it easily because of your kindness, if my judgment of you and of your character is correct. Farewell, and remain happy and always true to yourself.

24 May, at the source of the Sorgue.

Fam. XII, 16.

To both Niccolò and Giovanni, an appeal for harmony and* *for a return to their former friendship.*

I wish to bring you together, O most illustrious men and pride of Florence and Naples, I wish to bring you together if you will permit me to do so and will not shudder at the touch of a friendly hand. Rashness will not impede reason, nor envy charity, nor madness good counsel, nor finally the empty rumbling of detractors the binding effect of my love, with which this pen, indeed Christ as lover of peace working through the ministry of my pen, unites your hearts. Great is the power of friendship; nothing is difficult or impossible for it; and true indeed is that poetic saying that "love conquers all." It is for you to realize in yourselves what follows those words: "And let us yield to love." Do yield, I beg you, O most gentle hearts, do yield to him to whom monstrous beasts yield, whom even the insensible elements obey. I urge you to yield, for once you have done so, all things will then yield to you. Do not block your ears, do not turn away your eyes, do not harden your hearts which a just love will fill with better counsel. I take hope in the nobility of you both, which is so luminous that you shine forth like two bright stars in two cities and among two great peoples. Nothing is more certain than the fact that love distinguishes a noble heart from an ignoble one. Listen therefore to him who constantly inspires such things within your hearts: "Why do you part ways, O noble men, why do you rebel, what do you flee? I used to reign in you, dwell in you, and had pitched tents in you. I had increased your glory and you mine. Who drove me from your midst? Who separated your united hearts and, to speak frankly, made two hearts of one? Return to yourselves, return to me and admit me as I return to you; without this no good will ever result. Return to one another's good grace, discourse and embrace; join your right hands, unite your hearts, and once again form a single heart from two. This behooves your virtue, this delights others' virtue, this benefits your lands, this cheers good men, this terrifies the wicked. Let those who had conceived evil expectations because of your discord, now feel terror because of your reconciliation. Certainly if you continue the bitterness, the state of your affairs is such that, like it or not, you must dwell in some fashion in the same palace. How much more serene and peaceful your lives will be once the mist of anger is removed, if perchance vile whispers had

*See XI, 13 and XII, 14.

wafted any mists your way! This would be as desirable as it will be simple. No more serious than yours was the reason for reconciliation that joined Emilius Lepidus and Flaccus Fulvius for five years or for one year, for six or for eighteen months, in the office of censor; no more serious than yours was that of Livius Salinator and Claudius Nero during the year of their consulship, which consigned a dreadful affront to a merciful oblivion. Yours is not an association resulting from some office or other but a lifelong one that cannot be laid aside before the end. No more efficacious is your continuing relationship than the meal of the elder Africanus and Tiberius Gracchus, which hosted them as enemies but succeeded in uniting them, not so much in their former friendship, but in an even stronger alliance. What shall I say of the humaneness of Cicero who, unmindful of a justifiable hatred, was friendly even to his most relentless opponents? What shall I say of many others who laid aside very serious enmities, often for unimportant reasons? You need not lay aside any enmity, but simply renew the memory of an old friendship. Consider the evil that resides in discord; consider how it once destroyed great empires. The Roman Republic, which never was equaled in the world nor, and I hope that I am not mistaken, will it ever be, had rested on a foundation of countless virtues, yet fell only through discord. And I ask, through the discord of how many men? Of very few, no doubt. Scarcely more than a couple of men in any given age could have avoided the ruination of their state, had they been in accord. I confess, O Italians, that you have endured many harsh misfortunes at the hands of such men, and sometimes you went almost to the very limits. Yet no one would ever deny in my presence that your ancestors always managed to rise from their calamities. It was for this reason that the Indians, the Iberians, the Cimbrians, the Moors, the Scythians, the Ethiopians, the Africans, and the Teutons could not boast of victory over you; nor were Brennus, Pyrrhus, Philippus, Perseus, Syphax, Mithridates, Antiochus, Hannibal, and Jugurtha able to take pride in such a victory. Though victorious over other peoples and over kings, you were conquered by your own civil discord. If such discord subverts governments and royal wealth, what hope is there for private families and private wealth?''

If love or friendship were to say these words, or similar ones, to you, what would be your response? I believe that you would willingly put yourself into their hands and accept their sway. Yet love speaks these same words to you through me. I implore you by whatever is holy or pious or efficacious among mortals to offer one another the hand of friendship and to heed one another. It is nothing great that I ask, only that you not continue to oppose the search for friendship. Recall to mind and set before your eyes whatever moments of sweetness, trust, or pleasure you shared throughout your lives: the pleasant journeys, the delightful vacations, the enjoyable conversations, the tranquillity, the military service and campaigns, the days spent in the dust and the nights under the divine heavens when you enjoyed sleeping on the bare ground or on the sod, when you as soldiers would set your shield upside down to serve as a tent, finally your common hardships, your common glory, your common danger, or the reciprocal assistance, timely comforts, and helpful advice. On the other hand, if anything harsher perhaps intervenes than your sensitive minds can tolerate—something which I would say can be avoided in a lengthy friendship through good fortune rather than human prudence—uproot such an obstacle from your hearts. Two things create enduring friendships and add luster to noble spirits: the recollection of past kindnesses and the disregard of past offenses. Both of these I now request of you. If you do grant this, I shall achieve my greatest wish, and will have written with good fortune or, as they say, with the right foot. But if you prefer to remember all that has happened, I shall surely have to expend a little more energy; yet I would still hope that resentment will yield in the face of so many kind actions. For neither of you have such a nature that you feel greater hurt at the harshness of a single word than charm in the admittedly friendly deeds. If therefore the matter comes down to counting, I shall be the victor; but I would prefer not to travel that road. In fact many are the reasons leading you back to your former friendship and few, indeed hardly any, preventing you from doing so. You are bound by powerful ties, such as your age, your birthplace, your military experience, your virtue, your glory, your nobility, identical studies, the recollection of personal merits, and public interest, which is the most efficacious bond of friendship. Your motivations are the same: you serve the same king, you inhabit the same country, you have the same aspirations and desires: that virtue be rewarded and crime punished, that good men be esteemed and evil men put down, that justice flourish, strong men be honored, evil conduct be banished, and noble conduct be encouraged throughout your city. If such is the case, what slight offense, or rather what strong suspicion of offense, could dissolve a solid and sacred union of your minds? Go therefore with eagerness where your noble ardor calls you, follow this generous impulse, do not resist such fine drives, do not kill the spirit, as the Apostle says. Of necessity you must love one another; you struggle in vain, for nature itself makes you friends. Virtue is appealing and charming even in an enemy, pleasing wherever it may appear, incapable of not loving itself. The root of friendship is likeness of character. Intimacy among evil men is of brief duration, being built on weak foundations; among good men, in contrast, it forms an enduring and eternal alliance. What does it matter where indignation leads it or how anger tears it asunder? Your characters are alike; your virtue is sound, and it in turn orders your minds to become sound. Nothing is more greedy or tenacious than virtue; it possesses hooks, chains, prisons, and lures that entice very charmingly. The taste of pleasure is indeed flattering, but in abundance unpleasant; the taste of virtue is ultimately very sweet. Our custom is to use bait according to the kind of bird or animal we wish to ensnare, since we know their preferences. Pleasure is the bait of the multitude, virtue the bait of the few. You number among the few, so display openly what you are. What I offer you are not delights or conveniences, although true friendship abounds in countless delights and conveniences, not the enticements of pleasures, although virtue may also have its enticements. Ultimately I offer you nothing but naked virtue; if you are very hungry for it, as your reputations would indicate, grasp it eagerly and together hold it tightly until the very end. Just as the implacable stings of human indignation are now irritated by the smallest of offenses, so praise will be great for the distinguished exceptions. Otherwise, your infamy will be all the greater, the less the reason for impeding your friendship. So great is the charm of friendship that if—though offered to you in this unpolished vessel of my letter—it has not enticed your minds, however reluctant, one might suppose that you were inhuman and savage rather than angry. Such a mental strain should be avoided with the utmost zeal, not only by those seeking virtue or glory, but particularly by you who are so illustrious. I have no doubt what I have said thus far will have some effect on your noble minds.

Add to this that your coming together will be all the more pleasing the longer you have been apart; often a face, the eyes, and the sound of a voice can greatly influence the mind. Nor do I deny that I am prolonging my discourse not accidentally, but consciously, so that you would have to stay together longer. For this reason I had written on the back of this letter, as you saw, that no hand but yours was to touch it, that neither of you alone was to open this letter addressed to you both. I did everything possible to keep you conversing at length. I beg you that my attempt not be in vain, you in whose hands lies the effectiveness of my appeal. Consider me to be in your midst. I feel as though I am truly there, tormented by fear and burning with love. It would be extraordinary indeed if this flame burning in your friend's heart does not touch you. Let your kindliness, not to me personally but to my faith in you, bring it about that, were I to come to Naples, I should find you united; if not, that I should hear that it is so. Do not let it be said that more was granted to raging Veturius among armed enemy battle lines than to me, a suppliant among unarmed friends, or that more was achieved by the disheveled hair of the Sabine women than by my shedding tears. If I were to know that you had granted my wishes, I would be happy and would expect no more of life. So what will you do now, what is this delay, what are you awaiting, O wisest of men, bound by an enduring esteem, so alike in your pursuit of virtues and in your pleasant ways? Rush to embrace one another, I beg you, and weep for lost time; and do not allow yours not to be equal to the most famous friendships. Each time mention is made of the young princes, Tydeus and Polynices, Theseus and Pirothous, Hercules and Philoctetes, Pylades and Orestes, each time mention is made of the Pythagorean youths, Damon and Pythias, and of the greatest example of Roman virtue and friendship, Lelius and Scipio, let not posterity be ignorant of the illustrious names of Niccolò and Giovanni.

24 May, at the source of the Sorgue.

Fam. XII, 17.

To Zanobi, Florentine grammarian, * *a request for his assistance
in the matter discussed in the preceding letter.*

Scarcely had I finished responding in a single day to several letters
from friends that had been accumulating than your letter unexpectedly arrived at my door. If it had a voice with which to speak, it
would tell you how joyfully it was received. Accompanying it was a
fine poem which I admire and praise. First however, because of the
affection binding the two of us, I would like to suggest, before it falls
into others' hands, that you attend to one verse which I found
somewhat too long. To show my esteem for you, you will note that
it is marked in the margin so that you may delete what is excessive.
Lest you feel badly, I wish you to know that in the *Ars poetica* it is
recorded that "at times even good Homer may fall asleep." You
write that, burdened by the weight of your cares, you have real need
of my assistance, thereby proving your humility in this as in other
matters. I truly wish that it were within my power to afford you,
who implore my help and complain of my delay, a proper haven
against your misfortunes: I certainly would not allow you to be
weighed down any longer. My hope, however, is not in Thetis or in
Neptune but in the One who "is the lord of the sea and truly created
it," that with His helping trident He might quiet the swollen waters
of our mortal lives, agitated by the perpetual winds of human affairs.
He is the way and the goal, the leader and the companion, the labor
and the reward. As for your present state of affairs, I believe it was
sufficiently discussed with others' ideas, but with my own words, in
the letter which I recently sent you. In fact, I sent you the advice of
that great and excellent man which by now you have read and approved and, I am confident, will approve even more as the matter
itself develops. You ask me to thank him in your name, as if my
name could be of no little benefit, as you assert, in acquiring his
good graces. I ask you to note that, should I comply, it may be interpreted as arrogance or ignorance on my part, since it would appear
more appropriate for you to express your personal gratitude to him
than for me, a man unknown to him, to do so. Yet if you really wish
this, I shall comply with your request, but without any guarantee. It
so happens that at present I am writing to him concerning a very
serious matter. Next to virtue, what is greater among men than
friendship? It was about this very subject that I wrote him urging his

*See XII, 3.

return into the good graces of an old and esteemed friend. I used a method whereby I sent to both men one and the same letter so that they would at least have to meet in order to read it. Should my wishes prevail, I shall be proud of having offered a great and significant service to the republic and shall be eternally indebted to this pen of mine. I have sent the letter to you so that it may hasten to them in your hands, and reach them more securely with the support of your favor as well. I am also allowing you to do what I had forbidden on its cover to anyone else, namely, you may open it. If you feel anything should be deleted or added, you may do so, since you are acquainted with his character and mind, with what most easily moves him, and since "you know the appropriate times and approaches." Farewell.

24 May, at the source of the Sorgue.

Fam. XIII, 1.

To Gui, cardinal, Bishop of Porto,* condolences on the death of his mother.

I know to whom I speak; to one whom I have always known as a favorable judge and kind interpreter of my talents, and furthermore to one to whom I have no doubt my sincerity is well known; I shall not, then, because of the pressure of time be excessively concerned with making my style more sophisticated. Even my spirit is able to speak to you through silence. Moreover I hope that you will understand and be persuaded that mine cannot be a joyful style when you are sad. Add to this the fact that I have approached my pen with greater confidence and haste because of my experience with nearly all kinds of grief. There is no hardship, no sorrow unknown to me; nature made me ignorant and fortune made me learned in such matters. This alone I had not experienced in my writing, though I had in personal grief, namely, that I should console a son upon his mother's death. Until the present day, I confess, that kind of mournful subject was the only one left untried. In fact thus far that kind of comforting had been unnecessary for anyone I love or respect, except for myself who bore the misfortune in my earliest youth. But to return to our subject, dear father, I heard yesterday at eventide the sad and tearful news. I heard of your grief and of your tears, those true witnesses of devotion; not only do I not disapprove of them, but actually approve of them provided they be brief and moderate and restrained. So great is my approval, in fact, that I did not hasten immediately to you upon receiving the news, not so much because of approaching night which made it impossible, but because of this reflection: let us grant one night for a highly appropriate grief, let us allow time for pious devotion, let the nocturnal gush of tears flow, whereby the following day may dawn more serenely. What indeed shall I now say? How can I touch this rather recent wound of your spirit? Your dearest mother has perished. Had she enjoyed no other happiness or joy from life than giving birth to you, no one would deny that she was most fortunate. When the famous Cornelia, daughter of Africanus, mother of the Gracchi, beheld her sons crushed by a terri-

---

*Gui de Boulogne, cardinal, Bishop of Porto and apostolic legate, was of noble lineage. Endowed with great personal talents, he led many diplomatic missions in behalf of the pope. One of the two most powerful cardinals in the Curia, he played a central role in attempting to get Petrarch to accept the position of papal secretary. He lived from about 1320 to 1373.

ble death, she said to the mourning women who were with her, bewailing her misfortune with feminine laments: "I shall never consider myself unfortunate for having borne such sons." If she said this about her dead sons, what could your mother say about you who are alive and well? Pregnant, she bore you for nine months in her womb with difficulty and suffering; with joy and pain she gave birth to you; she brought you sleep with her soft singing while you lay in your cradle; she embraced you, her sweet burden, wrapped in your swaddling clothes and crying; she was solicitous when you crawled and anxious as you took your first uncertain steps; she was uneasy as you played with your young friends; she lovingly sought you out when you went to school, and she welcomed you happily when you returned a young man. As a young man, as a man, as a wise man, as a learned man, and as a man acceptable to God and to other men, you were a source of great joy to her. Shortly thereafter, earlier than usual because of your merits, you afforded her extraordinary glory by becoming bishop of the church of Lyons. Finally you gave her the greatest pleasure with your appointment by the Roman See as cardinal, and most recently as archbishop of Porto you provided her with a restful port for nearly all her prayers. Given this state of affairs, what can I say about the departure of your aged mother? Surely with her qualities, with her husband's renown, with the number and charm of her children, but especially with your high honors and devotion she was a happy woman, indeed so happy that she could scarcely have been more so on this earth. At the appropriate time she was taken from this mortal and transitory happiness to eternal blessedness. Now in heaven, with the misfortunes of mortal life behind her, she triumphs, having followed her husband, and preceding her children who in due time will also happily journey there. If by chance she is being delayed by some weakness of the flesh and is not yet in heaven, she ought to be assisted with devout prayers rather than tears. This is what she expects of you, this would be a more gratifying gift for her. Pray, do not mourn; if you loved her alive in this world, allow yourself with a calm heart, O most illustrious father, to ascend from your earthly, though lofty, position to the very highest summit of divine blessedness. What more could she do on this earth? What more could she have wanted to see you do, except perhaps become the Holy Pontiff? Indeed I am of the opinion that a person dies more happily enjoying the present and hoping in the future than when, by satisfying all hope and attaining everything that can be hoped for or desired on earth, fear gradually replaces hope. For it has been proven with nature's assistance that, just as those who desire possess hope, so those who have attained their desire fear its loss.

Consequently I feel that your mother could not have departed for the celestial abodes at a better moment. For she could leave you her survivor and a happy man—the twin desires of all parents—and also see in her dearest son a strength of mind and body, a substantial age, a position of honor and good fortune in his career. Therefore do not grieve beyond reason for her so that you may not seem to be faulting the processes of nature; it had to be that either she would survive you or you would survive her. She had hoped for the latter which was in keeping with the laws of nature, and this did happen. Console your spirit, O magnanimous sir, do not regret that the contrary did not happen, since it would have caused her indescribable sadness. Would that nature might carry out her other functions as well as she has in your case. We read and see that often mothers mourn grievously the deaths of their children, whereas the opposite is much rarer and more tempered. You will find that some mothers lamenting their dead sons have themselves met death as a result of their maternal grief. You will also find others who mourned a child's death throughout their lives until the last day without ever giving any heed to words of consolation. It was thus for those illustrious women, Livia the wife of Augustus and Octavia her sister, whom Seneca recalls when writing to his Martia. Cicero likewise mourned his Tullia to excess, consoling himself for his beloved daughter's death in a long work that Ambrose later imitated upon his brother's death and published as a work of consolation. It is certainly not strange or unusual that men lament the deaths of their children or of their brothers, and that learned men comfort one another in their sorrows. Unless my memory fails me, however, you will find scarcely more than one outstanding example of a son deeply lamenting a mother's death, not because of lack of devotion but because of the limits set by the natural order. Our Augustine wept over his beloved mother, who followed him on land and sea, and who shed solicitous and endless tears on all her son's journeys. Thus she gave birth thousands of times in her anguished mind to that son whom she bore but once in the flesh. She wept over him so sweetly that even today she brings tears to readers' eyes after so many centuries. Nevertheless, the same mother who had wept over him throughout his life he mourned only a single day. The grief he tried to soothe by reasoning and by accusing his mind of weakness, he was unable to alleviate, he relates, with reason or even with a bath: sleep alone extinguished it. Recalling this, I did not come to you at once nor did I immediately write you so as not to deprive you too soon, as I explained, of the pleasure of mourning—since mourning does have a certain, though unhappy, pleasure. I deliberately allotted you one night to devote with divine assistance to wiping away your tears, which, as I said, I not only do not condemn but even strongly commend as long as, in my opinion, you give them proper measure and limit. Since I have not the time to write the many things appropriate for such a subject, fearful of your spending a second night in tears, and desirous of bringing an end to this hasty letter, I beg your invincible spirit to turn its power upon itself and to drive away with mature reflection the desire for tears, which I personally know is very strong. At the same time I pray to Him who, dying for our sins, gave comfort to His sorrowful mother from the cross, that as another source of consolation and mercy He may comfort you on the death of your mother.

Avignon, 14 May.

Fam. XIII, 2.

To Rinaldo da Verona, poet,* a recommendation for the young man sent to him for educating.

I believe you know the young man I recently sent you and his blood relationship to me, unless his sudden growth, as often happens at that age, perhaps made it difficult for you to recognize your pupil. If you did recognize him, you know how dear he is to me and how I desire for him to become a good man. Unfortunately he was withdrawn from your school at a tender age and was compelled to go for a short while to Giberto, the well-known grammarian of Parma. I suspect that he does have some talent, although I feel incapable of judging him; whether he is disturbed by my presence or by the awareness of his own ignorance, he always seems to withdraw into an obstinate silence when we are together. One thing he does make clear to me: I have never seen a young man with greater hatred for letters. He neither hates nor fears anyone except the book, his only enemy. You will say, "truly a bad beginning"; a bad one, I admit, but nevertheless a true one. I do not intend to compose an epic about him or to describe a distinguished young man, but simply my boy. He has been raised in Parma and Verona and for a while in Padua. I often jest sarcastically with him, saying: "Be careful that you do not deprive your neighbor, Virgil, of his fame." Keeping his eyes fixed on the ground, he suddenly blushes, something which he certainly cannot feign. There is but one hope for him: he does seem very modest, and until now flexible and suited to any kind of learning under the guidance of an understanding teacher. Among other unfortunate experiences, the following recently happened to him. At my insistence—which will astonish you—he was taken out of the schools of Parma on the threshold of puberty to come with me to the so-called Roman Curia where he has already lost a year. It is an irreparable waste of time, I confess; it is I alone who am to blame, having done so not because I agreed with the Horatian saying "Wealth first and, after the money, virtue," but because I feared something might happen to me. Deprived of my assistance he would be crushed by a harsh poverty, that enemy of studies, that obstacle no less serious than excessive wealth for those wishing to rise above

*Rinaldo Cavalchini da Villafranca (or da Verona) was a close friend of Petrarch. His respect for Rinaldo's learning resulted not only in requesting to see rare manuscripts that he possessed but also in entrusting to him the education of his son, Giovanni.

the ordinary. In fact, it is an even greater one since we can free ourselves from the weight of riches if we desire, as many illustrious men did; but it is not within our power to shake off the burden of poverty. I therefore asked him to remain with me so that his constant presence, reminding me of his situation and silently gnawing at me, might prompt me to act. Divine mercy came to the aid of human deliberation. Thus, with sufficient means he returns to you as a canon of that Verona which gave him the rudiments in his childhood. I beg you to receive him with your celebrated kindness and insist, if possible, that in the manner of wayfarers who rise late, he make up for the loss of the morning hours with afternoon haste. What more shall I say? I entrust this man to you, whom, I hope, you will return to me a better man, as Socrates promised Eschines. So that you may proceed more willingly I shall say to you what Philip said to Aristotle: I indeed rejoice that he was born in your times, since you can make something of him if any man can. Nor do I conceal from you that, in my concern for him and in carefully considering all possibilities, I could have done otherwise, yet I preferred that he stay in Verona, believing nothing more desirable than you and your virtues. Farewell.

At the source of the Sorgue, 9 June, in a haste to which my writing will bear witness.

Fam. XIII, 3.

To Guglielmo da Verona, orator, on the same subject.*

I consigned the talents of this young man to our Rinaldo for his mental development; I consign him to you for his conduct. Although either of you may rightfully assume both responsibilities, I wished to share him between two friends. I beg you to work with him; and if you discover in him some good character, nurture it. If not, try to implant in his character some adult trait pleasing to you, which you may call of your doing. In his young heart, you can easily imprint whatever you please. Let him learn to love you, to honor you, to have respect for you; just as Virgil advises, "Let him admire you from his earliest years." Nothing remains to be said; if you always esteemed me as a brother, accept him as a son, and farewell.

9 June.

*See IX, 15.

Fam. XIII, 4.

To Francesco da Napoli, Apostolic Prothonotary, * *how restless and agitated are the lives of men of affairs, and yet great glory is unattainable without great toil.*

A greater audacity may conceal or excuse a lesser one. Therefore, bear with patience, O illustrious sir, if I say to you what I recall saying recently to the greatest of men, not without his approval. Although nearly everyone envies you, I pity you; and it certainly had often come to my mind to say so, but especially so today. Though distant as I usually am, I was with you in thought; for the memory of your occupations so increased the sweetness of my solitude that, almost without realizing it, I found my hand going to the pen. I am not so uncultivated and rustic as to be ignorant of the difference between an outstanding man and an obscure one, between an illustrious man and an insignificant one. But as much as I consider your lot honored and brilliant, I think it restless and agitated as well. Almost nothing of all that seems yours is yours, and more irreparable is the fact that not even time is yours because it certainly continues to fly, not through your negligence but, in Seneca's words, through being either stolen or snatched from you and dedicated to the service of others. No day or night can be called yours; nowhere is there any peaceful retreat for you. The gardens sought as refuges and relief from toil now abound with more business than grass or flowers, with more cares than foliage. Your bedroom and your bed, invented for the refreshment of human weariness, echo continually with the discordant voices of inconsiderate men. Thousands of such voices summon you but, even worse, after your long toil, either you cannot bring to a conclusion those projects already begun or countless others immediately emerge. Thus there is no end to your labors, no ports for your storms. If you mount a swift horse, some haunting care will cling to your buttocks; if you flee on some vessel, your anxiety climbs aboard on the same ladder with you. Finally if you were to cross the sea, there you will encounter yourself once again and will feel the truth of Horace's words, that you have changed your location, but not your spirit. This then is the source of my unusual sympathy for the state of your happiness. Who has called this kind

*Francesco Calvo da Napoli was apostolic prothonotary for Clement VI and for Innocent VI from 1347 to 1359. He became papal secretary after Petrarch's first refusal of the position in 1347. Little else is known about him.

of life truly happy? Who would not instead consider your destiny pitiful, however rich it may be in comfort? It is in fact filled with toil, lacking in repose, directed toward others, forgetful of oneself; the entire lives of men of affairs are wars without a truce. Such men lack peace; while they may appear tranquil, within they are agitated. Were sleep to intrude, their minds would remain awake with images of things to be done piercing their closed eyes. Their repose is disturbed by dreams; they begin weaving inextricable webs while awake, which they finish while asleep. Frequently they never extricate themselves, whether awake or asleep, from those webs, although they have begun them and woven them at length. Such men continue rolling the eternally falling rock of Sisyphus; they are driven by the wheel of Ixion; they contend with the Hydra which is born anew with its many heads when it is believed dead. Meanwhile the years flee, sweet youth slips away, old age quickly approaches, either preceded or followed by death. What can those men do in their distress, where can they turn, with what skills can they free themselves? They feel all things vanishing in time and themselves diminishing along with them. Only their affairs seem immortal, increasing daily in their hands; in vain they seek the file or the chisel, for their cares remain adamant. While men of affairs seem indeed to acquire many things, time slips by; while they seem to do all things, they always forget the one which is perhaps the most important—living. They are everywhere but with themselves; they often speak with others but never with themselves. What the multitude calls happy is the reverse of happiness, the more so because there seems even less hope of bringing an end to their cares. Just as pain seems less when punishment is brief, so does unending torment overcome and defeat even the strongest spirits. A military general indeed toils as does the soldier, but the former anticipates a victory and a triumph, the latter the stipend of a worthy soldier and a return to his peaceful home. The peasant toils but he thinks of winter, of the feast days and of the pleasure of an over-flowing granary. The hardened sailor toils, the untiring wayfarer toils; but the anticipated end of the journey enables both to bear the burden of their immediate labors. The miner of hidden gold toils, but within the dark and forbidding caves he compensates for his brief inconvenience with the hope of great profit and for the hateful shadows with his vision of welcome light. I ask, what hope is yours? Whenever you successfully bring many things to a conclusion, you are overwhelmed by still more tasks and subject yourself to a still heavier yoke. Yours is indeed a difficult lot, since the penalty for cowardice is shame and the reward for diligence is servitude. A truly unworthy and hardly new reward, especially among those whose lives do not depend upon their own will but upon that of princes or of their country. Industry is harmful to many men; I say harmful not with respect to fame but to that leisure and peacefulness considered the most lofty and incomparable pleasure by men of letters. Alcides could have lived in peace had his unparalleled virtue not driven him, not only to his famous twelve labors, but to a thousand other kinds; Ulysses could have lived in peace had his implacable desire for knowledge not driven him to many lands and shores. A laborious virtue it is, for it allows no rest to those who possess it. I call it laborious, but it is renowned and famed, combining love and admiration with hardship. If there is truth in their stories, this drove to Troy Ulysses from the shadows of a simulated madness and Achilles from the shadows of a secret love. Intelligence was of no benefit to the former nor a mother's talents to the latter; virtue, enemy of vacillation, uncovered all pretentions. Great men, like high mountains, cannot be hidden; the man granted some unusual gift of nature will have to spend his life in perpetual toil. Were he to flee the storms of affairs they would pursue him in the midst of his solitude.

Great things are not achieved at little price. Whoever is attracted by the appearance of virtue and wishes its companionship must know that he desires the greatest of all things, not procurable at low cost but demanding one's entire self in payment. I shall mention, therefore, some well-known examples drawn from our own past which perhaps will prove rather attractive to you. Fabritius could have grown old in his home although it was very small, Curius in the garden cultivated with his own hands, Quintius Atilius Serranus in his small fields, Camillus could have spent his life in peace and his remarkable fame would not have earned him the envy of his fellow citizens and exile, had the exceptional virtue of all these men not destined them to be lifelong leaders, worthy of the republic and needed against Pyrrhus, the Samnites, the Carthaginians, the Gauls, and an aggressive host of enemies on all sides, thus compelling them to spend their lifetimes in arms. The Scipios could have lived in Rome in congenial intimacy and could have been buried in the family tomb, had their enthusiasm for virtue not caused them to be buried in foreign lands after eight years of glorious deeds and incredible hardships. What shall I say about the two Africani? The first had no fear about crossing into Africa when scarcely anyone felt safe in Italy, and returned a glorious victor from enemy lands when all others had been defeated in their native lands; the latter in Africa and Spain conquered Carthage and Numantia, the two cities causing the most harm to the Roman Empire according to Cicero, and meanwhile wandered far and wide across many provinces to his great glory. What kept Marius from leading a peaceful life if not virtue and glory, especially the former, since all the hope and resources of the state had been assigned to him, according to a famous historian? His fame led him to be pitted against the Africans, the Teutons, and the Cimbrians. At one moment you could see him leading captured rulers from the south and at another incredible lines of captives from the north before his triumphal chariot, and shortly thereafter you could see the victor himself led to prison and hidden in marshlands. You could barely listen without weariness to the many hardships he bore with unwearying courage. What shall I say of Cato? Could he not have lived in his own home? He preferred instead to cross parched deserts, subjecting his life to Libyan serpents, so great was the virtue and the love of freedom which enkindled him; for this man his home was too confining. What can be said of Pompey, great in both deeds and repute? He forsook his enormous and opulent palaces and his country, where he was a distinguished leader, to wander as a conqueror throughout the world; did he not lay aside peace for himself in order to find glory? What shall I say about the Caesars, Julius and Augustus, what about Vespasian and Titus, what about Trajan and innumerable others whom I shall not mention in order not to belabor my subject? The day is not long enough to mention all the examples from our past. Let us give too a proper place to foreigners. The illustrious citizen of Carthage, Hannibal, crossed the sea in order to become more famous, passing through Spain, France, and Italy. Leaving the Pyrenees behind, he made his way through the Alps with fire and vinegar and steel; crossing the Iber, the Rhone and the Po, he conquered the heights of the Apennines and approached even the walls of Rome herself as an awesome conqueror. Why waste time giving all his accomplishments? Though so many times a victor he was finally conquered, yet even this did not cause him to abandon hope; on his own with foreign troops he renewed the war, traversing Syria and Bithynia. His end could be attributed to fortune, but the ardor of his spirit was without doubt his own. How just he was is not the question. What I was saying, unless I am mistaken, does demonstrate that his unusual superiority among his fellow citizens resulted in his suffering many hardships and dangers. What can I say about the Spartan Leonidas, a very brave man, what of the Theban Epaminondas, the glory of his country, what of the Achaean Philopemenes, one of the greatest generals, what can I say about the Athenian Themistocles, the most illustrious man in Greece as they say? What else did virtue do for all these men except cause a troubled and agitated life? The same is true of Pyrrhus of Epirus and Alexander of Macedonia, the same of Masinissa, king of the Numidians, and of Cyrus, king of Persia, and may also be asserted about many others. Let this sampling suffice. Pythagoras could have lived on Samos, Democritus in Abdera, Plato in Athens, Varro in Rome, except that their boundless desire for learning led them through many lands. Pliny could have died in Verona and Virgil in Mantua, except that the former's desire for experience crushed him under the cinders of your Vesuvius, while the latter's drive for fame caused his great talent to be felled by a painful death. His remains, whether taken from Taranto or from Brindisi, are now in the possession of your, and his, Naples. What do you expect this rash of examples to mean? Do you believe that I am bidding you to become lazy in order to live peacefully? That is far from the truth. Not only toil, but also death with glory is far more desirable than inglorious idleness. I do mean to say, however, that glory is not by any means gratuitous, for it must be sought and preserved through much labor.

For me those men lead happier lives who, while intent on some noble study, combine moderate labor with sober pleasure; they so spend their waking hours that they enjoy a fitting and peaceful sleep, however brief. Furthermore, they keep occupied but do not exclude needed rest; they dwell alone but they can intermingle with men when the occasion requires. But if given an option, they would prefer the country to the city, solitude to the multitude. They find delight in thick forests and green meadows no less than in marble and gold palaces; they do have lofty aspirations but so seek glory that they are burdensome to no one; they pursue glory and enjoy their deserving it rather than attaining it, being prepared at any moment to lose it with equanimity, provided they are aware of nothing that could make them not deserve it. While they are oftentimes affected by a desire for fame and a reputation with future generations, they understand nothing would be lost if their names are not known to posterity, as happened to our ancestors who were never known and who "were not fewer but certainly better men" according to Cicero. Leaving empty niceties to the ladies, they delight in noble and manly things; they do not mind sleeping either in a tree's shade or on a river bank. They are able to spend happily a good part of the day amidst the grassy hills, to postpone their meal until evening, to forget the principal meal, and if the occasion arises, to spend a sleepless night with pleasure among books. They have no less love for damp caves than for beds of adorned ebony or ivory, no less love for flowering turf than for a colorful bed covered with velvet. They esteem an ingenuous poverty; they do not so much hate wealth as place little value upon it. Gold neither frightens nor attracts them, and with the same spirit they can take or leave paintings and statues, Corinthian vases, Coan gems and Sidonian clothes, considering them not ornaments to be possessed but natural or artistic masterpieces. As was once the case with our ancestors—those excellent and true men—they consider the cook the worst servant and they dare to conquer through long fastings their mouths and stomachs, as if they were insolent and lazy slaves. They delight in hard, coarse bread, made from many kinds of grain; they do not shudder at drinking the waters of a pure spring or at rustic food which they consider the spontaneous product and gift of mother earth. They do not scorn herbs, berries from bushes, and sweet fruits, and they can oftentimes lead their lives without hunting animals. To aid their weary and sluggish stomachs, they seek not abundance and soft delights, but abstinence, hunger, and exercise. Finally they will have learned not to serve their bodies but to control them with rules and regulations; I would not dare count myself among this number. I am nevertheless striving, and seem to be making some progress. To pass over other things, I do not deny that by nature I am very desirous of glory, but I have so shaped my mind with study that I would be happy to attain it if possible. Yet if it escapes me I would not be sorrowful, being prepared should fortune wish to have my name spread far and wide, and also prepared to remain unknown within the narrow confines of my little country abode. I desire to be Demosthenes by nature but Democritus by imitation. We read that the former sought fame, the latter despised it. Meanwhile in order not to allow my talent to become feeble through neglect, I exercise my eyes in reading, my fingers in writing, and my mind in meditation. Finally, I am omitting nothing within my power to achieve this goal so that, should I not succeed, I may still believe that it was for the best not to have attained it. This is my life, which I thought should be judged by you through my letter since I had no other subject on which to write. It happened by chance that when I found myself alone late one day at the spring, meditating upon many things, and my ears had been struck by the immense roaring with which the Sorgue rushes happily from its imprisoning caves abusing the cliffs around them, there suddenly came to mind the rumbling that thunders without interruption in your ears. I then said to myself: "Here you have something you may write to that distinguished man whereby he may rejoice in your solitary freedom, just as you have compassion for his splendid servitude." I might add that, if this rather uncultivated writing of mine offends your eyes, accustomed to artificial and contrived lettering, you must blame a broken country seat, thick ink, rough paper, and a rural pen. I do, however, ask for forgiveness; may your politeness have pity on my fingers. Live happily and farewell.

At the source of the Sorgue, 10 June.

Fam. XIII, 5.

To Francesco, of the Church of the Holy Apostles,* concerning his misfortunes in the Roman Curia, and concerning the three styles.

Listen to a story worthy of tears and laughter. I was summoned to the Curia, this Curia which is not in the least Roman except in name; I came without knowing everything being plotted against me. Had I known, I would never have come, believe me. "Well then," you may say, "what dragged you there?" To be perfectly honest, nothing more than affection for my friends. I have long since put an end to most of my greediness; that is why I am now more preoccupied with abandoning and distributing the spoils of fortune than with increasing them, that is why I have absolutely nothing in common with the Curia. Never have our ways been in accord. If greed ever was a part of me, it has vanished. If hope is joined to it, it often keeps us in undesirable places, for hope and greed form a chain that overcomes the human spirit, snatching it from the control of reason and causing it to suffer many harsh and unworthy indignities. I came then not because of greed or any expectation but because of love, as I said. I came, however, knowledgeable about the place, unaware of the reason for my coming, and yet not unmindful of Seneca's words: "The shame lies not in going, but in being coaxed into going, saying with astonishment in the midst of whirling affairs, 'How did I ever get here?'" I clearly recalled these words; nothing came to mind more frequently in my deliberation about the journey. But what was I to do? I was being eagerly summoned by those two princes of the church whom the Dominican flock of the Lord now possesses as two powerful bulls grazing far and wide in the pastures of Christ: to one of them I was obliged for past favors, to the other for an unexpected and unusual kindness toward a man unknown to him except by reputation. To scorn their summons would have seemed arrogance since kings and princes venerate them, and especially since their words are said to carry pontifical authority. If I were then what I desire and strive to become, and to be perfectly honest, what I still hope to be, I could have scorned everything in order to preserve my peace of mind. But you will hear not what I ought to have done but what I did do. Will you believe it? Upon my arrival, the entire scenario of intrigues became evident to me. It would be a long tale to relate the various subterfuges which caused a year to elapse,

*See XII, 4.

despite my indignation and the embarrassment of my friends, in a place where I really did not wish to be. Everyone strove with all his might to make me wealthy, though busy and troubled; instead I became poor, miserable, and sad. Alone, I bitterly resisted, refusing the yoke of gold that was really nothing more than wood or lead. I called God and men to witness that they were depriving me of my freedom and peace, the only desire given me by nature and the only happiness granted me by fortune, that they were depriving me of all joy, all sweetness in life, and my literary pleasures, however modest, without which I despair of being able to live; I called them to witness that I had been a despiser of gold throughout my youth when I possessed it in moderate quantities and that I never had great need of it over a long period of time—if anything within the confines of this mortal life deserves to be called long-lasting. I called them to witness that the thirst for gold would appear shameful in me, now that I have it in sufficient quantity and have reached an age which usually softens and tempers desires, which considers greed even more disgraceful the briefer and the less the need for it; I called them to witness that a wayfarer ought to base his desire on the remaining distance of his road and that I am by now in my sunset hours with the thorny portions of the road behind me, and must consider my final destination more than the road itself. To these thoughts I added that, when I did have needier friends, my affection for them seemed to justify my eagerness and ambition for possessions. First among them was my brother, who then needed a great deal but now needs nothing, since he has truly come to despise everything in the name of Christ. I called them to witness that the needs of my dear ones have been resolved in part by death, in part by a kinder fortune, in part by religious poverty. Now, nearly alone and advanced in years, I would certainly appear shameful and unworthy of my name if I were to begin seeking still more wealth when as a young man, poorer and with dependents, I had no desire for it. I have what I consider sufficient, but that could swiftly disappear if the access to greed tempts me, for with wealth I will be subject to serious needs and concerns. Finally I prayed and implored them to allow me to finish my life's course in my own fashion, and not to cast so many obstacles before my tired feet, so near to their goal. Let them spare me any labor, let them spare my honor, so that I might not to my disgrace change the direction of my studies and make of myself a sad spectacle of senile greed. Let them not force me to spend a wretched and servile old age with those very companions with whom I passed a joyful and carefree youth; it is useless to seek with zeal unnecessary toil and reasons for toil. For them and for me, ultimate peace was at hand; that very day which makes them so restless could perhaps be the last, or surely not too far from the last. She who imposes an end to men's troubles and empty desires is fast approaching.

Such things I used to say, often angrily, often lamentfully and almost in tears. Pitted against me, however, was an obstinate band of friends, the advice and entreaties of many others, and the opinion of the multitude continually focused on earthly matters. Meanwhile I had come to the feet of him who opens the heavens with his fingers and tempers the stars with his miter. He appeared to rejoice at my arrival, but his words on many subjects clearly revealed that he was thinking of the impression on others and not of my freedom. To make a long story short, by myself I was unequal to the many persistent and eloquent men; nearly overcome and dejected, I was on the verge of submitting to the yoke when fortune came to my rescue. They had a certain esteem for my rather effective eloquence but even more for my capacity for confidentiality and trustworthiness. Let the sources of that reputation determine how true it is! Thus, I seemed suitable for guarding the pontiff's secrets for which purpose I had been summoned. They believed that just one obstacle stood in the way: my style might be too lofty for the humility required of the Roman See. Upon learning this from men particularly concerned about my situation, I was at first truly astonished. I feared they might ironically be ridiculing my humility, which I am aware resides not only in my speech but also in many other things. Subsequently it was confirmed by solemn assurances that the pontiff and the College of Cardinals so viewed me; they expected one thing of me, that I should, in their own words, humble my talents and subdue my style. When I heard this, not only from my two sponsors but from many princes of the church, I was filled with a joy that can only be experienced by a prisoner seeing an unexpected liberator on the threshold of his hateful prison. For I imagined a possible avenue of escape, and I was not wrong. I was asked then to write something to demonstrate how near I could fly to the earth by adapting humble ideas, for the men who had been pushing me into a truly lofty, but narrow, prison had firmly asserted that this would be easy for me. As soon as they gave me a subject on which to write, I unfurled the wings of my feeble talent, making every effort to rise far above the earth. As Ennius and after him Maro state, I flew so high as not to be seen, if that were possible, by those who had led me into captivity. You would think that the Muses were present, although it was hardly a Pierian labor, and that our Apollo was giving me protection. What I had written was considered insufficiently intelligible for the most part, although it was really very clear; by some, it was viewed as Greek or some barbarian tongue. Imagine the kind of men in charge of the highest matters!

We know that according to Cicero there are really three kinds of styles that he calls figures: the sublime, which he calls serious, the moderate, which he calls ordinary, and the humble, which he calls tenuous. In our day, the first is scarcely used by anyone, the second by a few and the last by many. Any style beneath these three certainly does not reach any level of artistic eloquence, but is rather a simple effusion of plebeian or rustic or servile words; although it may have grown over a thousand years through continuous usage, it still will never gain through the passage of time the dignity that it lacks by nature. In my opinion, if I appropriately turn to a humble style in writing a letter, it is a good thing. If anyone should urge me to ascend, I see the steps which must be climbed, and, despite the slowness of my talents, I can strive to achieve it. But if I am ordered to descend, standing as I do on the lowest step, I lack the capacity to obey. What therefore do they ask of me? Certainly what they order me to use, what they themselves call style, is not style. What indeed, I ask, would Juvenal now say, who laments the lost hope for serious studies in his own day? What would the great orator Seneca say, who laments the serious deterioration of eloquence after Cicero? What would the great flower of eloquence, Cicero himself, say, who even in his own day bemoans somewhere in his works the downfall of eloquence? It is fortunate that they, who viewed even the least fall from the highest style a precipitous one, do not hear such absurdities. To return to my situation, that is how it all happened. I have been given time to learn what I truly wish not to know, namely, to write frivolously, emptily, and abjectly; as an old man I am ordered to frequent the school that I always fled as a young man. But it is turning out well. For the moment, I am free, with those who had wished me to become a slave painfully conceding. If my expectation is realized, I shall be eternally free, far more happy with my freedom for having been so close to slavery. Let me add that liberty is all the sweeter the nobler its cause; my sole fear is that my liberty may not be real. But if it is, what more wonderful thing could I have desired than to obtain my freedom because I appeared too lofty to satisfy those who view themselves as the loftiest? I take delight in being so, if it is so; if not, why not desire to become so since the reason for it lies in loftiness and not in obscurity? It gives me pleasure to be noticed by few men; and the fewer they are, the more I take pride in myself. I do not wish dignity or wealth to be of any assistance to my reader; I wish that a pontiff or a king or anyone else pay equal attention to me, but especially someone who happens to have less talent. I shall repeat here one fitting example which I offered quite insistently as a counterargument to the insistent pontiff. You recall that Alexander the Macedonian requested his geometry teacher to explain more clearly some of the more abstruse axioms of his subject. His teacher replied, "These matters are equally obscure for everyone." Very elegantly put, for it is not a crown but intelligence aided by study that makes writings intelligible; otherwise, it would be preferable to be a monarch. There is much that majesty and empire not only do not aid but often greatly hinder. I am unworthy of a truly great and august reader; nor do I believe in impressing fastidious minds or delicate ears. If I am read and not rejected by humble men, I enjoy the choicest fruits of my study; I do not labor to be obscure, but to be clear, for I wish to be understood by those possessing intelligence, and even by these through a mental effort and application that is cheerful and not grudging. I do not exclude the wealthy man, if he willingly does this in the knowledge that his wealth is of no avail. What more can I say? If I were writing to anyone else, I would not be so indiscreet; but in writing now to my Francesco, I am writing to myself. I wish my reader, whoever he may be, to consider me alone, and not his daughter's marriage, not a night with his lady friend, not the wiles of his enemy, not his security or his home, not his land or his money. Even as he reads me, I want him to be with me; if he is pressed by affairs, let him defer his reading. When he decides to read what I write, he must lay aside the burden of his affairs and the anxieties of his home life in order to direct his attention to what is before his eyes. If these conditions do not please him, let him stay away from my useless writings. I refuse to have him simultaneously carry on his business and study; I refuse to allow him to learn without labor what I wrote with labor. But are you awaiting my conclusion? Finally, with difficulty, I obtained permission to live as I wish. Moreover, I intend to make use of it so that henceforth I shall put no one's judgment before my own in matters of supreme importance; I shall not bow to the pleas of friends; I shall never again allow my liberty to be jeopardized by any expectation or any hope for reward. I wished you, my dear friend, to know this so that you may both cry and laugh at my present state of affairs, so that you too may render thanks to Him who freed me from an opulent and splendid, yet painful, slavery that so many willingly embrace. Farewell.

9 August.

Fam. XIII, 6.

To the same correspondent,* concerning the manner in which poetry is profaned by the multitude and by the ignorant.

What could you expect to hear from me if not a continuation of my last letter, whose purpose was to make you weep and laugh? Certainly I have nothing more pressing to do at the present time; or rather I would have much, but lack of time prevents me from turning to more important ones, and even the little I have is not free, but full of unbelievable interruptions. I am constantly in motion amidst incessant noise, and am simultaneously here, elsewhere, and, therefore, nowhere—a common malady in those who continually move around. After my recent departure from Babylon, I stopped at the source of the Sorgue, my well-known port in stormy moments. Here I am awaiting my traveling companions and the end of autumn, or at least the season described by Maro when "the day now becomes shorter and the summer milder." In the meantime, then, lest my rural sojourn be wasted, I am gathering fragments of past meditations in order to add something each day to my major works, if possible, or to complete some minor one. What I intend to write today you will find set forth in this letter: poetry, a divine gift granted to few, has begun nowadays to be dishonored, not to say profaned and prostituted. Nothing makes me more indignant, and knowing your tastes I realize that you too, my dear friend, cannot bear this debasement. Never in Athens or in Rome, never in the days of Homer and Virgil, was there so much discussion as in this age on the banks of the Rhone; yet never was there a time or a place when in my opinion so little was understood about it. I wish you to soothe your anger with laughter and learn lightheartedness in your sadness. Recently there came to the Curia Nicola di Lorenzo—I should not say that he came but that he was led there captive—once a truly feared tribune of the city of Rome yet now the most miserable of men. What is even worse, miserable though he is, I know not whether he is worthy of pity. While he might have died with great glory on the Capitoline, he instead suffered imprisonment in Bohemia and shortly afterward in Limoges, to his shame and that of the Roman name, and even to that of the republic. How involved my pen was in praising and advising him is better known than I would perhaps wish. I loved his virtue, I praised his aims, I admired his spirit. I rejoiced with Italy, and I foresaw the sovereignty of the

*See XII, 4.

Holy City and peace throughout the entire world. I was unable to conceal my joy that sprang from so many sources. I seemed a participant in all this glory by sending him words of encouragement in his endeavors, words that he felt very strongly, according to the reports of his messengers and indications in his letters. All the more eagerly, I tried to think of ideas to enkindle his fervent spirit. Since I knew very well that nothing fires a noble heart more than glory and praise, I would include praises, perhaps overdone in the minds of many but truly warranted in my opinion; commending him on his accomplishments I would encourage him to other endeavors. I still have a number of my letters to him for which I feel no regrets; unaccustomed as I am to being a prophet, I indeed wish that he had not tried to be one! In any event, what he was doing and seemed about to do at the time I was writing him certainly deserved, not only my praise and admiration, but that of all mankind. I know not, then, whether these letters merit destruction simply because he preferred to live shamefully than to die honorably; but one ought not to deliberate on impossible things. Although I would very much like to destroy the letters, I shall be unable to do so; once in the public domain, they are no longer within my control. Therefore I shall continue my account.

He who filled evil men throughout the world with terror and fear, he who gave good men the most joyful hope and expectation, entered the Curia humble and despised. He who was once accompanied by the entire Roman populace and by the foremost citizens of Italian cities was unhappily walking hither and yon, accompanied by two guards, through a crowd eager to see the face of the man whose name was recently so celebrated. Moreover, he had been sent by the Roman king to the Roman pontiff. What an astonishing affair! I dare not say what followed, nor did I wish to say this much; instead I shall continue where I left off. Upon his arrival, then, the pontiff immediately assigned three princes of the church to hear his case. Their assignment was "to decide the appropriate punishment for a man who wished the republic to be free." *O tempora, o mores*—as I am compelled to exclaim again and again! I admit that he is indeed worthy of every kind of punishment, because what he wished he did not wish with as much persistence as he should have and as circumstances and necessity required. After his self-proclamation as the champion of freedom, he released all the enemies of liberty, still armed, when he might have crushed them—an opportunity fortune rarely grants to any commander. O fearful and hideous mist that veils the eyes of mortals in the midst of their greatest undertakings!

Had he decided to exercise only one of his surnames and not the one necessary for the well-being of the republic (he wished to be called both Severe and Clement), if then he had exercised only his clemency against the country's murderers, he could have kept them alive, after having deprived them of all their instruments for doing harm, and, above all, disarmed them of their arrogant skills. Thus they would either have become citizens of the city of Rome instead of its enemies, or despicable enemies to be scorned rather than feared. I recall having written him at that time a letter expressing concern about this; had he paid attention to it, the affairs of state would now be quite different and today Rome would not be enslaved nor he a captive. Certainly neither in what I have said nor in what follows can I find any way to excuse him. Not long after he had undertaken the protection of good men and the expulsion of evil ones, he suddenly changed his mind and conduct. He began seeking the favor of evil men, placing total credence in them, to the great peril and fear of good men. (He perhaps knew the reason for this, for I afterward saw no more of him. The fact remains that the reason for doing evil, even though it may be defended by eloquent men, can never be truly justified.) Would that he had not chosen the worst of evil men! Indeed I wrote him another letter about this when his shaky government had not yet collapsed. But enough of this, for I speak too passionately, interrupting the separate stages of my account and saddened, as you see, to have placed my last hope for Italian liberty in that man whom I had long known and loved. Once he had dedicated himself to such an undertaking, I had allowed myself to cherish and admire him above all others. Therefore the more I had hoped in him, the more I now grieve for my last hope, and I confess that, however this may all end, I cannot but marvel at the way it began. However, he arrived unshackled, spared of this public shame; yet he was so guarded that there was no hope of escape. Upon entering the city that unfortunate prisoner asked whether I was in the Curia, either because he perhaps expected some kind of assistance from me—which I know fully well I could never offer—or simply because he recalled our old friendship which began there long before. Now the welfare of this man, on whom the safety and well-being of many people used to depend, lies in others' hands. Both his life and his reputation hang in balance. Do not be surprised if you hear him declared in a ringing judgment guilty of infamy or sentenced to death. Indeed every human being, even the holiest, is subject to death, yet virtue fears neither death nor infamy. It is inviolable, not subject to any injustice or weapon. Would that he had not marred his dignity through idleness or through change of purpose! He would then have had nothing to fear from this sentence except corporal suffering, although even now nothing can diminish his reputation among those who weigh true glory and false disgrace on the basis of valid evidence rather than common opinion, and who measure the deeds of illustrious men according to their basic virtue rather than fortune's will. That this is so may be seen by the nature of the crime of which he has been accused. He is not being blamed for what good men dislike in him; and he is considered guilty not for the outcome of his endeavors but for their initiation. Nor is he accused of favoring evildoers, or forsaking liberty, of fleeing the Capitoline when nowhere else could he have lived more nobly or have died more gloriously. What is it then? Only one charge is directed against him, and if he is condemned for it, he will, at least for me, be not infamous but worthy of eternal glory. The crime is that he dared to have wanted the republic safe and free, and to have all matters dealing with the Roman Empire and Roman power dealt with in Rome. O crime worthy of the cross and of vultures, that a Roman citizen should grieve to see his land, the rightful mistress of all others, enslaved to the basest of men! This indeed is the nature of his crime, this is why his punishment is sought.

In this state of affairs, so that you may finally realize why I began as I did, wishing to offer you laughter after pain or sorrow, I have learned from friends' letters that one hope of rescue remains for him; there is a widespread report that he is an outstanding poet and that therefore it is terrible to punish a man dedicated to such sacred studies. They use that famous argument, among the common people, that Cicero used before the judges in defense of Aulus Licinius Archias, his teacher. I have not included the oration here since you possess it and eagerly read it, as is evident from your letters. Long ago I brought it back from the farthest reaches of Germany during a visit in my youth when I satisfied my longing to see those regions. Some time afterward, I sent it to you in your country because of your desire to see it. What more can I now say? I certainly rejoice and am delighted more than I can say that the Muses are still held in such esteem, and what is more astonishing, by those very men who are ignorant of them, and that merely mentioning them can save a man otherwise disliked by his judges. Could they have expected anything more under Caesar Augustus, when they enjoyed the highest esteem and when poets from every land gathered in Rome to view the face of that distinguished ruler, friend of poets and master of kings? I ask, what greater tribute could then have been afforded the Muses than to have saved from death a man, I know not how worthy of hatred yet certainly hated, I know not guilty of what crime yet found guilty, convicted, self-confessed, and by unanimous vote of the judges condemned to capital punishment. Again I shall repeat that I rejoice, and congratulate him and the Muses: him for having such protection, the Muses for enjoying such honor. Nor do I envy the saving name of poet to a defendant in an extreme situation with scarcely any hope. Yet if you ask my opinion, Nicola di Lorenzo is a very eloquent man, most persuasive, with a bent for oratory, even a pleasant and charming writer capable of delightful and colorful thoughts, though they are not many. I believe he has read all the poets who are commonly known. Still he is no more a poet than he is a weaver because he is wearing a mantle woven by others' hands. Writing one poem is insufficient to merit the name of poet, and that saying of Horace is very true, "You will not grant that to weave a verse is enough, nor will you consider that man a poet who writes poetic prose, like mine." Cola, however, never composed even one poem as far as I know; nor did he ever apply his mind to it, without which nothing, however easy, can be done well. I wanted to tell you this so that you may grieve at the ill fortune of the former defender of the republic, that you may rejoice over his unexpected release, that you may with me become equally indignant and amused about the reason for that release. If—were it only true!— Nicola escapes beneath the shield of poetry from such great perils, from what could Virgil not have escaped? But Virgil would perish for another reason at the hands of such judges since he was considered a necromancer and not a poet. I shall say something that will make you laugh even more. I myself, the greatest enemy of divination and magic, am oftentimes called necromancer by these excellent judges because of my admiration for Virgil. How low our studies have sunk! O hateful and laughable nonsense! So you may understand everything about varying tastes and may conceive how to judge inferiors by an example from superiors, I shall add something that is plainly ridiculous.

In Babylon I have a great friend whom I particularly cherish—to use the ancient and ingenuous manner of speaking with which Cicero intimately alluded to the great Pompey and with which Pliny the Younger greeted his Vespasian. For if the contemporary sort of servile and flattering style must be used, I do have a unique and venerable master. Nevertheless, however I shall express it, the truth remains that he is one in a million, a leader among leaders, most distinguished among the greatest men, an acclaimed honor of the

Sacred College, a man of rare prudence in whose counsel may easily be seen the ability to rule the entire world, and furthermore extremely well-read with a rare intelligence. But Sallust's words are also true: "Intelligence avails where you apply your mind." Thus, that illustrious man, in the intimate conversations with which he often deigns to honor me, each time mention was made of someone who had learned to address a few words to the public or, spurred by necessity, to write a letter with relative ease, would to my surprise and astonishment ask me the following question: Is this man of whom we speak a poet? I would remain silent, for what else could I possibly do? Several times he asked about some scholastics who write in a kind of stupid and disgusting style rather than with care. Once, I tried with difficulty to repress my laughter; being a sensitive man, he noticed the expression on my face, and began demanding even more insistently an explanation. Whereupon with the intimacy I usually enjoy in speaking with him about any subject—as was his desire—I respectfully reproved in a man of his intelligence his ignorance of something so beautiful. He did not know even the first and most general principles of an art in which we know the masters of the world at one time exercised their lofty talents with passion and constancy despite their involvement in public affairs. After offering him several examples doubtless familiar to you, I concluded by demonstrating to him that poets are far fewer than he thought. Because of the lack of time I briefly discussed with him the beginnings of poetry, its development and purpose, and above all the incredible rarity of true poets. This latest point was touched upon by Cicero in his *De oratore*. When the cardinal, so learned in other matters but so unlearned in these, had attentively listened, he seemed to embrace my words eagerly, often repeating certain ones, and after that day abstained from asking this type of question.

Meanwhile live happily and farewell; and unless you think otherwise, send today's letter and yesterday's, after reading them, to Naples to our Zanobi so that he and my Barbato, if perchance he has returned from the haven of Sulmona to the storms of Naples, may also enjoy our laughter and indignation.

At the source of the Sorgue, 10 August.

Fam. XIII, 7.

To Pierre, Abbot of St-Bénigne, * *concerning the same matter and the incurable mania for writing.*

Incredible as it may seem, I desire to write but I know not about what or to whom to write. Nevertheless, like an unyielding passion, paper, pen, ink, and nightly vigils are more pleasing to me than sleep and repose. What more can I say? Except when writing, I am always tormented and sluggish, whence (strangely enough) I feel belabored while at rest and rested while at labor. When my heart, so hard that you may think it born from the stones of Deucalion, is totally immersed in parchment and wearies my fingers and eyes, it feels no cold or heat; then does it seem covered by the softest blanket, and fearing to be uncovered it clings to my limbs though they refuse to obey. Once necessity compels it to quit, it begins at first to feel weariness, and subsequently has moments of idleness as a sluggish and overladen donkey ordered to climb a rugged mountain. Soon it resumes its work as eagerly as the tired donkey returns to his filled manger, and it finds refreshment in long nocturnal studies no less than does the donkey in his fodder and repose. What therefore can be done, since I can neither cease writing nor endure rest? I shall write you not because these things are of special concern to you but because I know of no one presently as close to me as you are, no one more eager for new information, especially with regard to me, no one more curious about obscure matters, better informed about difficult matters, more desirous of considering unbelievable things. You have already heard something of my state and my anxious mind; now I shall insert a short tale that will astonish you still more, in order to prove I was telling the truth. I had a friend who could not be dearer to me. At the time I had undertaken my *Africa* with a spirit that burned more than Africa ever does during the dog days, a work that has now long weighed heavily upon me and will alone, I believe, either lessen or quench the thirst in my heart, if there is any hope for that. Seeing me exhausted by excessive labor, he unexpectedly sought me out, asking a favor he said was very simple for me and pleasing to him. Unaware of his purpose I agreed, unable to deny him anything and knowing that he would only ask for something with the friendliest spirit. Instead he said, "Give me the

*Pierre de Rainzeville d'Auvergne was the seventh abbot of the Benedictine monastery, St-Bénigne, near Dijon. He was a member of the suite of Cardinal Gui de Boulogne.

keys to your cabinet." Surprised, I gave them to him, and immediately he closed all my books, gathered all my writing materials, put them in the cabinet, carefully locked it, and departed saying, "I want you to take a ten-day vacation and I bid you herewith not to read or write during this period." I recognized the trick. He thought I would remain idle, but he had actually left me crippled. What do you think happened? That day passed with great weariness as though it were longer than a year, and the next day I suffered a headache from morning to evening; when the third day dawned I began to feel a slight fever. When he heard about it, he returned and gave back the keys. Thereupon I immediately became well, and in the realization that I was actually nourished by work, as he put it, he restrained from making a similar request again. What, then, can I say? Is it not true that, as with other things, the passion for writing is incurable, as the Satirist asserts and, I must add, that it is also contagious? How many others do you think I, who am speaking to you, have infected with the same disease? Within our memory those who would write in this vein were rare indeed. Now there is no one who does not write this way and few who write on other matters. The blame, in the case of our contemporaries, according to some, rests in no small measure with me. Indeed I had heard this from many sources. But may it so happen that my prayer for deliverance from other diseases of the mind be answered, since I hold no hope for this one. Warned and, as it were, alerted in a thousand little ways I recently began to realize the truth that in an attempt to benefit myself I have inadvertently hurt myself and many others. Perhaps, then, the complaint lodged against me some time ago by the head of a family is justified. Sad and nearly in tears, he unexpectedly came to me and said, "Although I have always respected your name, see what you have given me in return; you are the cause of my only son's destruction." At first I was shocked and ashamed. The man's age and the expression on his face, indicating considerable grief, touched my spirit. When I had recovered, I replied that I knew neither him nor his son, as was the case. "What does it matter," answered the old man, "whether you knew him? He certainly knew you, and though committed to the study of civil law at great expense to me, he says that he prefers to follow in your footsteps. And thus I have lost all hope, while he, I predict, will become neither a lawyer nor a poet." At his words, I laughed, as did those with me; and he departed unamused in the least. Now I realize that I should have shown compassion and offered advice rather than laugh at him, and that his complaints and those of others like him are not unjustified. Furthermore, in the past young men of standing used to write for their convenience or that of friends about personal matters or business or the clatter and activities of the gossiping public. Now we are all doing the same thing, now the words of Horace are true, "Whether learned or unlearned, indiscriminately we are writing poetry." It is hardly any consolation to discover many partners in one's ills; I would prefer to be alone in my illness. Now I am engaged both in my own and in others' ills, and if I desire to breathe I am not allowed to do so. Every day letters and poems rain down upon my head from every corner of the world. What is more, I am bombarded by storms of letters from many foreigners, not only French but Greek, German, and British, asking me to judge all kinds of talents, though ignorant of myself. If I answer each one, I am the busiest of mortals; if I condemn them, I am a bitter critic; if I praise them, I am a flatterer and a liar; if I am silent, I am insolent and proud. They fear, I believe, that my illness progresses too slowly. Their pressures on the one hand and my ardor on the other shall soon satisfy their desires. All this would be of small concern, were it not that—who would believe it?—this latent disease very recently invaded even the Roman Curia. What do you think lawyers and doctors are doing? They no longer know Justinian and Aesculapius; they do not hear the moans of clients and patients; they have become deaf because they are hypnotized by the names of Homer and Virgil and wander through the wooded vales of Cirra to the murmur of the Aonian spring.

Why dwell on lesser wonders? Carpenters, fullers, and farmers have forsaken their plows and other tools of their trades to discuss the Muses and Apollo. I cannot tell you the extent of this pestilence, which until recently plagued only a few. The reason, if you were to ask, is that poetry is very sweet to the taste but capable of being grasped by very few minds, requiring a negligence and selective contempt for all things, together with an enlightened, abstract mind and an appropriate personality. Therefore, as experience and the authority of the most learned men have proven, in no other art is study to less avail. As a result—something perhaps humorous to you, but disgusting to me—you may see all the poets on the streets but almost none on Helicon, because all taste Pierian honey on their lips but no one digests it. Imagine, moreover, the great delight that art can give to its true possessors if it so delights those who dream about it, compelling them despite their busy life and greed to become oblivious of their affairs and of their wealth! Amidst the many vanities of our age and the great waste of time, the only thing over which I rejoice with my native land is that in it, amidst useless tares and sterile oats strewn throughout the world, there have arisen a number of fortunate and talented young people who, unless I am mistaken, can drink to advantage from the Castalian fount. I also rejoice with you, O Mantua beloved of the Muses, with Padua and Verona and Vicenza and my Sulmona, and with Naples, the Virgilian domicile, when elsewhere I see new flocks of poetasters always parched and thirsty, wandering widely over uncertain paths. As I said, my conscience disturbs me in this matter as though I alone supplied most of the stimulation to all this madness and did harm by example, although that is not the worst kind of harm. And I fear lest the laurel leaves that I plucked too eagerly and prematurely from their branches caused false dreams to emerge from the ivory portals for me and for many others in the darkness of an autumn night, even though they are said to make dreams come true. But it is as it should be; I am being punished for my own crimes. I seethe in my own home, scarcely daring to go out in public. From all directions, raving men hasten to meet me, inquiring, grasping, preaching, disputing, quarreling, saying things which the Mantuan shepherd and the old Maionian never knew. I am astonished, I laugh, I commiserate, I become indignant, and ultimately I fear that in the end magistrates may well seize me in the name of the law, accusing me of corrupting the state.

But where am I heading? A while ago I was saying there was nothing to write; here you now see a letter composed of mere trifles. I said I knew not to whom I should write; you seemed most suitable for reading these trifles. If you ask why, I have already given you one reason, and now add another: you will certainly be more apt to forgive me, to return to the serious from the ludicrous, if, besieged and overwhelmed by poems and poets from all over the world, I answer in a straightforward manner the letters from you and from our common lord which were sent to me en route. In the letters I noticed the most evident signs of benevolence and of your love, and I have followed the suggestions and advice contained therein. Since your authoritative word reaching me as I was about to depart, I postponed my journey, waiting anxiously as long as possible, but not, as God is my witness, because of the hope offered by the letters. I am not afraid to boast to you that no man is less subject to that passion than I. Indeed I hope for practically nothing, and you know the reason: I also desire almost nothing. I waited, however, to see at least once before my departure the face of that worthy and excellent man, not to mention yours. I surmised that once departed I would suffer a long and unpleasant desire to see him. Thus I wasted two months waiting where your letters reached me. When I was finally overcome by the tediousness of the Curia, I gave up, I confess, and departed, but no further than to that solitude I enjoy at the source of the Sorgue, which usually affords me relaxation in pleasing contrast to the weariness caused by the labors of the Curia. So here I am, and here I shall await you unless some urgent necessity arises. Here indeed I have spent many years since childhood, and though I know not why—whether because the air attracts minds less capable of fleeting thoughts or because it admits no foreign breezes, situated as it is in a closed valley—no one has yet become a poet through contact with me. The only exception is a peasant of mine who, though old, has begun "to dream of twin-peaked Parnassus," as Persius says. Should it begin to spread, we are lost: shepherds, fishermen, hunters, plowmen, and the oxen themselves will low and ruminate only poetry. Stay well, remember me and farewell.

Fam. XIII, 8.

To Francesco, of the Church of the Holy Apostles,* concerning his rustic and solitary way of life.

I am spending the summer at the source of the Sorgue. What now follows you would understand without a further word from me; but if you wish me to speak, I shall briefly do so. I have declared war on my body. May He be my witness without whose assistance I would fall, for I feel that my gullet, belly, tongue, ears, and eyes often seem wicked enemies and not fitting parts of my body. Indeed I recall that many of my misfortunes occurred because of them, particularly because of my eyes, which have always led me into some trouble. I have thus closed them, so that they behold barely anything but the heavens, mountains, and springs; they do not behold gold or gems, ivory or fine clothes; they do not see any horses except the two humble ones that carry me and my one servant around these valleys. Finally, they look upon no woman's face except that of my overseer's wife. If you were to see her face, you would seem to be looking upon a Libyan or Ethiopian desert, a face thoroughly parched and deeply sunburnt, without any vestige of energy or freshness. If Helen, daughter of Tyndareus, had had a similar face, Troy would still be standing; or if Lucretia and Virginia had had it, Tarquinius would not have been driven from his kingdom, while Appius would not have ended his life in prison. Yet I should not wish this description of her face to deprive her of praises worthy of her behavior, for I must say that her spirit is as pure as her face is dark. This is a fine proof that female ugliness is not at all harmful to the spirit. I could perhaps say a few words on this subject were it not that Seneca exhaustively treated it in letters about his Claranus. My housekeeper has a unique quality: although a shapely figure, rather than a masculine one, is considered a feminine asset, she feels so little this lack of shapeliness that you would think her ugliness becomes her. I know of no one more faithful, more humble, more devoted; under the hottest sun, when crickets scarcely tolerate the heat, she works entire days in the fields defying Cancer and Leo with her hardened skin. This little old lady returns late to her home and turns her unwearied and unconquered little body to household tasks, so that you could say she resembles a young girl just out of bed. Meanwhile there is no murmur, no complaint, no sign of a troubled mind, but instead an incredible concern for her husband and children, for

*See XII, 4.

my household and my guests, and complete disregard for herself. For this ironlike woman the earth covered with brush serves as her bed; hard bread is her food, and wine that resembles vinegar mixed with water is her drink. If she is offered something more delicate, she considers anything too dainty as disagreeable because of her long deprivation. But enough about my housekeeper, whose description could have been found only in a letter from the country. In this fashion, therefore, I mortify my eyes. What shall I say about my ears? Where is the sweetness of songs, of the pipe and of the lyre, which so profoundly enraptures me? The breeze has dispersed all such sweetness; now I hear nothing but the occasional bellowing of oxen or bleating of sheep, or the songs of birds or the continuous murmur of waters. What about my tongue, with which I often cheered myself and sometimes perhaps others? Now it lies still from morning often into evening, for it has no one to converse with except myself. Now indeed I have so disciplined my palate and my stomach that my plowman's bread often suffices, often even gives me pleasure; and when servants bring me white bread from elsewhere I let them eat it. This custom has now become a delight for me. My overseer, a most devoted servant and a man of iron, argues with me only over the fact that my food, as he says, is too coarse for anyone to bear for long. On the other hand, I feel that I can tolerate such food better than delicacies, which the Satirist says are very boring, and tolerable only for five days. Grapes, figs, nuts, and almonds are my delight, and I take great pleasure in the little fish with which this river abounds. Never do they delight me more than when they are freshly caught; I love to watch them and love to catch them with hooks and nets. What shall I say about my clothing and my footwear? They have all changed. No longer do I wear my usual clothing; I say "my" because of their exceptional rareness with which, I hope within the limits of modesty and propriety, I once liked to appear conspicuous among my peers. You would call me a farmer or a shepherd, though I still do not lack finer apparel. The only reason for the change is that what I once liked I now dislike. Untied are the chains that used to bind me, and closed are the eyes that I used to wish to please. I believe that they would not have their customary hold on me even were they open. I please my eyes in no way more than in being unattached and free. What shall I say about my dwelling? Where I live with one dog and only two servants you would consider the home of Cato or Fabritius. I sent the others to Italy; I wish I had sent them all to India so that they would never return to me since they cause the only storms that disrupt my peace!

My overseer has a cottage close by and is always available when he is needed. Lest his availability ever become tedious, I shall soon separate his lodgings from mine with a small gate.

Here I have acquired two small gardens perfectly suited to my skills and taste. To attempt a description for you would be too long. In short, I believe that no similar spot exists in all the world, and, to confess my unmanly fickleness, I regret only that it is not in Italy. I customarily call it my transalpine Helicon. The one garden is very shady, suitable only for study and sacred to our Apollo. It overhangs the source of the Sorgue, and beyond it lies nothing but ravines and cliffs, remote and accessible only to wild beasts or birds. The other garden, near the house, appears more cultivated, and is a delight to Bacchus. This one, astonishing as it may seem, is in the midst of the very beautiful and swift-running river. Nearby, divided from it by a very small bridge on the further side of the house, hangs a curved vault of native rock that now provides shelter against the summer heat. It is a place that inspires studies, and I suspect is not too dissimilar to the little hall where Cicero used to declaim his orations, except that his did not have a Sorgue flowing alongside. Under this vault, therefore, I spend my afternoons, and my mornings on the hillsides; the evenings I spend in the meadows or in my less cultivated garden at the source where my efforts have conquered nature and cleared a spot under the high cliff in the midst of the waters, narrow indeed but very inspiring, in which even a sluggish mind can rise to the noblest thoughts. What then? I assure you that I could perhaps settle here, except that it is so far from Italy and so near Avignon. Why should I conceal my two weaknesses? My love of Italy charms and tempts me, my hatred of Avignon stings and revolts me, along with its horrible odor that plagues the entire world. Is it any wonder that its excessive proximity pollutes the harmless purity of this country place? I feel the stench driving me away. Now you know my present condition. I wish nothing more than to see once again you and my few remaining friends, I fear nothing more than a return to the cities. Farewell.

Fam. XIII, 9.

To Zanobi, Florentine grammarian,* felicitations to him and to other friends who had followed his advice.

It is not easy to express how much I appreciate your esteem for me. I had advised you to leave your country for a time and your grammar school forever. Almost immediately you obeyed, magnificently breaking the powerful bonds holding you, namely, affection for your land and force of habit. So now you are enjoying the freedom justly due you, which is all the sweeter because it comes so late; just as slavery is most bitter for the person who has experienced freedom, so freedom is sweetest for the person who recalls his past slavery. May almighty God favor my advice and your compliance, and my hope is that He will. You have sat under a salutary shade, and you shall emerge more robust and energetic. For me, you are already deserving of greater honor and a more distinguished title because you are in my eyes not so much a grammarian as a poet. Along with your letter I have received one from that excellent and fine gentleman, and I know not what to do about it. For if I were to reply according to my sentiments—which I by no means wish to do—I fear appearing a flatterer. If I say less, I may seem ungrateful; if I say something more, I shall seem mad; if I say nothing, I shall appear proud. Therefore I shall respond with the same language in which it was written, and I shall tell him what is necessary. To you I shall only say this about his letter: in my judgment nothing can be more pleasant and more brief, more effective and more sophisticated. If I had previously entertained any doubt that eloquence for the most part comes naturally and requires somewhat less study than other arts, today I have none. But this is a serious question which cannot be dealt with here and now. I therefore turn to your letter. The advice I had previously given you regarding the small defect, doubtless inadvertent, that crept into one of your poems you accepted not only patiently, but even gratefully and joyfully. You have behaved in your usual manner, as behooves your lofty intellect, and you have displayed a learned and modest mind. Certainly you would never have said what you did unless this were true, nor would I have warned you unless I knew you had such a nature. As for your becoming a defender and propagator of my works, you have undertaken something necessary for me and honorable for you, but not

*See XII, 3.

easy, believe me. It will prove a considerable task, but I urge you to proceed and do as you think. Although you may say the contrary and perhaps may even believe it—since love is the greatest persuader—nevertheless I feel strongly that all my works need defense by friends and patience from readers, for they are fragile and unpolished, often emerging from my mind while it was very busy with other concerns. What you are doing voluntarily, then, do at my request: help their weak points as you can, offer polish to what is unpolished and cohesion to what is scattered. The first you will accomplish through the strength of your intelligence, the second with your eloquence and with the sweetness or sharpness of your words, the third through your skill in composition. I am indicating the weapons with which you can offer me assistance, for you cannot persuade either yourself or me that it is unnecessary. I believe that people who apply their intelligence only to the denigration of others' talent shall always exist. Neither through my retreat to the country, nor through solitude and idleness, nor through careful propriety toward others have I succeeded thus far in turning envy's covert glance away from my paths. And I have done everything possible to combat this plague except for one thing I have not done nor am disposed to do—surrender to laziness and cowardice. Aside from envy, I know not what else awaits me except perhaps the last day of my life; then, at least, I hope decency will prevent obstinate envy from approaching my tomb. Meanwhile go forth, my dear friend, and defend my reputation—this will redound to your glory. Even were I not to need the ardor of your mind I would still extol it, but now I do need it as I said. To cultivate the powerful is a common practice; to offer assistance to the weak is indeed an indication of true greatness of spirit. The protection of a destitute defendant earns greater praise, and the eloquence of a great advocate is especially recognized in his defense of a difficult case. Whence it is with general assent that we hear this short verse ringing out in the schools of grammar, "Eloquence provided strength to a doubtful case," although Lucan invented the entire story; for if Cicero did not visit the Thessalian camps, he understandably seemed to the poet most suitable for conveying everyone's feelings and preferences to the commander. There now remains for me to rejoice with myself and with my pen that, as you write, we have succeeded beyond all expectation in patching the friendship between those two illustrious men. I am indebted to them for this one thing, I confess, far more than for all the many favors they so generously bestowed upon me in the past. As for your final request that I convey your gratitude to that great and generous man, it shall be done, since I realize that you desire it so much. Farewell.

At the source of the Sorgue, 10 August.

Fam. XIII, 10.

To the same correspondent, * *an apology for an earlier letter.*

Let not any imperfection of mine displease you, my friend. I refer only to serious imperfections; otherwise everything is imperfect not only in me but even in the people whom the multitude consider most perfect. In my opinion the saying of the grammarian, which goes beyond grammar, is very true, "In human inventions nothing is perfect in all its parts"; and no less true is the saying of the lyric poet, "Nothing is perfect in all its parts." I confess that, in writing to those two illustrious gentlemen whose glory and friendship I desire to be everlasting, I failed to mention in my listing of eminent friends Nisus and Euryalus, a famous pair celebrated in Virgil's poem. I did that deliberately and not accidentally, first of all because my purpose was not to find and enumerate all such examples, but only to enkindle their noble minds to an imitation of models of extreme rarity. I thus considered it sufficient to list several pairs of friends, and especially more than did Cicero in his book entitled *Laelius*, which deals with true friendship; without mention of any names he says that scarcely three or four pairs of friends could be found throughout the centuries. In the second place, since I wished a firm friendship between our two friends established under happy auspices, and since I was speaking to honorable men much alike in their many virtues, I did not wish to include the brief and certainly unequal friendship of Nisus and Euryalus, inasmuch as the latter was a young boy. Furthermore, I hated making reference to a friendship with an unhappy outcome, considering it a dire omen to do so. I also expressly did not add the names of two men whose good fortune derived only from being mentioned by Virgil. I do not ignore the warm friendships of the Gracchi, or what Lucius Reginus did for the imprisoned Cepio, or what Volumnius out of faithful friendship did for the dead Lucullus. The first did not fear exile and the loss of dignity for the sake of his friend's liberation, while the latter with glowing faith embraced a death which was of no avail to his wretched friend, and so he followed to the nether world the man whom he had so highly esteemed. I know the quality of friendship Petronius enjoyed with Publius Celius, or Servius Terence with Decimus Brutus, but in these either personal devotion was placed before the public good or extraordinary faith resulted in a sad and unspeakable end.

*See XII, 3.

Alexander's general, Hephestion, aside from seeming destined to a friendship which was too unequal, fell in with a man whose character made it difficult to establish a solid foundation for friendship; while there is something quite sinister in the friendship of Achilles. Let what has been said thus far suffice in case you were perhaps puzzled. I did not consider that pair of Macedonian friends celebrated by a popular poet even worthy of mention amidst so eminent a list of ancients, seeing that all of us who now make our weary pens run along the dark parchment have become monkeys rather than imitators. Farewell.

At the source of the Sorgue, 25 August.

Fam. XIII, 11.

To Matteo Longo of Bergamo, Archdeacon of the Church of Liège,* concerning the nature and faithfulness of dogs.

At your departure your dog—blacker than pitch, faster than the breeze, more faithful than most dogs—"stopped and did not lose the way," as Virgil says of Creusa. But what follows, "he sank down from exhaustion," I suspect does not apply. No running, no difficult pathways, no rough roads could tire him, accustomed as he is to seize a bird in flight and outstrip a hare with his incredible speed. But such exercise is good for well-bred animals, while excessive repose is harmful. Therefore, having returned through error and not from weariness, he lost the tracks by which he might follow you. Not knowing what to do in his distress, he would certainly have gone alone into the woods in search of food—which he could have done with no difficulty—had not Mother Nature interposed her law saying that this animal may not live apart from man. Of all creatures under man's dominion, none is more faithful than the dog, as is generally known, and none can long be separated from man. We hear that some people used packs of dogs in battle instead of mercenaries. Whenever necessary, these dogs performed their duty most faithfully, never leaving the battlefield. We read that some died for their masters, while others vigorously and successfully defended them against harm. Still others, no less faithfully but less fortunately, protected them so long that they themselves were struck down, for there was no way to harm the master until the dog was killed. Others even survived their masters' deaths and continued to persevere, though badly wounded; and when they failed to protect the beloved bodies of their masters from men, they at least did so from beasts and birds of prey. Some avenged their masters' deaths; in fact, others with eager paws dug up their buried masters from the earth, and even identified the slayers hidden in the crowd, compelling them, through constant bites and distressful howls, to confess. Still others abstained from food after their masters' deaths until they too died. This recently happened in Padua to that most illustrious man to whom I owe so much both in life and in death. After his cruel end, which brings tears to the eyes, his dog, whom I knew

---

*Matteo Longo, of an ancient family of Bergamo, was a friend from Petrarch's youth in Bologna where both studied law. He later became Archdeacon of Liège. He had been living in Vaucluse but had left shortly before Petrarch's arrival in 1351.

well, behaved in the same fashion. We have heard of others who have obstinately clung to a tombstone and could not be pulled away before dying of starvation; others jumped on their masters' funeral pyres and burned to death with them. Pliny the Younger and Solinus narrate a wonderful episode in which the king of the Garamantes returned from exile with the assistance of two hundred dogs who fought his opponents in his behalf. They also tell a more pitiful story which happened in Rome: the dog of a condemned man could barely be prevented from following him to prison. When his master had subsequently been executed, the dog displayed his grief with loud howling. At length, when sympathetic onlookers offered him food, he put it in his master's mouth; when his master's body was thrown into the Tiber he swam to it and tried to keep the beloved burden afloat, not without effect, "because a multitude gathered to behold an example of animal fidelity," to use Pliny's own words. As I said previously, there are innumerable examples of canine fidelity. After your departure, where was your dog to turn, since he was by nature mindful of his master, and on the one hand shuddered at his loneliness, on the other scorned to serve anyone else? Only one remedy remained for his wretchedness. He returned to his familiar home where he had lived happily under you, where he had often won praise for his running, where he had often brought back bloody roebucks and hares. But finding there none of your people, he pitifully kept leaping at the locked door, thereby arousing, with his desire for your presence, the compassion of all those who saw him. Then did we begin to feel our loss and to realize that you whom we thought were always present had departed. And indeed he growled when he first saw me, but when he heard me calling him with a kind voice he soon followed with his tail wagging. Now he goes into the woods with me, hunts with me and at my commands attacks wild creatures, often bringing me welcome game. He is ready to come to you if you so order, but he is happy that fortune has brought him to a friendly door. Farewell.

At the source of the Sorgue, 25 August.

Fam. XIII, 12.

To the Abbot of Corvara in Bologna,* that his thirst for new works must be tempered by patient anticipation.

It is not easy for me to express my happiness at hearing that a man of your stature found such satisfaction in my works that, after carefully examining your situation with yourself, with me, and indeed with both of us, you are directing the prow of your restless spirit from life's many storms to this solitary and rustic dwelling and to me as if to a secure haven. I hope you made the right choice! But bear in mind that an ardent and intense thirst may find satisfaction in any fountain. Consider how Pythagoras and Plato, thirsting for the learning with which they were to flood the entire world, went first as beggars to the Egyptian shores and then to the Italian ones. How great your thirst must now be for it to compel you to turn to the meager and turbulent stream of my learning! You asked to learn from me when I am more desirous of learning than of teaching. But you do not consider this, and inflamed with a noble desire you often tap with your voice and pen at my withered door. Well then, I am opening it for you. If you find anything in my mind capable of quenching your thirst, make use of it as you please. Otherwise do as genial guests are wont to do: take into account the good will of a hospitable host and not the food he serves. As Seneca says, "I wish to pour all I possess into you." If I am not mistaken, you are so attracted to my works that you have put all your faith in my Scipio and in the title of my *Africa*, being as you are a cultivator of virtue and a devotee of letters. My Scipio is not fully developed in the poem, and my *Africa*, which I have long possessed and cultivated with greater toil than I thought possible, has still not been given its final hoeing. I have not yet broken down its useless clods with my rake; I have not yet evened off with a harrow the mounds of my uncultivated fields; my pruner has not yet checked the growth of the overgrown vine leaves or my sickle its thorny hedges. Therefore do as you please with everything else I possess, but for this work alone you must have patience. Allow me, while there is still time, before making you the possessor of African land, to review it and revise it a little to the extent that my tired and fragile talent will permit; allow me to see whether it contains anything disagreeable for the eyes of my more severe critics—I would not say for your eyes,

---

*Nothing is known about this Abbot of Corvara, a monastery near Bologna, except his enthusiasm for Petrarch, and his learning as seen in his request for a copy of the *Africa*.

which approve all my works—or, since I consider that very difficult, whether it contains at least more that is pleasing than displeasing. I confess that Africa is a very fertile region of the world, that Scipio is the most illustrious of men, but there is no virtue in man or fertility in earth so great that it does not need a solicitous cultivator. Nor is it sufficient to cultivate only once: one must be persistent if he wishes a truly unique kind of fruit either of the field or of the mind. I might add that you should not judge in haste my writings but be indulgent with whatever you read and ascribe any faults to time. If I have not answered your particulars, I beg you to forgive me my many occupations; were they known to all men, everyone would forgive me, many would commiserate with me, some perhaps would envy me. Farewell.

At the source of the Sorgue, 1 September.

Fam. XIV, 1.

To Cardinal Talleyrand, Bishop of Albano,* concerning the difficulties and perils of the higher life.

You bid me be clear in my style; and I am indeed disposed to obey you in all things. But we are clearly not in agreement on one point, since you call clear the style that skims the ground and I consider clearer that which flies higher, provided it does not become enveloped in clouds. But you are my father, you are my lord, you are my teacher, and it behooves me to do your will and not you to do mine. Surely I cannot accomplish this in a better fashion than to speak about human life. For whenever style pursues the intricate path of rational philosophy or the hidden one of natural philosophy, it is not surprising that busy minds have trouble following it. Yet once style emerges from those narrow byways and returns to the field of moral eloquence, who has a mind so dull as not to grasp easily, hearing it from others, what he knows to be true even if everyone were silent, and what he sees in himself and recognizes in others, examples of which abound before his eyes and in his mind? Therefore I shall speak about this matter, which no one has ever been able, or will ever be able, to discuss sufficiently, or in fact is discussing or considering enough. Wherefore, there exists a tremendous difference between words and actions, for according to Cicero, "Speech battles wondrously with life." How else should I begin, O most illustrious father, if not with those matters that especially affect your life and mine, so that you may understand that I, though preoccupied and besieged by many concerns, still often turn my eyes to you? Although at times I may perhaps appear inflexible to the multitude, I feel the toil of this journey and think about its end. We are indeed, as you see more clearly than anyone else, all wayfarers in this life, perfectly aware of the difficulty of the road and uncertain of the goal. No one can avoid this condition, whether an unlearned farmer or a rude shepherd, a wandering merchant or a stationary hermit, a suppliant beggar or a haughty man of wealth, a French king or a Roman emperor. Or again he may be a humble priest, a proud archdeacon, a more exalted prelate, one destined to the Roman cardinalate (as was your case) or

---

*Elie de Talleyrand (1301–64), of the noble family of the Counts of Périgord, had such wealth and learning in law and the sciences that he was made cardinal at thirty by John XXII. One of the most powerful cardinals of the Curia under Clement VI and Innocent VI, he often sought to engage Petrarch more directly in the service of the pope.

finally the supreme pontiff to whom the people have given the name of pope out of admiration. We are all equally wayfarers, I repeat, except that you may be generally viewed on a lofty road, while we seek our goal via a more humble path. It is still true that far beneath our feet there is a huge and indescribable multitude of wayfarers. Consequently, while they proceed through the deepest and darkest valleys and you proceed along lofty and toilsome summits, we fall in the middle as though on mountain ledges. By different footpaths but with similar dangers we all sigh for a single goal. Consider carefully and try to understand, so that the splendor of your good fortune not impede your clear judgment. You will see—and what I say about one you must understand about all having your station and good fortune—you will see, I say, that, though distinguished and possessing a happiness capable of being enjoyed here, you are still subject to common misfortunes and dangers in life. For that reason your misfortunes may perhaps be all the more serious, since a fall from on high is more serious and the danger of falling is greater for those wandering among precipices. One might add that not the least of evils is the difficulty of concealing your actions from any direction, since all eyes are fixed on you alone. There follows from this that, as everyone must toil with great energy, it is especially true of you so that your progress may be blameless and upright in God's presence and in men's eyes, so that you not fall or turn aside or hesitate, or stop, or become weary, or finally allow anything to remain hidden. Whatever you alone do, everyone will know. This is the affliction of famous men: they can keep nothing hidden, everything is revealed. The homes of powerful men are full of cracks, permitting nothing to be concealed, for everything pours from them into the public eye. Everyone knows what they eat for lunch, for dinner, and for supper, what they converse about at table and in bed; whatever emerges from their mouths is studiously reported; every word is an opinion, every chance remark is considered premeditated; every joke is taken as a serious statement. In short, with so many onlookers intent on reading their minds they can scarcely keep their thoughts hidden.

Are you asking my advice about this? What else can it be, if not to live always as though you were in the public eye, to do everything as though everyone were watching, to think as though your thoughts were transparent and your home a stage for the public, to believe that your heart is the temple of God. This I think you should do, this I believe should be done particularly by all great men. Otherwise they will not avoid the judgment of the multitude or the censure of fame, not to mention pricks of conscience. Unless they not only watch with their every step what they do or what they say, but foresee constantly what men think of them, they will inevitably be denigrated by the basest men, a fate no high station can ever avoid. It is true that the needy and the obscure can do almost everything in silence and in the shadows; for the successful there are no shadows or silence. "Do you believe any privacy exists for the rich man? Though his servants may be silent, his cattle will speak, as well as his dog and his walls. Lock the doors, extinguish the light, let all be on watch, let almost no one sleep, yet whatever he does at the rooster's second crowing, the innkeeper will know before daybreak." If these words of the Satirist were ever true, they are especially so in our day. The lofty deliberations of the Roman Senate were kept in deep secrecy and were revealed only after what was decided in the inner chambers was brought to fruition in magnificent deeds. Often the people heard that the greatest battles were being waged before learning why they had to be declared, and this is why news about the war preceded reports about the preparations for war. Nowadays our senators do not maintain that secrecy. You may hear everything before it happens through the tattling of little old ladies, and, what is even worse, much that will never happen. But it is better that I return to my argument instead of improving no one and offending everyone with my digressions.

Many things indeed, O greatest of men, are part of this mortal life from which moderation, humility, or a lofty station cannot deliver us; and in fact among them is found much more that is bitter than sweet. Thus it was rightfully said that in the vestibule of life there are two vases, a small one containing sweet liquor, and another very large one containing bitter draught. Because of the variety of possible interpretations, the words of David can perhaps be recalled without sounding foolish, "the cup in the Lord's hand is filled with spiced and foaming wine," signifying that the Lord's cup from which we wretched ones drink in this exile partakes of a certain sweetness and purity, yet in its fullness it is mixed with much that is bitter. Sweet things, as I have said, are few and short-lived; joy is brief, delight is brief, in short anything pleasing is brief. Anyone who has traveled even a small distance on the road of this pilgrimage has admittedly had this experience. On the other hand, no one can relate with any ease how old and how serious are the battles against fortune, how varied the kinds of adversities, how numerous and how diverse the forms of torment; no one can deal with this infinite subject in a brief discourse. The matter is truly well known, and there is no need to summon witnesses from afar. Everyone has his own conscience to bear witness to his sorrows and toils; aside from known and obvious troubles no one is capable of scrutinizing its hidden torments, hidden wounds, and hidden ulcers. Singing in his sublime voice, Virgil mentions many things about the infernal condition that a number of readers understand as applying to the condition of our present life. As they affirm, it is indeed infernal compared to the celestial life. Since there is a common vestibule to the entire structure, in it is placed quite effectively, if these readers are right, whatever is common to almost all those who cross the threshold into this life. In the more hidden circles, however, are particular punishments for particular faults. For the sake of example, every man is not guilty of yielding to adultery or of committing incest with a daughter, or bearing wrongful arms or of making and unmaking laws for a price, of selling his native land for gold or of deceiving his "master." May God help us to avert such plagues! Mankind would be in the worst condition if those actions were true of all men. On the very threshold of life, however, those vices are still indiscriminately cast as obstacles before all men, although some may admittedly be avoided through God's special grace. You ask what these may be. I beg you to allow Virgil to appear before you since you just now deemed Juvenal worthy of it. Although your innumerable and lofty responsibilities make it difficult for you to be familiar with him, Virgil is nonetheless a great man, among the greatest in intelligence and second to none in eloquence. If you begin acquiring a taste for him, you would perhaps begin sensing his appeal and regret not having known him earlier. Who, I ask you, could have better expressed this thought with better words?

> *See! At the very porch and entrance way to Orcus*
> *Grief and ever-haunting Anxiety make their bed:*
> *Here dwell pallid Diseases, here morose Old Age,*
> *With Fear, ill-prompting Hunger, and squalid Indigence,*
> *Shapes horrible to look at, Death and Agony;*
> *Sleep, too, which is the cousin of death; and Guilty Joys*
> *And there, against the threshold, War, the bringer of Death....*

You know, O illustrious father, how difficult is the road we have taken and how many misfortunes along it besiege us; you know what an inexorable crowd of difficulties we encounter on the threshold itself. There is no advantage in being born a wealthy man or a king; ultimately poverty follows even the greatest riches, and often, as the Psalmist says, "The wealthy become poor and hungry." Grief enters even the most gleaming bridal chambers; trouble, fear, illness, and toil even climb into the most secure strongholds; wars strike even the wealthiest of kings; a sluggish sleep overtakes even the most vigilant minds in the midst of exciting deeds; the most moderate are disturbed, whether they like it or not, in the midst of their joys. Finally unexpected old age follows days spent in pleasure, and death offends even the most bejeweled royal crowns. No one is spared, no one enjoys respite from trouble; every man's home has its griefs, its hatreds, its mournings, and its laments. Great eminence rarely avails against misfortunes and often does harm; the greater it is, the more it is exposed to the storm of circumstance. A more humble condition also has its burdens, for poverty pricks with its burning nettles; but wealth has even sharper thorns, and worldly power the thorniest briars of all. Every man who has experienced both kinds of fortune knows this to be so. You, my dear father, cannot judge these matters except insofar as you can supplement with your intelligence your inexperience. Born into a magnificent and famous household, reared amidst great wealth and pleasures, always accustomed to presiding and never having to obey, you happily ascended with the aid, on the one hand, of your virtue and, on the other, of divine clemency through most of the official ranks nearly to the very highest position. You are thus not a fitting judge of a humbler destiny; yet no one is more qualified to judge loftier destinies, either because of your experience, the greatest of teachers, or because of careful observation and study, or because of the strength of your mind and the agility of your intellect. Although I have already said much about this, I should still like to say, unless you disapprove, a bit more about something much better known to you than to me. I shall be expressing, I believe, what you will consider so true and obvious that, had you not known me, you would believe me a person with power. First of all, how much indignation and anger, I ask, is inherent in the higher state when powerful men lament their powerlessness, experiencing even in their least affairs difficult beginnings, troublesome progress, unexpected outcomes, and ruined expectations; or what daily indignation they experience at the discovery that they are not as powerful as they think, that they are not feared as much as they wish, and that the more humble dare to resist them! For what man is, or ever was, so powerful that he did not often suffer grave injustices from inferiors, servants, subjects, and friends? I speak of the men who wear the false name of friend, for true friends are rare and do no harm. But so as not to become too involved with minor examples, I shall limit myself to the more famous ones. How many and how great are the conflicts experienced by that class! No one was more illustrious in war than Julius Caesar—thus history asserts and facts prove—who had resolved during his last days to wage war against the Parthians in order to control through force the Dacians who had poured into Thrace. He would have done so except that death prevented him, compelling him to leave these and other magnificent plans unrealized. Thus the man so feared throughout the world, the man who had conquered Germany, subjected the Gauls and Britons, trampled Spain, Africa, Egypt, Pontus, Syria, Armenia, nearly the entire world, and finally in the greatest of all his victories, conquered and subjected the Republic and city of Rome herself, mistress of the world, to the rule of a single citizen, this man met in Parthia and in Dacia what he feared, or rather, since he is said to have feared nothing, what worried him. Caesar Augustus, the greatest of mortals, heard of the defeat of his legions and of Quintilius Varus, their commander, when he was enjoying the height of his success; everyone knows the sadness and the dignity with which he bore this misfortune of the Republic. There now come to mind a great number of examples both ancient and modern. What nations or leaders are so fortunate that they cannot be engaged in sudden warfare, or do not constantly fear a swift collapse, or lacking such fear, do not expose themselves to even greater peril since their precautionary measures are minimal? If you have doubts about the frailty of success, consider above all the examples of the Roman Empire. Who would ever have thought that it would have fallen from such great heights to its present state of lowliness? The empire nevertheless did fall because, although admittedly boundless, it was still human, and for that reason it could never endure eternally. Never did a people have so many enemies internally and externally. Thus its troubles and perils in peace and in war always increased in proportion to its successes until it reached the point where at present scarcely any danger exists of its falling any lower. And this empire, unconquered by any people, could be conquered and destroyed from within, while all others were overcome from without. But so as not to entangle you in long and ancient histories, I shall return to what we ourselves have seen. Our age has had outstanding rulers, who seemed both to themselves and to others to touch the very summit of the heavens. Suddenly wars began to arise where they least feared them, and they were not only assailed by lesser peoples—previously no one had even suspected this possibility—but defeated time and again as they weakly defended their borders, until we finally saw them overcome in battle and thrown into enemy prisons. What can be considered more unfortunate than this kind of destiny, which indeed exists at all levels and in all places yet rages more openly and fiercely at higher levels, since, as learned scholars agree, every fall from on high is precipitous?

What shall I now say about domestic misfortunes? Two illustrious names must be again repeated. There is Julius Caesar, than whom "no one was ever more moderate in victory," to use Seneca's words. He witnessed the drawn and flashing swords of his men on his threshold, and once surrounded, he was killed by those very hands which he had filled with victories and gold or spared because of his innate piety. Augustus, a most benign ruler and most deserving of the love of all mankind, led a disquieting life amidst the conspiracies of his supporters. I am recounting what is indeed well known and commonplace among historians. Consider how serious are the discords and contentions caused by words when a totally unrestrained statement stings and offends delicate ears! We are ashamed to yield, we are ashamed to be won over; though this may be seen at all social levels, that saying of Sallust is nonetheless true: that pride is "the evil common to the nobility." Therefore the greater the preeminence, the greater the indignation; and that opinion of Caesar that must be resisted from the outset is implanted in minds—that it is more difficult to force rulers from first to second place than from second to last place. Consider also their imitation of ostentation, their concern with dress and their fancy banquets, their hypocritical manners, their caution in speech, their constant repression of affections! Troublesome indeed is human ostentation when you must either seem what you are not or strive to disguise what you are. It is a double task to attempt to overcome nature in two fashions when it is so difficult to overcome it in only one. What of the longing to propagate one's name and the constant vigils to capture the attention of posterity? What of the devotion of one's children or the uncertain future of one's grandchildren and of one's ancient lineage, that tremendous anxiety for noble hearts? What of the governance of one's unruly servants and the hatred of their most unruly members, often concealed and sometimes erupting against the master himself? It is indeed a difficult situation to have to feed someone who hates you, who can perhaps cause destruction and certainly weariness; to be unable to be alone when you wish; to be haunted eternally by domestic enemies; to know that you will be prey to various ambitions; to be cultivated by many men because of expectation rather than affection; to be esteemed rather than loved; to have your good fortune count more than yourself; to appear terrible to many,

amiable to a few, and never to know who loves you because the saying of the Spanish poet holds true: "The successful man knows not
whether he is loved"; to know that your death is prayed for, your
inheritance sought, your days numbered and time's passage so slow.
Do you consider all this freedom from danger? Indeed you will recall
the three vices taught by philosophy to be avoided above all others
so as to live without annoyances: hatred, envy, and contempt. From
this last one, dear father, you are exempt since your wealth and
power, dignity and knowledge, nobility and virtue make you immune to it. Through what means, however, can you extricate
yourself from the first two? How is it possible that you have not
often offended many men when your purpose has always been to be
a champion of forsaken justice? On the other hand, it is unavoidable
for the lover of justice to be hated by the enemies of justice.
Moreover, amidst such partiality of fortune, amidst such great glory
and glimmerings of honors, how can it ever be possible that envy
does not look at you askance? All things may come to pass before
success will lessen envy. Add to all this pangs of conscience and various
mental turmoils, modesty, repentance, hope, sorrows, secret
fears—torments familiar to everyone, but in particular to men of
power. Amidst these difficulties everyone must live, especially those
persons of lofty position who are illustrious either because of fortune
or because of their virtue. While these troubles may be annoying to
every man, they are particularly contrary to your intentions, for
they hinder a mind disposed to better things. I know, as you wanted
me to know, the burning movements of your mind and its noblest
concerns: its zeal for letters, its intellectual activity, its love of
moderation, its attachment to religion, and its appetite for solitude.
But your good fortune is at variance with your intention, for what
you ought to do is far different from what you consider expedient or
pleasurable. I can imagine your state of mind and its upsets, and I
measure the storm in your heart in comparison to my own upsets. If
you are seeking a remedy, I have but one. If it is truly impossible to
be outwardly what you desire, be inwardly what you must be. Let
your good fortune make you display an ostentatious exterior, but
conceal your humility within; you may sit in the court but let your
mind wander in a hermitage; love poverty amidst riches and fasting
amidst banquets; let gold glitter on your table and gems on your
fingers but let a contempt for them glitter even more in your mind;
let your body be dressed in fancy clothing but your spirit in
haircloth. While riding a horse in fancy gear, recall the donkey of
the Lord and the worn feet of the apostles. While wearing on your

head the ornamental red felt cap, recall the crown of thorns worn by the Lord. When you lie in your gilded bed, contemplate the sepulchre of Christ and your own. In short, whatever you do, always keep before your eyes the last day of your life. Whether it be today or tomorrow is uncertain, but that it cannot be too distant is certain. Such is the diversity of fate and the brevity of life, and so as not to let that day unexpectedly cause you terror, you must now become intimate with it through continuous meditation.

The most magnificent acts of virtue are three: to scorn pleasures, to love poverty, not to fear death. Know that there is nothing more fortunate than the last. As for the other two, I believe there is no less merit in scorning present pleasure than in protecting one's self against it by avoiding it, in loving poverty amidst wealth than in being poor. There are indeed countless poor for whom poverty is itself a punishment, but they are few who became poor after being wealthy out of love for Christ, who consider poverty both glorious and pleasant. Can you show me any man who remains poor in spirit amidst wealth? It is wonderful to make one's way through obstacles, and it is more glorious to overthrow an enemy at hand than to avoid one approaching. Likewise it is the mark of a more noble mind to despise pleasures than to shun them, to scorn the sight of gold than to avoid looking at it. It is possible in any state of life to love virtue, whose cultivation deserves greater praise and reward the greater the effort involved. You will find many who honor you with flattery and exalt you to the heavens; as agents of popular beliefs, they will order you to admire yourself and your affairs, to preserve your dignity through artifice, to remember your bloodline, to consider your wealth and to have regard for your power; finally by dint of words they will almost make you immortal. In truth I urge you to forget none of these and to render thanks to God for them and much else with which He made you truly unique among the few. I also urge you to glory in none of them but in the Lord, to have faith in Him, and to place in Him all your hopes and concerns. In the meantime I exhort you to disdain yourself and perishable things, and always keep in mind your end, a salutary habit. For nothing is more efficacious than this to make you hold equally in contempt life itself and death. Whether you ponder carefully the miseries of this life and do not, as I believe, wish to live too long or fear to die, or whether you behold its brevity and pay no attention to the harshness and flatteries of such a limited stretch of time (scorning magnanimously the bitter with the sweet), you will know this exile to be not only brief but difficult, one in which good fortune deceives and bad fortune casts down. You will easily overcome all difficulties if, finding consolation for this exile's trouble in its brevity, you sigh always for that fatherland where you have been enrolled as a citizen, if you so desire, where all the greatest and eternal things are to be found. This, my lord, is what I intended to write you for now. If something more comes to mind—and much comes to mind daily—it must be postponed for another time. You be the judge of this letter's style; the content is without doubt clear; therefore even if you do not approve of the style you will not condemn the content. Live happily, O you who are a glory of our age.

At the source of the Sorgue, 22 September.

Fam. XIV, 2.

To his Socrates,* that he deliver the preceding letter to the person to whom it is written.

You certainly know that magnanimous man of high position; no one is in fact more exalted in the Church militant except the Roman pontiff. Indeed if I did not fear incurring envy for him, and for myself the accusation of flattery, not even the pope stands higher—for to make popes would appear a somewhat loftier power than to be pope. He himself is silent, but his reputation speaks clearly; he himself denies it, but everyone affirms that he created two Roman pontiffs in a row. If anyone were to boast that either one has been mindful of and grateful for that great favor, the entire church would deny it. Judging from his words and from his appearance he overlooks this ingratitude with high-mindedness, striving not to let others' vices mar his own virtue. I have spoken about his greatness, and I have done so rather briefly because the matter is well known and mention of it, I noticed, is without question hardly pleasing to him. To speak to you of his affection for me would also be superfluous; this applies not to me alone but to you and to all those dear to me. This man, so great and so kind to me, though he could order me to do whatever he wishes, pleads each day that I write him something, always adding that it be clearly written. At the same time he requests something which scarcely harmonizes with the clarity he desires: that I cite in my writings verses from other poets in whom he has begun to take delight at my urging. He requests this, not to indulge in them, but to make use of their work for his purposes, and to season and embellish with poetic colors his civil eloquence, in which he is quite competent. Therefore this matter has its difficulties, which can hardly be called insignificant. I feel that he has so accustomed himself to the plain language of law that whatever may be expressed in another fashion he considers obscure; and yet I must speak in that way since I cannot speak or express myself otherwise. It is indeed astonishing that with his comprehension of all things beneath the heavens, as Pliny the Younger says of the elder Caesar, with his lofty and acute intelligence whereby—overlooking his distinguished skill in action and unique cunning in deliberation—he so mastered civil law on his own in a brief time, for which years of study scarcely suffice, that he equaled or surpassed the fame of all the legal minds of our age. What is even more remarkable is that he ac-

*See I, 1.

complished this amidst the greatest concerns and in circumstances where men usually unlearn what they know rather then learn something new, for he had come to the cardinalate rather unlearned. That man, I say, so well endowed by nature and cultivated by study, so very capable and quick at understanding any matter, is rather awkward only in the use of words. Any style not his, that is not a legalistic style, frightens him as if it were barbaric, often causing him to repeat: "Make me understand you as I understand a legal text." I answer him that a legal text, which I myself studied as a boy, is not as easy for all as it is for him, but for many it is really more difficult than other texts that seem most difficult to him. All things are easy for experts but difficult for nonexperts. He next says: "Let yourself be readily understood by everyone." I then object that what is grasped without any mental stretching is without value or merit; I also add what I said to Clement VI, who had taken a similar stance many times before, as well as many other things which seem to fit the occasion. Among others I referred especially to the concept that I prefer being understood and approved by the few than to be understood by all and approved by no one. Learned men have always been few, but in our age they are very few indeed, and soon there may be none at all if divine wisdom does not provide them. Therefore, as long as they are few—inasmuch as I do not expect them to be many, since they never have been—I do not mind being judged by them. But the judgment of the many, that is, of the multitude, I have taken rather lightly, and continue to do so. I no more prefer to be understood than praised by them, for praise by the multitude is disgraceful among learned men. Moreover I have often used Cicero's saying, found in his *Tusculans*: the greastest proof that something has not been expressed with refinement is that the ignorant easily learn and approve it. In the end, however, I am overcome by the man's authority and, after a long struggle, I yield and often subject my reason to his will. As a result, I displease myself in order to please him. But I am making use of a new procedure so as not to displease too many; I write for him without keeping copies for myself. This time, however, I have so succumbed to his fervent and long insistence to be clear in my style that I fear he may accuse me of being too submissive. Whatever his judgment, you will give him the lengthy letter enclosed which I thought of sending first to you so that you might have an opportunity to present yourself to that man from whom no one ever departed without being a better, or happier, person. Farewell.

At the source of the Sorgue, 22 September.

Fam. XIV, 3.

To Luca da Piacenza, clergyman, condolences for the
untimely death of a young man in the prime of life.*

Had I not long since cleared my eyes, fought against tears, and
determined not to mourn the deaths of mortals, the contents of your
letter would have caused me to shed many tears; nevertheless I could
scarcely keep them from welling up and quietly approaching their
usual threshold. All because our friend's death seemed to me so extraordinary and astounding, if there is truly anything astounding that
happens in Mother Nature's realm, so untimely and harsh, if any
day might be thought the fitting moment for death, and finally so
unexpected and precipitous. That such an incredible flower of
youth, such a brilliant light of heavenly beauty as he seemed, in the
firm vigor of his youth and in the best of health, should have died in
less than three hours, as you say, all this has served to remind me,
with a recent, clear, and well-known example, of a truth that we daily
repeat and yet never apply in our conduct and activities: we ought
not to place any hope in transitory things, and, except for a good life
and a pure conscience, there is no remedy against death. To what
avail are the promises of doctors whom we see dying everywhere,
who are always pallid—by now this is proverbial—and are just as ill
as anyone else? Virtue alone does not know death. But what, I ask,
did our friend lack; of what avail was his age to him? What good was
his beauty, his elegance, the cultivation of his body, his splendid
garments; what good was his very pleasing voice and mellow singing;
what good was his wit with words, the divine bearing in his walk, in
his taste, in his leisure, in his games, and in his serious moments?
With all these qualities was he able to defer even for a moment the
hour of his death? O unpredictable affairs of men, O unforeseen
departures, O deceitful hope and unstable fortune, O delights of ours
hanging on a very tenuous thread, O fatal day never known to mortals, always suspect and feared! So what am I doing? Here am I
gradually entering the waters when I am hardly safe on shore; I must
therefore turn back. Our friend has perished; the city had never
begotten anyone more splendid, for he was to it as Scipio to Rome,
Leonidas to Sparta, Alcibiades to Athens. I used to admire his
character second to none, I cultivated him, I delighted in him, I
never knew more clearly how dear he was to me until I lost him.
This is why I could not bear such a misfortune in silence, and yet

*See IX, 6.

one should not indulge in such long lamentations. Our friend has perished, or rather he has discovered an end to perishing; he has departed, but in fact he has gone where he may now abide without concern and fear about his departure; he has left, but indeed has returned whence he had departed, whence he had wandered, whence he was in exile; he has returned to Him by whom he had been sent to occupy a perishable, though very beautiful, body; he has died, leaving behind us who are continually dying, and now he is the first to live; he has been buried, but indeed delivered of his heavy chains he has returned what was his to earth and what is his to heaven. His body does indeed lie lifeless; it now terrifies onlookers whom it once knew how to charm. Freed of its fleshy prison, however, his spirit, more joyful now, more beautiful than before and more vigorous, has ascended to the stars in the company of his other virtues. There it now dwells, and in due time it will receive in a much more resplendent form, I hope, its body entrusted to the earth. I thus consider what happened to him so fortunate that to weep for his sake may seem envy rather than sympathy. As Lelius laments at the death of his Africanus who was of like age, I feel quite troubled that as the first to enter this life I am not the first to leave it. But together with Lelius I nevertheless console myself, for I loved that man's virtue, which was not destroyed; otherwise inconsolable grief would have overcome me. For that reason, as I have said, upon reading your letter, I forced myself to control my inconsolable mourning with all the power of my reason—however small that may be—but I have been unable to control my grief. I have grieved, I confess, nor am I hiding my weakness. I say that I have grieved, and I am grieving considerably more than I had now thought myself capable. I grieve, moreover, not his change of destiny but the rare honor that he represented for his homeland, the extinguishing of a remarkable constellation so near to us and the departure from us of a pleasant solace for our cares. But since profound grief ceases only with effort, and since lamenting because of irreparable losses leads to nothing but an increase of loss and grief, I lay all this aside to address the section of your letter where you ask me to pray for him, a reminder which I truly praise. Yet prayer is more appropriate to you as a priest. As a surviving friend of the dead man, I ask you to pray for him, I ask you to pray so that if he lacks anything in his blessed state you may request it in his behalf from our common lord, Jesus Christ. Farewell.

At the source of the Sorgue, 25 September.

Fam. XIV, 4.

To the same correspondent, * *a reply to various accusations of envious rivals.*

I received two of your letters at the same time. One was an exhortation that was most pleasing to my spirit, not only agreeable but almost necessary amidst the torments and troubles of these days; the other was really a censure that would have been no less pleasing if I thought it justified. The latter, you say, is not yours but the multitude's. While it indeed disturbs me to hear this, it does not affect my spirit; just as a new kind of false accusation does not upset me—you know that I have been subject to a great deal—so it does not surprise me that I displease the public. I am rather astonished when I hear the public extol me with praises that are unexpected and displeasing. Since the first cause of love is a certain likeness, I have dedicated myself to being as unlike that multitude as possible. If I could ever fully achieve it, then I would at last consider myself most fortunate. How then could I please those whom I have always labored with great zeal to displease, when the multitude's servile flatterers with their different goals and intentions can scarcely achieve with all their skills what they desire. After a large number of these flatterers had, through shameful means, won some long-coveted praises, a sudden reversal in public favor not only brought them dishonor, but often, as with those who caress panthers or tigers or lions, even attacks or snares on the part of the cajoled multitude. But let us return to the matter at hand. I do not wish you to be surprised if the multitude uses the same rights against me, now that I have become its notorious enemy, as it does against its own friends. It is the sign of an experienced and self-assured traveler, on the other hand, not to be frightened by barking; and I certainly am not frightened, often calling to mind Cicero's words: "Whatever men may say about you is strictly their opinion"; and further on, "If you wish to aim high, disregard the multitude's talk and place no hope for your welfare in human rewards." I recall too Seneca's words: "Men speak evil of me; they do not what I deserve but what they are wont to do." What do these lazy and useless dogs, mangy through want, accomplish by barking at the moon? Why do they involve themselves in the affairs and plans of someone who never thinks, not even once, about their lives or deaths, or about them at all except as one often does with cadavers, not to mention beasts?

*See IX, 6.

But for many it is pleasant to indulge in such madness, to search the secrets of someone else's heart while neglecting their own, and to probe the deepest recesses of the mind, which is the most difficult undertaking of all; they perhaps divine what cannot be known through human effort. I wonder which Apollo, after fleeing Delphi, has entered the hearts of those beasts? It is indeed a great wonder that, ignorant of their own affairs, they know mine, which I, so very distant from their view, have hidden in an arched valley, as Aeneas did with his pledges and household gods.

It is worthwhile examining closely what they are saying; for now we have gradually arrived at our main point. First of all, while they feared my departure from Italy as fatal and even dangerous, they are now finding cause for complaint, you say, at the rumor of my return. They are insolent if they wish anyone to be nowhere when no one prohibits them from being anywhere, or mad if they complain at one and the same time of a person's departure and return. What can I say? Since I must even now give reasons for my actions—for any responsible person properly does nothing for which he cannot give some reason—I shall relate in brief to you, but certainly not to the multitude, a summary of my departure, conduct and return, and of this entire affair. As you know, I recently came to the Curia, indeed I came to Babylon. They marvel, amazed, because I think of leaving a place where, as God and my conscience bear witness and as you often heard me say, I was always sad and reluctant to be, even though I was held by rather strong ties; but I did come. Now unless they were devoid of all reason they could have imagined that it was not without good cause, which they ignore and will continue to ignore, that I would move to a place known and hated by me since childhood, having for a time abandoned my pleasing residence and my solitude, for which no one was ever more desirous than I, if I really know myself, and having left my Italian Helicon and the tranquil idleness of letters, harmful to no one but envied by many, and even hateful to some as I have begun to notice; and that I would prefer to these many comforts the unpleasant business and inextricable labyrinth of the Curia, unless it was perhaps poverty or wealth, the double distress of mortals, that drove me here, or enmity or rivalry or perhaps contempt, which is most annoying to lofty minds. Clearly they could suspect any one of these, had I not striven to remain equidistant from great riches and shameful want; had I not always been held in esteem and cultivated with unusual kindness by all good men, not only by those with whom I happen to live, but even by those at a distance; had not the greatest rulers of Italy tried to retain me with entreaties as they grieved at my departure and anxiously awaited my return. I believe it was another reason, more hidden, that urged me on despite the many protestations and attempts to restrain me. How could they know whether I have already realized the reason for my coming or whether I ever will? Either one could be sufficient cause for my return. Again, how could they know whether my purpose is to remain here longer in order to ridicule them in the meantime? Now indeed I have discovered the cause of their grief and the crux of the matter. It is this, believe me, that bothers them: they complain, not because I am absent from there, but because they fear my presence here. While I am there I can only offend their ears and their eyes; by my staying here they imagine much more serious consequences. Thus I have become not only likable to good men, as I had always desired, but also formidable to fools, which I had never wished at all. But now consider this new kind of malice (for even madness has its cunning and its stings): my stay, which they curse and fear for being too long, they pretend to fear for its brevity in order to accomplish what they desire. They know, however, that I have always disagreed totally with their views, accustomed as I am to strive against the opinion of madmen. I have also been of the belief that no easier path to the truth exists than to abandon the headlong and oblique ways of the blind and rambling multitude.

Let us now see how they color the figments of their imaginations. For not even in this do they agree, a common fault of the multitude, whose folly is at variance with itself. Therefore my return—which has not occurred, although I wish it had, in order to relieve my spirit's longing rather than their fear—they attribute to fickleness, as if anyone who knows me does not realize that no fault is less likely for my character. For me the accusation of obstinacy leveled by unjust critics of my affairs ought to be feared more than fickleness. Others ascribe this crime of my hasty return, you say, to avarice; I shall silently let my life respond to that charge. Who has ever seen the kind of miser who preferred to be poor when he could be wealthy? And yet, to desire and to scorn are opposites, but they, blind with envy, do not see their self-contradictions, and being accustomed to calling me disdainful, they call me greedy as often as they open their mouths. What does this matter to me? Let them call me a thief, a robber, or a hunter of last wills and testaments. I shall no more become what they believe than they would become just and high-minded and reasonable, if I could say this of them with a lie that is not smaller than theirs but certainly more honest. Ancient indeed is their boldness in disparaging those whom they formerly praised; ancient is that impudence and carelessness about lying. It is perhaps more excusable because in the manner of dogs, whom they strive to resemble, they bark at each and every one without distinction. Perhaps the charge might be called more justifiable when we consider that there are two kinds of avarice, one damnable for excessive appetite and the other for excessive stinginess, and that I am accused of the second, not of the first, as if I neither dared to bear, nor was able to bear, the abyss of Curial expenses. While this may be true, it is fortune's fault and not mine. The size of my patrimony, which has not increased but rather diminished with time, clears me of the suspicion of the first kind of avarice. I have always felt that, though I needed little, I needed still less as my end approached. I feel in my bones Cicero's words: "I do not understand what the avarice of an old man means. Can there be anything more absurd than to desire more provisions for a journey the less of it remains?" I would confidently say that these words are a commentary on the hostile and unfounded accusation of my critics. To the dying man the last day will serve as witness, when he is not allowed to carry off or hide anything. Unshaken by conscience and by detractors, I promise one thing in good faith to my faceless accusers. I call to witness this letter and you, together with whoever sees it, that if I possess at present or at my departure from this life anything besides my books, in which I find nearly all respite from my labors and all solace for my life, and besides my modest furnishings and daily expenditures, which I have never or rarely been without, if besides these things, I say, my detractors were to dig up mounds of gold and amassed wealth that their envy causes them to imagine, let them feel free to grab and divide whatever there is among themselves. For me, my patrimony could not have a worse end. With these words I hereby lay down the law for my heir, who must not dare mutter even a whisper against it. Let the shame of coveting my treasure be theirs, let my only shame be that of having amassed it, and let my simple name and empty expectations be my heir's. Sensing a bit of hidden gold for themselves because they see my way of life as perhaps less wretched than theirs, they suspect that a considerable portion of my wealth lies hidden as huge treasures in the earth; they are incapable of believing that I have not amassed a fortune, as they have, almost from nothing. Truly foolish and unjust judges are they who measure others' minds against their own when they are totally unlike. Though mortal and dying, they hope to live forever while I, though healthy, recall my mortality and the fact that life itself is brief and uncertain, in the words of Seneca. Their fear is to be left with nothing, mine on the contrary is to have more than enough for my well-being. Yet their error can in some way gratify me if it deceives and torments them; but if their error is simulated I will be deprived of the greater part of my delight. I abandon their minds to their poisonous mouthfuls of envy and to the secret torments of their cares as to so many torturers and hangmen. But now let us hear what others either imagine or think. They say that I return because of being suspect; by whom, I ask? Who does not know that no man of such humble status as mine has come here in these times and has been received with such joy and delight by the Roman pontiff, to begin at the top, and by the highest and most important people? I ought to boast, but only in the name of the Lord who allowed me to deserve or to gain without merit such a great and rare favor. It was indeed astonishing to many, and especially to me, that people whom I had never seen, men resplendent in their cardinal robes who usually disdain everything equally from above, including princes and worldly lords, viewed my arrival with so much pleasure, sincerity, and kindness that I could scarcely believe that it was due to my fame alone. Therefore there is no suspicion, there is no cause for suspicion. Believe me, I could really expect great things if I wished. I desire nothing, however, beyond peace of mind, and desiring nothing I expect nothing. Even if this can be considered one of those things beyond belief, it has still often been proven to you on many occasions, unless I am mistaken; and I shall now prove it with fresh evidence as yet unknown to you.

You certainly know that for some time four ecclesiastical benefices of nearly equal value have been assigned to me on which I live, since it is my fate and since I chose this kind of life because of parental wishes or personal interest. After determining that only two portions of the benefices sufficed for me, I so divided the other two between my oldest and most deserving friends that, although until then I may have been wealthier than both of them, each may now be wealthier than I. The memory of this deed affords me as much joy as it would arouse bitterness in my detractors, not were they to do something similar (this would be setting impossible conditions), but were they compelled to do so. There was a fifth portion of these benefices that I have been discussing, smaller indeed than the others, but seemingly more fitting for you because of its proximity. I have taken this benefice, recently given to me, and turned it over to you. Thus by this same messenger you will receive some apostolic letters in which you will read of your appointment as the canon of Modena, and with them will also be my letter of recommendation for you to the lord of the city, whose great esteem for me you well know. Observe now and judge in silence how much faith one must place either in their curses or in my defenses. You now know all the particulars: judgment has been rendered and the scales of justice balanced. But if you wish my opinion, I offer Seneca's words: I give no more weight to their words than gas escaping from their bowels. For what does it matter, I ask, from which part of the body their foul sounds emerge? Without doubt a fool has no more obscene part of the body than his mouth. Why do these raging and famished dogs disturb me with their troublesome barking when I am intent on other things? Do they perhaps hate me and give vent to their hatred with words? It is indeed a shameful and unfit multitude that has no weapon but a sordid tongue. But why should they hate me when I have never wronged them in any way, unless they think my contrasting way of life harmful to them? Or do they envy me instead? But as the saying goes, envy is usually present among peers. Or perhaps they dream as drunkards, speaking in their sleep? I would rather believe this, and prefer to think this, since dreams excuse insanity; they say and do much while asleep which they would be unable to remember when awake, and for many their lives are a dream until the very end. I am writing you these things in great detail and in anger, my dear friend, so that you who have assumed the defense of my reputation against these gossiping magpies—if by chance the name of dogs offends them—may be sharper in your defense, repeatedly warning them that they ought to begin looking at themselves, black ravens that they are, rather than questioning the spots of swans. Only then will their conduct cause them shame for slandering those whom they have scarcely met; then will they cease lying about others' affairs when they have found much to discuss in their own homes and ample material to ponder in their own calamities and griefs. But in order not to remain silent about anything on my mind today, those men seem to me nearer the truth who give another reason for my return—indignation; this opinion too was also in your letter. These men are not so insane, and seem indeed to have looked quite deeply into my mind, provided they know what indignation is. It behooves me then to define it; whether I do so correctly you can judge for yourself. Unless I am mistaken, indignation is nothing more than a rather disturbed state in a generous mind resulting from the perversity of human affairs; this state I confess is rarely, if ever, absent from me and is present even more strongly when there is just reason. But I have said much too much about a small matter, indeed a minimal one, perhaps one of no consequence. Let them roar as they please, and let their howling into the ground throw dust in their eyes. Either deriding them as they deserve or sympathizing with them as they do not deserve, and proceeding to the matter at hand, let us as much as possible retain reason as the guide of our lives. As for me, I shall continue on my present course, undeterred from my purpose by the buzzing of these flies; proceeding with a deaf ear beyond their insane rumblings, either I shall achieve what I have longed for or, if that perchance is not to be, at least the multitude will not glory in my misfortune. I certainly hope that will be the case. In the meantime my plans, which I strive to conceal from them, I am certain will receive your approval and that of all my friends, although for me the witness of my conscience suffices in all matters. Farewell.

19 October, on the banks of the rivers of Babylon.

Fam. XIV, 5.

To the Doge and Council of Genoa,* an appeal for peace with the Venetians and for civil harmony.

Forgive me I beg you, O most distinguished doge and you most brilliant luminaries of the Council, if I speak to you informally. I do not indeed fear to broach prematurely this discussion, which I have postponed for good reason. Until now, I confess, I have anxiously awaited to see the end chance might give to the many preparations. Just as it would be inhuman to enkindle with words spirits already burning with anger and hatred, so did it seem untimely to me to persuade armed men already standing in battle lines to abandon their arms. For I knew that it was too late for an armed soldier about to do battle to have regrets, and I seemed to have partially performed my duty when, before the beginnings of this war which has shaken both east and west, and even before the fleets from both sides had set forth from their homelands, I intervened rather forcefully and almost tearfully with the illustrious Doge of Venice (to whom I am well known and was at the time even closer) in the hope of quelling the surging flames of anger. I do not fear being told that I am interfering in others' affairs since it is not unseemly for a man to interfere in human ills or for an Italian to be touched by Italy's ills and to render assistance if possible; in such matters I consider myself second to no one, unless I am mistaken. With the war presently underway and with the flames of hatred unsoothed, I believe, by diminished bloodshed, it would hardly seem untimely for me to sound a retreat so to speak; and I would not be doing it so confidently had I not been familiar with the characters of the men whom I am addressing: no people is fiercer in battle yet more humane and benign in victory. You did win; let that be enough lest some people believe that you have betrayed your customs. And indeed not only for illustrious men and peoples but even for noble beasts it suffices to win; it is an ignoble passion to desire to rage on, nor does victory quench one's thirst for blood. Therefore, most generous hearts, it is time to restrain your victorious hands from bloodletting; the fortunes of warfare have taken those who fell in battle. Let that be the proper reward for martial valor, but it does not become your benevolence

*Giovanni di Valente was Doge of Genoa in 1352 during a period of conflict between Genoa and Venice. Their great naval battle was fought on 13 February, 1352, in and around the Bosporus. The Genoese were the victors despite being outnumbered by the Venetians and their allies.

to pursue the survivors with arms. Amidst the glimmering battle lines of armor it is difficult to weigh singly and precisely whom you should wound with your dripping sword, whom you should spare; the drive and ardor of the combatants overwhelms everything. When this subsides and the tranquillity of spirits is restored, then freedom of judgment, interrupted for a time, returns; then is it fitting to check your spirit and demonstrate through acts of notable humanity that you are worthy of victory. This is not easy for those who find victory something new and unusual. Fickle minds are easily given to arrogant joy, and unexpected delight wrests the bridle from reason. For you victory has now become a habit; the many wars waged by the Genoese throughout the world have resulted in as many victories. With your triumphs and victories you have made famous the seas of almost every people—the Tyrrhenian, the Adriatic, the Black Sea, the Ionian, the African ocean, and the Aegean; the ocean itself fears your banners, while the Indian Ocean rejoices that it cannot be penetrated by your fleet. The only thing lacking for us had been to see the Bosporus foaming with your enemies' blood; and we did see it. What difference is there between us who read about it and the warriors who fought in it if not that for them, while they fought, the danger was without terror because of their greatness of spirit whereas for us, while we read, our terror was without danger? Whose mind would not be permeated with horror upon hearing or reading of the event on that dreadful night when between Constantinople and Chalcedon at dusk in the midst of a violent southern wind you were attacked by three very powerful peoples? They proceeded from the south—having set forth from Gallipoli—and assisted by the wind, with full sails, they compelled you to fight against the enemy, against the wind, and against the sea. The ensuing battle was so unrelenting that neither the storm nor the following night was able to interrupt it. What a tempest of winds, what a sound of sail stays, what a clamor of horns, what an outcry and groaning of men, what collisions of ships, what sounds of metal, what hissing of arrows flying through the darkness! Throughout the night the battle continued, making it worthy of the poet's verses: "That night! What words can render its death and its disaster? What tears can rise to the level of all that was suffered then?" The battle raged without interruption until the following dawn, and it was a winter night which will be even more amazing to posterity; the next day the battle continued. Who has ever heard of anything similar, who has even seen or read anything comparable? For the greater part of one day and of a second, and throughout the night, you battled against the sea, the wind, and the enemy. You were opposed by three fleets and three independent countries, united but from different regions; in the middle stood only the courage of the Genoese, only their destiny.

I am not complaining about external enemies, for why is it they intrude in Italian affairs with their weapons? They are mercenary peoples, perfidious and insolent, motivated by money to form long-lasting and miserable militias while forgetting their solemn peace agreements with you. To confess the truth, however, one ought to feel compassion for the wretched public inflamed by their leaders who sold for small gain in a shocking and inhuman commerce the blood of their countrymen. Yea indeed, not only do I not grieve, but I greatly rejoice over the deceitful and indolent Greeks who dared nothing noble on their own. I desire to see that infamous empire, that seat of error, destroyed at your hands, if by chance Christ has chosen you avengers of their wrongs, if He assigned to you that vengeance which all Catholic peoples have unfortunately deferred. On the other hand I feel deep compassion in my heart for our Italian brethren whom I wish had truly heeded my warnings to them while there still was time! But at present would that—to mention what I scarcely dare to desire openly—you both, with heaven's inspiration, will begin bearing in mind that you are Italians; that you were friends and could be again; and that you undertake war not for capital offenses but for glory and power, as has always been true of powerful people and will always be equally true of those seeking leadership; and that, once you have roused yourselves, you will quickly turn from this Italic and civil war to external ones, and at the same time turn your avenging arms against faithless instigators. After they have been driven in iron fetters from the seas, something that could be done in very little time, you could soon thereafter undertake a pious expedition to liberate the Holy Land, and joyfully demonstrate your allegiance to Jesus Christ, thereby presenting to the world and to posterity a most pleasing spectacle! But let me continue where I left off. You did win, O powerful men; now prove to all mortals that you fought with Italians, not out of hatred or ambition, but in the name of peace; compel your enemies to confess, be it even in silence, that you have conquered them not so much with your arms as with your conduct. Let those who fear your power revere and esteem your virtue; he who overcomes an adversary through virtue of spirit rather than through the sword ought more rightly to be considered superior. He is the true victor who conquers his own spirit, surrenders to reason, controls his actions, mitigates his victory, and checks his indignation. Often he deserves victory who becomes a better person in victory, and he possesses the highest military reputation who is not shaken by adversity or exalted by good fortune. The first of these you have demonstrated in the hardships of war; demonstrate the second after the victory so as to make the world realize that you maintain the same spirit in all kinds of fortune. Add to your virtues the embellishment of constancy and firmness, and let nothing that mars perfect glory be lacking to you in war and in peace.

I now come to the matter that greatly disturbs and concerns me; if your moderation could free me of it, I would fear nothing else in your government. As with apparently healthy and sound bodies that are wont to abound with hidden illnesses, so with the peace of great cities; when such illnesses seem arrested they are at work within the deepest recesses of the body. When a disease does break out, then for the first time it is understood that it is preferable for it to remain on the surface than to penetrate to the region of the heart. Just as exercise aids heavy bodies, so for a great people wars serve as medicine; and just as excessive repose burdens and corrupts the body, so excessive tranquillity affects the city. It begets changeable humors in a body, and in a people changeable rivalries, discordant minds, and opposing feelings. Controlled activity is a friend of health, whereas abundant rest causes ill health. Roman virtue would never have perished had Carthage remained secure; once that fear was gone, it led the way to strange vices and civil wars, for the end of that great struggle marks the beginning of still greater ones. What do we think harmed the Athenians? Certainly what ravaged that flourishing city was not so much the war against the enemy, or the destruction of its fleet in the waters of Syracuse, as it was her dangerous citizen Alcibiades, and the raging civil madness of the thirty tyrants. External ills can be handled more readily than those hidden within; there is no question, moreover, that the unseen is most dangerous in every illness. Here, I beg you, establish the battle line of your prudence for which you are so well known; here hold firm and with the greatest zeal try to avoid having spirits become dissolute or wanton in victory. It is best to live in peace, but if that is impossible, it is far more desirable to clash with an enemy than with fellow citizens. Mine is not a prophet's inspiration, nor do I foresee future happenings from the course of the stars. Still, to the extent that I foresee the future from past events with the aid of reason, your virtue and fortune will render you invincible in foreign wars, and you have no sword to fear except internal enemies and civil war. Rome could not have been conquered by anyone but herself; the same will happen to you unless you show civil equality and a restrained spirit. If you do, you will always enjoy good fortune and be invincible; and once your fleet acquires self-confidence, it will be considered formidable on all the seas. I could further demonstrate which cities unconquered by enemies were destroyed by internal hatreds, but I have assumed that in this well-known matter a few of the most outstanding examples drawn from antiquity would suffice. In our age I find nowhere a more famous example than yourselves. Therefore, recall that time when you were the happiest of all Italic peoples. I was then an infant, and I can remember, as if in a dream, when that shoreline of your gulf that looks both eastward and westward used to appear a heavenly and not an earthly dwelling, such as poets describe in the Elysian fields with their hilltops full of delightful pathways, green valleys, and blessed souls in the valleys. Who would not marvel from on high at the towers and palaces, and at nature so artfully subdued, at the stern hills covered with cedars, vines, and olive trees, and under the high cliffs marble villas equal to any royal palace and worthy of any city? Who could behold without astonishment those delightful recesses where amidst the cliffs stood courtyards with gilded roofs? Resounding with the heavy waves of the sea and wet from stormy rains, these would attract seafarers' attention because of their beauty and would cause the sailor struck by the view's novelty to abandon his oar. But if the journey were by land, who would not be greatly astonished at seeing the majestic and truly superhuman quality of your men and women? What traveler would not halt in the midst of his journey to observe among the shady forests and remote countrysides delights never seen in the cities? When one finally arrived in your city, truly a regal city as it was said of Rome, one would think it was like entering the temple of happiness and the doorway to joy. Not long before that time, after your defeat of the Pisans in a major battle, you undertook another naval war with the Venetians. Ask your own elders—for there are survivors who saw both battles—how much trepidation there was in the ports, how much reverence from the people, how much din on the shores at the return of your victorious fleet in those days when hardly anyone dared navigate the seas for long without your permission. Slowly turn your minds and memories from that moment to another, when extravagance, envy, and pride, those companions of success, invaded your blessed city and its victorious people. These accomplished what had never been accomplished by outside forces: such great misery that the appearance of your city, now forsaken, uncultivated, and filthy, and the beauty of your shoreline, transformed from magnificent villas into as many dens of thieves, inspired terror and dread in travelers. Finally your city was besieged by its exiles, with the assistance of the Milanese, and long troubled by a serious war. It was then that Robert, the Sicilian king of cherished memory, that shining star of his age who had come to its aid, spent nearly one year within its walls, and daily fought—something which sounds incredible and was never seen elsewhere—not only on land and sea but at times even in the air and underground. After that, you had no peace for many years, no security, although meanwhile you had nothing to fear except your victorious citizens and your own weapons. At length, taught by your ills, you had turned for assistance to a single, just ruler, doubtless the best government for a state. Then for the first time, with your rivalries laid aside, your happiness returned, and with the dispersal of the clouds of evil, your coveted tranquillity was restored. Whence resulted peace at home and justice, the friend of peace; whence resulted the sweet harmony of citizens, which certainly promotes a city's growth, and the desire for no other kind of victory except against the enemy. With this achieved, unless I am mistaken, it is simple to take precautions for the future. Ancient is the proverb that many things are badly done because they are done only once, nor is there any recourse for those who err once. You, who have been twice fortunate in one lifetime, recall what ruined you, what deprived you of your original happiness, since it is not in the distant past. You have learned from a local example, memorable and recent, that the greater your happiness, the more need for protecting it; for human prosperity is a delicate thing, uncertain and slippery. You know that nothing can hurt you except your own arms and internal discord. Begin to live once again; recognize your digressions, and be careful not to slide back into your old ways. If you avoid this, all other things are secure; you will return victorious from all battles. Love each other, love justice, love peace, and if you are possessed by a desire for war, go into war happily, for there is never a dearth of enemies. But abstain from civil wars.

Avignon, 1 November.

Fam. XIV, 6.

To the same correspondents, an appeal to do battle against
external enemies.

What I desired I now see; from east to west you are spreading
your victorious banners. I beg you to devote yourselves to this, O
valiant men; attend to it, for this is a patriotic, just, and holy war
that is not in the least Italian. I urge you to exercise your military
skill and valor and to press the attack; through it you must uproot
with battleaxes the primary cause of your troubles. Here is that lying
king; to his search for legitimate causes for war you replied with
equal boldness and truth, following his incipient warlike actions, that
he was really inventing pretexts with empty words, that the true
reason for his madness was avarice, but that he was selling his honor
and his men's blood for a petty price and soon with a belated repentance would come to deplore what he was then doing. Now that
time promised him has arrived. What was lost in the Hellespont will
now be reacquired in the Tyrrhenian and African seas; the western
sea reeks with slaughters and burns with fires; landing on those
shores, destroy with your swords and with your flames the shelters
of those miserable robbers. I beg you, persist and do not desist, pursue your enemies and overtake them, and do not turn back until you
have made an end of them; in the words of the Psalmist, smite them
until they are unable to resist and they will fall under your feet. Exhausted from their lengthy expeditions in foreign lands, they will
again be defeated in their own territory; recognize the power of a
favorable fortune. I used to say: "Check your spirits, restrain your
anger, moderate your victory." But with the change of subject matter, I am changing my style; I now exclaim: "Press closely upon the
terrified enemy, pursue them in their flight, offer the weary no time
to catch their breath, give this war its final blow; have no fear of a
royal name, for often that which glitters externally is dark within.
Greater than royal sway is the power to punish the pride of kings;
you have not a king, but regal spirits. Rome was small while she had
a king, but as soon as she did not, she became boundless; and she
who had been a slave under one king ruled an empire without them.
Attack this king; the sceptre neither bestows nor eliminates virtue.
He is a king, but a man and a mortal; he has done you many wrongs
for which he should be given well-deserved punishment by a fair
judge. Finally, whatever we may wish to imagine about him, he is

*See preceding letter.

still only one person; how many of your own people can wear the crown more splendidly since they are stronger and more illustrious because of their glorious deeds! Go forth undaunted, for you are at war with a mere name. You have conquered live bodies, do not fear mere shades. Go forth undaunted, then, for you go not to war but to the rewards of war; go quickly while there is time; to know how to use victory against one's citizens is cruelty, but not to know how to use it against the enemy is folly. He is, I say, an insolent king who despises treaties and pledges; his is a people impatient with peace and a fleet that is infamous and wicked; these are your enemies as well as the people's. Avenge both yourselves and your republic, and compel the barbarians to recognize that they have foolishly undertaken an unworthy and abominable war against justice and against a people expert in arms, that bedazzled by Venetian gold and blindly desirous of others' wealth, they have meanwhile been unmindful of their own condition. Let them publicly repent for the madness and hasty counsel of a few men, and let them direct against their own betrayers the arms which they unsuccessfully bore against you. Let them fear eternally not so much your arms as your name." I am speaking contrary to my custom: I am enkindling already burning embers, and goading men already rushing to the fray. You have already begun what I am urging, and fortune too favors your glorious beginnings. Follow her voice with unwearied virtue. I who am accustomed always to preach peace shall now confidently say the following: it is advantageous to you not to let just wars such as this fail; the rust of civil strife is cleansed by external involvement. I know not your intentions, but I confess that the wrongs you have suffered exasperate me; therefore may I perish if you find in this letter any mention of peace. For you I desire a bloodless victory over a treacherous enemy.

Fam. XIV, 7.

To Gui, cardinal, Bishop of Porto.

Your permission to leave, which you verbally granted me at your departure, you have now withdrawn in a letter sent en route. In it you request and advise, in keeping with your usual consideration—and I in keeping with my devoted humility have accepted your request and counsel as commands—you request and advise, I say, that I not leave here until you return or write another letter about a most important matter dealing, you say, with my situation for which you offer your services with much kindness and liberality. Indeed, who can now imagine my joy or measure my gratitude? That a great man should do such things for such an insignificant person and, redounding to your credit, without any request from me and without my having any knowledge of it whatsoever, can only lead to the belief that you must be kind and magnificent! With all due respect to our century I should say that today this is hardly the usual way of acting. I am therefore compelled to marvel at your virtue and to praise my good fortune: you never forget your friends whether present or absent, nor do you ever cease thinking of their well-being and their honor. If I deserve to be one of your followers, I am fortunate; surely no one deserves that without the assistance of virtue. If this has happened to me undeservingly, I am at least fortunate, as they say, because of a benevolent and propitious star. Eager to obey, then, I have waited in vain for two months, and not for the one month which you had set as the length of your absence. I postponed my departure, waiting for nothing more than to see you once again whom I always keep present. But as for my eager eyes which hope to behold your serene face, once I have departed, they will not see you again for a long time, unless I am mistaken. It is for this reason that I willingly looked forward to satisfying my desire. And so? The greatest of kings, to whom you are joined in love and blood, together with Paris and the more flattering Seine, are detaining you, forgetful of your promise, beyond the time set for your return; gloomy Avignon and the violent Rhone have thus far painfully detained me. At length weary and satiated with Curial matters, incapable of waiting longer I have undertaken this very day a journey with the intention of going a short distance; I shall stop at the source of the Sorgue as long as possible in the hope that the happy news of your return in the meanwhile should reach me. If you con-

*See XIII, 1.

tinue thus, I shall depart quietly and secretly, deceiving my friends, who wish to detain me here eternally, if they can, despite my contrary determination and opposing fortune; while my friends satisfy their own desires they really overlook mine. My love for them has compelled me to endure much that ambition could never have done; it was that love that forced my hand and detained my weary body where my spirit was not. Recently, however, as I have said, the weight of your command was added, which bound any movement of my feet with chains; if all toil and difficulty become more burdensome the closer their end, you will be persuaded that this two-month delay has been longer for me than spending a year in these parts. It is because of this one merit, since I lack others, that I ask a last favor: that my friends not be held accountable for my absence. If you were going to plead for anything significant on my behalf—for you do not usually do small favors—you will please me so much if whatever was destined for me be passed on to them, and thus they may not feel my absence while you are with them. As for me, I have all I need for this very brief journey of life, more than enough, even too much, and I require no more. I beg you, O most benevolent father, to forgive me if just as I willingly and joyfully obeyed you while I could, now unwillingly I must obey sadly that necessity to which even kings and leaders must submit. Farewell, you who are a glory to the church.

At the source of the Sorgue, 8 November.

Fam. XIV, 8.

To Ponzio Sansone, Canon of Cavaillon. *

May your kind disposition forgive me, O worthy sir, if I departed without saying farewell; I was remiss in this because of my long-standing allegiance and recent promise. There is nothing that a mind conscious of a great love does not presume; I confess that my hope was for forgiveness. I said to myself: "He knows my ways and my affairs and my heart; he will not deny forgiveness to my many concerns, of which he is well aware." Although I am always busy with new and unusual kinds of preoccupations, as you know, I have in these last days found myself even busier than anyone can imagine; as a result, I often marvel and become angry, asking myself what is the reason in this short life span for all these preoccupations of mortals and why does anyone wish so much anxiety upon himself. Still I sometimes flatter myself that my concerns proceed not from the ordinary crowd of daily cares but from a purer source. I find comfort for my labors through this means, except that I clearly know that all of us living beings gladly deceive ourselves in judging our own affairs. Therefore it is very near the truth that just as I ridicule the many about my studies, so in turn I am ridiculed by them; nevertheless I have always scorned the judgment of the multitude, disdaining not only their scorn of me but even considering it a considerable portion of my glory. What preoccupies me still more is that I sometimes scarcely approve of my own studies and vigils; and I feel I would be acting more wisely if I abandoned everything for which I labor and waste such valuable time, in order to begin doing the one thing I have long meditated, for which alone I came into this short and wretched life. But often another thought follows upon this excuse: that my studies are in no way harmful to that purpose and are perhaps even useful. Amidst such doubt and hesitation I am only troubled by the lack of time; and so I try to find ways to free myself, but meanwhile I become more involved and preoccupied. May truth find a place amidst these alternating mental deliberations! But returning to my initial excuse, I was called home for personal affairs that I consider of some significance. I knew that by coming to you I would depart too slowly; my cares ordered me to make haste; the swift and

---

*Ponzio Sansone, Canon of Cavaillon, intimate friend of Philippe de Cabassoles, was a friend from Petrarch's boyhood. He is known only from Petrarch's description of him in the *De vita solitaria* (II, tratt. 10 cap. 1) where he is eulogized for his Samson-like qualities.

brief day flew by; the approaching night pressed upon me, overtaking me en route as I was riding a very weary horse. Do forgive me, I beg you; so that you may not have new cause for complaint, I wish you to know that my intention in the coming days is to depart for Italy, for—since plans often go awry—I have decided to complete in the wintertime what I had determined to do in the autumn. Were I even to go to India, I shall always and everywhere be with you. Farewell.

At the source of the Sorgue, 13 November.

Fam. XV, 1.

To his Lelius, an appeal to pursue with resolve the projected
reform of the Republic.*

Our long-standing love, indeed ever fresh and never allowed to
grow old, which bound us from an early age with indissoluble
bonds, has often prompted me in recent days to write you, and to
renew our interrupted relationship; and yet I was restrained on the
one hand by the entanglements of my cares and on the other by the
recollection of your silence. After all, who but a madman speaks to a
deaf person? There are men who are not troubled by wasted words,
and to them the Ovidian saying certainly applies: "The loss of words
is not serious." Whoever considers the brevity and swiftness of time,
however, knows how sparingly and frugally it must be distributed,
how it must not be wasted in useless actions and words. The head of
a family who beholds himself near to poverty abstains from needless
expenditures; the traveler who sees the day waning doubles his
pace; the plowman who notices a storm's approach urges on his exhausted oxen, continuing his plowing with more vigor than usual;
the prudent sailor who sees his sail collapsing catches the waning
puffs of the dying breeze; and friends who are about to depart try to
speak hurriedly with a continuous stream of words at the last moment, allowing no moment to be lost. You will find this to be so in
nearly everything; we love our goods all the more when they hasten
toward an end. You know that the same happens to all elders unless
they are victims of senility; they love time, and because they wasted
its first fruits, they gather together their remnants. For me too time
has become dearer than it once was, and it appears swifter and more
irrecoverable; I see its flight without return, I recognize its deceits
and I fear its flatteries. I feel myself reaching the end with each passing hour, and strive to turn to better use what remains of my time,
despairing not of success despite the great labor involved. Had I had
this goal in mind from my youth I could perhaps, now that my life's
duties are discharged, live securely, which is more pleasant than
anything else. But to come to the main point, I wrote you quite
often and always found you—whether because of preoccupations or
laziness, for I do not wish to suspect pride in the heart of such a
friend—I always found you, as I was saying, unyielding and slow in
your responses. And yet if I may boast with you as I often do with
myself, I have often been considered worthy in these intervals of let-

*See III, 19.

ters and messages from kings and rulers. Recalling all this, I resolved to give respite to my pen, wearied to no avail in dealing with your affairs; the well-known fame of your virtue now spurs me to return to the task. I speak according to my convictions, for among the powerful of this world yours is a serious disgrace and an inexcusable crime; you should know that they are convinced that whatever happens in the new senate, regardless of the person truly responsible, is all your doing. Such is everyone's opinion of your abilities, and mine is even greater since you are closer to me. Therefore I hope your shoulders will be sufficiently strong not only to bear these few things offensive to insolent minds that consider nothing unjust except what opposes their desires and nothing just except what serves their pleasures, but also to raise your collapsed and prostrate republic from the mud, provided the republic itself entrusts itself to your counsel and that you lay aside all personal feelings and turn to the common good. In this I differ from the opinion of many great men because what they consider an enormous dishonor for you is for me the source of your greatest honor; with subdued grumbling they threaten temporal punishment for you for the very reason I predict eternal fame. How I wish that my weary and busy pen could accomplish something for you along these lines! If you continue as you began, you will doubtless deserve such fame because of your own virtue, not because virtue demands the reward of fame, but because it cannot be without it even though it may wish to be; for just as a shadow follows the body so does glory follow virtue. In short, as far as they are concerned, there is nothing for me to warn you about, for you know all there is to know. I want you never to forget one thing I often heard from that high-minded and wise old man, despite his opinions that differed from ours; what he said seemed memorable not because of the elegance of his words but the truth of his opinions. On the basis of his experience he would say very forcefully: "The Roman church is wont to esteem the powerful." Nothing briefer, nothing truer can be said. Thus if you wish to be acclaimed by the people and be dear to God, which is even more desirable, O Romans, cultivate the virtues, love religion, observe justice, use your ancient skills: spare your subjects and vanquish the proud. But if you wish to be esteemed by the church, your only need is power without which, believe me, you accomplish nothing, however great your virtue. As far as you are concerned, I shall say only this: of the two who seized control of our republic in recent times I wrote at great length to the one and nothing to the other because the former had given me great hope, though premature, and the latter hardly any. But if you persist, my dear friend, if you do not fear the threats and hissings of serpents, I believe you will give birth to many and various accomplishments in due time. For now let this suffice as a reminder: those entering this path are harmed equally by too much moderation and too much fervor; you have before your eyes domestic and recent examples of both kinds, and as Ovid has it, "You will proceed most safely in the middle of the road." Farewell, and since you are a man, act as one.

Fam. XV, 2.

To Francesco, of the Church of the Holy Apostles, * *concerning the obstacles encountered at the start of his journey.*

Night brings counsel: the proverb is ancient and true in my experience. At the source of the Sorgue I had packed my few belongings which in these times I often carry around with me, and set out from there on 16 November, relying on a clear winter day, which can be truly fickle and uncertain. My hopes had been raised because throughout the autumn and long afterwards, even to that very day, no clouds, much less rain, had been seen. My usual fate worried me because it never allows me to travel anywhere without heat or rain, and it now appeared quite likely that the heavens would pour out what they had been storing up. What do you think happened? Scarcely had I stuck my foot out the door than rain began to fall, at first a light rain very much like drizzle, but soon it turned into a steady downpour. I became irritated and began to recognize my usual luck, and in the meantime I began to look back and consider the possibility of returning. But meanwhile, as often happens, my body still continued on its way as my mind turned back. This state of mind did not last long, for as day came to an end I found myself near a harbor. I came to Cavaillon, a small but quite ancient neighboring town. I found to my surprise that the local bishop, Philippe, the best of men, more concerned than anyone else for my comfort and honor—more so than I am myself—was ill; but he received me, nevertheless, in his customary way, not as a man but as an angel of God, and he wept with joy. He thought that I was bringing him his health again, and that with me a remedy for all his ills was crossing his threshold. When he heard, however, that I had come not with the intention of remaining but to say my last farewell, he became very sad and all his joy changed to lamentation. Using all his authority, he prevailed upon me to remain under his roof, or rather under my roof as he always showed in word and deed. He insisted that I grant him that one night so that he could, as he said, enjoy by my presence the remnants of the solace he had hoped for and I the remnants of my weariness. I willingly obeyed, since the hour for the lighting of lights was near and the rain had by now become a deluge. That night I slept very little; for in the middle of the night, at first very faintly, then more loudly and finally continuously the murmur of the servants caring for the sick man permeated the house, spreading the rumor that a band of raiders from

*See XII, 4.

the mountains had descended upon Nice-on-the-Var and that already the road was blocked by enemy scouts who ranged far and wide. Initially I believed the story to be the kindly father's invention so as to prevent me from proceeding with my plans, since great love is ingenious, as those experienced in it well know. Having thereupon sent some of my servants to inquire into the matter, I learned that the report was not at all fabricated but well known and widespread. I began to waver and to ponder a number of possibilities, and to ask the bishop's advice, while he increasingly urged me to abandon my plans if I desired his safety and my own. I nevertheless clung to my intention of departing although I could easily have been persuaded to change my itinerary; for, though more inconvenient and longer, I had chosen this route simply because I wished to visit my brother whom I had not seen in five years, and who lives near that road in the service of Christ. While discussing all this with that excellent father, the deluge continually grew in intensity; weary in mind I retired to my bedchamber and slept scarcely one entire hour, I believe. I awakened earlier than is my custom and immediately turned to the recitation of matins, as is my wont; everything seemed flooded because the roof tiles could not keep out the rain; once again I began mulling over with the sleepless bishop and myself what to do and what course of action to take: one road was blocked because of war, all had been blocked because of the flood. What else need be said? The matter, to use the words of historians, was beginning to assume religious proportions: it appeared that my departure did not please God. There also arose in me the fear of seeing my books ruined, which formed a large portion of my baggage. I realized that possessions obstruct one's freedom, since I feared, to use Maro's words, for what I carried rather than for my body. I would certainly have left if I had been unimpeded; now I had to remain. I yielded to the bishop's pleas, and changing my plans I sent on to Italy some of my servants and returned to the source of the Sorgue. Here I am almost alone, with some hope that this delay will lead to some unexpected good or avert some unexpected evil. With little faith in human counsel, I have entrusted the vessel of my affairs, as the helmsman of a ship overcome by a storm, not to the winds and the waves but to God, under whose guidance no shipwreck can occur. Farewell.

At the source of the Sorgue, 18 November.

Fam. XV, 3.

To Zanobi, Florentine grammarian,* concerning the same matter.

I know that you are surprised and saying to yourself: "Where in the world is he battling now?" unless perchance that alter ego of mine in name and in fact, who is keeping watch over my nest in my native land as I wander far away, sent you from Florence to Naples my letter addressed to him, which dealt more or less with this subject. If he has done so, the present letter is useless. But since I fear he may be very busy, and know your desire to hear from me, I decided it was preferable to spend an hour writing an unnecessary letter than to withhold news about myself from a friend because of my greed for time. Where I am, what I am considering, what I am doing you have heard; and rumor had it that I was fleeing the storms of the Curia to return to Italy where the fates seemed to offer a quiet retreat. I was making my way along the road to Genoa with the sole purpose of seeing after five years my only brother, dearer to me for his virtue than for our common blood, who has chosen a solitary and wooded place named Montrieux near that road to become a servant of Christ and to mortify the flesh. At the western boundary of Italy near the river Var I learned that the road was blocked by a war caused by certain armed Alpine peoples who had poured down onto the shore. Moved by these reports and by friends' entreaties, I was about to change my plans and take another route. I was already mentally turning leftward in order to go to Mont Genèvre when an unexpected cloudburst poured down everywhere—and this was all the stranger because before and ever since that storm we have had a great drought in the heavens and on the land such as we have never seen and can hardly find recorded. I stopped anxiously. Rarely had I ever realized more clearly what Virgil meant by his fear for a dear burden. I had with me a precious bundle of books, and in with the old books was a small number of my own trifles with which I too cover sheets of Egyptian parchment, not because doing so is the best of occupations, but because for me doing anything else is difficult, and doing nothing at all is harmful, almost impossible, and against my nature. In that situation I feared not for my body, hardened enough for anything and long accustomed to bear not only rain but ice, heat and hail, and experienced in all labors or danger; I feared not for myself *and* for my burden as Aeneas did, but only for my burden as Metabus did; for I confess that my fear was for that little bundle so dear to me. What

*See XII, 3.

could I do? "Turning all things over in my mind," as he says, it seemed evident that God's will was somehow forbidding me to depart at that time; it would seem almost irreverent if I, on my own authority, resisted divine prohibition. Recalling the saying of Cleanthes, "the fates lead on the willing, but drag the unwilling," I willingly yielded in order not to yield unwillingly, and sent several of my servants to Italy, not so much to attend, with their presence, to certain urgent matters for me, as to afford me, with their departure, a more perfect solitude and a more tranquil idleness. They had scarcely departed and had proceeded just so far that there was no way to recall or overtake them, when the skies suddenly cleared. It has now been this way for several months, as it had been previously, and it seems likely it will continue thus, unless the heavenly ruler changes His mind or, since the will of the Lord remains in eternity, decides to reveal His will in a new way. Therefore, the more I think about it, the more it becomes evident that my strong desire attracting me to Italy has been checked by God with earthly and celestial obstacles in order to counteract human dangers; for what we desire is merely pleasing, whereas for God it is also known. What else could I think, given the war in regions where in the memory of our fathers there had never been one, and given the only cloudburst this year on the very day at the very hour of my departure? And so, checked in this fashion, I returned to the source of the Sorgue a few days after my departure. Before the swift moon had twice completed its immense course, one of the servants whom I had sent ahead, as you heard, returned. "What in the world," he said, "are you trying to do? While fleeing Charybdis, you turn your prow toward Scylla: you shudder at the problems in the Curia, as you should, but you do not know what a mass of troubles await you if you set foot in Italy. What a bevy of friends the rumor of your return has created for you; in how many ways you will have to divide your mind, which you hope to collect; in how many affairs it will have to become involved that are really not concerns of yours but of your friends; and how much time you will have to lose, of which you have so little and need so much; how many annoyances you will have to bear in order to satisfy the desires of others!" After this rather general statement, he carefully elaborated each point, presenting explanations that were brighter than the sun, and added much else which must remain unsaid. Why do I detain you any longer? He seemed to me to be speaking not as a servant, but as a philosopher and a divine being. And so, pondering and reconsidering much within myself, perceiving that where I had believed to find a port was a turbulent sea, and forced by the storm of affairs to redirect the ship of my mind, I tied the halyards, dropped anchor, tied fast the helm, and moored amidst these cliffs the ship of my life, wearied by storms, until a port appears, with no intention of returning to the Curia or of seeking Italy unless I hear otherwise.

If you were to ask what I am doing here, I would answer, "I am alive—to be sure." Do you expect me to complete the verse with: "I spend my life amidst all kinds of adversities?" God forbid! Indeed I am well and happy, and I reject everything that distresses most men. Here is how I live: I rise in the middle of the night, go outdoors at sunrise, but both in the fields and at home I study, think, read, and write; I keep sleep from my eyes as long as possible, softness from my body, pleasures from my mind, sluggishness from my actions. Every day I wander over the rocky mountains, through the dewy valleys and caverns; I often walk along both banks of the Sorgue without meeting anyone who disturbs me, without a companion or guide except my cares, which day by day grow less insistent and troublesome. Mindful of the past, I deliberate on things to come and consider them from every angle. Let Him decide how wisely I do this about whom it is written: "In Your light we shall see the light," without whom blind humanity peers in vain through the shadows. My every hope lies in His guidance; certainly with all my might I strive to make my spirit ready and willing, forgetting as did the Apostle the past as best I can and turning my attention to the future. One important consolation has been granted me in each place of exile; just as I seem to have succeeded in adapting myself to this place, I could do the same in any other as required, with the exception of Avignon which overhangs the windy and turbulent waters of the Rhone. I could no longer bear your not knowing all this, my dear friend, if it was indeed unknown to you until now, for fear of having your letters perchance wandering in search of me here and there over uncertain paths. As I said, I am at the source of the Sorgue; and since fortune has so decreed, I seek no other place, nor shall I do so, until she shifts her changeable edicts as is her wont. Meanwhile here I have established my Rome, my Athens, and my spiritual fatherland; here I gather all the friends I now have or did have, not only those who have proved themselves through intimate contact and who have lived with me, but also those who died many centuries ago, known to me only through their writings, wherein I marvel at their accomplishments and their spirits or at their customs and lives or at their eloquence and genius. I gather them from every land and every age in this narrow valley, conversing with them more willingly than with those who think they are alive because they see traces of their stale breath in the frosty air. I thus wander free and unconcerned, alone with such companions; I am where I wish to be. As much as possible, I remain alone with myself; often too I am with you and with that illustrious man whom, strange to say, I see at all hours although I have never met him. Whenever you are able to speak with him, I beg you to keep my name alive for him. Farewell.

At the source of the Sorgue, 22 February.

Fam. XV, 4.

To Andrea Dandolo, Doge of Venice,* a justification for his frequent moves.

What I had silently suspected, I now hear from you: you are surprised that I am wandering here and there, never settling down, that seemingly I have not yet selected a steady abode for myself, that after spending scarcely one year in Italy I have for the past two years been migrating from Italy to France and from France to Italy. Since there is no denying this, I must report the reason, to you so that you will commiserate, to other men of good will so that they will forgive, and to the public so that it will not tear me to shreds. I applaud the words of Annaeus Seneca, "The first mark of a well-ordered mind is that it can stand still and commune with itself;" but I also know that many who have never left their little towns are still ever aimless in mind and incoherent in thought, while others in continuous movement have been men of great seriousness and stability. Many great generals and philosophers have been wanderers, as you well recall, whereas Vatia, though still alive, was hidden and buried in his country home and Buta snored all day and lay awake all night, never leaving his bedroom; you too know of this pair whom Seneca makes famous in his letters and immortal through his mockery. The apostles travelled far and traversed barefoot the most distant regions; one was sent to Ephesus, another to Syria, another to Greece, several to Rome, another to India, and still another to Egypt; their bodies wandered through the roughest regions and were hurled about on land and sea, but their hearts remained fixed on heaven; the bodies of our present apostles repose on gilded beds while their minds wander over land and sea. I therefore ask, among all these men, who shall we say possesses the mark of a well-ordered mind? Those who do not change locations or those who do not change their purpose? There is something else I must mention that I have often said and am happy to repeat; the Greek poet and our own who followed in his footsteps, whom no philosopher ever surpassed in the depiction of human affairs, make the perfect man, in their descriptions of his character and actions, travel the entire world always learning something new. They did not believe that the man they shaped with their eloquence could be what they wished of him were he to remain continually in one place.

Because these examples perhaps do not apply to me, I omit excuses

*See XI, 8.

that would indicate pride or provoke envy, in order to return to the one for which I urged your compassion. Since you, my dear sir, so devoted to good men did travel at one time and did acquire knowledge of many places and things, since through the merits of your excellence you have now finally ascended in glorious fashion to the highest office of your renowned republic while still in your youth, and since you have willingly enclosed yourself in a splendid but everlasting prison for the sake of the liberty and welfare of the people, I know that I would be acting in a way more pleasing to you if, after the wandering campaign of my life, I too were to begin pitching camp somewhere near you, to spend whatever remains of my days in peace. Know that for me also nothing is more pleasing or more desirable, and yet nothing seems more difficult. For this reason, I have long steered my helm in this direction, but the raging waters push me unwillingly elsewhere as I struggle in vain. Since I feel your great affection and have known your great modesty in listening, in the midst of your occupations, to discussions even by your humble friends, I confess that it was my youthful ambition to follow the advice in Homer's poem: to behold the mores and cities of many people and to contemplate with curiosity new lands, lofty mountains, famous seas, celebrated lakes, hidden springs, noted rivers, and various other sites. I believed that thus I might become learned, something which has always been my primary desire, and might do so expeditiously and briefly, without much trouble, indeed with great pleasure; it seemed that I would in some way deliver myself from ignorance by exercising the mind and body. But I have wandered enough now, enough have I gone in circles, enough have I humored my desire; it may be time to address the standard-bearer of my mind as that Roman centurion addressed his: "Standard-bearer, lay down your banner, it is best for us to remain here." Surely either my wandering and rambling through many lands to a point of saturation or my youthful ardor, now slackening and gradually cooling, and leading to my desire for peaceful surroundings, which is more becoming to my calling, has killed my appetite for wandering and roving. But what shall I do? If anyone were ever to believe anything about me, let it be this: should I ever find a good spot under the heavens—or at least not a bad place, not to say a terrible one—I would go and stay there gladly and permanently. At present, like a man on a hard bed, I toss and turn, not finding the desired repose despite all attempts; and so, because I cannot relieve my weariness with a soft bed, I do so with constant change; and thus I wander and seem to be an eternal pilgrim. Weary of the hardness of one place, I try another, and it is not softer; but its hardness is meanwhile at least softened by novelty. Thus am I tossed about, in the knowledge that there is no resting place here, and that I must long for such rest through many difficulties: here indeed I must perpetually toil and groan and—what is perhaps worst of all—amidst so many trials and fires of life I must still dread eternal strife and everlasting fires and hardships. "Well then," someone may say, "how many live tranquilly and know how to stand firm in those very places where you are agitated?" To this I answer: "How many in those same places live more restlessly and are continually in motion?" I shall not, as did Virgil, speak about the celestial origin of souls nor, as did Cicero, about the mind given to us by those eternal fires which we call planets and stars, to justify, with a metaphor pleasing to Seneca, our mutability with the mutability of the celestial fires from which our souls are born. But I do say this: that our souls are created and at once joined to our bodies by God, that the abode of God is in heaven, as the Psalmist says, that the movements of the heavens are truly perpetual, as we can perceive with our own eyes. It should therefore not be surprising if we reflect some similarity to the place inhabited by our Creator. I do not know whence its origin, but I do know that innate desire, especially in superior minds, to see new places and to change domiciles, something which I do not deny should be tempered and regulated by reason. Believe me, however, and you will believe me more readily when you have experienced it, there is something truly pleasant, though demanding, about this curiosity for wandering through different regions, whereas those who remain in one place always experience a peculiar boredom in their repose. What is best in all human endeavors I believe is known only to God. But if anyone places the highest virtue not in the mind but in places, giving immobility the name of constancy, then sufferers from the gout must certainly appear constant, the dead must appear even more constant, while the mountains are the most constant of all.

Enough of this. I shall perhaps be accused of searching for arguments to excuse my disease; I do not deny that I am ill with a rather serious disease of the mind, and I hope that it will not be mortal; nor can I, in order to offer some excuse, place all the blame for my disease on my bed. Once more I repeat what appears evident even were I to remain silent: I am ill; make me well. I shall be stronger, but my bed will not for all that be softer or unrumpled—the bed of this life on which I lie exhausted—but rather rough, unpleasant, soiled, uneven, lumpy, such as would torture even the most healthy body. How anyone can find rest in such a bed

I know not, unless perhaps those who sleep more deeply do not feel what oppresses me, or they find in torment certain pleasures unknown to me! And yet what prevents us from believing that I am suffering from a fever of mind, while they are healthy? I could easily believe this of learned men, but neither I nor anyone else is about to believe that the multitude possesses a healthy mind when it is instead insensible and sluggish. Finally, let others know the causes of their tranquillity; let it suffice for me to have revealed the causes of my restlessness. Either I am mistaken or I am not as ill as I appear; and even though I may be somewhat ill, why should I not stop being so were it not for inconveniences of place and circumstance? It would be well for me to adopt, if possible, a remedy I have recommended to others, namely, that I find within myself a peace not found without, and that I find that repose, which cannot be found in places, within my own spirit, or rather in the Master and the Illuminator of the spirit. But more of this at another time. For you, O wisest of rulers, whom love alone has driven to worry and wonder about my affairs, let this be the answer for now. Farewell.

At the source of the Sorgue, 26 February.

Fam. XV, 5.

To Pierre, Abbot of St-Bénigne, his disappointment over
the Emperor's delayed journey, and other matters.*

You have indeed used a wonderful and utterly new technique; with
the pretext of a reverence for my style, my dear father, you
magnificently excused your tardiness, or more properly your affairs
that made you fall behind in much of your correspondence owed me.
While you express in elegant words and with wonderful refinement
your admiration for my writing, you truly surprised me with your
own. Can it be that either you do not realize, or you hope, that I
would not perceive that you have now betrayed—as often happens—your own talent and revealed your guilt, particularly through
the excuse you offer? Your letter bears witness that henceforth you
are capable of responding magnificently on any subject even to Cicero
himself, much less to me; and the foregoing testifies that you neglected
to answer me only because of lack of time or will. I knew this to be
so, but your letter assured me that never again will you be able to find
excuses. But to gloss over all this for the present, I now wish to express my deepest gratitude for the books you sent me, you who are
now my father and were once my brother, but even more for the
brief warning with which you arm and fortify me about a considerable part of my expectations; I assure you that your counsel will
be followed. I had previously and silently felt and noted this very
thing, but it has much more meaning when a master's authority is
joined to one's uncertain knowledge. What I used to suspect I now
know: I am sorry to hear that my letter to the Galens of our day,
who claim dominion over our health and illness, over death and mortal life, is arriving too late at its destination. For I knew their madness;
they will feel that they had uttered something wonderful, and thus will
be easily persuaded that I perspired long and much in answering
them. A windy and empty kind of animal are they, always inclined to
believe what they say of themselves, imagining and nourishing
astounding opinions of themselves; what they are in reality, credulous
mortals daily learn with peril to their lives. But let them imagine what
they please, for it will be a small error in comparison to their more
serious ones. You know the whole truth as far as I am concerned: that
I required only one day, not an entire one, and the latter part of one
night to write that letter, although it did remain for several days in the
hands of copyists.

*See XIII, 7.

Your letter brings me news about the passage into Italy of our leader, yourself, and all of yours, which I believed imminent; it rid me of my false hope but I do regret that it was false. For his journey seemed glorious and his efforts fruitful for the entire world, but "destiny resisted", in the words of the poet. I fear our Caesar may simply be satisfied with living out his life, that he may feel by his disdain of the crown destined for his sacred brow no concern for the empire or desire for greater glory. What is he doing, or what is he thinking? Surely if he is content with his Germany and the mere limbs of the empire, he has forsaken its head, Italy; he may be the German king, but he cannot be the Roman emperor. Foolishly I hoped that my two letters of appeal, written with scarcely any artifice but with much trust and ardor, would move him, not to say fire his spirit. But why be astonished that mere words do not affect one unaffected by the splendor of glory, by immense reward, or by the simple opportunity to accomplish magnificent deeds? I would be downcast in spirit except that I had learned through much experience not to be troubled by transitory matters. Nearly all hopes and cares, not only my own but all mankind's, have but one end: they vanish into nothingness, for whatever is woven under the sun is very like a spiderweb. What do you wish me to say? "Not all of us can do all things," says Maro; "whoever can understand, let him understand." Rulers should certainly possess that heroic virtue which Virgil calls "glowing" and Lucan calls "fiery"; unless it is given at birth by the heavens, it is difficult to acquire. But why am I upset, being the smallest particle of the republic? Why do I torment myself? Why do I rack myself to pieces? I am a newcomer and a pilgrim on earth, as were all my forefathers; I am an exile and a wayfarer anxious about the journey's brevity. How much longer I shall live, I know not; I shall die and return to my true fatherland. Italy will remain between the Alps and the two seas as she has since the beginning of time; and if the aid of an earthly ruler is not forthcoming, she will implore the mercy of the eternal Emperor. Believe me, then, my dear father: it is a serious matter to sit in the chair of Peter, and a serious matter to sit on the throne of Caesar. Enjoy good health and farewell.

At the source of the Sorgue, 3 April, with my pastoral pen.

Fam. XV, 6.

To the same correspondent, * *against unjust critics.*

My controversy with doctors is indeed great. "What then," you might say, "don't you fear fevers?" I do not feel so secure as that, but I place no hope in these doctors. Someone else might say, "And what do you have in common with them?" Nothing at all except that I have offended their minds with the truth, nor do I regret having done so; indeed if the truth makes enemies, I shall always either remain silent or never be without enemies. My quarrel is not with all doctors, however, but the worst of them: the very title of my letter shows this, for it is addressed to a certain impudent and mad doctor. Whoever is disturbed by it is himself impudent, mad and the one whom I address, not because there is only one such person, but because the singular is often more significant and because one of that group had stood out above the others in his madness. Thus I had to wage war against that one man, punishing in one the impudence of the many. There are those who become arrogant at an adversary's moderation and receive encouragement to speak out from another's silence; such an unfit species and gang of revilers must be checked by abuse. What is the present status of this literary war? If you desire to know, I can tell you clearly what goes on in my camp. I scorn the entire matter, ridiculing my garrulous and powerless adversary. The matter stands as I stated at the end of my longer letter; I have not laid aside my darts; if he makes a move he will feel them and thus understand this pen; if he wishes to attempt revenge, it will not be without punishment. I believe, however, that he wishes he had not started this battle, but bygones are not changed through repentance; and so he is ashamed to yield and displeased to fight, and thus, you may see him agitated and worried. Because of his inability to speak out he goes about the city seeking the undependable assistance of public scribes; for I recently learned that the letter you saw in which he first attacked me with impudent words is the work of some peasant writer. I pity his madness, and I confess that often it crosses my mind to become more friendly and, laying aside our quarrel, to reveal him to himself. If I could, I would also suppress the man's arrogance; but it is very difficult to implant new ideas into a hardened heart. First the man must be freed from error so that at length truth can find room in his busy mind; for this reason I despaired and decided against such action. In the beginning I had not known with

*See XIII, 7.

which enemy I had to do battle, and, as if struck by Nisus in the shadows, I could unknowingly have fought with my drawn pen against Euryalus; nevertheless I guessed—nor was I wrong in my guess—whence those spears of words were directed at me. Finally with the discovery of the plot, I recognized the personal identity of my poorly disguised enemy, and upon close examination I read in his countenance the marks of his obstinate and arrogant ignorance. Now I seem to have recognized that hardhead; in the knowledge that people can be broken more readily than bent, I leave him to himself. I shall retain my habit of never making a rash affirmation; he shall retain his habit of continuous quarreling and of judging with confidence those unknown to him.

What else do you expect? Would you like another example of his temerity? Recently I wrote you a letter in which near the end, because the subject required it, I said: "It is a serious matter to sit in the chair of Peter, a serious matter to sit on the throne of Caesar." When you showed him the letter, this sentence annoyed him. Why so? Was I telling a falsehood? Let those who occupy those seats be questioned; I believe they will confess the truth of these words. But how does that untrustworthy interpreter twist it? He says that I meant that the chair of Peter ought to be nowhere but in Rome. But this is not a matter of what I meant to say, but what I did say; unless I am mistaken, what I meant to say cannot be known through Hippocratic prognosis. I know that the see of Peter was wherever Peter sat, and now it is wherever the successor of Peter sits; nor am I ignorant that Peter first sat in Antioch and then in Rome. Although it may still be true that one place may be more sacred and salutary than another, nevertheless it is the prerogative of the head of a household to decide where his abode may be located; and even if he could perhaps live elsewhere more honorably, still whatever place he deems worthy of being his abode, he will grace with honor. That is how I feel, nor while writing did I think of any reproach from my envious critic. I did not suggest the place where he who is the master of all places must necessarily sit. Without drawing from the waters of the Decretals, I have taken this draught from the fount of Jerome: "When it is a matter of authority, the world is more important than the city; and wherever the pope may go, whether in Rome, Gubbio, Constantinople, Reggio, Alexandria, Thebes, or Sarmatia, the place possesses equal authority and the same priesthood." Therefore, with this knowledge, I abstain from stating that sort of nonsense. This I meant to say and this I have said: it is a serious matter to sit in the chair of Peter, wherever that see may be; and I said this not on purpose but incidentally. My subject was really the throne of Caesar, and not the chair of Peter, as you are aware. Know therefore that the accusation was the work of a clearly poisonous mind rather than a keen one; let him, then, rant on and bite as freely as his teeth allow. Live happily and farewell.

At the source of the Sorgue, 17 April.

Fam. XV, 7.

To Stefano Colonna, Provost of St-Omer,* concerning the unsettled condition of nearly the entire world.

Either I am mistaken, O noble sir, or whatever you behold in nearly every region of the world is contrary to your own goals and convictions. Consider Rome, our common fatherland, our mother: she lies there—O shameful spectacle!—trampled by all whom she, the conqueror of all lands and seas, once trampled; and if perchance she leans on her elbow as if to rise again, she soon falls, struck down by the hand of her own sons. Therefore either no hope remains for her or, if there be any, I greatly fear that it lies beyond the present century. Perhaps He will have compassion; perhaps He who selected her as the see of His successors, who established her as the temporal head of the world and as the foundation of His religion, will have compassion for this sacred city. Someday He will have mercy on her, but beyond the limits set for our brief lives. There is nothing in her, then, to render joy to your eyes or to your spirit. What shall I say of the rest of Italy, with her cities and states too numerous to list? Let us therefore limit ourselves to her provinces. Cisalpine Gaul, which includes what the public calls Lombardia but the learned call Liguria, Emilia, and Venetia, indeed whatever lies between the Alps, the Apennines, and the Rubicon—the ancient boundary of Italy—is almost totally in all its vastness oppressed by an undying tyranny; even that region looking westward and sitting at the foot of the mountains—O cruel fortune!—has become a passageway for transalpine tyrants. There you will not find one place where a lover of virtue and tranquillity may seek repose, save that most noble city of the Venetians; though she has remained until the present the sole sanctuary of liberty and justice, she is now so shaken by warfare and is furthermore so much more dedicated to merchant trade than to the Muses in order to regain her former well-being, that I doubt whether she could be a pleasant abode for you. Tuscany, once the most flourishing of lands, which had filled all the universe with its renown and wealth, according to Livy, whose success long before the Roman Empire is amply attested to, especially in the fact that, although countless peoples inhabited the lands near the two seas that gird Italy, Tuscany alone with general consent gave

*Stefano di Pietro Colonna, provost of St-Omer at the time of this letter, became apostolic prothonotary and eventually cardinal under Urban VI in 1378. One of the younger members of the large Colonna family who were Petrarch's patrons, this Stefano was grandson of Stefano the Elder. He died in 1379.

to both seas its name, which will endure forever; today, I say, she proceeds with staggering footsteps between an uncertain liberty and a dreaded servitude, and knows not on which side she will fall. The seagoing Ligurians who dwell, as Florus attests, between the Var and the Magra, whose capital was once Albenga and today is Genoa, are so managing their affairs and their time that, in accordance with their ancient custom, the end of a foreign war means the beginning of a civil one. Would that my recent letter urging them not to let this happen at the present time be as effective as it is sincere! Nevertheless, thus far their stretch of land and the area bordering Illyria on Italy's other shore are raging with the loud thunder of wars and storms of great slaughter; as you know, even today, the Genoese and the Venetians are in battle. And so, in order not to lose any of our ancient ways, we gnaw and are gnawed in turn, tearing each other apart. Every region of the Piceno whose capital is now Ancona but formerly was Ascoli, as Florus again has it, is caught in the ebb and flow of the changeable waves of passions, and the natural fertility of its fine soil spoiled by the nature of the inhabitants. Beautiful Campania, which the great Plotinus once chose as his domicile to enjoy noble leisure where it looks upon the Ernici and Monte Algido, is now not only unsuited to philosophical retreat, but is barely safe for travelers, beset as it always is by roving bandits. On the other hand, where it embraces Capua and Naples and was once called the Land of Labor with much too ominous a foreboding, it now shares a common fate with Apulia, Abruzzi, Calabria, and the entire Kingdom of Sicily: within and without its boundaries, it is shaken and belabored. Once, indeed, that portion of the world had as its sun Robert, greatest of men and kings; on the day he departed the human condition, the sun seemed to have fallen from the heavens, as was said of Plato. If you do not believe me, ask its inhabitants how long the eclipse lasted, how much foulness and sadness pervaded the darkness. I need not say even one word about the city where you dwell, which some call little Rome but which I customarily call the newest Babylon, since it is so well known, not only to its neighbors, but to the Arabs and Indians.

Now bear with me a little longer. All of Gaul and Britain—the very extremity of our part of the world, jutting even beyond its confines—are weakening each other with serious warfare; Germany no less than Italy is sick with internecine riots, burning in its own fires; the kings of Spain have turned their arms against themselves; the largest of the Balearics has lately seen its king, first in exile, and shortly thereafter his body miserably beheaded; Sardinia labors under an inclement heaven and a shameful servitude; primitive and squalid Corsica and the smaller islands in our sea have become notorious and infamous for pirate raids; like fiery Etna, the whole of Sicily is parched by great flames of hatred, deliberating whether it prefers to be with Italy or with Spain, but meanwhile remaining neutral, in a wavering state of mind but in a certain and unmerited slavery, except that whoever wishes not to be free deserves to be enslaved. Rhodes, protector of the faith, lies inglorious without wounds; Crete, that ancient center of superstitions, is living with new ones; Greece travels its wandering path alone, threshes for itself, feeds itself, and poorly ruminating the food of salvation has deserted our fold; in the rest of Europe Christ is either unknown or hated. Lacking an armed enemy, battered by a weakening and easy idleness, pleasures, lust, and other ugly enemies, Cyprus is an unfit abode for a strong man; lesser Armenia fluctuates between the danger of temporal and eternal death, besieged on all sides by enemies of the cross. The garden and sepulchre of the Lord, the twofold haven and repose of Christians, is being trampled beneath the feet of dogs; nor does it have any secure or easy access for those wishing to visit it, surely an enormous disgrace and perpetual shame for our age. Ought death not to be preferred over this crime, unless perhaps we are already dead? About all of Asia and Africa I speak not, although the testimony of histories and of the saints proves that once they were subject to the yoke of Christ, but the damage wrought by the passage of time has resulted in dissimulation and contempt, and what we should have avenged with arms, we have mitigated with oblivion, consoling ourselves with silence. We are more gravely distressed by nearby evils: who would believe that Genoa's little fleet with its hostile prows would reach the Venetian shore, and who would believe that Britain would attack France with a small band of men? Within a very short period of time we have heard of both. Where, I ask, can one now find a safe dwelling place? Venice and Paris seemed the safest of all cities in our region of the globe; the former was a fortress for the Italians, the latter for those beyond the Alps. Recently an enemy easily invaded both these cities, causing profound trepidation. Who would ever have thought that the French king would be vanquished in a British prison, perhaps even to die there? At present we are certain of his imprisonment, but in suspense about his end. Who would have guessed that the British army would reach the gates of Paris? Now it has happened, although who could be astonished at the king's imprisonment or the city's siege, unless he be truly ignorant of the course of history? A Roman emperor grew old in a Persian prison in the most abject servitude; the city of Rome herself saw Hannibal with his army standing in hostile array before the Porta

Collina; she would have borne that shame with greater restraint by comparing it to more serious ones, since many centuries later she was to be captured by the Goths, as she had been many centuries before by the Senones. From all these examples, I draw one conclusion: in mortal affairs there is nothing so miserable that it cannot happen even to those considered most fortunate.

Since this is so, O worthy sir, your course is clear; and therefore I approach you as a faithful adviser, perhaps unneeded, seeking to persuade you to do what I wish I had done long ago. Do then what men accustomed to cleanliness are wont to do, indeed not only men but some white animals that dislike filth; upon emerging from their lairs and perceiving their surroundings covered with dirt, they retreat and remain inside their hiding places. Seeing peace and rest nowhere in all the world, you too return to your room and within yourself; be on guard with yourself, speak with yourself, be silent with yourself, walk with yourself and stand firm with yourself; do not think you are alone if you are with yourself: but if you are not with yourself, though you may be amidst people, you will be alone. Make for yourself a refuge within your mind where you may hide, rejoice, rest without interruption, and live together with Christ, who through the sacred priesthood made you in your youth His confidant and table companion. You will ask, "and with what skills do I do that?" It is virtue alone that is powerful enough to accomplish it all; through her you will be able to rejoice and to live happily wherever you are; no evil can approach you in the midst of evils, for you will choose nothing except what brings you happiness, you will fear nothing except what brings you unhappiness; know, however, that what brings you happiness or unhappiness exists nowhere except in your own heart. What lies outside of you is not yours, only what lies within you is yours; nothing outside of you can be given to you, nothing that is yours can be taken; in your hand alone is found the course of the life you choose. The multitude's opinions must be fled and those of the few followed; with a noble spirit you must scorn fortune, knowing that she possesses more threats than power, that she threatens more than she wounds, that she rages more than she injures, that she has no control over your goods, that her flatteries are not to be trusted, for whatever she gives must be possessed with uncertainty. If you ever assume a higher position, attribute it to divine mercy; if not, note with equanimity that in fortune's realm the good are crushed and the evil exalted, understanding "their final destiny" as the Psalmist says, and recalling that this life is the fatherland of hardships, not of rewards. Farewell.

Fam. XV, 8.

To his Lelius, * a discussion on the selection of a suitable place to live.*

What I shall write will at first seem astounding, but if you turn
your mind to the past, to a consideration of my ways, known to you
from my earliest years, and to my purpose in life, then it will not
seem so astonishing. In sum, no place in the world is pleasing to me;
wherever I turn I find everything thorny and hard. I believe the time
has now come for me to pass to the other life, for, to be honest, I
find myself badly off here, whether it be my fault or the fault of the
location, or of men, or of all these together. I wrote extensively to
our illustrious Stefano, that for these reasons I have been traveling
this earth for such a long time, and I recently wrote in justification to
the eminent doge of Venice, Andrea. I have sent you both those letters, since they seem pertinent to the advice I ask of you; not that I
am uncertain that many points could be argued against me in this
regard, but I feel confident of being able to respond adequately to
them all. With considerable effort and strenuous mental exercise I
have found one consolation amidst so many difficulties: wherever on
earth I may be, though a terrible or even an ugly spot, I persuade
myself that it is fine, and deceiving myself, I force myself not to feel
as I do. Often this is a useful or necessary remedy for ills, yet an extreme one. What good does it do to struggle against an inevitable
destiny, multiplying with the mind's impatience and aversion the
disgusting qualities of the places? You truly know my mind: if there
is any place on earth pleasing to me, it is in Italy. Nor will this
astonish you; for there is our fatherland, there the nature of places is
such that it delights even foreigners and barbarians. On the other
hand, because of my fate or the inconsiderateness of its inhabitants I
have long been a voluntary exile—perhaps this astonishes you unless
you already knew it—and not even here, at the source of the Sorgue,
can I find peace as I often did other times. It is a modest country
place, confined, yet solitary and tranquil; and if you were to compare it with many more splendid ones, it would stand out as a place
eminently suitable for pursuing noble and peaceful studies. Similarly,
insofar as the location is concerned, I could live here most peacefully
except that external winds buffet me. Thus even in this haven I must
be fearfully wary of many things, but above all I am frightened by
the neighboring Babylon which is called the Roman Curia; a strange
name indeed since nothing is less Roman and nothing more hated in

*See III, 19.

it than Rome. Its proximity, its sight and stench, are quite disturbing to my well-being; that alone is enough to drive me from here, not to mention the remnants of other past storms which from nearby have pursued even into this port the battered ship of my life.

In short, all this leads to the conclusion you have known for more than twenty years, unless you have forgotten: there is no place I would rather dwell than in Rome, and I would have remained there forever had my destiny allowed. No eloquence could express how highly I esteem those glorious remnants of the queen city, those magnificent ruins and the many impressive signs of her virtue that afford light and point the way for those who have entered upon either the heavenly or the earthly journey. It is in that very city—I would like to be able to say half ruined—that I would prefer to spend now even more eagerly than is usual whatever remains of my life. Having tried almost all places, my heart inclines primarily in that direction; and though I was often there as a foreigner, I now desire to become an inhabitant. After having long wandered throughout other parts of the world, finally I yearn in my weariness to abide in its head and, to the extent this is possible, to find some rest there. If I must still live, it seems that nowhere could I live better; and certainly nowhere would I rather be buried. I am now awaiting my departure from this life and thinking of my final home. For the present it remains to be seen whether I can attain my desire; thinking about it, I cannot see what difficulties could stand in the way, but beginners usually see difficulties in everything, although on the other hand it is also true that some things are more difficult than they seem. Because of such uncertainties, I have referred the entire matter to you. You, my dear brother, know me very well and know my affairs, my abilities, and my fortune; you better than anyone else know Rome and are familiar too with her present state of affairs. If one man from among those three were still alive—that wonderful old man, that illustrious young man, or that magnanimous youth—and if we had not deserved losing at one and the same time all our luminaries and our fatherland's, I would entertain no doubt; you would not hear me seeking advice but would see me there in person. Now in need of advice, I ask first of all what Rome, our common mother, is now doing. And then, what is our other young man contemplating in whom lay the hope of a great family? What flowers of virtue, what signs of glory does he reveal? To what degree does his elders' fame affect him or their example inflame him? How does he remember me, and how does he love his own? His is an age that is wont to forget easily its love for the family. Finally, I hope to discover whether you have decided to remain there until the very end, for it is of no small moment in my arriving at a decision. If you have, I shall praise you; if not, I shall be astonished: long enough have we been wanderers, not to say tossed about; at vespers it is time to halt and cast anchor lest the night overtake us in our wanderings. How much I like the Babylonian Curia you have known since that period when we lived there in our youth and it was less detestable. But now my indignation has increased with time, and the Curia has become such that those who have thus far eagerly lived there now flee from it even more eagerly.

But so that you know all the facts and can deliberate more effectively, I am being summoned and tempted at one and the same time by different parties. I am being called to Naples by the Sicilian king, but I mistrust its climate, which is perhaps beneficial for its inhabitants, as their health and great comeliness indicate; for me it is warmer than I wish. Furthermore, he is a new king, and although Lucan states that "most placid is the state of kingdoms under a new king," I still recall his predecessor and constantly sigh at the thought of him. All else would indeed easily suit me, for the countryside is very beautiful and I am promised—since all know what I crave above all else—a great deal of freedom and solitude by those who can deliver their promises, whose words ought rightfully to be trusted. I am also summoned to Paris by the French king, an excellent and benevolent ruler, who loves me, as you know, more than a person unknown to him deserves; yet neither do the customs of the inhabitants agree with mine nor does fortune yet agree with him. Yet another obstacle is my lack of obedience long ago at the summons to receive the laurel crown there. If I do go now, I may appear to critics of others' lives to have been called twice but to have accepted only once, at a time when it was a matter of my profiting tremendously from the city and not when the city could perhaps have gained some glory because of me, if any were involved. So much for recent invitations; the following are older. Presently I am expected in that part of Italy where I once spent many years, enjoying a large share of the gifts of fortune: indeed there everything is delightful, if it were not for numerous civic disturbances. I am summoned once again to the nearby Curia: there nothing is attractive, everything is hateful. Amidst all these complications I have anxiously clung to these cliffs, and here I stand fast, not knowing toward what parts I should most likely set sail; if I remain here, I shall certainly become a man of the woods. You have heard what I am doing; listen then to what I am considering. I shall await your reply; if you dissuade me from coming to Rome I shall turn my helm to that part of Italy of which I have spoken, and I shall learn whether fortune or reason can offer me some refuge between the Alps and the Apennines on that sea. If the voyage seems too perilous, then I shall not only cast my anchor here where I am, batten down and beach my little ship, but as do men terrified of shipwreck and weary of the sea, I shall place it under cover, or even burn it to avoid ever sailing again, should I change my mind. Here, though the neighboring noise and smoke of the ungodly city may hamper me, I shall block my ears and eyes, enjoying as I have begun to do the pleasing idleness and desired solitude. If any nuisance from there should come here, something which is unavoidable, he will understand that in the woods I am oblivious to and unmindful of urban cares; he will say that it was like speaking to a deaf man; I shall listen to nothing at all, I shall say nothing that is against my wishes; I shall wander solitary and free as I now do, the only difference being that, while I used to think of the Tiber and the Po, the Arno and the Adige, and the Ticino, hereafter I shall keep in mind nothing but the Sorgue. Here I shall live and be buried among these peasants, and on the very last of all my days, I shall rise again at least outside, but alas all too near, that Babylonian confusion which even now upsets me. But enough of this discussion, which has been so lengthy because of my desire for conversation with you. Having gathered all this together, and even if I have forgotten something, I beg you, my dear brother, to write what you think would be preferable for me to do, keeping this in mind: given a free choice, I would by far prefer Rome to all other cities. This I have always indicated in words, and I would have demonstrated in deeds as well, had I been my own arbiter. I was instead subject to the will of fortune to which kings and princes of all lands are subject, from which nothing can be entirely exempt in human affairs, except an enduring and perfect virtue, which I certainly do not possess. Now I am drawn there by a desire which burns all the more by being postponed; therefore believe this and fix it in your mind: once I have entered the Holy City, never again will I leave it, not if Juno were to summon me to Samos, or Venus to Cnidus, or Jupiter to Crete. Farewell.

At the source of the Sorgue, 24 April.

Fam. XV, 9.

To the same correspondent,* a discussion of certain accusations that many people seem to have directed against the glory of Rome.

I had already said farewell and had folded my letter on the date indicated when a new thought secretly stole upon me, prompting me to write at greater length. What was I to do? The first sheet was full without any space for additions, and "the very last line had touched the margin," as Naso has it; I shall pursue here, then, what I omitted. We must be all the more careful in everything we do, the more our actions are likely to be subject to public judgment and the more they must dwell amidst envy and ignorance. Above all I must see to it that my explanation in the previous letter satisfies, as much as possible, those who disagree, and I must demonstrate that I am attracted to Rome by a truly powerful and worthy desire. I shall not speak of the civil wars and the belligerence of the ever-unsatisfied masses; I omit the many evils that city has in common with the entire world, particularly the sensuality that seems rampant everywhere; I do seek a modest dwelling, not a sumptuous one, recalling that Scipio in his exile preferred the roughness of Linterno to the pleasures of Baiae, for which he received great praise. I come to that one point that recently came to mind, compelling me, as you have heard, to go beyond what I decided to write. For it occurred to me that my choice could be opposed by the opinions of many for whom Rome is a Babylon and—it so enrages me to say this—her virtue detestable and her glory disreputable; nor will I deny that many great men also held the same opinion. Thus, in erecting his City of God, Augustine in a certain place touches upon the time of Abraham's birth, which we know occurred among the Assyrians during the reign of Ninus: "He had been ruling," he says, "for forty-three years when Abraham was born, which was about twelve hundred years before the founding of Rome." I would prefer that he had not said what follows that statement: "which rose as though another Babylon in the West." Not satisfied with saying it once, he says in another place, when he comes to Romulus through the lineage and succession of the Albans, "to be brief, Rome was founded as though another Babylon in the West." He then not only repeated his previous words but went still further by saying, "as if a daughter of the older Babylon." But indeed, I would not wish at this point to conceal what follows: he says that "through her it pleased God to sub-

*See III, 19.

due the entire world and, after uniting it in a single alliance of states and of laws, to keep it at peace." You then learn that, just as the divine city is infamous because of the name of Babylon, so is it glorious because of its origin and the special regard of divine providence when he says, "through whom it pleased God to vanquish the earth." Certainly He could have accomplished this through another city but He desired to do it through her, eternally destined by Him as being fit about all others for such a great task. Nor was it easy to provide leadership to an untamed world, a fact that Augustine himself does not overlook in his reasonable assertion that "there were already powerful and strong peoples and warlike nations that would not easily yield and that had to be conquered at great peril and devastation, with an enormous and dreadful effort on both sides." These then are the means whereby divine providence forged the Roman Empire to be the indisputable head of the world; while it was the lot of the Assyrian kingdom, either because of its shorter borders or because of the rude and cowardly barbarism of the people to be subdued, not to be the head of the world, but of Asia, as the same Augustine demonstrates in many words. Since the responsibilities given to the Roman Empire were more serious and more difficult, God wished it to be as great as was required by the great labor and difficulty involved in settling human affairs. I believe that in all this nothing is unclear thus far except the name of Babylon, which many historians have used, and among the first after Augustine was that chronicler of the world's ills known as Orosius. In a letter, Jerome praises the tranquillity and silence of his Bethlehem; and in his desire to prove that poor place more pleasing to God than the Capitoline, famous for its many triumphs, he rightfully states that the citadel was often struck by heavenly thunderbolts; nor is he mistaken, as anyone who peruses a history book can easily learn. I do not deny that not only the Capitoline but other Roman citadels were struck by similar disasters, the most notable being Mount Celius, not because of its own ill fortune or the hatred of the lightning-bearer, but because of the victim's fame, which has often caused a minor disaster in one case to become a major one in another. Thus that hill about which I speak became infamous as a result of a single event, terribly sad and horrifying, that befell Tullius Hostilius, a Roman king. We read that, following an impetuous and indeed fulminating life which he lived in the same fashion to the very end—O death befitting each man's life!—he burned to death there together with his home and all his belongings in a fire caused by a lightning bolt. I am omitting other critics who have insulted the Roman name, for they are not few in antiquity, in the recent past, and even in our own age. Many of them—as their words reveal—are motivated not so much by their desire for truth as by their hatred and envy of the city. In my opinion they do not deserve an answer; they deserve to be destroyed by their own poison. If they are literate and read books, I believe that the illustrious name of Rome occurring in every line will compel them to sigh and, to cut short their charges, they will find its name in books written by foreigners and not by Romans. As Crispus says, the Roman people never had writers in abundance, and in fact they more appropriately led others to write about them than vice versa. They sought fame in deeds and actions rather than in words. What more need be said? Whatever misfortune strikes the city of Rome, her name will live as long as any memory of Greek or Latin letters survives, but the envious will never lack reason for complaint. Let this indeed be the response to Augustine and Jerome, who cannot be taken lightly.

I do not deny that Rome was founded in the West as another Babylon so that it would be clear that the oriental empire, centered in Babylon for many centuries, once removed from there, would in time and in accordance with God's will, likewise go west where Rome was. It should be noted, however, that the customs of the two cities were different and that the oriental empire did not become the western empire but a universal one, the only genuine monarchy of all peoples. But were it to be called Babylon, meaning confusion, because of the concourse of all conquered peoples into a single city and the great confusion of affairs—especially the crowd of gods and sacred ceremonies—then I neither oppose nor question the name. Yet I dare say that it lost the name as soon as it excluded false gods and accepted the worship and name of the one true God. To borrow the words of Pope Leo, "from a teacher of error she became a disciple of truth." As for the statement that the Capitoline was often struck by lightning and the argument that it was a place unacceptable to God, I shall maintain with all due respect to the holy and learned man that it should be attributed to the wrath of nature, not to God. Otherwise God loves above all other lands Egypt, seat of impiety and every evil superstition, which used to worship and venerate not only Isis and Osiris but Apis, Serapis, and the crocodile, but now venerates Mohammed, who is less sacred than the crocodile; in any event, by all reports, it rarely, if ever, thunders there. Conversely, God must have tremendous hatred for the Pyrenees, where Christ is worshiped, but where we well know how frightfully and frequently it thunders, having spent a summer there in our youth, often seeing country homes go up in smoke from the flames of lightning bolts. Although every thought and opinion that prompts a pious and sobering awe may be useful and praiseworthy, it is still true that the sound and fire of lightning is the result of nature more than of any wrath. To use the words of the Satirist, it falls to earth by chance according to the fury of the winds. Some writers, especially the very learned Pliny the Younger, maintain its cause to be the nobility of the air; if true, then the air in the Pyrenees can be considered truly noble. For this very reason he says that it often thunders in Italy. If all this is true, I would for my part most willingly exchange this nobility with the Egyptians or the Irish, in whose lands it thunders very rarely and softly, according to the testimony of those who write about them or who have returned from there. But let us return to Rome.

Does God not love, O glorious Jerome, the Tarpeian Rock which often, to cite Maro, "He blasted with the searing breath of his lightning-flash?" I respectfully beg you for permission to converse with you in the name of truth. Does God not love the Tarpeian Rock? How then could He have wished, I greatly wonder, that place to be the head of the world which you cannot deny. Indeed I do see what might be your reply and thus will not mount a defense. Let us therefore concede that God hated a place which, if He did not love it, would not exist; but He did hate it and let that be so. Do you still conclude from this that He seemingly attacked it with lightning? Note, I ask you, the strength of this argument. I do not wish, nor is it necessary for me, to offer examples at great length; surely if God does not love the Tarpeian Rock, which He struck with lightning and has often allowed even in our day to be a refuge for robbers—this I would consider a clearer indication of His hatred—though it was once the capital of the world, He loves at the very least His dwelling in the Lateran and the dwellings of the Virgin Mother and of His apostles, which we see that He has spared. Though destroyed by flames in our day, the Lateran is even now being restored through enormous toil and at tremendous expense; yet anyone will say that it was man's fault and not the object of divine wrath. It is four years since the total destruction of the church of the apostle Paul by a terrible earthquake, when the Virgin's dwelling on the highest hill was severely shaken. Can anyone perchance say that an earthquake is not as clear a sign of God's wrath as a lightning bolt? The present year saw the tower of the apostle Peter so destroyed and burned by lightning—incredible as it may seem—that scarcely a trace of that huge tower remains, and no one would believe that a tower once stood there if he had not seen it. Furthermore, to mention an incident that provokes religious awe, the famous bell, the work of Boniface VII and named after him, is said to have so melted that not even its remains could be found. I relate this last example not as one who knows and wishes to reveal it to someone who does not know, but as one ignorant of the facts inquires of one who knows them. I believe through report what you have personally witnessed, for I have not been in Rome since the Jubilee Year three years ago. But if the unanimous reports by people arriving from Rome, who usually do not lie, are true, the Tarpeian Rock has never suffered a similar disaster. I believe that God hates none of His creation; but if He does love one place more than another, then it is where He knows He is more loved, sometimes striking the most holy places to frighten unbelievers. I should add that customarily I have no fear of thunder, because the longer I live the less I fear to die, or because I have begun emptying my conscience of its hidden ills and no longer fear external rumblings and dangers. If what I am contemplating does happen, I have selected for my dwelling the same Tarpeian Rock, not to avoid being suspected by the people, as we read about Publicola, but not to fall once again as a result of boredom into what I am determined to avoid. Moreover, you know which of the seven hills, more famous than all the world's mountains and valleys, has long been my favorite and is most suited to my studies. Therefore, to return to my point and to conclude, I have not changed my mind and I am still attracted to that city; the matter lies in the hands of God. Certainly if I ever enter the sacred city, you will behold the truth of what I promised in my other letter. Farewell.

Fam. XV, 10.

To Ponzio Sansone.*

An enkindled love knows no restraint: this I have understood as never before from your delightful and courteous letter. I would be astonished if that more than brotherly affection of yours for me were really new and not the one which began in our younger years and has increased continuously to the present day. I thank you and heartily accept your offer to make use at any time of your property as though it were my own. I consider your excuse an accusation against me, for I should have come to you, not you to me; and if you stay a little longer, I shall come to visit the one whom I always see in my mind. I would like to write at greater length, but your messengers whom you sent to give assistance to your very eloquent letter are silently waiting and, with deep signs, counting in silence the number of words as they look skyward. The sun has fled, and I fear being unfair to them, should I yield to my desires. Farewell, and remember me.

*See XIV, 8.

Fam. XV, 11.

To Philippe, Bishop of Cavaillon, that envy ought to be shunned by retreating from it.*

You are about to hear something extraordinary but nevertheless true: I know not what others are doing, but I am still incapable of deciding what I want at this age, not because I am unaware of my wishes, but because many obstacles impede my desires. Therefore I cannot fully want what I see myself wanting in vain, whence my distress and my infinite perplexity. Daily I experience more deeply that saying of the wise Hebrew, so brief and weighty, which the majority of readers bypass without wetting their feet; but each time I read it, I thrust my foot into it, and keep repeating to myself with many sighs what is there written: "All things are difficult." Consider the difficulties now present even in small matters: what I want I cannot do, what I can do I do not want to do; and so I seek something that I can and want to do, and do not find it. Meanwhile, buffeted by countless considerations as if they were waves, expecting some resolution, and with the rumor of my departure invented and spread abroad, I secretly left Babylon, as though to return to Italy, and came here; and I would have come to you not so much to satisfy your eyes as my own, which seek almost nothing with greater eagerness than your face. But you must know that I come here, intending to hide and flee, if possible, not only others but myself—my vices and my errors, which have hounded me from infancy to old age. So great is my desire to avoid envy, which everywhere haunts me, that if, in this hiding place of mine, I could free myself from it and from all mortals, and could not do so in any other way, I would be prepared to remain here without all my friends, who are my greatest delight, but without being the object of envy, which is my greatest displeasure. To achieve this goal of mine, that corner of your countryside appears as always most suitable; allow me, then, to take refuge under your wings. Hide me, I beg you; if you do this, you will often have me at night or on rainy days as a guest, certainly an insignificant one, but grateful for your welcome; on the other hand, as we read in fables, if you begin publicizing it, you will lose me. Farewell.

*See II, 1.

Fam. XV, 12.

*To the same correspondent.**

Here are three small gifts, all very different, my dear father. One is a fish, bright gold in color and spotted with silvery scales; some call it a *torrentina* while others call it a *turtra*, but you will find its taste better than its name. My steward's son and your servant caught it today in these limpid waters. The second gift is a fat duck, until a short while ago an inhabitant of this pleasant spring, who found neither the freedom of the air nor the river's hiding places sufficient to save itself from the expertise of my fine dog, and thus was unable to swim or fly to safety. To these I am adding a recent letter which lately I also caught for you in your countryside with the hook of my weak intelligence amidst the billows of my mind and the reefs of my affairs. While the first two are to remain with you, however, the last gift must be returned. Do you know why? Because "truth begets hatred"; if this was true in the age of Terence, how much truer it is in our day! Therefore read it thoroughly if you like, doing so secretly, and send it back until such time as we know what God or fortune is preparing for the world. Only then shall we decide what should be done with the letter, whether to commit it to the flames or to add it to its sisters. Meanwhile, rest assured, and from this measure my trust, that I would never have shown it to any other eyes but yours. Farewell, O you who are an honor to me.

At the source of the Sorgue, 14 December, in the silence of a still night.

*See II, 1.

Fam. XV, 13.

To the same correspondent. *

It occurred to me to add a fourth little gift to the three of yesterday. You did read and immediately send back that letter written to you, whom I knew to be a foremost enemy of vice; I rejoice that you liked it so much, and thus it has become more pleasing and precious to me because of your approval. Now I am sending another letter, written to the clergy of the church of Padua on the passing of Bishop Ildebrandino of holy memory, whom I knew you were wont to praise and admire although, by the miracle of his divine virtue, he transcended in my judgment any human admiration. You loved him, or rather you loved his virtue, since you had no dealings with him, I believe, except that it necessarily follows that a hater of sin is also a lover of virtue. Dear father, in comparing these letters, you will be able to judge whether my pen is capable of writing on subjects of such diversity as censure and praise, but meanwhile you must remember that, whatever their failings, the fault lies with my talent; on the other hand, if they have any merit, it is due to the subject matter and not the style. For who is there who cannot praise one man or censure another, or who is so incompetent in other matters that he is incapable of eloquence in either of these? Farewell.

At the source of the Sorgue, 15 December, at dawn.

*See II, 1.

Fam. XV, 14.

To the clergy of the Paduan Church, * *on the death and virtues of Bishop Ildebrandino.*

We have lost our father, my beloved brethren, indeed we have sent ahead our shepherd whom we hope to follow, our leader, our comfort, and our glory, truly a light and lantern for our feet and our pathways. Our Lord has, alas, extinguished our spark and the torch of Israel so as to relight it in heaven; I speak of Bishop Ildebrandino, whom I know not whether to call an earthly angel or a heavenly man. We have sent him ahead, brethren, where we too must go under the leadership of Christ, following in the very footsteps of our father; we have sent on ahead one who will prepare for us a dwelling place in heaven, who will placate with his prayers the King displeased with our sins. He went happily. What can I say? Every thought of mine is inadequate for what is needed to eulogize him properly. Shall I say "he has left the earth?" But he never was of this earth except in body, that is, only with the least part of him. Shall I say "he has left his body?" But he inhabited it only as a prison. Shall I say "he has escaped from his body?" Perhaps this seems more suitable for the occasion. Yet it too would be improper, for how can anyone say he has escaped from his body when, in Cicero's words, "though he may have been in the body, he really stood outside of it, contemplating what was external, and he always separated himself as much as possible from it." Shall I say "he sought heaven?" But he always dwelled in heaven with his pious thoughts, even when he seemed to be here with us. Shall I say "he went to the stars?" Indeed he himself was a shining star on earth. Shall I say "he went to God?" Indeed he was never without God; to cite what is quite astounding from the mouth of a pagan, Seneca, "God comes to men, for no mind is good without God." If this is true, when was the most gentle father of our souls without God. What then shall I say? Without doubt he went to God, who was with him and who is everywhere; he went to Him, despising his own body, leaving us physically behind who were so dear to his spirit and who were for a time in exile with him. And with what words, O most blessed bishop and, as no one will deny, a bishop who was the outstanding glory of our age, with what words shall I rejoice at your happiness and weep for

---

*As a canon of the Paduan Church, Petrarch is really addressing his fellow clergymen. Ildebrandino Conti was Bishop of Padua from 1319 until his death in 1352.

our solitude? I beg you to aid my style, unequal to the task and insufficient for the subject, with your prayers, for you can do so. And so, our bishop, the leader of our ranks, has gone to heaven on the straightest possible path; he so simplified his difficulties and troubles, straightening the crooked path with the mallet of his fiery virtue, that I believe nothing whatsoever could impede his footsteps. Moreover, he went very joyfully as do blessed souls, with the sweet songs of angels resounding among the stars and throughout the heavens, to be welcomed into the bosom of Abraham, or rather into the lap of Christ Himself. If there be any true hope, any true faith, our bishop is in the empyrean, from which he had never departed in thought; of special import is the fact that the very place to which all his thoughts were directed until the present now contains his soul in fullness; freed from bodily slavery and the earthly prison, he lives joyfully with his desires satisfied in the very place for which he had once piously sighed. He dwells where no hostile power can touch him, from which no weary burden or old age or death can remove him, where illnesses do not torment, need does not distress, troubles do not affect, cares do not disturb, and wars do not terrify; where anger does not kindle the mind and hatreds do not inflame, luxury does not befoul, and the stomach does not tempt; where no gloomy envy gnaws, no vain prosperity charms, no misfortune stings, no pleasure overwhelms, no elation inflates, no hope exalts, no fear dejects, no pain is felt, no grief overcomes, and no despair oppresses. Although even here he was immune from such ills, leading an absolutely celestial life on earth, his saintly soul still could not at times avoid being affected by the human miseries among which he had to dwell; and although sound and strong, it was at times compelled to become sick because of others' ills, to pity and to heal, to advise, to aid and to toil. Now at last he is fully happy where neither his own torments nor those of others can touch him, and in fact his great joy even increases by beholding the happiness of others.

I believe only one thing grieves our beloved father amidst so many joys: his departure has left his church widowed and us leaderless. Who will henceforth resolve for me thorny passages from Scriptures? Who will clarify its mysteries? Who will explain the enigmas? Who will illuminate the shadows? Who will henceforth shape conduct, eradicate vice, and sow virtue? Who will raise the fallen, strengthen the timid and exhort the strong? Who will exalt the humble, restrain the proud, frighten the bold, confuse the wicked, reveal hypocrites, and honor the worthy with just praise? Who will reward the deserving, punish the guilty, destroy evildoers? Who will sustain

Catholics, guide the strays, overthrow the heretics, and keep the thieves away from the sheepfolds of Christ? Finally, who will care for the orphans and the widows? Who will feed the hungry? Who will clothe the naked? Who will comfort the afflicted and visit the sick? Who will bury the dead and be the common father of the poor? With him we have lost all these good things in equal measure, my dear brethren, or rather we have transferred them from one place to another, as I have said. We had him as a teacher on earth, we shall have him as a mediator with Christ in heaven, whom he did his best to please while living, from whom nothing is requested in vain. What do we believe to have been his prayer above all others, if not what any good shepherd would ordinarily desire: that his flock, delivered from the attacks of wolves and thieves and from every kind of disease, may reach the home of the Lord where, being summoned, he himself has now gone? Indeed what else would he request from the Lord in heaven than what he used to request from his vicar on earth? A few days before his death, as he felt his end approaching, he sent a letter filled with human charity and concern to the Bishop of Rome and some members of the college in which he humbly requested a suitable successor for himself, something which I cannot recall without tears. As an anxious father lying on his deathbed entrusts the care of his unwed daughter to a faithful friend, he too committed his widow, the church, to their trust. O most blessed and holy soul, O truly perfect man, O truly solicitous and vigilant bishop and pastor! While some seek doctors or consult with soothsayers or prepare and alter their complicated wills, while others do nothing but groan silently or twist around in their beds, weeping and complaining, or, astonished and immobile, become numb at death's approach, he, in his pity for the condition of the church, and not his own, thought about its future bishop and felt that his beloved bride, with whom he had harmoniously spent thirty-five years, should not be forsaken even as he departed. Who would not praise this faith, who would not desire to have this spirit, who would not admire this constancy of a dying man? Among the many things Roman historians admire about Julius Caesar is that at his death he let his toga fall to his feet in order not to expose the lower parts of his body, in order to fall with greater dignity; Pompey too is praised for having shown at death a concern for his own dignity; among the Greeks, Queen Olympia, mother of Alexander, is similarly said to have dropped her toga over her bosom when she was killed, but modesty is less admirable in women than constancy. Epaminondas, a Theban highly respected by the Greeks, asked as he was about to die from wounds received in battle whether his shield had fallen to the enemy; upon learning that it was safe, he ordered it brought to him, embraced it with a martial delight as if a witness to his military valor, kissed it affectionately through his tears, and died happily. How much better our bishop, who considered not his toga nor his shield while dying, but his soul and his church; exactly like Martin, he neither feared to die nor did he refuse for his people's sake the toil and weariness of an exceedingly long life! Having entrusted concern for all this to divine providence, he meanwhile, as best he could, prayed to God and entreated the men to whom he could turn to provide for his bride's widowhood and solitude.

We have read that some men really did think about their successors; indeed who is there that does not? For the sake of making a greater impression, however, let us limit ourselves to more famous examples. After considerable uncertainty, King David, judging surely and maturely, finally made heir to his kingdom his duly begotten son, a very learned man as everyone knows. The deified Vespasian, Roman emperor, had as his successors to the empire two sons, one a very fine man but the other a truly evil one; it is said that he had such a presentiment and had publicly predicted this. Their successor, Nerva, was unable to do likewise because he had no children; he adopted Trajan, a strong and vigorous man who was beneficial to the Republic; the latter also adopted someone who in turn adopted another. In the Roman Empire there long continued the tradition of adoptive succession that was common much earlier among the first emperors: Julius Caesar was succeeded by his adopted son, Augustus, and Augustus himself, for lack of children, chose his stepson, Tiberius, as his son and successor, although I am aware that he became suspect for purposely selecting such a successor so that the state would feel his own loss more deeply after his death. Even if true, this opinion is indeed unworthy of such a ruler; in fact, distinguished historians consider it unlikely, and so exonerate him from suspicion. There is no doubt, however, that the virtues of the dead are wont to be much more deeply missed as a result of the weak qualities of their successors; for the more disparaging their successors' lives, the more praiseworthy the glory of their predecessors. Consequently, Philopemenes, the Achaean leader, does deserve praise; after his capture by the enemy, as he was about to suffer death by poisoning and was holding the deadly cup in his hands, he asked whether Licortas, the other Achaean leader and the most powerful after him in Achaea, was still alive. When he heard that he was, he said, "That is good; dear fatherland, you have a fine leader"; and thus he died contented and undaunted. To return to our subject, it was through prayer that our prelate procured his successor, since neither nature nor adoption allowed it. He was really concerned, not about his own fame, but that of his church; I have no doubt that, had it been in his hands, he would not have wished a successor whose idleness would increase his own reputation. He would rather have as successor a reborn Ambrose or Prosdocimus himself, through whose efforts the diocese was founded and established, and flourished from the early days of our faith. But since, I believe, that age is reaching its twilight, he selects the best from among the late workers in the vineyard of the Lord, and requests from Christ one gift above all others, next to his own immortality—that he choose a successor who through his works and the splendor of his life may obscure his own fame rather than brighten it, something in my opinion he requests in vain. Let Verona send her Zenonus, Modena her Geminianus, Ravenna her Severus, Nola her Paulinus, Capua her Germanus, Aquitania her Prosperus; let Africa give her Cyprianus, Spain her Isidorus: and you, Padua, select from this holy company whomever you wish as bishop. He may be brighter than the sun, but never so much as to obscure the luminous name of your Ildebrandino, whom Rome recently sent you as bishop, as she once sent Ambrose to Milan; and never will his reputation die which he now dwelling in heaven left alive on earth. Abounding in ineffable happiness, he does not desire the favor and applause of popular acclaim, which he disdained high-mindedly while in the flesh. This is the nature of glory: it pursues those who flee from it, it exalts those who do not seek it, often abandoning through flight those who desire it to excess. But how could a mighty stream descending from an unfailing spring dry up, or how could the shadow of a solid body struck by a sun ray disappear? Virtue itself, the source of man's glory, which is but its shadow, does not die. My dear brethren, in this letter I am doing what is commanded by the authority of divine discourse; I am not praising the man while he was alive but, as Ambrose advises, I exalt him after his perils when he is safe, I praise him as a successful sailor of the world who has cast his anchor in the heavenly port, I praise him as a leader famous for his terrestrial battles yet triumphant in his celestial palace within the ethereal vault. Not that I am worried that vanity will cause him to be spoiled by my praise, for there never was vanity in his heart, that well-known bastion of humility; nor that adulation may harm the praise, for I only fear my praise to be insufficient and lukewarm, since the words of a sinful man cannot equal the sanctity of the best of men, but I hope to speak the truth and I know that I am not lying. How could I flatter a dead man if I refused to do so when he was alive, or how could I dare lie in his presence when he can see all things, whereas I had not dared to do so while he, as a human being still enclosed in his corporeal prison, could perhaps have been deceived? I call God to witness that I only used to speak to him as if he could read my face and my mind, although, after accepting me as an intimate friend, he tried to instill in me a sense of confidence. But there was in him a divine quality which made me more reverent and astonished, the more he was courteous and gracious to me.

Often in my presence, but more often in my absence, he would adorn my name with praises that I wish were merited. He thereby gave me delight and considerable incentives toward glory; yet much greater was my wonderment that, as they say, blind love could even lead astray the judgment of such a great man. When he could, he was a most indulgent father to me, and I had entered more intimately than anyone might believe into his secrets, as if into his Holy of Holies; and so I consider myself a better man than before and can speak of him with greater confidence. While alive, he loved me because he perceived with his spirit the ardor of my heart, nor did his feelings for his dear ones, I believe, diminish with death. Never did I have such hope in his assistance as today when I trust that he wishes no less for me and can do even more. And because the mere remembrance of illustrious men is pleasant, I shall continue a little longer with this discussion. He began to have great affection for me several years ago when, having availed himself of my talent for some of his short works, he perchance discovered some things that appealed to him, not because such a master lacked a helper, but because he delighted in conversing with me while the minds of those greater than I were as usual occupied with more serious matters. In fact when I recently visited his church, "that man of God received me as a father would"—to use Augustine's words about his Ambrose— "and gave me his episcopal blessing for my journey." Indeed he was my Ambrose; and he sustained and strengthened my spirit through his words and through his life. I wish that he had come into my life earlier; if only I had had more opportunity to profit from his saintly conversation, which no one ever left without being a better person. I feel shame and regret at not taking greater advantage of it while I could. But my expectation that he would enjoy a longer life deceived me; I did not consider his age, already greatly advanced, but his moderation, his conduct, and the pure and vigorous body of an elderly man. What happens to most men happened to me with regard to him: we assume that whatever gives pleasure will be eternal.

While I was preparing for my journey, and without my realizing that I would never again behold on earth his venerable and holy face, he tried, as if aware of all this, to dissuade me from it with a variety of arguments; this I sadly recall now that I am alone. Given all the above, with what can I repay him except with remembrance and love and trust, whence I beg him to pray for me, since I believe it to be not only vain but foolhardy for a sinner to pray for a saint. Lest my personal grief, unmindful of my purpose, distract me from the public mourning, I return to you, dearest brethren of mine in Christ. What shall I now say? I know not how to stop remembering him; the more I think of him, the greater my desire to do so; the more I speak of him, the greater my wish to do so; the longer I continue, the more I find things to say and the less I find a way of ending; yet this letter demands a conclusion. I dare not urge you, indeed I dare not allow you to weep over the death of such a man, lest you seem to be weeping over a happy man out of envy rather than friendship, as Cicero has it. For who except an envious person would mourn a friend who has passed from the flesh to the spirit, from the earth to heaven, from toil to peace, from death to life, from tribulations to eternal blessedness? Furthermore, I dare not forbid you to mourn the serious and irreparable damage suffered by the church. Confidently, then, I exhort and implore you to act thus: that you cherish our father's memory and follow in his footsteps, that you endeavor to cultivate a sanctity such as his and observe the ceremonies he prescribed, that you complete what he had started and strive to preserve what he had accomplished, so that at all times, but especially now when our church is widowed, our prayers to God may be so ardent and devout that He may ever grant us shepherds like Ildebrandino. And so consider him an angel of God in our midst rather than a man. And you, O noble Padua, blessed in your location and your mild climate, near to the sea and encircled by rivers, wealthy with fertile fields, famous for the genius of your inhabitants and celebrated for the splendor of your ancient name, if you have any faith in me, forever rank among your greatest bishops and the glorious names of your confessors Ildebrandino far from the last.

Fam. XVI, 1.

To the Cardinals Talleyrand, Bishop of Albano, and
Gui, Bishop of Porto, * request for a leave, with an*
admittedly weak but feasible justification for it.

When Marcus Atilius Regulus, the first terror of the Carthaginians, was in charge of a large and dangerous operation in Africa in behalf of the Republic, he was not ashamed to ask the Senate by letter for a leave, the reason being the death of his steward who had cultivated his few acres outside the city. Why then should I, who deal with no public affairs and few private ones, be ashamed to request leave for the same reason from you two nobles of the church? My steward, a man not unknown to you, who likewise cultivated my few parched acres, passed away yesterday. Nor do I fear that either one of you will now answer me as the Senate did Atilius when it ordered him to continue the operation and leave to it the care of his abandoned lands; his land was in Rome, mine is at the source of the Sorgue, a place known to you only by its small reputation. It so happens that I have greater reason for concern than he did. It is not so much that I hate to see that parcel of land uncultivated, but just as the other African scourge, Gneus Scipio, because his daughter lacked a dowry, sought a leave from Spain where he was enjoying a great success, so I, who combine the reasons of the two famous commanders within myself, feel the need of a guardian for my library, which is my adopted daughter. My steward was a peasant, but he possessed more prudence and refinement than a city dweller, and no more faithful creature lived on this earth than he, I believe. What more need I say? With his exemplary fidelity, he alone tempered and compensated for all the iniquities and perfidies of servants about which I daily complain, not only in conversation, but often even in writing. And so, to him I had entrusted myself and all my possessions, as well as all the books I have in France. Although I had many and various volumes of all kinds, and some large ones mixed in with small ones, even upon my return after a long absence of three years, I not only found nothing ever stolen but nothing even misplaced. A great lover of letters, he was illiterate and he took particular care of the books he knew were more dear to me; through long practice he had come to know the titles of ancient works and even distinguished them from my own modest writings. He was filled with joy whenever I happened to put a book in his hands; he would hold it

*See XIV, 1 and XIII, 1.

close to his breast and sigh, sometimes softly addressing the book's author. Truly astonishing it was that merely by touching or seeing the volumes he would appear to become wiser and happier. Thus such a guardian of my possessions, with whom I have been sharing my concerns for fifteen years, whom I had used no less than a priest of Ceres, as they say, considering his home nothing less than a temple of fidelity, left me yesterday evening to join a better master. The day before yesterday, at your bidding, I left home, believing that he was slightly ill; though he was old, I considered his old age, in Maro's words, still green and fresh. May he be granted peace for his soul after so many physical labors! He sought and desired but one thing from the Lord: do not deny him this, O Christ, that he dwell not in my house but in the house of the Lord all the days of his life which is no longer mortal; that he behold not my will but that of the Lord, and visit His temple and not my fields, where his tough body has worked for many years in cold and heat. He grew weary in my service, I pray You that he find repose in Yours; freed of his old prison through Your will, he comes to You. One of my servants, who had by chance seen him die, brought the sad news with utmost haste; he arrived late last night with the announcement that my steward had expired with my name on his lips and invoking through his tears Christ's name. I was distressed, and would have grieved even more deeply, had I not foreseen that this would happen because of the man's age. Therefore I must go; give me leave, I beg you, most venerable fathers, and allow your humble servant to leave this city, where he is not needed, for the country where he needs to make provision for the care of his library even more than for his fields. I wish you a peaceful and happy life.

Avignon, 5 January.

Fam. XVI, 2.

To his brother Gherardo, Carthusian monk,* an appeal.

I happened to be dining at the home of that saintly and illustrious man, Ildebrandino, Bishop of the Paduan Church, who then illumined the city with his manifold rays of virtue but now is a new star in the heavens, when suddenly there arrived by chance two monks of your order, one Italian and the other from beyond the Alps. One was the prior of the monastery of Casula overhanging Ligurian Albenga, the other was from Valbonne near the right bank of the Rhone. After the bishop, in his delight at the arrival of such guests, had courteously welcomed them, as was his custom, and had conversed on many subjects long into the evening, he asked in particular their reason for coming to Padua. They responded that their order had sent them to found a Carthusian monastery near Treviso, provided the bishop and other worthy and devout citizens of the region favored the project. I do not know how the project has proceeded thus far, or if it will succeed. At length, after covering a number of subjects, our host, whose life was as exemplary as his learning and eloquence, mentioned your name and asked whether you were content with your lot and your vocation. They eagerly took up the subject, giving wonderful reports of you, but one in particular: when the plague that had spread over all lands and seas had in turn reached you, invading those fields where you serve Christ, your prior, otherwise a holy and zealous man as I personally know, was so terrified by the unexpected affliction that he urged flight. In the manner of a Christian and philosopher, you replied that his advice was good, provided there was any place inaccessible to death; at his insistence that everyone leave nonetheless, you answered more resolutely that he might go where he thought proper, but that you would remain in the post you believed Christ had entrusted to you; when he insisted again and again, warning that among other terrors you might not even have a grave, you said that was the least of all your concerns, and that the kind of burial received was of no interest to you but only to your survivors; they said that the prior finally retired to his paternal home, and not long afterward was overtaken by death which had tracked him there, while you indeed remained safe in the care of the One who is the fount of life; within a few days death had borne off the thirty-four men who were there and you remained alone in the monastery. They also added that you were not at all

*See X, 3.

deterred by the contagious disease, that you stood by your dying brothers, receiving their last words and kisses; after bathing their cold bodies, often in a single day with untiring piety you buried three or more of them with your own hands, carrying them on your own shoulders, since there was no one to dig their graves or to give the dying their just due. Finally only you and a dog remained. Using only part of the daylight for necessary rest you were vigilant every night, for prowlers who are rampant in that area would often mount attacks in the deep silence of the night. They were kept out by you, indeed by Christ who was with you, at times with gentle words and at others with stinging ones, and thus were unable to inflict damage on the sacred dwelling; when the terrible summer had passed, you sent requests to the nearest monasteries of the servants of Christ that they send someone to stand guard in your place. Once this was granted, you went to the Grande Chartreuse where you, a nonprior, together with eighty-three foreign priors, were received with extraordinary and unusual honor by the prior of the monastery, who is the only religious leader in those parts; you were successful in getting them to assign you a prior and some monks whom you chose from several monasteries, and with them you would rebuild your own, which had been laid waste by the death of your brothers. The visitors further reported that you returned very joyful as from a mighty triumph; that thus through your care, your wisdom, and your faith the once venerable monastery of Montrieux, then deserted, returned to its former condition; and that amidst these and countless other difficulties you managed to keep your body strong, your health good, and your appearance dignified, as befits a religious. This would have surprised me, had I not known the saying, "saintly men earn bodily virtues as well"; indeed good spiritual health often helps to maintain bodily health, strong limbs, and facial comeliness. In any event, as the visitors were telling these stories and similar ones about you, the bishop looked at me with tears of joy in his eyes; and as I stood there, not knowing if my eyes were dry, yet certainly not tearless in my heart, they suddenly turned to me, saw your image in my face either through divine prompting or mental intuition, and embraced me with sighs of joy, exclaiming, "O blessed are you for the piety of your brother!" They said much else besides which is better expressed through silence.

Farewell, my dear brother, and because of all I have written here, I beseech you to strive to be to the very end as you have begun.

Fam. XVI, 3.

To his Socrates,* against advocates of worldly pleasures.

I had much to say to you today that I am deliberately omitting since it is said more frankly and easily in person; my tongue, so long silent and motionless in this solitude, will save my weary fingers from the task. One subject I did not wish to postpone, which must be said not to you but to our common friend who, in his customary way and in the common fashion, is prodding me with letters, some by his hand and some written by others, continually trying to inflame my cold heart with worldly desires; as Horace has it, he is "intent on destroying me with love," an evil common to all ordinary friendships. For such reason, though my affection for him is still intact, my esteem is certainly diminished; and as Brutus says of his Cicero, "I abate nothing of my love, but much of my favorable opinion." Indeed, while I cannot help loving a man of such proven loyalty, with whom I have long been bound in friendship, I also cannot help disliking a mind set on earthly things and offering unworthy counsel. Know then, you and all my friends everywhere who may consider me rather indolent, that I have set limits to my wishes and that I care little, indeed have no desire, for any new developments in my life. I have enough to live on, enough with which an honorable man can strike a truce with fortune and with which he may feel content. Quintius had less, as did Curius, Fabritius, and Atilius, and all these men, conquerors of kings and nations, enjoyed even greater triumphs when they conquered themselves and the impulses of their rebellious spirits. And what would this all lead to? If I should yield to avarice, I shall never feel that I have enough to keep me from appearing very poor and indigent to myself and to others; luxury and avarice and ambition know no bounds: they are all full of false opinions, to be resisted if they are not to drive a man into the extremes of misery. It is difficult to resist them, yet ruinous to obey them; whoever surrenders to them, however, cannot free himself when he wishes.

I have enough to live on, to use the common phrase; indeed I have more than enough, much I might better do without. What more would you have me desire or hope for? I have my own ground where I could be buried if needed (if anything we have here can be called ours); I have a place where I can live for a short while or for a long time; I have something to eat and drink, shoes for my feet and

*See I, 1.

clothes for my body; I have someone to serve me, keep me company, and carry me, something to cover me, a place to rest and a place to roam as I please: what Roman emperor has more? Furthermore, my body, disciplined through long labor, is sound, no longer the rebellious slave of my mind as it once was. Books of all kinds, not the least portion of my wealth, surround me; added to this is an intelligence, however small, a love of letters which nourishes the mind with delight and exercises it without trouble; then you must add yourselves, my dear friends, whom I number among the foremost of my blessings, provided your counsel does not destroy my freedom, without which I would not wish to live; there is also security, a great boon, since to my knowledge I have no enemy in the world except those spawned by envy (these I duly despise, but it is perhaps unwise to expect to be without them); there is the general affection of all the good men of the world, even of those who have never seen me and never will, an affection owed to divine favor, I confess, and not to any personal merit. This may all appear insignificant to you, and thus you want me to become a usurer, sail the seas, shout in the forum, or sell my tongue and my soul. What else would you have me do to become wealthy? Would you have me live in poverty so that I may die in wealth? Do you urge me to wander around, assembling what another wastes without moving, or to seek painfully what someone unknown to me will enjoy, or to acquire with toil what I abandon with sorrow and guard with anxiety? Believe me, in your solicitude you have undertaken a difficult task: to satisfy avarice. It is insatiable, implacable, thirsting after and devouring all things, and bottomless. Human cupidity needs no external punishments, for it is its own: if its undertakings fail, it is downcast; if they begin to succeed, it becomes inflamed; if they are fully realized, then indeed does it become anxious, needy, and wretched. But let us lay aside this philosophy, hateful to all men yet certainly true, and return to some commonplace ideas. Although I may appear poor to the rich, to myself I appear rich. What do you advise? Shall I toss and turn until I appear rich to them also? There would be no end to it, not if I were to possess all the lands and the seas; as long as there is something to be desired, avarice will never be satisfied. Allow me, I beg of you, to be wealthy in my own fashion; after all, it is my own affair. Why do I need anyone else's judgment? What free person eats according to someone else's taste? You have your own opinions, but leave mine to me, I ask you; you are digging at them in vain, for they are rooted in the hardest rock. What hope, then, as you indicate at the end of your letter, does our friend wish to enkindle in me? Even if what he says were true—which I rather doubt—what would it amount to? Suppose the new Roman pontiff loves good men, what is that to me? Certainly if he does not love the others, he loves very few, and I am not of that number, which I would prefer to be than to be pope. Farewell.

At the source of the Sorgue, 28 March.

Fam. XVI, 4.

To a friend wavering in his Catholic faith.

I am omitting other subjects which I hope we shall have the opportunity to discuss in person; I shall write about one of much greater seriousness, which admits no delay. I am worried about your doubts regarding ultimate salvation, which I have often discussed in your presence, yet not as often as I should have, I see, or as much as was needed to break your stubborn heart. How could I now possibly believe that amidst the complexities of life and the snares of the devil your mind could begin meditating on something no one can deny: the human race is unworthy of what we know heaven has done for it, inasmuch as one man is a thief, another a perjurer, still another an adulterer; all the earth is so filled with them that we read the Creator was forced to say, "I regret the creation of man." How, then, could such a great power have done so much for creatures so unworthy? Perhaps this you are now asking yourself. You ought to realize, however, that such thoughts ought to lead to humility and gratitude, and not to disbelief; I admit that few men, indeed none at all, are worthy of the favors of God, except him whom He made worthy: this makes His kindness all the greater, His generosity all the more manifest and His mercy all the more remarkable. Perhaps your doubts are intensified still more because of the common belief that many men distinguished in intelligence or in moral virtues lived before the coming of Christ. Would that it were less obvious today to us all that virtue and intelligence have completely disappeared! At this your mind wavers, and because it cannot see why this should be, it does not believe that it has happened. Yet this too leads to the same conclusion, which ought to increase piety and love, and not produce disbelief, for the more we perceive our unworthiness, the more we perceive and admire His great munificence toward us, but we ought not to marvel so much as to deny it. Who except the worst kind of person when receiving a great honor, though undeserved, from his master rebels against him or forgets the favors received; he should rather say, "For no reason have you loved me, you preferred me, unworthy as I am, to those better than I, and I render my gratitude, I recognize you as my devoted master, I recognize the excellent advantages you have obtained for me, I accept the rewards of virtuous men without being virtuous, I am happy beyond description; all this I sought through your good will and not with my own labor, and I owe it not to myself, not to another, but to you alone." In all Christian teaching handed down from Christ by those who love truth, which is Christ, what is either impossible to God or incredible to us except that God's great humility, consummate mercy, and compassion toward mankind are shown in such measure that the human mind can barely comprehend it? Indeed true are Augustine's words on Psalm 147: "Though certain, unusually happy events are barely believed." Therefore, O mortal creature, if you lay aside incredulity, you have the wherewithal to begin rendering your gratitude. You have been made happier than you would have thought possible. Believe what has happened. "God's very wisdom, the only consubstantial and eternal Son of the Father," came to free you; from the throne of His majesty He could have sent forth commands which had to be obeyed in heaven and on earth, but He wished to act more efficaciously and humbly. As Augustine has it, "He deemed it worthy to take on all of man, and the Word was made flesh and dwelt among us." The reason then follows: "For thus to carnal man, incapable of seeing truth with the mind and dedicated to the senses, He showed the lofty position of human nature among all the creatures, and He not only appeared visibly—for He could have revealed Himself as some ethereal body, tolerable to our sight—but also as a true man." For this too Augustine gives an explanation: "For He had to assume that very nature which was to be set free." So much for Augustine.

Therefore, my dear friend, when God perceived you to be in peril, He did not allow you to perish; though He could have raised you with His word, He preferred to do so with His hand. As do lovers, He bent to the earth where you lay, raising you up in His embrace, and Himself assumed the crushing burden that weighed you down. Thus were fulfilled David's words, "As far as the East is from the West, so far has He put our transgressions from us." As I said, what He could have done with His word, He did with His blood; another has said, "He struck a covenant with you through His blood." Do not break it, for He is a very dependable keeper of promises. If you are certain that He could free you, why do you doubt that He wished to? Why do you hesitate to believe what you need and what is easy for Him to bestow and most worthy of His majesty? Why do you fear admitting what you strongly desire except that your mind is too narrow to accept such great joy, as I have said, and you feel unworthy of such a gift? Rejoice now with your entire spirit, for you have just cause; so much is there to rejoice over that you can barely comprehend it. Certainly you should derive from this as much faith as comfort. You are unworthy, He is kind; you are a sinner, He is merciful. Recognize the favor, welcome the gift, cast off your doubts. You deserved lasting punishment; instead an eternal glory is promised you if you do not refuse. You feared a strict judge, you found a devoted father: "As a father has compassion on his children, so the Lord has compassion on those who fear Him," not because our sins merited it, but because "He knew our frailty and remembered that we are dust." And thus He is not as angered by our sins as compassionate of our fragility, giving assistance to our needs. So incredible is this that it seems difficult to believe: good is returned for evil and reward for punishment by the very Person who has been so unworthily offended, who could so easily take vengeance. And yet it must be believed beyond doubt, and the Redeemer's mercy must be recognized; for as our father Augustine writes in his profound book, *De vera religione*, "The holy assumption of human nature and the virgin birth, the death of God's son for us, the resurrection from the dead, the ascension into heaven, the sitting at the right hand of the Father, the redemption of sins, the day of judgment, the resurrection of the body, the knowledge of the Trinity in eternity and the changeableness of creatures are all not only to be believed, but are also to be judged as examples of the compassion the highest God extends to the human race." For all this, my dear friend, I confess, we must embrace and retain a great admiration, a wholesome astonishment, and a reverent fear, since truly "powerful is the Lord on high," truly "He is great and awesome above all who surround Him," truly "He is terrible in the decrees toward the children of men"; and yet He is "good and forgiving, abounding in kindness to all who call upon Him;" the Lord is "pitying and compassionate and slow to anger," and "patient, merciful and truthful," "good and upright is the Lord, and the One who gives the law to those who have lost the way," this law indeed by which they may return to Him and be saved. What more need be said? Surely, as there is no one more awesome, so there is no one more merciful or peaceful. He causes many to toil so that they not fall prey to passion, He allows others to be in peril so that He may correct them, He wishes no one to perish and does everything so that we not perish. Therefore, despair should be banished, hardness abandoned, irreverence cast off, disbelief left behind. As everyone in his right mind knows, nothing is impossible or truly difficult for God; no one who has faith doubts that anything pertaining to the salvation of His creatures seems difficult to Him. The indication of a perverted intelligence is to doubt that God will, or can, have compassion; from this source alone despair usually arises. Since the first denies His "goodness" and the second His "omnipotence," both are blasphemies against the Holy Spirit—a blasphemy that is not pardoned in this life or in the future one, since one is accusing the highest power of impotence with regard to our salvation, and the highest good of envy. The opinion about Cain is that he fell into this very sin when he said, "My sin is too great to gain pardon," for the misery of the creature could not be greater than the mercy of the Creator. Unfortunate Judas committed this same sin when he went and hanged himself after throwing his pieces of silver into the temple; although his sin was much greater than Cain's, it was still his despair alone that prevented him from finding mercy. If he had sought it from Christ, he would have obtained it, in Ambrose's opinion. But he did not seek mercy, he confessed his sin to those who rejoiced in it and cared not for his punishment, and finally, according to Jerome, he offended Christ with his despair rather than with his betrayal, something certainly worth remembering. What then can God do? Anything He wishes, but He desires everything that He knows is good for us: this must be believed with a strong faith and a constant trust. Let empty and shaky conjectures cease, and let believing ears be blocked against the whisperings of the devil; it was a wondrous thing indeed that because of us God was born in such a miraculous manner; greater still, that He lives amidst our necessities and miseries; greatest of all, that in His mercy toward us, He died in a way more common to us but miserable for Him. Who will deny this wonderful and ineffable sign of divine love? Is the magnitude of His benevolence such that it makes us ungrateful? May this madness not enter devout minds! Let us realize that we are unworthy of such great favors, and recognize that we are completely incapable of expressing our gratitude in words in payment for such favors. Let us confess that our frailty was overcome by the immense mercy of God, but let us, as much as we can, be grateful in mind, obedient and believing and faithful, and let us not despair that, because the gift is great and we are unworthy, He cannot, or will not, watch over us on account of the unapproachable perfection of His power and majesty. Farewell.

29 March.

Fam. XVI, 5.

To an unknown correspondent, that one is always going toward death even while seemingly returning from it.

I hear that you have come back from the threshold of death to which, amazing as it sounds, you hasten to return. I should express this more clearly: we who have entered upon the journey of this life are all hastening, we are hastening, I say, and we never cease; indeed we are running when we seem to be slackening our pace. This is an understatement; we are not running but flying, and so our goal cannot be too distant. But let us be of good heart, proceeding undaunted and without delay: the goal is not the threshold of death but of eternal life, truly hidden because of our sins yet revealed by the blood of Christ and opened by His wounds. Oh, would that we be allowed to sleep there in peace, would that after lengthy and countless labors we may finally rest in Him who in a most unique manner provided us with a hope that could not be false, coming as it did from Him! I indeed rejoice that you have returned to good health, nor do I wish us to be separated in this exile of life, although wherever we are flung we must all likewise come under the sway of the eternal Leader. But since the mind favors man's good fortune over man's nature, so I rejoice in not having known about your dangerous condition until it was no longer dangerous, if indeed to be ill or to die is a danger and not instead the road to true and enduring peace. You must know that recovery has been according to that law which not only allows you to remain mortal but at the same time to approach death with every passing hour, and so with each hour you are continually dying; yet what is death for the multitude is the end of death for philosophers. A truly astonishing matter for rejoicing it is, that death, which we so fear, becomes longer merely by speaking of it! Oh, what incredible stupidity! At one and the same time we fear death and its end, preferring a long-lasting death to a momentary one, yet all to no avail. What you believe to have evaded will come, I say, it will come; it will come a little later, but it will be swift, perhaps at this very moment. You cannot turn your back on that condition. After having carried it along with you for a while, will you be surprised that, when you have finally dragged it where you must of necessity return, you have both avoided and found it? Clearly, it is as I always say: the day of payment has been postponed for a time, but the reckoning of the natural debt has not been erased; once contracted at birth it must be paid at death. Farewell.

Fam. XVI, 6.

To Niccolò, Bishop of Viterbo,* some words of comfort in his illness.

A strong man needs no one to encourage him in order to face with fearlessness a known enemy and the usual kind of battle. He goes to confront him, being quite certain of victory and very certain of praise; he often delights in trials of his own choice, preferring to exercise his valor in difficult undertakings than to languish in effeminate idleness. Therefore, he dwells amidst dust and perspiration, amidst swords and wounds, not only without pain but often even with pleasure; he worries not about the present, he is totally immersed in his goal and, though weary in body, he finds rest in peace of mind and the hope of glory. You, my brother in love and my son in age but my father in dignity, whom virtue made a man of a boy before his time and whom dignity made an old man of a young one, you have no need for a lengthy sermon to understand what is written in Sacred Scripture: "The life of man on earth is warfare," and not only warfare but a constant battle, deadly, without truce or peace. This war you entered as a soldier of Christ, and at length you deservedly became one of its leaders. It is not enough to have made a good start, for if you covet the crown of victory you must remain in the battlefield from dawn to dusk to assail the raging enemy with both hands, raising on high the shield of your untiring virtue. Indeed we are attacked by all kinds of weapons: on one side tormenting poverty and on the other heavy riches weigh us down; on one side unforeseen misfortunes, either our own or our friends', and on the other a heart burning with anxiety, mental and bodily illnesses, and the numerous and various blows of fortune that are all not only difficult to bear but even to list. Nowhere is there any security for man; often when the sea's surface seems most tranquil, a tempest is raging in its depths, and when the world most seems flattering to you, then it is lying in wait with its hidden snares; every road is beset with traps, each branch is smeared with lime, and each clod of soil covered with burrs and thorns; hardly anywhere can you set your foot without danger. It did you no good to have climbed higher, for wherever you turn there is equal peril and trouble; and indeed it is all the greater the more your lofty position is exposed to fortune's arrows. Thus in this field of life where we descend to do battle, there is

---

*Niccolò di Paolo dei Vetuli, prior of Sant'Angelo de Spata, was elected Bishop of Viterbo in 1350. At the time of this letter (1353) he had been gravely ill. He died in 1385.

no hope of flight, no byway of peace; everything necessarily depends on divine protection and on the virtue of the unconquered spirit. But to return to the matter at hand, I have heard, my dear father, the sad news, which has reached even into the shadows of my solitude, that you are suffering from a serious illness; but I do not speak as to a sick man, rather I hope that by the time the news of your illness reached me you were already well and that when this letter reaches you there will be no sign of illness; and so I shall speak quite frankly. I must at least confess to you my frailty: at the arrival of the sad news—to show you that I am a man rather than a philosopher—I, as a man, grieved so much that the happy tranquillity of my peace suddenly turned to sorrow, and I repeatedly reproved my mind for its weakness. But in reality, I grieved more for your most loving father than for you, who I am certain have always borne, and will continue to bear, all vicissitudes with moderation and manliness; he now feels the ills of your body even more, I imagine, than you, who by now as I said are probably out of danger. You may feel badly about my grief and my unnecessary fear, but he will certainly not feel well again until he sees you recovered. He is hastening to you after laying aside all his affairs in which he is forever involved, and you know their importance and number; furthermore, he has left his home, despising the sea, disregarding the Alps, and scorning the winter, and is unmindful of all the difficulties and cares, and even of himself, thinking only of you as a dutiful father should. Now the son can properly say to his father what that father in Virgil said to his son: "Devotion has overcome your difficult journey." Unless I am mistaken, this knowledge should give you strength, making you realize that your father lives in you and even suffers in you, not to mention your mother, brothers, sisters, and friends, among whom I dare number myself not the least. Who among us can be well while you are ill; for who could ever enjoy bodily health when the health of the spirit is languishing? I have found delight for a little while in using these kind words, and my devotion has nearly brought tears to my eyes. Now it is time to counsel you manfully to remember that you must endure and despise with a noble spirit all mortal things, you must scorn present things, hope for better things, and have no faith in the world—for it is deceptive; you must believe that you and your fate are in the hands of God, place all your hope and cares in Him, and know that from the day you entered this life you came not for banquets but for wars and illnesses, troubles and toils. Nevertheless whatever happens, yours could be the victory if you wish, provided you not cast off your weapons or become faint of heart or fall to the ground; to be born, to live, to be ill, to grow old, and to die are natural occurrences, but to endure them manfully without change of expression or heart is the result of virtue. I am not saying what some men have said, that there is no real difference between the greatest pleasure and the worst sorrow. That seems much too rigid and heartless an opinion to me; nor do I agree with the assertion that physical pain is not an evil, as was held by the celebrated school of the Stoics. With their words they do indeed prove that nothing can be properly called evil unless it stands in opposition to the good, and that the only good is virtue to which vice, and not pain, can be contrasted; and yet in the real world it is very difficult to prove such an assertion. It is better then to speak more commonly and listen to the Peripatetics, who consider pain an evil but not the greatest; however great, it is subject to virtue: in this everyone agrees, and certainly more illustrious is that praise earned through great hardship and brighter is that fame originating from an uncertain fortune. Everyone knows how to rest in peace, to rejoice, to feast, and to abound in pleasures; but man must toil tirelessly, bear illness patiently, stand firm amidst dangers and, if need be, die fearlessly. While enduring all this is certainly unpleasant, its recollection is pleasurable. Virgil's words are well known: "One day—who knows?—even these will be grand things to look back on." Amidst my difficulties, I admit, this saying often comes to mind and proves useful. But unfortunately I lack the time at present to write at length, so let this be a general summary: you must place your hope in God, you must seek the aid of the Almighty, and you must firm and strengthen your spirit against all you have endured, or can endure, so that it may grow a callous against adversity, as hardened men usually do on their feet.

So much for my advice with regard to your mind; it seems useless to give advice on the care of your body, since your episcopal dignity did not keep you from the field of medicine. As a physician and the son of a renowned physician, unlike the many dishonest practitioners of that art who plot against others' lives and who like to frequent only the homes of the wealthy, you know the causes of your illness, I believe, and its remedies, if Cicero's words are true—doctors believe that, once the cause of an illness has been discovered, they have already prepared the medicine. Allow me to express something beyond the boundaries of this discussion: an infinite number of illustrious examples confirm what mental feelings, joy or grief, can do for good or for evil to bodily health, but I shall restrict myself to the most famous. The mental joy experienced by the elder

Africanus contributed to his physical well-being; as he took pleasure in his son, so can you in your father. At that same time, mental distress caused the illness and death of Philip of Macedonia, the king who waged war against the Roman people. Surely, although there is no one to whom the world did not give some reason for complaint, nevertheless if you think about yourself and the abundance of celestial gifts bestowed upon you, you will find yourself among that number who have cause to rejoice; wherefore you must exhibit a patient, yet joyful, spirit. And above all meditate on this, which perhaps may not be too hard to do, that among the many gifts of God with which you were blessed before your time but not without merit, you know that you are a man with a mortal body and that as a result of your illness your health will be dearer to you and you to your friends. Meanwhile, do bear in mind that nothing, as far as I know, compares with the solitude in which our Socrates and I are eagerly awaiting you, where by God's favor you may easily strengthen and restore your body, bringing peace to your mind. Here there is no threatening tyrant, no insolent layman, and no foul-mouthed detractor; here no wrath, no political factions, no complaints, no perfidy, no clamor and shouting men, no sound of bugles and clashing of arms; furthermore, here you will find no greed, envy, ambition, or thresholds of arrogant men to be crossed with fear, but instead joy and simplicity and freedom, that desirable state between wealth and poverty, a temperate and humble and gentle rusticity, a harmless folk and an unarmed people, a peaceful region whose bishop is an excellent man, such a friend of good men that he will consider you a brother, since he treats us as sons. What else shall I say? Here the air is mild, the breezes gentle, the land sunny, the waters clear, the river full of fish, the groves shady, and the grottoes mossy, here there is many a grassy retreat and smiling meadow; here you will find oxen lowing, birds singing, and nymphs murmuring. All this is hidden away, and for this reason bears the delightful name of the Closed Valley; nearby, however, are hills pleasing to Bacchus and Minerva. In order not to dwell excessively on food and drink in the manner of parasites—which is not my custom—I shall merely report that all that grows here on land or in the water is such that you would consider it grown in the paradise of delights, to use the words of theologians, or in the Elysian fields, to use poetic language. If this little village really lacks anything—since often man's taste is more expensive than it need be—it may easily be supplied from the bounty of the neighboring region. In short, so as not to give too many details, here you will find the peace and tranquillity you crave and an abundance of books (the greatest wealth for the studious mind) and the fellowship and regard of friends. You will consort with saints, philosophers, poets, orators, and historians; the two of us will remain nearby without being in your way; already we are running in spirit to meet you, preparing this harbor against the storms of your busy life. Meanwhile, weeping and distressed, your father is coming to you, and with every step repeats David's words: "Had I but the wings of a dove, I would fly away and be at rest"; that is, "when shall I have the joy of seeing once again my first-born son restored to health, my son who has become my father?" And we who are awaiting you with the utmost eagerness are doing as lovers usually do: we are counting the days one by one, constantly straining our ears and wondering whether we shall receive happier news of you.

Amidst the good wishes of your friends live happily, I beg you, O loving father, and farewell and come quickly, exalting your mind above your strength and repeating to yourself and to all your powers the famous verse: "Be patient, and preserve yourselves for better things."

Fam. XVI, 7.

To his Socrates, * *concern about the disappearance of a friend.*

Our friend came to me as you had promised. After exchanging greetings, I asked whether he had a letter from you; at his reply of "nothing," I began to think it pointless to ask for a letter when I had recourse to his human voice. In short I want you to know my great pleasure at his arrival; you know the kind of people I usually like: the harsher fortune was to him, the more welcome he is to me, and similarly the more he dislikes himself or is disliked by arrogant men, the dearer he is to me. I received him as best I could and as the place allows, namely, with rustic simplicity, yet with a regal spirit, and showed him as much of this mountainous solitude of mine as time permitted: what I had lately sowed and reaped in my mind, in my garden or in my small fields. While we were thus getting along so well that nothing except your presence seemed missing—your name did occur several times—a desire, common to saddened spirits, seized him to go walking for a while. He said that he would particularly like to visit the island located about three miles distant, delightfully bathed and encircled by the Sorgue. I approved, urging him to accept one of my servants as a companion, but he pleaded with me not to burden him with one, since he really hoped to find some peace of mind; for nothing pleased him more in his particular condition than solitude. This did not surprise me, for everyone who knows me realizes my great love of solitude. I let him go, and he left saying he would return for dinner; it has now been two days and he has yet to return. What am I to do? What could possibly have happened? When shall I expect him? Where can I ask anyone to search for him? Can it be that he has returned to you? Has he gone on a longer journey? He is not where he had said he would go, and I know not what to think. His depression worries me; solitude does not help a dejected spirit. If you have any news of him, please set my mind at ease. There is nothing more to write except those words of Ovid, "Love is full of anxiety and fear," adding the words of Flaccus: "and it becomes greater for those who are absent." Farewell.

At the source of the Sorgue, 1 April.

*See I, 1.

Fam. XVI, 8.

To his Lelius,* concerning the noble manners of Roman ladies.

On the nineteenth of April, while on my way to visit once again my brother, your brother, indeed our brother in Christ, to use his own words, I was between Aix and the church of St-Maximin when by chance I saw advancing down the road a large group of Roman ladies. Strange as it may seem, from a distance I recognized their lineage and origin by their appearance and stately walk, but I still wished to know if my assumption was correct. But as I drew near and heard their voices in conversation, no doubt remained. I halted and, as if in ignorance, asked them in Italian Maro's question: "What is your country and where is your home?" At the first sound of Italian, they happily stopped, and the eldest answered, "We are Roman ladies on our way to the shrine of St. James in Spain. And you, are you perhaps Roman and going to Rome?" I replied, "Indeed I am a Roman at heart, but at present I am not on my way to Rome." Then, gathering about me in a friendly manner, they began speaking informally. First I inquired as to the state of the republic; their answers mingled cheer with sadness. When we came to particulars, I first asked about you; they said that you were well, happily and honorably married, and the father of a fine boy. Although I already knew this, I was as glad to hear it from them as if I had not known it, or as if I saw you and your wife and your son face to face. They added some details about the dangers you had encountered; while they were well in the past, their story so renewed my fear that I listened in great anxiety. Thanks to God, the outcome was favorable. Then I asked about our young friend, and learned of his escape from a deadly peril when his colleague, Senator Bertoldo, had fallen into the hands of an angry mob and been stoned to death, according to their account. Immediately Lucan's words came to mind, "You will pay with your own blood for the wrongs done to your wretched city; with your lives you will pay for the slaughter you have wrought." When I heard the cause of such a misfortune, I recalled the saying of Solomon: "He who hoards corn shall be cursed by the people." That wretched man had poorly learned these sayings of Caesar: "The highest favor is won by providing plentiful food," and "a hungry mob knows no fear." I then asked whether they wished me to do anything for them, for I intended to satisfy any of their requests to the best of my ability, for the sake of God, of honor and of our fatherland, and for your sake. I offered to

*See III, 19.

share with them whatever money I had brought for my journey. You can well imagine what they all answered: they wished nothing for themselves except my prayers to Christ for a safe return to their homeland and for a ready entrance into the heavenly city, since they were well supplied for all their needs. I did my best to persuade them to accept something from me, but they repeatedly refused. What could I do? I recognized in them the true character of the Roman lady, and I happily reflected that women of many nations would not only not have refused any gifts offered them, but would have clamored insistently for anything refused then. But truth begets hatred, so I shall name no names. Our Roman ladies, however, gratefully acknowledged my good will and graciously declined my offer of money. Let whoever wishes say that men are importunate in asking and ungrateful in receiving! With all due respect to such a slanderer, I shall say that I have known Romans who are splendid in their scorn of gifts offered them and mindful of those received—and not only men, but women as well, who are said to be more greedy by nature. I do not wish to detain you today with this letter for as long as I kept those ladies that day from continuing their journey; indeed I would gladly have detained them until evening, even though it was not yet nine in the morning, except that I feared to slacken the sacred zeal of the ladies' devotion. Besides, I too was in a hurry, intending, after a visit with my brother, to take a longer journey to Italy, God willing. I resolved to hasten and by my eagerness perhaps elude my usual fate, which has always forced me to wait for July or December whenever I am about to travel abroad. And so we said farewell and parted. Only then did I realize where I was, for during the course of the conversation I seemed to be in Rome, beholding Cecilia wife of Metellus, Sulpitia wife of Fulvius, Cornelia wife of Gracchus, Cato's Martia, Scipio's Emilia, and the entire troupe of illustrious women of antiquity, or, to use examples more appropriate for our present discussion and more suitable to our present age, the Roman maidens of Christ—Prisca, Praxedes, Pudentia, Cecilia, and Agnes.

I went on, and the next morning saw my brother, who of all men I have ever known—unless my love for him deceives me—has sailed more successfully among the storms and miseries of life, and is so raised above earthly cares, so spiritually disposed, that his very life gives praise to God. Although so inferior to him in my way of life and my ideals that I should blush being outdone by my junior, I still rejoice and glory that we are of the same blood and born of the same womb. Reunited for the first time in five years, we had a long and eager conversation, speaking of many friends but of none more than our Lelius: he wondered how you were faring with fortune and how she was faring with you, what you were doing, where you were, what kind of life you were leading, what preparations you were making for your final day, and whether you were proving true to yourself. After answering all his questions, I left him happier than I had found him; I believe you know without my saying so how greatly he wishes that all may go well with you. Farewell.

At the source of the Sorgue, 24 April.

Fam. XVI, 9.

To Zanobi da Firenze, * *a request in behalf of the Carthusian monastery of Montrieux.*

Halfway between the new Babylon and Nice-on-the-Var, ten miles to the right of the main road as one goes toward Italy, hidden between wooded mountains and mountain streams there is a place that I believe is named after its location. It is in fact named Mont Rieux, and is an ancient seat of the Carthusians that was built nearly at the order's beginning. It is said that twin brothers came from Genoa who were navigators and successful exchangers of goods, to use Lucan's words, one in the east and the other in the west. Others tell a different story, but let its credibility remain with the authors, as is commonly said: I shall only report what I have heard. The brothers usually left home at the same time, and upon their return after a long period, one from the east and the other from the west, they would meet in their city; there they would settle accounts and, as such men usually do, after making the necessary arrangements, they would once again set sail on the high seas. After a number of expeditions from which they had amassed tremendous and well-earned riches, it happened that the brother returning from the orient was the first to return home, only to learn that the other coming from the west had landed in Marseilles. After awaiting him for some time and vainly urging him by letter to return, he became suspicious. Impatient at the delay and very jealous of his time, as merchants are, he finally went to Marseilles: there he found his brother almost a different man with changed cares and interests. In astonishment, he asked the reason for his more than usual indolence; the response was that he had sailed the seas long enough and wished no longer to entrust his life to the wind; therefore his brother might do what he thought best for himself, but he personally had reflected upon this, had sought a harbor and on the shore, indeed at the entrance to paradise, had built a house where he might rest his weary body until his departure for his eternal home. Still more astonished, the other brother continued to inquire more deeply into the meaning of his brother's obscure statement. Whereupon his brother without any reply took him by the hand and led him to the place in a hidden valley amidst these wild woods where he had built the monastery of which I have spoken. Once he understood his brother's intention, the other brother also underwent a conversion and, burning to im-

*See XII, 3.

itate his brother, built a second monastery on a nearby hill; they amply endowed the place, renounced the world and its pleasures, and dedicated the remainder of their lives to Christ, persevering to the end in the fulfillment of their vows. Now the twin buildings house a single Christian community, and its appearance seems to reflect that the founders were indeed twins, yet of one mind. That then is the story.

There, as you well know, lives my brother, my dearest and only pledge, in whom can be clearly seen what the Psalmist calls "a change by the right hand of the Most High." Suddenly he was transformed from a wayward and unstable young man into a firm and constant one; in short, he has daily risen so swiftly from virtue to virtue and so manifested the ardor of his changed resolve through ten years of perseverance that he now fills me with great amazement and joy, he who was once my fear and anxiety. Since I had not seen him for more than five years, and since I know not when I would ever see him again, should I return to Italy, I stole a few days from my occupations and recently went there to visit him once again. What can I tell you? Of my brother's loving tears or of the humble gatherings with the servants of Christ, of their blessed hospitality and inspiring words, of what I said or heard or saw, of what was said and done during my stay and at my departure; how the entire angelic flock gathered under the sacred roof to extend all possible hospitality to their guest; how they all accompanied me at my departure to the monastery gates and how my brother with a few others went with me on the wooded path down to the foot of the mountain; how he hastily warned me of many things, as time allowed, and asked and told me many things for which an entire day and night had not sufficed? As I say, you can well imagine all this without my writing it, but I must tell you of one matter about which you cannot have any knowledge. If amidst the many sobering and sacred consolations that blessed place and my brief visit afforded me I also experienced bitterness, I believe it was intended to help me understand the truth that "all who live piously in Christ shall suffer persecution," and that the wayfarer has no hope of peace wherever he may rest his head until he reaches his fatherland. This innocent company of saintly men, scorning honors, riches, and pleasures, and spurning our invisible enemy, is now being molested by visible enemies; sad to relate, having fallen prey to the avarice of tyrants both secular and ecclesiastical, they are often compelled by extreme need to interrupt their divine praises. The tale would be too long were I to include all the indignities they are forced to suffer; I give it to you in brief, which will allow you to infer the details. They are surrounded by petty tyrants, a most unfit type to be avoided by any means possible. For while powerful tyrants often plunder they are at least generous; petty tyrants are never so, being forever parched, famished, and thirsty, and emboldened by their petty thieveries they live in the hope of still greater plunder. In any event, for the servants of Christ who are cloistered in voluntary servitude there is no hope of escape or mercy from these tyrants; their only hope lies in divine or royal assistance. And thus once in the past they humbly approached Charles II of blessed memory, King of Sicily and grandfather of the present king, with the request that he send them one of his officers, whose very presence, in the name of a just king, might protect them from harm; after the manner of Caesar, the king could not deny a deserving plea and thus willingly agreed. With such protection for many years they lived in relative peace under that king and then under his son, Robert, the best of kings and the best of men. Later, however, there was appointed in Marseilles, the diocese whence came their worst trouble, a new bishop who was such a good friend of the order and such a just man that they chose to deal with him rather than to have recourse to a superior force or authority. For many years, then, they lived in harmony under him while the others refrained from doing them any harm out of respect for the good bishop, and thus there was no longer any need for royal protection. After a time through the simplicity of these humble servants of Christ—a simplicity considered folly in the eyes of the worldly-wise, yet wisdom in the eyes of God—the patronage of illustrious kings became obsolete and antiquated. After the bishop's departure from this world, his successors were increasingly worse and everything began to deteriorate until it gradually returned to its original condition; now the diocese of Marseilles has a tyrant, and now the local lords near the monastery, since it is human nature to imitate evil models rather than good ones, exercise a tyranny even worse than before. While the monks are singing matins to Christ, in comes a weeping shepherd to complain that his flock has been stolen; while mass is being celebrated at the altar, you can hear a farmer crying out that his crop, vineyard, meadow, and garden is being torn to shreds by the tyrants' cattle; when it is time for their frugal breakfast or brief slumber, a sacristan, that servant of the servants of Christ, interrupts the monastic silence to lament his beating at the hands of the tyrants' men. The monks try to make use of their former remedies and to take refuge under royal privilege; their appeal to an antiquated authority is ridiculed, and now they are enslaved even more than before for nothing but their belief that they deserved freedom under the yoke of Christ. What more can

I say to you? Should you hear what I heard, you would hold back your tears no more than I did; they still have an abundance of chalices, garments, and books, which thus far they have defended against the thieves but only with difficulty. In short, there is no hope or remedy for them unless our king looks with royal compassion upon this ravaged hut of Christ, and renews the privileges granted by his grandfather and his uncle, and through his benevolence frees and restores that monastery founded by others, thereby deserving as much credit as the founder—even as the glory of Brutus or Camillus is no less than that of Romulus, if one believes their virtue to be true and the latter's divinity not to be false. In tears, then, they begged me to do what I could to have a royal officer or some protector reinstated so that they might be safe from attack. I replied that I had no claim upon the king beyond my respect and trust in him; that at the court was an illustrious and excellent man having great influence with the king, who holds me dear because of his benevolence rather than my merit; that I had hope in the justice of a man so disposed to do good, who has proven his affection for their order by recently having constructed at his expense and under his supervision a remarkable cloister near the walls of his native city; that therefore I would intercede with him, using you as intermediary because of my fear of writing him a letter whose length might prove annoying, since he is so occupied with highly serious matters. Your tongue will be my pen, and thus their justifiable pleas will be transmitted by my fingers to your eyes, by your tongue to his ears and through him to the king's attention. Do advise our friend to imitate Caesar Augustus, "the founder or restorer of all temples," as Titus Livy calls him, or rather to surpass him so that here he may restore the temples of the true God—he has already founded one—as Augustus restored the temples of false gods. Now you have the essence of the matter, now you see the request and its justification, the dignity of the petitioners and my own wish in this regard. I shall not burden you with entreaties that would indicate a lack of confidence, but if you succeed, as I hope, you will accomplish something most pleasing to Christ and to me. Farewell.

Fam. XVI, 10.

To the same correspondent. *

  The letter you are reading, in which I intercede in behalf of the Carthusians—I am using our meaning and not that of the ancients for whom the word intercede meant "to hinder" or "to oppose something in order to make it fail"—that letter then which you are reading, or have read, was conceived at that holy hermitage; a few days later I began writing it in our Helicon. I completed it this very day—so much does fortune envy my tranquillity—in Babylon where I came the day before yesterday never to return again. For I have once again sent scouts to Italy, and, although there is no tranquillity to be found anywhere, I hope to find there some semblance of a harbor for me in my weariness. I shall bear whatever comes of it as long as I keep in mind that nothing in the world is more upsetting, nothing worse, than Babylon, whose stormy madness allows nothing within its proximity, not even my Helicon, to remain tranquil. Mindful of this, wherever overbearing fortune whirls me I shall find solace as long as I am not here. Does this surprise you? Do you perhaps believe that the nature of the place or my own fortune has changed? Here no happy news ever comes, or ever will come. Thus, immediately upon crossing the threshold of this infamous city, I was twice shaken with terrible news: I learned of your accident and of that illustrious man's death. I see what my pen ought to do, but my affairs are interfering with my duty. The place and the time, my difficulties and a crowd of business matters that pursue me in my flight—for nowhere in the world could they so interfere with my freedom as they do here—and even the journey which, God willing, I shall soon undertake in the manner of someone escaping from prison once this brief letter is finished, all these things are preventing me from writing you a friendly letter, yet not from feeling badly about it. Upon my departure, in keeping with my old custom I shall stop at my solitary dwelling, but only for eight days, no more. And I shall view my journey as follows: to have left here represents more than half the length of the road as well as its most difficult portion; the remainder ought to be short and simple. Farewell.

Babylon, 28 April.

  *See XII, 3.

Fam. XVI, 11.

To Francesco, of the Church of the Holy Apostles, *
on the preciousness of time.

Once time was not so precious for me; for although it always is uncertain, my expectations then were undoubtedly much greater, but now time and hope, together with all other things, are diminishing. Yet it is scarcity that gives value to things: if we imagine the world abounding in pearls, then they would be kicked about as stones; if we imagine as many phoenixes as doves, then the fame of that unique bird would perish; if we imagine forests of balsams blanketing the mountains, then balsam would become a common balm; in short, the more their availability, the less their value. On the other hand, scarcity causes even the more ordinary things to be valued. For this reason, in the parched Libyan deserts a little water in the hands of a Roman commander was viewed with great envy; for this reason, during the siege of Casilinum that filthy beast, the mouse, was held in high esteem; for this reason, to give an example superseding all others, the mere lack of men caused the greatest cowards to flourish. I shall forgo examples, since my pen scorns to write such foul names; besides, what need is there for examples when the alleys and avenues abound in such monsters; indeed there is no pestilence more rampant in our times. If I may say so without boasting, never was time as worthless for me as it was for some of my contemporaries, even though I never did appreciate it as it deserved. I should like to be able to say that I never lost a day, but I lost many; if only they were not years! I am not afraid of saying this: as long as I can remember, I never lost a day without being aware of it; time did not slip away, but was instead so snatched from me that I could still say amidst the snares of affairs or the flames of passion: "Alas, this day is irreparably stolen from me." Now I realize that it happened because I did not yet appreciate the value of time, that value which Seneca mentions in writing to his Lucilius. I had known days were valuable, I had not known they were invaluable; listen to me, O young men in the prime of life, the value of time is incalculable. This I did not know at your age, when it would have been the best and most useful thing for me to know. I did not esteem time according to its value: I would cater to friends, I would complain about physical labor, mental boredom, and spending money; time came last. Now I realize that it ought to have been first; while repose does indeed alleviate weariness, and money lost can in-

*See XII, 4.

deed be regained, time never returns once it has slipped away. Its loss is, in short, irreparable. And so? Now I have begun—this is a change wrought by the right hand of the Most High which I truly desire but dare not express—and indeed I am beginning to appreciate time only because it is forsaking me; I think I shall understand it more clearly when it has slipped away from me altogether. O wretches that we are, what hardships await us! Do you realize the value of a single day for the soul of a dying person? At present I am truly beginning to value time, not yet as I must, but as I can; I recognize its incredible flight and its precipitous course which no reins can restrain except those of a growing and diligent virtue. I behold it forsaking me and with my eyes I can barely take measure of its damage; often I recall Virgil's words, "My day is already shorter and my summer milder." For a goodly portion of my time is now behind me and my affections are waning; from that vantage point I compensate for the damage wrought by fleeting time. As a result, it behooves me hereafter to make my letters shorter, my style humbler, and my opinions simpler; ascribe the first one to the brevity of time and the others to a weary mind. Lest you think that today I have been philosophizing in vain, I know your mind and your ways, concerned as I always am about my friend's welfare, and I know the depth of your friendship for me. You burn, you are distressed, agitated, and afflicted; and when you are most silent, your humanity cries out; your incomparable devotion makes you inquire about my affairs, my state of mind, where I may be, what I am thinking and what I am striving after. Accept then this briefest of summaries, which contains a long table: I am in good health, as is customary with bodies composed of contrary elements. Indeed I am making every effort—and I wish it were with success—to be of healthy mind; otherwise, my good intentions are deserving of praise. You certainly know my ways; I refresh my mind, wearied by affairs, through a change of location. Thus, after two years in France I was returning to my homeland when, at my arrival in Milan, that illustrious Italian graciously welcomed me with an honor such as I neither deserved nor expected, and to be perfectly truthful, never desired. As excuses I could have used my preoccupations and my hatred of crowds, as well as my natural desire for peace, except that he had anticipated all I might say and promised me above all the most perfect solitude and leisure in his teeming city—so far he has kept his promise to the best of his ability. I therefore yielded with the understanding that there was to be no change in my life, scarcely any in my dwelling, and no more infringement upon my freedom and leisure than was absolutely necessary. How long this will last, I know not; I predict it will be brief, knowing him and myself, our concerns and our lives, which involve such differing preoccupations. Meanwhile I am living in the western outskirts of the city near the basilica of St. Ambrose. My dwelling is very comfortable, located on the left side of the church, facing its leaden steeple and the two towers at the entrance; in the rear, however, it looks upon the city walls and in the distance fertile fields and the Alps covered with snow, now that summer is past. Nevertheless, the most beautiful spectacle of all, I would say, is a tomb which I *know* to be that of a great man, unlike what Seneca says of Africanus, "I believe it to be the grave of a great man." I gaze upwards at his statue, standing on the highest walls, which it is said closely resembles him, and often venerate it as though it were alive and breathing. This is not an insignificant reward for coming here, for the great authority of his face, the great dignity of his eyebrows and the great tranquillity in his eyes are inexpressible; it lacks only a voice for one to see the living Ambrose. For the present, this must suffice; as soon as I have any idea of the length of my stay, I shall make certain you know. Farewell.

Milan, 23 August, before dawn.

Fam. XVI, 12.

To the same correspondent,* a friendly letter.

One brief night scarcely suffices for household concerns that keep me busy at all hours, for the necessary repose which, though unwanted, every man requires, and for those nocturnal praises of God that human piety opposed to ungrateful mindlessness so that each day we may once again recite our prayers; I say then, a brief night scarcely suffices for the many important matters just mentioned and for responding to letters from you and other friends. Your messenger has threatened to return at dawn, and will do so because his self-interest is involved and because I read haste in his face as he handed me a bundle of letters late yesterday evening. Yet why am I so concerned? Shorter was the night for Vulteius when he was successful in infusing a love of death into his trembling companions; thus great deeds are often brought to fruition in the shortest time. Indeed time is not as brief as they say, although it may seem quite brief; I believe it would suffice for most things except that we shorten it through our own laziness; I am determined to lengthen it, and hope another time to write you of this and many other subjects. As for this very night, I shall try to deceive my weary eyes with a short nap and to express lengthy thoughts with few words. Indeed, my dear friend, the splendid content of your letter revealed its author's mind more clearly than the sun: you are distressed and tormented over my affairs, for you are uncertain where to seek me, when to summon me, what to hope and fear for me. Try to rid yourself of such mental uncertainties with the thought that everything will finally turn out well for me and in accordance with your wishes and your sincere hope, which I would want to be as real as it is friendly to me. Your most kind affection, I confess, has afforded me great pleasure, although hardly new. There was no need to express in words what I already knew; I see you, though absent, and I hear you, though silent. What indeed shall I call you except, to use Cicero's words, "almost a brother in affection, a son in obedience and a father in wisdom"? Each one delights me as it should; but since this discussion is of the deliberative kind, I shall make use of the last category, embracing your counsel as that of a most prudent father and thus agreeing on the matter you asked me to keep secret. As for the rest, fortune will decide where it will all lead, what outcomes and events will result, and where this all will be dragged by the

*See XII, 4.

multitude's distorted judgment; my intention is to do nothing for which I cannot advance a plausible reason. Indeed I feel as I used to feel before you wrote, and I recognize the remnants of my destiny: I have fallen into the hands of the multitude, my ancient lot! But despair not, I beg you, for I shall emerge brighter from the rubbing. The multitude may sometimes see what I do, but it does not see what I am thinking; and thus, with my better part, I conceal nearly all of myself from them. Yet even if the multitude were to judge me only by my actions, what does it expect to gain? After a thorough examination of all possibilities, I did what was best; if there be any doubt about it, at the very least I did what I considered less evil. In my opinion, there is scarcely any good done on earth, as the Psalmist testifies: "There is not a single man who does good, not even one." Ultimately, whether good or bad, I doubtless did what had to be done. Who will dare cry out, I shall not say against my judgment, but against the power of necessity which fastens ironlike nails, in the words of Flaccus, to the highest crowns, weighing down the arrogant shoulders of kings with a bronze yoke? What then could I do, what words could I use and what escapes could I seek, over what paths could I flee and with what skills could I shake off the authority of such a suppliant, for whom slow obedience meant rebellion? One must recall the words of Liberius about Julius Caesar: "How could I, a mere man, deny anything to him whom the gods themselves could not refuse?"

At his first words I thought of these verses, and at the same time the fairly noble ones of an obsure poet: "A request from leaders is a violent kind of command, and the man of power beseeches as if with drawn sword." One thing really obliged me more than the many other reasons, increasing my great respect for him and the weight of his authority: he was also a man of the church and, as much as could be expected at such an elevated level of good fortune, he was most devout; an honest man could not avoid involvement with him without seeming arrogant. Consequently I would not wish to conceal from you what prevented me from resisting him and even from refusing him, although it would be more modest to consign it to silence. When I asked exactly what he wished of me, since I was ill suited or ill disposed for anything he might need, he replied that he wished nothing but my presence, in the belief that I would do honor to himself and his state. I must confess that, overcome by such kindness, I blushed and remained silent; and by so doing, I consented or seemed to have consented. There was nothing, or at least I could find nothing, to say against it. But why go on? Would that I could persuade the multitude of this as easily as you! And yet, good God, what is this I desire? Am I perhaps forgetful of my conviction: let the multitude think as it wishes and myself as I can? Farewell.

Milan, 27 August, in haste, in the dead silence of the night.

Fam. XVI, 13.

To the same correspondent, * *that a man can do nothing without being criticized.*

Is there anyone so endowed with wisdom in human affairs that he can avoid the stings of critics? Can you name me even one person free of this curse? Christ Himself was disgraced and killed by the very men whom He had come to save; fortunate are we if, escaping from their axes and lashes, we are assailed only by their words. Lest we consider the ancients more slanderous than we are, never was an age as insolent as ours. Let me tell you a story, popular with the multitude, which old ladies use to while away wintry nights before the hearth. An old man and his young son were traveling with a small donkey, which each in turn would ride to relieve the demands of the journey. While the old man rode the donkey with the boy following on foot, other travelers jeered at him, saying, "Look at that dying and useless old man, thinking of himself while destroying that handsome boy!" The old man jumped down and made the reluctant boy take his place. A crowd of passersby remarked, "Look at that lazy and strong young man, giving in to his own laziness while killing his decrepit father!" Stricken with shame, the boy forced his father to mount the donkey, and thus both were carried at the same time by one beast. Then the muttering and indignation of onlookers increased because one small creature was weighed down by two heavier ones. Why delay any longer? Disturbed by such criticism, both dismount and begin following the donkey. Then the mocking really becomes more biting and the laughter more intense because in sparing one ass, two asses don't spare themselves. So the father says to the boy, "See, my dear son, you can never do anything that will win everyone's approval. Let's go back to our first way, and let these keep their way of discussing and slandering everything." I shall say nothing more, nor is there any need: the tale is simple but effective. Farewell.

*See XII, 4.

Fam. XVI, 14.

To the same correspondent, * *that men have greater concern for style than for life.*

I laughed as you wished, yet not for your reason but for another; I considered laughable not that you made a slight error in your Latin discourse but that the error shamed you so deeply. I noticed you were so preoccupied by one word, or rather one syllable, in truth just one letter, that had slipped from you but had scarcely seemed a slip to my ears that I said to myself: "O the anxieties of even the most learned men!" To whom, I ask, could something similar not happen? Our Cicero is the great father of the Latin language, and Virgil the second; but since not everyone agrees with this order of importance, then Tullius and Maro are assuredly the fathers of Roman eloquence—whoever denies this is a person with whom I could agree about nothing. Yet both men are troubled by grammar, even in entire passages; Cicero seeks relief from such tediousness in his letter to Atticus, asking him to deliver him from that great annoyance. If there is anything for which someone who hesitates or errs may be pardoned, it is in the uncertainty of the preterite construction since, in the words of the prince of grammarians, even the most adept writers do not know how to treat it according to set rules. But am I not looking for excuses for you as if that slip was yours rather than your pen's? If such an error had escaped your skillful and golden eloquence, would you not have certainly noticed it even if you were sleeping? The pen commits many thefts, more often against great talents and great writers; nothing can be stolen from the person who has nothing. He who possesses great riches does not notice small thefts, but as Naso remarks, "'tis the poor man's lot to count his sheep." As is the case with the wealth of a house, so it is with a rich intelligence—the more it increases in value, the more it is subject to thieving servants. Therefore, you wished to say *perfluxi*, and you certainly did; but weary from its demanding labor, your pen let slip a double consonant. Lay aside your fears, for you are too great to have slipped into such an error through ignorance, despite the opinion of your detractors. But take note, I beg you, consider and learn through experience how it need not interfere with your style but may even be useful to your mind.

Note, my dear friend, how we who soil our hands in this field are concerned about eloquence rather than life, and about the pursuit of

*See XII, 4.

fame in the fashion of ages past rather than virtue. I ask you, how vigilant are we in avoiding a base and uncultivated discourse, while being negligent in the meantime about life, where we leave uncondemned what is truly squalid and wicked. Faithful servants of human laws, we transgress divine commands despite its being the inexorable law of God that we live well. For it is only human whim and convention that would have us speak in a particular manner which is often changed, and must be changed, by the needs of daily usage. If it is true that, as Flaccus says, "the language of Cato and Ennius enrichened our native tongue and produced new words for things," then it is also true that Cicero, Virgil, and their successors changed many things, and would have changed many others, either through their authority or through usage. In fact, this is the source of the error deplored by Augustine in his *Confessions;* since his words so pleased me, as I believe they will please you, I am including them here. "Behold, O Lord my God, how diligently the sons of men observe rules of letters and syllables handed down by ancient writers, while they neglect the eternal rules of everlasting salvation taught by You. The learner or teacher of established rules of pronunciation is held more contemptible if he drops an 'h' and speaks of a 'uman being'—thus breaking a law of language—than if, though a man, he hates another man—thus breaking a law of God." In the same passage, he complains about many other things on the same subject, and not without reason. Hence, while eloquence is certainly reserved for the few, and virtue belongs to everyone, all seek what is of the few and no one seeks what belongs to everyone. Lest you think this reproach holds only for grammar, can you name me a poet who would not prefer to limp in real life rather than in his poetry? Or can you name me a historian who, after transmitting through his writings or through recollection the events of all ages and the deeds of kings or nations, the succession of events and of ages, wishes or is able to justify what he himself does or to render an account of his own actions and of his brief life? To run through a few others, show me a rhetorician who is not more afraid of ugliness in his speech than in his life; show me a dialectician who does not prefer to be conquered by his own passions than by an adversary's syllogism. I shall not mention mathematicians and geometricians who number and measure everything, yet neglect the numbers and measurements of their one and only soul. Musicians apply numbers to sounds, spending all their time in this pursuit; these are men who despise morals and deal with sounds, forgetful of Cicero's words: "Greater and better is the harmony of actions than of sounds." Tirelessly they must labor to avoid disharmony, yet they would scorn harmony of action where so much toil is required. Astrologers examine the skies, number the stars, and, in Pliny's words, "dare things that appear bad even to God"; they so boldly predict far in advance what will happen to kingdoms and cities, yet give no heed to what may daily befall them; they foresee the sun's eclipse, yet do not see the present eclipse of their souls. Those who bear the illustrious name of philosopher seek with empty arrogance the causes of things, yet neglect to know what is God, the creator of all things; or else they describe virtues in words, yet desert them in their lives. Finally, note the great fall of those who usurped a more noble name and professed a knowledge of divine things: instead of theologians, they are dialecticians, sophists at that; instead of lovers of God, they are knowers of God, nor do they wish to be that, but only to seem to be so; thus although they could follow Him in silence, they pursue Him with raucous voices. Behold the level to which the studies of mortals have descended! Oh, if you only knew the drive I feel and the passion that inflames me to speak at length on these matters! But the garden of such matters is too extensive and entangled for this pen of mine to weed out; and besides, long enough have I built on the humorous foundations of your brief letter.

You have heard how much the unpleasantness of hated gatherings and unwanted affairs has recently infringed upon the sweetness of my long-desired solitude and tranquillity. For too long I had been happy, for too long I had been my own man. Fortune envied me, or perhaps it was an act of heaven, lest the gratification of my desire would begin to make my spirit insolent. I confess that solitude, tranquillity, and freedom are useful only for the person of perfect virtue and sound mind, which I feel and lament that I am far from possessing. For the mind obsessed with passions there is nothing worse than leisure, nothing more damaging than solitary freedom, since they lead to obscene thoughts, deceitful lust, flattering evil, and that familiar plague of idle minds, love. I thought I was free of such fetters, but perhaps I was wrong. The merciless hand of a trusted doctor is perhaps necessary, but what does it matter if he cures hidden ills, if he attends to recurring diseases, and if he promises in the future after brief discomfort the lengthy pleasure of a tranquillity now past? Certainly I, in Virgil's words, "while the fates and God allowed," enjoyed my idleness with great pleasure, and would have enjoyed it if it had continued. Thus, I am not impatient at the changing course of events although I am ignorant of their cause and effect. As for the desire expressed at the end of your letter that you be allowed to be numbered among my followers, what is it if not an exceedingly friendly, modest, and humble request? You will be numbered among my friends, not those called friends by the rabble but by learned men, friends whose great rarity you know. Just as I consider you a sharer in my studies and all my wishes, just as I consider you a sharer of my name and my native land, so if at all possible would I wish you to share in my glory. And happily, I well know that I am acquiring this companionship at a good price and am purchasing with a small investment of fame a rich association and a great expectation of profit. Farewell.

Milan, 16 September, before dawn, in haste.